# RELIX

*music for the mind*

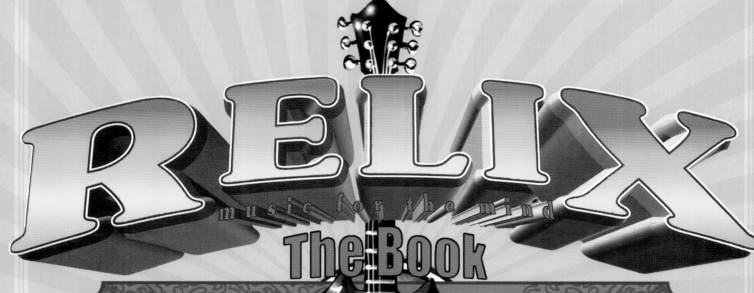

## The Book

## The Grateful Dead Experience

*I spent my whole life dancing, might have missed a step or two*
*But the music was always with me, part of all I'd live to do*
*The rhythm set me twirling, always got my bones to shake*
*Each show was like a thrill ride it was my destiny to take!*

*The people that danced with me were my brothers, lovers, friends*
*We're linked as kindred spirits in a dance that never ends*
*And though now the silence echoes, there are those who keep the flame*
*In my soul, they'll live forever—Grateful Dead! Long live the name!*

From *Rabbit Hole Soul*, "Live Dead Dance" by Toni Brown © 2000 Toni Brown Communications

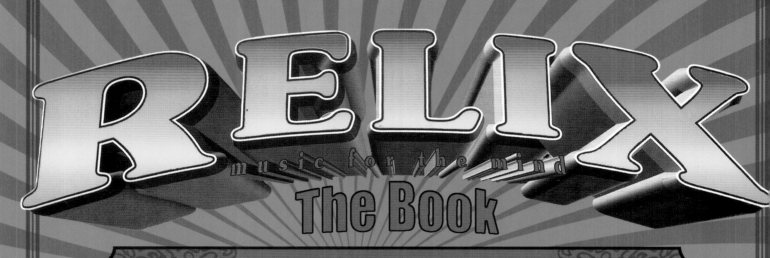

# RELIX
### music for the mind
### The Book

## The Grateful Dead Experience

### 30 Years of Mind-Melting Art, Interviews, Anecdotes and More!

# Compiled by Toni Brown with Lee Abraham and Ed Munson

Backbeat
Books

An Imprint of Hal Leonard Corporation
New York

Published in 2009 by Backbeat Books
An Imprint of Hal Leonard Corporation
7777 West Bluemound Road
Milwaukee, WI 53213

Trade Book Division Editorial Offices
19 West 21st Street, New York, NY 10010

All material for *RELIX, the Book: The Grateful Dead Experience* was used courtesy of and with permission and cooperation of Relix LLC, 104 W. 29th Street, New York, NY 10001, www.Relix.com

Every reasonable effort has been made to contact past Relix contributors to secure permission for all materials reproduced in this work not originally designated as work made for hire. We offer apologies for any instances in which this was not possible and for any inadvertent omissions.

Printed in China

Book design by Ed Munson

Library of Congress Cataloging-in-Publication Data

Relix, the book : the Grateful Dead experience / compiled by Toni Brown with Lee Abraham and Ed Munson.
     p. cm.
  Includes bibliographical references.
  ISBN 978-0-87930-986-2 (pbk.)
1.  Grateful Dead (Musical group) 2.  Rock musicians--United States. 3. Deadheads (Music fans)  I. Brown, Toni, 1954- II. Abraham, Lee. III. Munson, Ed. IV. Relix magazine.
  ML421.G72R45 2009
  782.42166092'2--dc22

                          2009017402

ISBN 978-0-8793-0986-2

www.backbeatbooks.com

# CONTENTS

# CONTENTS

# FOREWORD

IT'S HARD TO BELIEVE 35 YEARS HAVE PASSED since the first issue of *Relix* magazine hit the streets. In those early days, it was obviously geared toward Deadheads specifically, but we know today that the nascent jamband scene was lurking in the pages waiting to be born. A community that had not yet truly defined itself had already found a home. A musical scene that mainstream America was hardly aware of was on the move. In those days it was about shows and tape trading. The readers of *Relix* and the fans of the music seemed to move in a parallel universe. There was no Internet, no e-mail. *Relix* provided the connective tissue that kept a community together.

Folks such as myself found a home on the Relix Records label for a while as they made our music available to the world. The magazine kept our vision alive in the public eye. To get an article in *Relix*, much less a cover, was always a big deal . . . it still is! As years went by, the jamband scene took off big time and took its rightful place as an art form, and *Relix* was right there to chronicle the journey. As more music from different corners of the musical universe surfaced, the magazine kept us informed. *Relix* kept its focus without ignoring emerging artists from other realms. It was a magazine for our time then as it is today, and there are now many more of "us."

Thirty-five years . . . where do those decades go? It's all good, though. Without change and growth there is nothing but stagnation, and this pool is filled with clear water.

I can hardly wait to see what happens next.

—Jorma Kaukonen, 2009

BUSINESS PLAN? I REMEMBER BEING ASKED by a business student about the birth of *Relix*. He wanted to see a copy of our "business plan" for a term paper. HUH?

We were hippies. We did things because they felt right. *Dead Relix* started as a tape exchange in my head somewhere between "Dark Star" and "St. Stephen." There was no business plan, just lots of good people who thought the idea of a tape exchange and a magazine about the Grateful Dead was a cool thing.

The first issue of 200 was printed in a high school printing shop as a lesson for students about printing a "real" magazine. A friend provided the postage. My mother, Florence, typed the material. My father, Philip, and I would drive all around New York to deliver the issues.

We shipped magazines to Tower Records in California. They sold like hotcakes in San Francisco and San Rafael.

A business plan couldn't have anticipated our need to sell bumper stickers, buttons and T-shirts to keep the magazine alive. A business plan couldn't have predicted Bill Graham's creation of Winterland Productions and *Relix*'s direct involvement with rock merchandising.

A business plan couldn't prepare us for face-to-face confrontations with organized crime (who were bootlegging T-shirts, threatening us in an effort to get us to stop selling Winterland's licensed rock products).

But we believed. And with people like artist Gary Kroman, who I met one spring day in Bay Ridge, Steve Kraye, who took me to my first show, friends like Monte Dym and Jerry Moore, my brother Gary and sister-in-law Ronnie, and all our great contributors, *Relix* grew even when the Grateful Dead took a year off from touring.

It has been a long strange trip and it continues today.

This book, a multiyear effort by Toni Brown, brought tears to my eyes when I saw the first pages. I hope you enjoy it and maybe remember when things weren't planned, but just happened!

Gratefully,
Les Kippel, Founder,
The First Free Underground
Grateful Dead Tape Exchange,
*Dead Relix*, Relix Records

# NOTE

*Relix* AND I FIRST CROSSED PATHS BACK IN September of 1977. I was in high school, living on Long Island, and although I was aware of the Grateful Dead, I didn't know much about the band or its music.

One day in the cafeteria a bunch of kids (who I later found out had just returned from the Dead's huge outdoor show in Englishtown, NJ), were wearing tie-dyed T-shirts with the Dead's "Steal Your Face" logo and images of Jerry Garcia in a star-spangled top hat, smiling an illegal smile. I was intrigued! I liked the look. I liked the vibe. I wanted to be part of that scene. Somebody handed me a *Relix* magazine and I mailed off my subscription that afternoon!

*Relix* opened my mind's ear to more than just the Grateful Dead. From day one, Hot Tuna, Commander Cody, the New Riders, and many others, rocked my world, instantly becoming the soundtrack of my life.

But *Relix* was more than music. *Relix* was community. Months before flying to Europe for a six-week adventure in the early '90s, I contacted all the tape traders from overseas who placed ads in the "Have/Want" tape trading section at the back of the magazine. In addition to sending a tasty tape, I let my new trading partners from far and distant lands know about my upcoming trip, asking for suggestions on things to do or places to go.

The results were overwhelming! Bottom line: I stayed with Deadheads, my brothers and sisters, every single night! The people and experiences I had were amazing. And they never would have happened without *Relix* providing the gathering place every community needs to exist.

Years later as a writer for *Relix*, I was fortunate to gain press passes and backstage access to more shows than I can remember. Interacting with the musicians, as well as the people behind the scenes who make the music possible, was what I treasured most.

The opportunity to meet and spend time with my musical heroes, Jorma Kaukonen, Merl Saunders and Bob Weir, were life-changing experiences, enabling me to appreciate these musical giants as real people rather than just abstractions. Writing for *Relix* was the vehicle that took me on a road I never could have traveled alone. For that, I am eternally grateful!

Congratulations to Toni not only for the incredible body of work she created during 20+ years at the *Relix* helm, and all the musicians, bands, writers, photographers and artists she opened doors for, but also for creating this wonderful retrospective featuring the best of *Relix*'s early years! While the old saying "There is nothing like a Grateful Dead concert" remains true, I know for a fact that there has never been a magazine like *Relix*!

Enjoy the celebration of music and community on the pages to follow. Let your mind wander playfully and your spirit dance freely with the collective joy of memories deeply held, reliving a magical time we shared together. . . .

Rock steady,
"Mr. Lee" Abraham

PHOTO BY ED MUNSON

THERE ARE SO MANY ROADS TO FOLLOW ONCE you find that first step. Sometimes, the path is laid out for you, and you follow it without question. So it is that my life evolved. One well-timed Grateful Dead concert—and you find yourself with a magazine in your lap. Well, at least I did.

I never set out to publish *Relix*, but I was a pivotal player in taking it where it needed to go. Twenty-plus years with my head buried in music was not a bad place to be, but it was a job, and I took the responsibility seriously.

There is a long, strange story to tell in documenting *Relix*'s colorful history. I was given the opportunity to revisit a previous time in my life, and was overwhelmed by what I found. The first 27 years of *Relix* provided a treasure trove of material, a timeline documenting the history of the Dead and Deadheads through editorials, letters, stories, interviews, artwork and photos. There is so much that doesn't appear in this volume, but I went with my heart on the selections. You now hold a portrait of the early years of one

of the most enduring music publications ever.

Started as a tape-trading newsletter to connect Deadheads, *Relix* went on to become the birthplace of the jamband scene. Many musicians got their first exposure in our pages, and I am proud of the role we played in supporting music, old and new.

I went to my first Dead concert in 1969. I was hooked! I met *Relix* founder Les Kippel in the late '70s. From the first day I spent at Les's Brooklyn apartment, it was obvious that the roller-coaster ride was just beginning. He'd gone off to his job at the New York City Housing Authority, and the phone rang. And it kept ringing. Les had no answering machine and no way of knowing that people were anxiously trying to reach him to do *Relix*-related business. I happily left my job as an insurance broker, and wound up living with Les, answering the phone and working with then editor Jeff Tamarkin. The *business* of *Relix* began at that moment.

**Philip and Mom**

helped supplement the endless outflow of cash that it took to run a record label. Les became the East Coast representative for Bill Graham's Winterland Productions. Successful sales of music paraphernalia helped support all of our other enterprises, and ironically, it was New Kids on the Block that ultimately made us enough money to keep things afloat.

There were many ups and downs in the scene, and *Relix* was there to document the many transformations. News of the Dead during their 1975 hiatus, Garcia's illnesses, the overwhelming success of the Dead's 1987 release, *In the Dark*, the targeting of Deadheads by the DEA in the war on drugs, increasing problems at shows . . . and through it all, the beautiful thread of music kept us riveted and coming back for more.

Jerry Garcia died in 1995, a bitter loss. It was time to move on to my next love, playing music. I started recording and touring with my own band, and when we were mentioned in *Relix* reviews or ads, readers criticized me for using the magazine to exploit my own trip. I realized then that in order to get out there and perform, I needed some distance from *Relix*. The decision to leave was in no way easy, and I miss *Relix* to this day.

Steve Bernstein came along at the right moment, and bought the magazine in 2000. In early 2009, Peter Shapiro (former owner of Wetlands) took over at the helm, and continues to put out the most dedicated music magazine ever!

It has been an amazing ride, and it still is. People continue to thank me for the many years, the smiles, the parties, the joy. And in turn, I thank *you*! The axis has been realigned, but we are still members of an extended family that lives on. At the end of the day, it was all about the Deadheads, at least for me. History will tell the story of the Grateful Dead the way it does, but *Relix* is the real testament to who we Deadheads are.

Thank you for a real good time!

In peace, love and light,
Toni Brown

[On a personal note: Les and I got married in 1980 and had our beautiful son, Philip, in 1982. Philip was diagnosed with Asperger's syndrome, a high-functioning form of autism, one of the earliest cases documented in the United States. My long days got longer, having to devote many of my daylight hours to providing for Philip's needs. I have been rewarded in the fact that he is now 27, living on his own and working at a place he enjoys.]

In 1980, the magazine was finding its footing, and in an effort to keep up with the growing expenses of publishing, we formed a merchandising company. We were present at many shows, and got to know many of the musicians I admired—Hot Tuna, Robert Hunter, Commander Cody, David Bromberg, members of the Dead, Kingfish, New Riders, Peter Rowan.... It was Hunter who suggested Les start a record company, which made sense at the time. Relix Records was formed in 1980, and we released over a hundred titles by musicians we loved.

*Relix* was a full-time job, but the peripheral companies needed much attention because, after all was said and done, the magazine always struggled to break even. Our merchandising division not only kept the magazine going, it

Relax with Relix

Artwork by Gary Kroman

# PART ONE

# DEAD

# RELIX

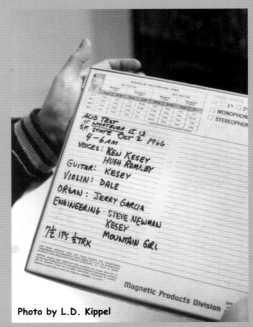

Photo by L.D. Kippel

# AND SO IT BEGINS...

Les Kippel went to his first Grateful Dead concert in 1970. The Brooklyn-born college student was inspired, and his fascination got him thinking. He wanted to spread the word of this mind-blowing musical experience, and he needed to take that music home (bottle it, as it were). Les found others who had the same passion. That idea blossomed into the First Free Underground Grateful Dead Tape Exchange, a grassroots group of Deadhead tape-trading enthusiasts who sought to collect and trade live Dead concert tapes.

In 1973, Les was featured in an article in *Rolling Stone*, "Mr. Tapes of Brooklyn," and the demand for tapes grew too fast for him to keep up. The idea to start a newsletter came as a way for him to help other tape traders connect with each other, so he could step out of the loop and still play an active role in getting tapes of the Grateful Dead into circulation.

An old friend, Jim McGurn, helped come up with a name. They decided that Dead tapes were like relics, and *Dead Relix* came to mind. Jerry Moore came on as editor and chief writer, and they started working on the first issue. Hand-typed and mimeographed in 1974, 200 were printed. Free tape-trader ads were offered as incentives, and the subscriber list grew.

That first issue was, of course, dedicated to the trickiest taper of all time—Richard Nixon!

Ironically, the first issue of *Dead Relix* hit just as the Grateful Dead announced a hiatus. Exhausted from touring and hauling around the "Wall of Sound" (a monstrous sound system that was light years ahead of anything used in live concert previously), the band and its extensive road crew decided to take a much-needed break.

Deadheads were frantic with worry over the implications of this news for the band that they adored. Questions about the future of the Dead and the scene poured in to the newsletter, which was rapidly becoming a crude yet viable magazine, a pre-Internet clearinghouse of information for a growing community of Deadheads who had nowhere else to gather. Were the Grateful Dead calling it quits? How long would they remain off the road? What do we do now? *Dead Relix* quickly gained a reputation as the place to connect while the band was planning a next move.

Another unexpected bonus of the Dead's respite was *Dead Relix*'s role—thanks to a sudden scarcity of material for the predominantly Dead-related publication—in promoting other bands and musicians who appealed to the same fans as the Dead.

The New Riders of the Purple Sage had opened up for the Dead and featured Jerry Garcia on pedal steel. Okay. Commander Cody opened for the New Riders. Yes. It started to gel. Then the individual Grateful Dead band members stepped up to the plate and got busy! They each took on projects, got involved in other bands, released all sorts of amazing music, toured and gave *Dead Relix* lots of news to share. The magazine was up and running!

—Toni Brown, 2009

Cover Artwork by Jerry Moore    Nov./Dec., 1974

Cover Artwork by Jerry Moore    Jan./Feb., 1975

# Watch Your Speed
## by
## Bruce J. Brass

"The Dead have really changed my life," Christine Keeler once said. Lots of people have said that, or things like it. The religious zeal with which many have approached the band for years is legendary. So, with rumors of imminent breakup spreading like acne across the country, it was time to get the (or at least some) official word on the status of the Dead. I recently spoke with Andy Leonard of Grateful Dead Records and he graciously gave me an outline of the band's activities for the next year.

First, and most important, the Grateful Dead is not breaking up. After years of touring throughout the U.S.A. and, more recently, Europe, they have decided to come to a halt and catch their breath.

As they gradually evolved from a San Francisco phenomenon into a corporate musical institution, the whole business of being the Grateful Dead has grown far more complex than they desired. Putting out your own records and booking your own tours is a costly operation and requires, among other things, money. In order to bring that money in, they had to go on the road. Due to increased popularity as well as business needs, they had to play larger halls. In order to make the music work in these larger surroundings, more and better amplification equipment was needed. This, in turn, required money, so, it was on the road again, this time in arenas and stadiums hardly built with the Dead (or any music) in mind.

This cycle of having to play in larger surroundings for more people for more money was careening out of control, so they simply stopped the machine before the momentum swallowed them whole.

There will, however, be plenty of activity on records. Garcia already has one album in the can and has started another. The Godchauxs have been working on their own album (along with the ever-present Garcia) for the past four months. There has been some talk of an electronics music album along the lines of the "Warp-10" interludes between sets during the Dead's last tour. Weir has just put the finishing touches on his new home studio and will be working on his new album, tentatively scheduled for release next spring. Nobody knows what Kreutzmann's going to do because he's a drummer. Mickey Hart (!) is also at work on his second album... Come the new year (January 3, to be precise), they'll all wander into the recording studio and get reacquainted in the form of a new Grateful Dead album.

But the big project is going to be the movie. Yes, the movie. One of the most camera-shy groups in America has finally surrendered to the cinema and hopefully will be appearing on the screen in about a year. All five nights of their final 1974 concerts at Winterland were filmed and recorded for purposes of producing a 'canned concert' experience in the theater. On the first few nights of filming, the band was somewhat uncomfortable with the cameras around, but they finally got into it and by the last concert, were really getting off on this new (for them) dimension in performing. Andy Leonard, a photographer by trade, was quite excited about the movie and felt that they had caught the essence of the Dead on film. In all they shot 27,300 feet of film and will spend the upcoming months turning it into a coherent movie. A live album, with no present commitment as to how many discs it will take, will also result from the movie. It will not be called "Ladies and Gentlemen, the Grateful Dead."

While it's true that you won't be seeing the Dead for a while at your local neighborhood sports complex (Nausea Coliseum, barf!), they'll still be out there keeping in touch one way or another. And remember, if none of these things actually take place, this is where you heard it first.

**Cover Artwork by Jerry Moore**

**Cover Photo Courtesy Relix Magazine**

The
Commander
And His
Airmen

Lost
In The
Ozone

**Cover Artwork by Jerry Moore**

# The Golden Road
## (To Unlimited Collection)
### by Steve Kraye

FOR all intents and purposes, practical or impractical, this whole tape trip started the first time I asked Les, "Hey man, you want to see the Grateful Dead?" Getting an affirmative answer, I went ahead and picked up a couple of tickets for the Fillmore East show, Midnight, May 15, 1970. Having seen the Dead before, I figured on showing my pal a good time. I was wrong. It was so much more than just another pleasant evening that we were both hopelessly hooked. The first mellow acoustic tune floored us, and we remained plastered to the Fillmore's greasy tiles right through the New Riders and a pull-out-all-the-stops electric set.

The night ended, as all magic moments eventually must, and we stumbled forth to meet the rising sun and the light of a new day on Second Avenue. On the lonely road back home, the echoes of "Saint Stephen" and "Good Lovin'" fading away, we swore that the next one would be more than just a happy memory. By hook or by crook, by murder if necessary, our next Dead show would be recorded.

We tried. In July of 1970, Les smuggled a small portable cassette machine into the Fillmore, and gave it to a friend in the first row, who recorded the show. I'd like to be able to say it was a great tape, but, in all honesty, it was pretty bad. It sounded like the show was held in someone's garbage can, and consisted mostly of comments like "Hey Bobby, pass the Kool-aid." Bad as it was, though, it was a beginning.

Les taped a few more shows by himself, and was just knockin' around, waiting for the next show, when Art Carlyle introduced him to Jim Watson. It turned out that Jim had also taped some shows, so they arranged a trade, bringing them both up to twenty hours or so. This was a taste of what was to come. As one Dead freak can only do just so much, it gradually became clear that the solution to the problem of how to get more tapes lay in cooperative effort.

So, in late 1971, Les, Jim, Art, and Harris Mulnick were sitting down, taping concerts, and trying to decide on their next step. They decided that there must be other people out there who were recording shows, and that there had to be a way to get together with them. Everybody should have access to any existing tapes, and exchanges should be free, to avoid the stigma of bootlegging. These dicussions resulted in the FIRST ORIGINAL UNDERGROUND GRATEFUL DEAD TAPE EXCHANGE. The idea caught on, and now people are exchanging everywhere.

The idea caught on everywhere, that is, but with the Grateful Dead family. Initially, we were treated rather coldly. Letters went unanswered and discussions with their business people proved to be fruitless. The concert halls and sports arenas of the nation became battlefields. The Dead's roadies, men of *much* muscle, enjoyed themselves, cracking skulls, stealing tapes, cutting microphone cables, and so on. This nonsense reached its peak in Waterbury, Conn., in September of 1972. We were hanging out in our room at the local Holiday Inn, where the Dead were also staying. We were listening, of course, to Dead tapes. Augustus Owsley Stanley III, commonly known as "Z. Bear" was roaming down the hall, when he heard the strains of music. He steamrollered his way in, made off with a set of tapes (including one of Art playing guitar), informed us that we would never get away with taping, told us that we'd be stopped, and let us kow that our tapes were shit anyway compared to his.

For a short time thereafter, hassles were truly intense. Still for every one of us they've caught, twenty have never been bothered. Like the starfish, cut us and we multiply. Maybe the roadies have gotten tired of fighting us, or maybe The Bear just liked Art's guitar work, but lately we've rarely gotten hassled. Our equipment has gotten much better, we've learned more, and our tapes have gotten to be quite excellent.

Now, since The Bear was so proud of *his* tapes, we'd like to hear them. All that older stuff, and all the shows that we don't have are in the can someplace. We exist (in rather considerable numbers) and we want those tapes. We'd like to be able to listen to a Dead concert at home without having to record it ourselves, and we'd like to be free to attend concerts without being nailed to our seats by a tape recorder. Is anyone listening out there?

---

**Toni's Note:** Post--Beat generation author Ken Kesey (*One Flew Over the Cuckoo's Nest*), pushed the envelope of nonconformity via legendary exploits aboard the Further bus with his band of coconspirators, the Merry Pranksters. These psychedelic pioneers took their message public by way of the "Acid Tests." Their personal stash of the then legal chemical compound LSD-25 was created by Augustus Owsley Stanley III, a.k.a. "The Bear."

Owsley became a vital contributor to the direction and growth of the '60s counterculture revolution. He brought a popular Bay Area rock group, the Warlocks (later known as the Grateful Dead), into the psychedelic arena as the house band for the "Acid Tests." He also kept the band afloat financially with the proceeds of his LSD sales. He proved to be visionary as a sound engineer for the group and, along with Dead soundman Dan Healy, was a major contributor to the concepts of stereophonic PA systems and the monstrous Wall of Sound equipment that the Grateful Dead trucked from show to show in 1974.

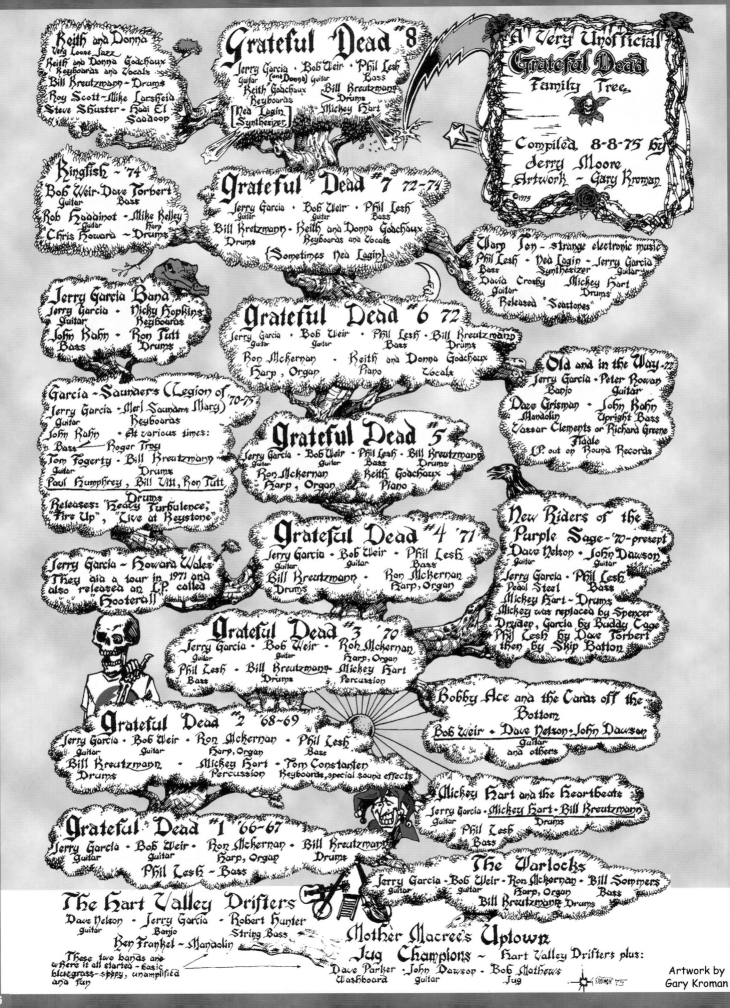

**A Very Unofficial Grateful Dead Family Tree.**

Compiled 8-8-75 by Jerry Moore
Artwork – Gary Kroman
©1975

**Keith and Donna**
Very loose Jazz
Keith and Donna Godchaux
Keyboards and Vocals
Bill Kreutzmann – Drums
Roy Scott – Mike Larsheid
Steve Shuster – Hadi El Saadoon

**Grateful Dead #8**
Jerry Garcia · Bob Weir · Phil Lesh
Guitar (and Donna) Guitar Bass
Keith Godchaux Bill Kreutzmann
Keyboards Drums
Mickey Hart
Ned Lagin Synthesizer

**Kingfish ~ '74**
Bob Weir · Dave Torbert
Guitar Bass
Rob Hoddinot · Mike Kelley
Guitar Harp
Chris Howard ~ Drums

**Grateful Dead #7 72-74**
Jerry Garcia · Bob Weir · Phil Lesh
Guitar Guitar Bass
Bill Kreutzmann · Keith and Donna Godchaux
Drums Keyboards and Vocals
(Sometimes Ned Lagin)

**Warp Ten ~ strange electronic music**
Phil Lesh · Ned Lagin · Jerry Garcia
Bass Synthesizer Guitar
David Crosby Mickey Hart
Guitar Drums
Released "Seastones"

**Jerry Garcia Band**
Jerry Garcia · Nicky Hopkins
Guitar Keyboards
John Kahn · Ron Tutt
Bass Drums

**Grateful Dead #6 '72**
Jerry Garcia · Bob Weir · Phil Lesh · Bill Kreutzmann
Guitar Guitar Bass Drums
Ron Mckernan · Keith and Donna Godchaux
Harp, Organ Piano Vocals

**Old and in the Way ~ '73**
Jerry Garcia · Peter Rowan
Banjo Guitar
Dave Grisman · John Kahn
Mandolin Upright Bass
Vassar Clements or Richard Greene
Fiddle
LP out on Round Records

**Garcia – Saunders (Legion of Mary) '70-75**
Jerry Garcia · Merl Saunders
Guitar Keyboards
John Kahn · At various times:
Bass Roger Troy
Tom Fogerty · Bill Kreutzmann
Guitar Drums
Paul Humphrey, Bill Vitt, Ron Tutt
Drums
Releases: "Heavy Turbulence",
"Fire Up", "Live at Keystone"

**Grateful Dead 5**
Jerry Garcia · Bob Weir · Phil Lesh · Bill Kreutzmann
Guitar Guitar Bass Drums
Ron Mckernan · Keith Godchaux
Harp, Organ Piano

**Jerry Garcia ~ Howard Wales**
They did a tour in 1971 and
also released an L.P. called
"Hooteroll"

**Grateful Dead #4 '71**
Jerry Garcia · Bob Weir · Phil Lesh
Guitar Guitar Bass
Bill Kreutzmann · Ron Mckernan
Drums Harp, Organ

**New Riders of the Purple Sage ~ '70-present**
Dave Nelson · John Dawson
Guitar Guitar
Jerry Garcia · Phil Lesh
Pedal Steel Bass
Mickey Hart ~ Drums
Mickey was replaced by Spencer
Dryden, Garcia by Buddy Cage
Phil Lesh by Dave Torbert
then by Skip Battin

**Grateful Dead #3 '70**
Jerry Garcia · Bob Weir · Ron Mckernan
Guitar Guitar Harp, Organ
Phil Lesh · Bill Kreutzmann · Mickey Hart
Bass Drums Percussion

**Bobby Ace and the Cards off the Bottom**
Bob Weir · Dave Nelson · John Dawson
Guitar
and others

**Grateful Dead #2 '68-69**
Jerry Garcia · Bob Weir · Ron Mckernan · Phil Lesh
Guitar Guitar Harp, Organ Bass
Bill Kreutzmann · Mickey Hart · Tom Constanten
Drums Percussion Keyboards, special sound effects

**Mickey Hart and the Heartbeats**
Jerry Garcia · Mickey Hart · Bill Kreutzmann
Guitar Drums
Phil Lesh
Bass

**Grateful Dead #1 '66-67**
Jerry Garcia · Bob Weir · Ron Mckernan · Bill Kreutzmann
Guitar Guitar Harp, Organ Drums
Phil Lesh ~ Bass

**The Warlocks**
Jerry Garcia · Bob Weir · Ron Mckernan · Bill Sommers
Guitar Guitar Harp, Organ Bass
Bill Kreutzmann Drums

**The Hart Valley Drifters**
Dave Nelson · Jerry Garcia · Robert Hunter
Guitar Banjo String Bass
Ken Frankel ~ Mandolin

These two bands are
where it all started – basic
bluegrass-skippy, unamplified
and fun

**Mother Macree's Uptown Jug Champions** ~ Hart Valley Drifters plus:
Dave Parker · John Dawson · Bob Mathews
Washboard Guitar Jug

Artwork by Gary Kroman

*Vol. 2 No.5*
*Sept-Oct 1975*
*$1.25*

BOULDER, COLO. 909

Sundance Exp.

LETTERS, HOT TUNA, JEFFERSON STARSHIP, GRATEFUL DEAD, TOUR HAPPENINGS, BITS AND PIECES, PHOTOS, WANT PAGES AND MORE!

Artwork by Gary Kroman

*Vol. 2 No.6*
*1975*
*$1.25*

*Anniversary Issue*

*Nov.- Dec.*

Artwork by Gary Kroman

# LETTERS

Les,

I am deeply involved in obtaining and sending "Underground" tapes of the Grateful Dead, and I have come to discover, again, how incredibly powerful these recordings actually are. I must assume that all of "US" people, who are involved in such an adventure, have had the same kinds of incredibly joyous and "cleansing" experiences that I have been having with my family over here in paradise. We have, what one could call "Dead-Ins" often, and these intense experiences of togetherness are the exact same as we have all repeatedly had seeing the Dead "Live" when we used to live in the Bay Area.

Anyway, I thought of how rich and entertaining it would be to have "Dead Relix" include a section that contained copies of letters that transpire between Dead Freaks. (Especially the ones that pass between collectors of the rarest performances by the band.) Maybe it would be a column that gave people the opportunity to briefly describe "what the Grateful Dead means to me".

As I think about it, you probably have already thought about this possibility and subsequently discarded the idea as naive and immature. But I do know that whenever I get to thinking about such a question, as what the Dead means in my life, I find myself thinking, saying and writing about the most basic things in my life; and if that is immature, then I better stop thinking now!

Your magazine is so necessary to me, being so far away from the center of it all. Hawaii has absolutely everything I want, except getting to see them at Winterland, or wherever; and I have yet to meet any Dead Freaks over here. All those in my family came over here with me. If you are ever coming over to Hawaii I could show you some very fantastic things. (Not to mention how much cheaper your vacation would be if you stayed with us! )

IN LOVE, DICK LATVALA
PAHOA, HAWAII
**October, 1975**

**Toni's Note:** Dick Latvala was a longtime friend of *Relix*. He wrote this letter while living in Hawaii. He came back to the States to see the Dead play in 1979, and he met Bill "Kidd" Candelario (of the Dead's road crew) backstage at Red Rocks. It changed his life. Latvala went on to be the Dead's tape archivist, one of the most intense jobs behind the scenes. His task was to sort through and organize the vast tape vaults, and come up with what eventually became the *Dick's Picks* series of releases.

The first show Dick remembered absolutely was the Trips Festival in 1966. It was soon after he had taken LSD legally in a research project in Menlo Park, a defining moment for him.

Dick became aware of live tapes in 1974. By the time he entered the Dead's vaults in 1985, he had 900 reels of his own live material, and felt "like a kid in a candy store."

The first *Dick's Picks* release came out in 1993, taken from a 12/19/73 show. He convinced the band to release more material, and his *Dick's Picks* series continued to flow until his death in 1999 of a heart attack.

David Lemieux has taken over the archive's helm and continues to release music.

Artwork by Gary Kroman

$1.25

Vol. 3 #1          Jan.-Feb. '76

N.R.P.S. SPECIAL!
History of the Riders!
History of the Good Ol' Boys
Interview with Dave Nelson
Riders at the Fillmore - 4/29/71 and
Salt Lake City • Concert Reviews
Bits and Pieces • Rumblings from the Bay City
Dead in Wichita, - Nov.,'72 Plus Moore!

Artwork by Gary Kroman

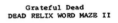

Grateful Dead
DEAD RELIX WORD MAZE II
by
Ronnie and Gary

Hidden in this maze are the 36 words which are written
below. They read forward, down, or diagonally

```
R O W A N S K E I T H U N E
U S T E L L A B L U E A O S
S N E L S O N U R I P P L E
E A B G R A N T N G A R Y A
L B E R T H A R T D W O O S
U L R C O A E L E V E N S T
B O D A R K S T A R I R T O
S O O N B W E N D Y R T S N
T S N D E V I N T A G E T E
L E N Y R R O N C W A L E S
B L A M T I A K A H N Y P T
S U G A R B E C H R A C H A
H C O N T R O L E S L I E P
B Y N T H E O T H E R O N E
```

| ACE | GRANT | RIPPLE | THE OTHER ONE |
| APRON | HART | RON(in 2 places) | TORBERT |
| BERTHA | KAHN | ROWAN | UNBROKEN CHAIN |
| CANDYMAN | KEITH | SAUNDERS | U S BLUES |
| CONTROL | LESH | SEASTONES | VINTAGE |
| DARKSTAR | LESLIE | STELLABLUE | VITT |
| DONNA | LOOSE LUCY | ST STEPHEN | WALES |
| ELEVEN | NELSON | SUGAREE | WEIR |
| GARY | REBT | TAPE | WENDY |

**Puzzle by Ronnie & Gary Kippel**   Artwork by Gary Kroman

*Nugents to the Dugents
*Rowan Bros. in Concert
*Rowan Bros. Family Jungle
*Nitty Gritty Titty Committee
*Review: Old and in the Way
*Rumblings from the Bay City

Plus Moore

Vol. 3, Number 2
March~April 1976
$1.25  © 1976

Artwork by Gary Kroman

# NEW RIDERS OF THE PURPLE SAGE

An abbreviated history of that group of illustrious pickers known collectively as THE NEW RIDERS OF THE PURPLE SAGE.

## The PINE VALLEY BOYS around 1962

| DAVID NELSON guitar / vocals | JEFF LEVIN gtr / vocals | BUTCH WALLER gtr / banjo / vocals | HERB PEDERSEN vocals / guitar |

When the Pine Valley Boys split up, Butch Waller went on to form High Country, Jeff Levin was in People (a one-hit pop group), and Herb Pederson joined the Dillards and was in Country Gazette too.

The Wildwood (Black Mountain) Boys, based in Palo Alto, California, were a folk-cabaret act playing at the Jabberwock in Berkeley, the Tangent in Palo Alto, and coffee houses in San Francisco's North Beach. Also did several bluegrass / folk festivals.

## The Wildwood Boys, later the BLACK MT BOYS around 1963

| ERIC THOMPSON gtr / vocals | PETER ALBIN bass / guitar | DAVID NELSON gtr / vocals | JERRY GARCIA banjo / vocals | BOB HUNTER gtr / vocals |

In 1959, Jerry Garcia was thrown out of the Army and, together with friend Hunter, began to discover the joys of bluegrass and folk music, particularly old-timey country and jug band music. He helped to found several groups; the Wildwood Boys (later the Black Mountain Boys), then The Thunder Mountain Tub Thumpers, then (in 1963) The Hart Valley Drifters, the Asphalt Jungle Mountain Boys, and his last acoustic group — Mother McCree's Uptown Jug Champions.

Did a few solo coffee-house / folk club gigs

## The HART VALLEY DRIFTERS

| DAVID NELSON guitar | JERRY GARCIA banjo | BOB HUNTER string bass | KEN FRANKEL mandolin |

## NEW YORK RAMBLERS Spring '64 to late '65

| DAVID GRISMAN mandolin | GENE LOWINGER fiddle | FRED WEISS bass | WINNIE WINSTON banjo | ERIC THOMPSON guitar |

Initially formed for fun — to compete in the Union Grove Fiddle Contest..... they won! Presented with cup declaring them World Champion String Band! David Grisman later founded EARTH OPERA and is now in OLD & IN THE WAY (also on the new 'MULESKINNER' album with Richard Greene & Clarence White).

## The Asphalt Jungle Mountain Boys, later MOTHER McCREE'S UPTOWN JUG CHAMPIONS

This group, formed in 1963 (they changed their name in late 1964) had a very fluid line-up.

| JODY STECHER mandolin | ERIC THOMPSON guitar | PETER ALBIN bass / guitar | DAVID NELSON guitar / vocals | JOHN DAWSON vocals / guitar | JERRY GARCIA banjo / guitar / vocals | BOB WEIR jug / guitar / vocals | RON McKERNAN (PIGPEN) harmonica / piano / vocals | BOB MATTHEWS guitar / vocals |

Became a solo folksinger for a while

Left the field of performing (but later played in the New Riders), and now runs Alembic Studios & Electronics.

## BIG BROTHER AND THE HOLDING COMPANY 1965

| JANIS JOPLIN vocals | JAMES GURLEY lead guitar | SAM ANDREW guitar | DAVID GETZ drums | PETER ALBIN bass | DAVID NELSON guitar |

David Nelson was in the emerging Big Brother for only the first few weeks. It wasn't until after he'd left and Janis Joplin had joined that they began to get any national acclaim. (Listen to the group's, and Janis's solo, albums on CBS.)

## The WARLOCKS — later THE GRATEFUL DEAD (changed name in Feb 1966)

| JERRY GARCIA | BOB WEIR | PIGPEN | PHIL LESH | BILL SOMMERS |

THE NEW DELHI RIVER BAND, which included all sorts of itinerant musicians at various times in its relatively short life span, played mostly at a club called The Barn — 'out on Route 17'. Dawson left after a while ("it didn't work out") but Torbert, formerly in various blues and R&B bands, stayed till the end.

## The NEW DELHI RIVER BAND 1966

| DAVID NELSON guitar / vocals | JOHN DAWSON guitar / vocals | DAVE TORBERT bass / gtr / voc | CHRIS HERALD guitar |

THE GRATEFUL DEAD went their merry way and, until Garcia got a pedal steel guitar, had no connection with the New Riders - except that Dawson played a few gigs with Weir's occasional group BOBBY ACE AND THE CARDS FROM THE BOTTOM

## The JEFFERSON AIRPLANE formed in August 1965

after founder Marty Balin had seen the Beatles. One of the earliest rock groups in San Francisco - only the Mystery Trend & Charlatans pre-date them.

| SIGNE TOLY ANDERSEN replaced in Autumn '66 by GRACE SLICK vocals | MARTY BALIN vocals | JORMA KAUKONEN guitar | JACK CASADY bass | PAUL KANTNER guitar / vocals | SKIP SPENCE drums replaced by SPENCER DRYDEN drums (previously in The Ashes - later The Peanut Butter Conspiracy). Left the Airplane in March 1970 |

Left in Sept 1966 to join MOBY GRAPE (who made 4 albums for CBS)

## The MESCALINE ROMPERS (1968) was a very short-lived group;

their only gig appears to have been at Pinnacles National Monument. Following its demise, Dawson did solo gigs at 'The Underground Cafe' in Menlo Park and Torbert retired to Oahu Hawaii to lie in the sun.

| JOHN DAWSON guitar / vocals | DAVE TORBERT bass / gtr / voc | MATTHEW KELLY gtr / banjo / vocals / harmonica |

Despite various personnel changes, the Airplane still flies today (though, some say, fading gracefully after a long and illustrious career spanning almost 9 years).

## The NEW RIDERS of the PURPLE SAGE #1

Spring 1970 to Spring 1971. The first New Riders (including 3 members of the Dead) played as guests on Grateful Dead gigs & remained very much under their wing. The personnel changed "largely by accident and at convenience". According to the hype, David Nelson and Bob Hunter (now the Dead's lyricist) named the group "by numerological transposition" from their old name (the New Delhi River Band)! Hardly likely, considering the Zane Grey novel and Gene Autrey's song.

| DAVID NELSON vocals / acoustic & electric guitars | JOHN DAWSON acoustic guitar / vocals | JERRY GARCIA pedal steel and banjo | MICKEY HART drums / percussion | PHIL LESH or BOB MATTHEWS bass |

## The GREAT SPECKLED BIRD

A Canadian based group which (with different line-ups) also worked as Ian & Sylvia's backing band. Recorded with Ian & Sylvia and made solo album on Ampex

| KEN KALMUSKY bass | AMOS GARRETT guitar | N.D. SMART drums | BUDDY CAGE pedal steel guitar |

Joined Paul Butterfield's Better Days and does sessions — he's a fabulous guitarist..... amazing.

## The NEW RIDERS of the PURPLE SAGE #2

Spring 1971 until November 1971. In June 1971, the group signed with CBS and subsequently released their first album 'NEW RIDERS OF THE PURPLE SAGE' (CBS 64657) on 3.12.71 (England). Still toured with the Dead, doing support and intermission spots — and Jerry Garcia continued to play in both groups.

| SPENCER DRYDEN drums / percussion | DAVID NELSON lead guitar / vocals | DAVE TORBERT bass / vocals / guitar | JOHN DAWSON vocals / rhythm guitar | JERRY GARCIA pedal steel guitar |

Having launched and nurtured their off-spring, Jerry Garcia and the rest of his cohorts were able to concentrate fully on THE GRATEFUL DEAD once more. After various changes of personnel and some dozen or so albums, the current line-up is as follows:

| JERRY GARCIA guitar / vocals | PHIL LESH bass / vocals | BOB WEIR guitar / vocals | BILL KREUTZMANN drums | KEITH GODCHAUX keyboards | DONNA GODCHAUX vocals |

## THE BYRDS #7

Skip was in the most stable Byrds line-up, and flew with them from Oct'69 to Feb'73. Also made solo album (Signpost).

| ROGER McGUINN guitar / vocals | CLARENCE WHITE guitar | GENE PARSONS drums | SKIP BATTIN bass |

Family Tree re-searched and drawn by Pete Frame. June 1974

## The NEW RIDERS of the PURPLE SAGE #3

November 1971 to February 1974. With Garcia's commitments restricting their activities, they decide to separate from the Dead and survive independently. Having met Buddy Cage during the notorious Trans Canadian Festival Express of 1970, they invite him to join on pedal steel.

| BUDDY CAGE pedal steel guitar | SPENCER DRYDEN drums / percussion | DAVID NELSON lead guitar / vocals | JOHN DAWSON vocals / guitar | DAVE TORBERT bass / vocals |

Left to form his own group

This line-up (New Riders #3) cut 4 albums:
'POWERGLIDE' CBS 64843, released 19.5.72
'GYPSY COWBOY' CBS 65008, released 16.2.73
'PANAMA RED' CBS 65687, released 16.11.73
and their new one, released here on 21.6.74,
'HOME HOME ON THE ROAD' CBS 80060

## The NEW RIDERS of the PURPLE SAGE #4

February 1974 to the present. With the arrival of Skip Battin we see the beginning of a new era for the New Riders — look out for them when they tour here later this year

| SKIP BATTIN bass / vocals | BUDDY CAGE pedal steel guitar | SPENCER DRYDEN drums / percussion | DAVID NELSON guitar / vocals | JOHN DAWSON vocals / guitar |

"Once upon a time, when things had fallen apart but not quite everyone knew it, some few hundred entities who lived and moved upon the San Francisco peninsula did there establish between themselves obscure bands of understanding, decision and hope. Within this particular stream of life, events came to pass and phenomena flowered and much music was played. From this age, the 1960s, came forth THE NEW RIDERS OF THE PURPLE SAGE."

Printed With Permission of Zig Zag Magazine

Cover Artwork by Gary Kromam

October, 1976

NOBODY FOR PRESIDENT IN '76

*Photo Courtesy Wavy Gravy*

Wavy Gravy

Fellahs:

For the past two years I've had this strange disease of which there is only one known cure. I believe this disease is Labeled DEAD FEVER .... the cure .... A DEAD concert. When, on June 1st, I heard the announcement of a Dead concert, I blew my last brain cell. Finally, I thought, my fever would be cooled on any one of the eves of June 21, 22, 23 or 24. At the Tower Theater in Philadelphia, no less, the best possible place to experience such a high point in my life. Nothing could stop me now, I thought, and I started to plan which two or even three nights out of the four I would attend.

On the morn of June 2nd, well before 10 a.m., I started my trek to the Electric Factory ticket outlet. When I arrived approximately 400 people fainting with fever pushed and shoved for the one known cure. I stood for two (or was it 6?) hours in the rain, leaving the scene with nothing more than a cold.

Will I have to wait another two years ?????????

The saying goes "There's nothing like a Grateful Dead concert." How will I ever know ???? Although I've seen them several times singularly, I feel this groping need to experience the life force of the universe. good ole Grateful Dead (as a whole). This, you know, was my major goal for 1976 and I dislike wholeheartedly the thought of having to make it my LIFE goal.

Now that you've heard my story I'll get to the point of this little note. It is my understanding that only 1,200 tickets were available in that little room they squeezed four people into at a time. Now... the Tower holds approximately 1,965 people multiplied by four nights to get a grand total of 7,860. What happened to the other 6,660 tickets? huh? I have been told they were distributed by some kind of mail order. MAIL ORDER????? WHAT MAIL ORDER ???????

Renee L. Benjamin

**A** lot of you have written to us requesting the address of the Dead Heads organization, so that you won't be closed out again if the Dead once more put tickets on sale through the mail.

Instead of answering each letter individually, we are just going to print the address here so you can send them your name.

Send them your name, address, and zip code. Don't forget that last item, or your mail will get held up by the post office.

Here it is:

DEAD HEADS
P.O. Box 1065
San Rafael, California

Relix Editor Jerry Moore & Founder Les Kippel during their weekly late-night Dead radio show at WQIV in N.Y.C. Courtesy Relix Archive

Artwork by Gary Kroman

Artwork by Gary Kroman

# pieces by Les

A friend of mine told me that I should never try to use logic in the music business, and that there is no way to try to figure out the thought processes of musicians and the music industry. After hearing the stories that I am going to tell you now, I think I understand.

The New Riders signed with M.C.A. Records in January. In February, Skip Battin left the Riders for the Flying Burrito Brothers. Natch, that left the Riders without a Bass player.

Meanwhile, Commander Cody and His Lost Planet Airmen came back from Europe where they had a fairly long tour, and decided that it was time to end everything. John Tishy, decided he had enough and wanted to farm. He didn't even go to Europe. So, Commander Cody, and the Airmen, are now lost in the ozone, and might never be seen from again. There might be a joining of the souls in a few years, but no plans are even being thought about now. But, there will be at least a double live Cody album out soon, with music recorded on the European tour.

And Cody himself will be going on a lecture tour put together by Rolling Stone Magazine with maybe Dylan and a few other folks.

Meanwhile, back to the Riders. Now, that left Buffalo Bruce out of work. He could have fit in with the Riders, and would have added a little something to the group, but it seems that the Riders didn't think so.

So, the Riders were still without a Bass player.

Enter The Grateful Dead. The Dead started to plan a tour of small theaters in June, and then to hit the road for the biggies in July. The initial arrangements were already made, places picked to play in, and dates solidified.

Back to the Riders. There was this bass player who played with the Riders a long time ago, no, not Torbert, but Phil Lesh, and Lesh hasn't been doing anything lately,.....

So, now it looked like Phil was going to help out the Riders and do the album with them, as well as a show or two.

Also, The Dead then changed some of their June dates. When Bob Weir was recently asked about their tour plans, he said that the Dead might play in South America, Australia and Africa....

Now, all of this sounds strange, and a lot of this can cause outrageous rumors, and all of the aforementioned could be the result of rumors. So, I decided to call up the Riders and the Cody people.

The Riders office told me the that Skip was still with them, and that the tour plans were going ahead. They didn't admit to the fact that Skip left, or might be leaving the band in the future....so, ??????

As for the Commander, some people are saying that the group has split up, but they are scheduled for a show somewhere in the mid-west, at least according to Performance magazine, so, again ???????

Don't ask me to explain, but this has been PIECES, by Les.

FROM OUR USUAL SEMI-RELIABLE SOURCES: ANOTHER OFFICIAL DEAD RELIX RUMOR:

Grateful Dead tour's approximate dates are June 10-24. The tour will consist of 2 nights in each of 5 cities, with no nights off for the band, all in theatres of less than 5,000 seats. HINT TO EXACT LOCATIONS: All tour arrangements are being made by John Scher.

The tour will be publically announced in middle May (unless the word leaks out before that).

Vol. 3 No. 6

Nov-Dec

ANNIVERSARY ISSUE

$1.50

RELIX

November/December, 1976

Interviews with

Rick Griffin
Mickey Hart
Paul McCartney

STARSHIP
Photo Section, History & Family Tree

Cover Photo by Dave Patrick

# R.Crumb
## by Dave Patrick

"**H**onest to G-D, I tried," explained underground cartoonist Robert Crumb in his usual half apologetic manner. "I went to the Fillmore. I hung out in Golden Gate Park. I took the drugs. I even went so far as to buy the records, but the Grateful Dead, the Airplane and all those other San Francisco psychedelic bands just put me to sleep."

Could this be heresy, direct from the mouth of the man who created Mr. Natural, Flakey Foont, Honeybunch Kominsky, Creem magazine's Boy Howdy and the artwork for Janis Joplin's lp, Cheap Thrills? Call it what you will, but Mr. Zap's not kidding.

"As far as I'm concerned, good rock music died with Jan & Dean, and the early Beach Boys," he continued. "To tell you the truth, I never really even liked the Beatles."

RECORD FACTORY
555 FRANCISCO BLVD. IN SAN RAFAEL
PRESENTING

GRATEFUL DEAD
ARTWORK and MEMORABILIA
AUCTION
SUNDAY · SEPT. 26th at 3 P.M.
PREVIEW of AUCTION ITEMS BEGINS AT 1 P.M.
PLUS
LIVE MUSIC
1 P.M.
BY
ROADHOG
GRATEFUL DEAD LYRICIST, ROBERT HUNTER'S NEW GROUP
·ITEMS TO BE AUCTIONED TO THE HIGHEST BIDDER INCLUDE·
ORIGINAL ARTWORK
SIGNED PRINTS BY·
·KELLY MOUSE · PHIL GARRIS·
·VICTOR MOSCOSO · RANDY TUTEN·
(PROCEEDS GO TO THE RESPECTIVE ARTISTS)
·ADDITIONAL ITEMS INCLUDE·
·PROMOTIONAL POSTERS·STICKERS·MOBILES·STAND-UPS·
FROM GRATEFUL DEAD and ROUNDER RECORDS
(PROCEEDS FROM PROMOTIONAL ITEMS GO TOWARD
FORTHCOMING GRATEFUL DEAD PROJECTS)
EVERYONE WELCOME!!
DEAD HEADS, COLLECTORS, AUCTION ENTHUSIASTS & MUSIC LOVERS

Photo by Dave Patrick

Robert Crumb

Photo by Dave Patrick

Starship

Photo by L.D. Kippel

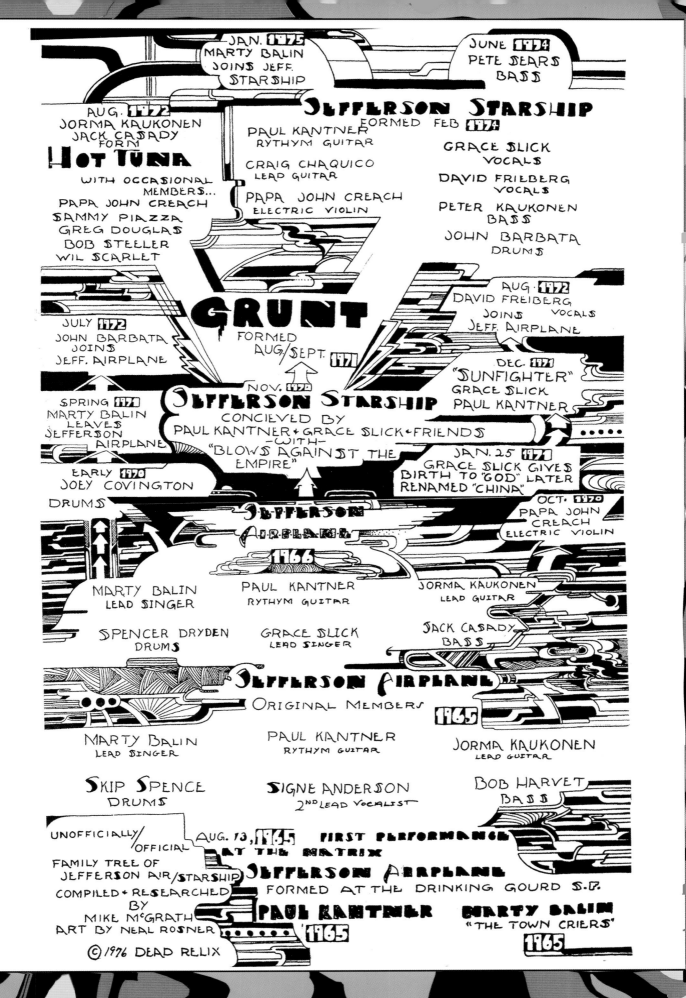

JAN. 1975
MARTY BALIN
JOINS JEFF.
STARSHIP

JUNE 1974
PETE SEARS
BASS

AUG. 1972
JORMA KAUKONEN
JACK CASADY
FORM
**HOT TUNA**
WITH OCCASIONAL
MEMBERS...
PAPA JOHN CREACH
SAMMY PIAZZA
GREG DOUGLAS
BOB STEELER
WIL SCARLET

**JEFFERSON STARSHIP**
FORMED FEB 1974

PAUL KANTNER
RYTHYM GUITAR

CRAIG CHAQUICO
LEAD GUITAR

PAPA JOHN CREACH
ELECTRIC VIOLIN

GRACE SLICK
VOCALS

DAVID FRIEBERG
VOCALS

PETER KAUKONEN
BASS

JOHN BARBATA
DRUMS

JULY 1972
JOHN BARBATA
JOINS
JEFF. AIRPLANE

**GRUNT**
FORMED
AUG/SEPT. 1971

NOV. 1970

AUG. 1972
DAVID FREIBERG
JOINS     VOCALS
JEFF. AIRPLANE

DEC. 1971
"SUNFIGHTER"
GRACE SLICK
PAUL KANTNER

SPRING 1971
MARTY BALIN
LEAVES
JEFFERSON
AIRPLANE

**JEFFERSON STARSHIP**
CONCIEVED BY
PAUL KANTNER + GRACE SLICK + FRIENDS
—WITH—
"BLOWS AGAINST THE
EMPIRE"

JAN. 25 1971
GRACE SLICK GIVES
BIRTH TO "GOD" LATER
RENAMED "CHINA"

EARLY 1970
JOEY COVINGTON
DRUMS

OCT. 1970
PAPA JOHN
CREACH
ELECTRIC VIOLIN

**JEFFERSON**
**AIRPLANE**
1966

MARTY BALIN
LEAD SINGER

PAUL KANTNER
RYTHYM GUITAR

JORMA KAUKONEN
LEAD GUITAR

SPENCER DRYDEN
DRUMS

GRACE SLICK
LEAD SINGER

JACK CASADY
BASS

**JEFFERSON AIRPLANE**
ORIGINAL MEMBERS
1965

MARTY BALIN
LEAD SINGER

PAUL KANTNER
RYTHYM GUITAR

JORMA KAUKONEN
LEAD GUITAR

SKIP SPENCE
DRUMS

SIGNE ANDERSON
2ND LEAD VOCALIST

BOB HARVET
BASS

UNOFFICIALLY
OFFICIAL
FAMILY TREE OF
JEFFERSON AIR/STARSHIP
COMPILED + RESEARCHED
BY
MIKE MCGRATH
ART BY NEAL ROSNER
© 1976 DEAD RELIX

AUG. 13, 1965   FIRST PERFORMANCE
AT THE MATRIX
**JEFFERSON AIRPLANE**
FORMED AT THE DRINKING GOURD S.F.
**PAUL KANTNER**
1965

**MARTY BALIN**
"THE TOWN CRIERS"
1965

## THE WEIRDEST THING THAT EVER HAPPENED TO ME AT A DEAD CONCERT

Tower Theater, Phillie, June 24, The Dead just played an excellent show. It was a very hot night, standing outside I noticed a wierd guy walking toward me coming from the back door. OH G-D, Phil Lesh approaches. I didn't know what to do. I was very wasted, so was he. I tried to start a conversation with him. "Hey, you know you look familiar?" I said. He looked at me, smiled and said, "So Do You." I was freakin out. He had a brown paper bag in his hand. I was wondering what could be in it, so I asked "What's in the bag?" He reached slowly into the bag - he was acting really weird. I was really wrecked. He suddenly pulled his hand out of the bag... I jumped back about 5 feet-in the hand was an icecold can of beer. He gave it to me and then he split. He went back inside laughing. He left me standing there holding the can. I kept saying to myself "That didn't happen, did it?" All the way to Canarsie. By the way, I still have the can.

CLIFF GOLDFARB
CANARSIE, BROOKLYN.

## DAN HICKS  by Jerry

They don't call him Dangerous Dan for nothing. Dan Hicks has a reputation for being slightly, shall we say, "eccentric." Actually Dan's best known groups, the Charlatans and Dan Hicks and his Hot Licks, made their marks more as comedians than as musicians. Old Dan himself goes gonzo at fairly regular intervals.

Danny boy was booked into a Long Island club called "My Father's Place" for a 2 night stand beginning January 7th, when his reputation got the better of him once again.

He was well prepared. His backup was a cassette tape, and he was drunk, as usual, when he staggered to the stage for his first show. The first thing he had to say on taking possession of the stage was "O.K. I'm going to play my 45 minutes, collect my $1,000.00 and leave." He only made it to about the half hour mark.

After a lively exchange of insults, he left the stage, leaving a genuine, knock 'em down bar-room brawl behind him. It was great-like something out of a sloppy John Wayne movie, chair swinging and all.

The rest of Dan's stay was cancelled, but the whole thing was so much fun that the club wants him back again. We can't wait to see what he does next time.

January/February, 1977

Cover Artwork by Gary Kroman

Gary Kroman

Photo by L.D. Kippel

## Interview with Jorma

### by Nick Ralph

NR: What were you and Jack doing in the early 60's?

JK: I was playing coffee houses. I did that for about 8 years before I got in the Airplane; folk clubs, coffee houses, bars, and teaching guitar. That was in California. Jack was back in our old home town, Washington, D.C., and he was teaching music in a music store and taking classes at some college.

NR: When and where was the "typewriter tape" recorded? (this question refers to a recording of Jorma with Janis Joplin, with a typewriter providing the percussion).

JK: It was recorded in San Jose, in late '64 or early '65.

NR: Three of those tracks were broadcast on the radio. Can you remember any other titles?

continued .......

RELIX

Vol. 4 No. 2

$1.50

Mar.- Apr.

March/April, 1977    Cover Artwork by Gary Kroman

plus
New Year's Eve
at The Cow
Palace

Jethro Tull
Commander
Cody

& much
Moore!

HOT TUNA

# Interview with Jorma (Continued)

JK: No, I can't, and I'm really pissed. We did around 14 songs. Janis and I were old friends, and just before we came to England in '68, Janis and this guy came by, and she said she'd really like to borrow the tape. I said "sure", and gave them the original copy of the tape. For some reason she only liked the three cuts that came out. I remember I thought they were all really good. I don't remember what's on it, I never got the original back. I keep trying. I know who has it, and I'd really like to get it back. There's some really good playing on it. It was taped when I was at my peak of that kind of guitar playing, and I think Janis was singing better than she ever did with Big Brother.

NR: How early did Hot Tuna start playing gigs?

JK: Right around the time the accoustic record came out, Grace didn't wanna work, and Jack and I got bored. So, we made an acoustic record and started getting some ideas together for a band.

NR: Who wrote "Keep on Truckin' Mama?"

JK: I really don't know. I've known the song for 15 years, and I've never seen any credit- I mean credits that really belonged to the original writer. I've seen some people claiming arrangments, but I have no idea who wrote it.

NR: Does Jack write at all?

JK: Not really, he just plays around with ideas. We've collaborated on tunes and worked things out in the studio, but he doesn't really write songs. He doesn't sing, and it's kind of hard if you don't sing, unless you play a melodic instrument.

NR: Which is your favorite Hot Tuna album?

JK: Usually the latest one. I really like Quah a lot, and I like the first one a lot. It's hard to say; I can think of something I like about all of them.

NR: Don't you think those two have a similar feel about them?

JK: Yeah, mainly because, except for the stuff I wrote myself on Quah, everything was something I'd known and wanted to record for a long time.

NR: You played acoustic guitar on both those albums. Do you prefer playing acoustic or electric?

JK: I like both: One of these days we'll get the technology so that I can get a good sound on the acoustic guitar, and then I'll do that with bass and drums too.

NR: You use a picking style on many of your electric songs that makes me believe they were originally intended to be acoustic. Were they?

JK: That's because I usually write on the acoustic guitar. There is an acoustic song on the new album.

NR: Now that you seem to be more oriented toward electric playing, does it bother you to be questioned about your acoustic music?

JK: No, 'cause I really like it. It's just that I can't do both things simultaneously. It really is physically different for me to play electric as opposed to acoustic. When I'm adapted to one, my playing on the other is a little stiff. I don't like to have to think when I'm playing, so I either play only electric or only acoustic. When we did our acoustic guitar tour, I didn't play any electric at all for months, because I didn't feel confident switching from one to the other.

NR: Quah could have been a Hot Tuna album. Why did you record it with Tom Hobson?

JK: Because I wanted to try it acoustically. We perform all the songs with the band, and one of these days when we get around to doing another live album, some of them will probably be on it, but it's a different trip. I've known Tom for many years, and I think he's really great. He does a lot of really fine stuff. Originally the album was supposed to be one side of Tom and one side of me, but RCA didn't like a lot of Tom's stuff and wanted more of me. I thought the idea was great, but they had more cards than I did, so I wound up doing more songs and he wound up doing less. We had to change the format around considerably.

NR: Do the lyrics of Quah and Phosphorescent Rat indicate a religious influence or spiritual enlightenment?

JK: Spiritual enlightenment, yeah.

A. Klosterman

May/June, 1977

Cover Artwork by Gary Kroman

## On The Road Again

Cut back in time to June 24, 1974. We could pick up the trail in any one of a number of automobiles, all trying to make the trip from Miami to New York in negative time. We choose to zoom in on one ancient heap, traveling at lunatic speed through a torrential downpour. The spirit of Neal Cassady lives on in the maniac at the wheel. This gent went to the Sunshine State to see the Dead, but got behind so much acid that he somehow forgot to go to the shows. As we find our precise focus in time, the heap is flying across the state line into Savannah at 85 miles each and every hour, as rain beats upon the highway in solid sheets. Our car contains, besides the nut, two more guys, one of whom proudly wears the handle "Crazy." The third guy is our observer, and there are also two young ladies in company with these three fools. The observer cringes in the back seat, paralyzed by fear. He isn't bothered much by the rain, or by the possibility of being picked up by the Georgia state troopers for traveling at 85 per, in company with four stoned freaks and nine or ten assorted chemicals and herbs. After all, he is a Dead freak, and used to such circumstances. Besides, what sensible cop is going to be cruising the highway in a monsoon? Our helpless participator in this event merely wishes that the driver would now and then glance at the road instead of the young ladies in the back seat with him. Deciding that, if death is inevitable, he might as well exit with a smile, our reporter eats a tab of a green tranquilizer. He eats another every time he feels a fresh twinge of anxiety. Five or six hits later, he is reliving every set he has ever heard the Dead play . . .

**Oh, Gosh!**

. . . By the way, while reading the March-April, Vol. 4, No. 2. I saw the list of dates on which the Dead would tour. I called the New Haven Coliseum and found out that they had many tickets left. I went by Amtrack train and bought ten tickets for May 5th. Thanks to your magazine, I'm finally gonna go see the Dead — live. Thank you.
STEVE FIORE

I think the work you people are doing is great. The only thing I like reading better than **Relix** is reading the first 3 digits on my paycheck. (Thank you all)

(Relix Reader Forever)
ANDY SANTASINE
Staten Island, New York

Gary Kroman

Gary Kroman

Vol.4 $1.50
No.4
July–Aug.

Scattered
Recollections
of the
GRATEFUL
DEAD
Tour

Interview
with
George
Frayne

July/August, 1977

Cover Photo by Les D. Kippel

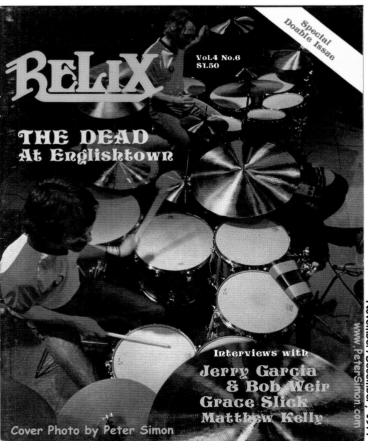

Vol.4 No.6
$1.50

Special Double Issue

THE DEAD
At Englishtown

Interviews with
Jerry Garcia
& Bob Weir
Grace Slick
Matthew Kelly

November/December, 1977
www.PeterSimon.com

Cover Photo by Peter Simon

Gary Kroman

Darkness Falls
&
Seasons Change
by
Jerry Moore
and
Monte Dym

Excerpt from
Vol. 4, No. 6 , 1978

Bob Weir, rhythm guitarist and vocalist for the Grateful Dead, stood pinned by the eye of a CBS camera. He assured the interviewer (who very obviously knew less than nothing about the Dead) that he could indeed play guitar and sing at the same time. The interview and the afternoon heat were part of the price he had to pay for being at that site on that particular day. Ten years ago the Dead were among the acts unleashed on the world at large at Monterey Pop. Eight years ago they played for 400,000 people at Woodstock, but bowed out of Altamont after feeling the ugliness in the air at the Speedway. Four years ago they woke 600,000 at Watkins Glen. The media built legends around those events, but somehow managed to miss the fact that the Dead were the only chain linking them all. On this past September third, 125,000 people showed up at Raceway Park, in Englishtown, New Jersey, to hear the Dead, the Marshall Tucker Band, and the New Riders of the Purple Sage. The networks came along too, and they have finally caught the notion that the Dead themselves are news. Bob Weir has been interviewed on national TV. God help us all, Andy Warhol was right. Everybody *has* been famous for 15 minutes.

Bobby Weir, when asked by the interviewer to what he attributed the Dead's 12 years together and the tremendous turnout for their show, replied, tongue in cheek and hand on heart: "Dedication."

Dedication it must surely be. The Dead have survived together through 12 years of total confusion, some of those years remarkably lean. They have always worked close to the edge, for, whenever they have made money on one project, they have lost it on another. So, after 12 years the Dead are still struggling, but they endure, having weathered tempests that would have destroyed any band less determined. They have become an institution the hard way.

RELIX Vol.5 No.1 Mar.-Apr. $1.50 1978

Cover Photo by Dave Patrick

Hot Tuna

McGuinn, Clark & Crosby

Papa John Creach

...more!

Grateful Dead lyricist: Robert Hunter

## The Man Behind The Words
### Excerpt From Volume 5, Numbers 1 and 2
### by Monte Dym & Bob Alson

Robert Hunter, of course, is lyricist of long standing to the Grateful Dead. More recently he has been a recording artist, with two albums under his belt, **Tales of the Great Rum Runners** and **Tiger Rose.** Lately he has become a performer in his own right, first with **Roadhog** and **Barry Melton's** band, and now with **Comfort.** He has in the past been shy of any publicity, so we feel honored and extremely grateful that he has chosen to unburden himself here.

**Jerry Moore**

**Relix: You have been known as a recluse. In fact, you once wrote a piece for Crawdaddy explaining that you didn't give interviews. What is compelling you at this moment to come out front and be more of a public figure than you have been?**

**Hunter:** Having an eight piece band to support, and a road crew, engineers, management and everything. If you're going to do a number like this you *have* to do it. There's no holding back. I have to get out, get my face seen, and make up answers to questions. That's the sad but true tested method.

**Relix: You must be at a point where you're trying to do something to get your energy flowing in a different way. Have you wanted to perform all this time?**

**Hunter:** I felt that I *was* performing with the Dead over all that period of time, and I woke up to find myself pretty much unknown. This is a big surprise to me. I thought I was quite well known.

Oh well, you actually have to get out there and do all that stuff. You have to promote yourself and make sure your big ugly face gets out in pictures and all that, or you just glide by and your opportunities to do things are gone. I had always intended to actually perform, and before I did this Dead thing I *was* performing; I had a band with Garcia and Nelson. It had at least half a dozen different names. And before that I had performed in high school, in my own band called the Crescents in which I played trumpet and . . . back to my Harry James fantasy. I did my last year of high school and my first year of college in Connecticut, but I was always performing. I was in the army for a while, and I was always hanging out in the service club, working in the shows playing folk songs and stuff. But the Dead as a performing unit were just so heavy there was really nothing to do if I didn't join them, which I didn't or couldn't. I couldn't play anything well enough to join *that* band. I *don't* know why I didn't perform.

Now I regret not having performed for a couple of years, except possibly that I'd be burned out as a performer at this point. It may be that I needed not to have done that in order to have the right ring of energy to write at the time.

**Relix: If you were good enough to perform with the Dead would you have?**

**Hunter:** I suppose I would've. There wouldn't have been any reason not to.

**Relix: There's a mystique about Robert Hunter the recluse, who doesn't want to be public. It would be great to get it down in your own words and lay all those myths to rest.**

**Hunter:** I *was* paranoid for a while, around the time of **American Beauty** and **Workingman's Dead,** of having my face seen. I thought we were such a phenomenal number that I would lose my identity by feeding it to the public. My face wouldn't be my possession anymore. There was definitely an element of this. I guess I was chicken to be known at that point. *Yellow.* I don't feel that I could lose my identity out in the public world at this point, because I kind of have it socked away.

**Relix: I think a lot of your lyrics relate to something deeper than the Grateful Dead. They're an understanding of the life principle. I've always elevated your lyrics, rather than bringing them down strictly to being about the Grateful Dead.**

**Hunter:** That's my work. That's what I do. Some of it relates to Dead, some only relates to me, some to horrible attitudes, good attitudes, *whatever*. It's not specifically Grateful Dead, in the sense that "Truckin' " is, or something like that. That song is legitimately about the Dead.

**Relix: Seeing that song work so beautifully last night, I have to ask about this continuing thing with "Truckin'." I'm sure there was more written than was sung. Do you think they'll add some verses to that song on stage?**

**Hunder:** I hope so, because I wrote a whole bunch more on demand a couple of months ago. I don't know if they're going to do them or not. I was against the idea to begin with, thought we should just let it lie. I *was* asked to do it, so I sat down and found it was very easy to do and I enjoyed updating it. As to whether they'll do it or not, I have no indication. There is *no* communication within this group as to what gets done.

**Relix: Let's go back to the crazy 60's again. A lot has been written about the Acid Tests, Kesey, Garcia, the Dead, and what everybody was doing then. Where were you in relation to the whole trip at that time?**

**Hunter:** I wasn't part of the Kesey scene. We were all living in a house in Palo Alto on Waverly Street and Jerry was there. The crew kind of just picked up Jerry and his wife and split. They went off with the Kesey crowd to L.A. to do those acid trips, and I didn't go along 'cause I wasn't in the band. I wasn't into acid in *that* way, as a show. I was into it as a kind of personal trip 'cause I'd been through those things at the Stanford Hospital. I was the only one I knew who had taken the stuff, and I was a bit surprised that they took it to that level. When they brought it back to San Francisco and made the Acid Tests, I can remember being at the Longshoremen's Acid Test, and I was thinking, "This is **Hell**, this is the worst thing I've ever seen." Then Kesey was writing on an overhead projector, and on the ceiling it said: *"Outside is inside, how does it look?"* I went *"Aaaahhhhhhh . . . . "* because it was true, and I was seeing hell projected out there, and all of a sudden I did that whole little flip around. That's been one of my little guiding mottos ever since, because it became very, very ecstatic and very groovy after I stopped projecting my own hell out there. It became very nice indeed and I had a wonderful time — so that was *my* Acid Test flip-over. The other thing that always happened at those Acid Tests was that at the end of them I'd always run into Paul Foster sweeping up afterwards. That's something that always seems to me to occur in eternity: at the end of all these trips I'm going to run into Paul Foster sweeping up and we'll exchange a few words about this and that . . . .

Artwork by Glenn Harding

**Relix: What were the government experiments with Kesey like?**

**Hunter:** Well, I didn't know Ken at that time, although he was on those tests also. Peter Dema also was involved in them.

**Relix: How did they approach you on it? Draw your name at random?**

**Hunter:** I heard from Heath Moon that they were doing tests with LSD and Mescaline and what-not at Stanford, and he had the phone number. I called up and volunteered. They took me in and gave me a battery of psychological tests to see if I was stable enough to go through it. They paid me 140 dollars for the four tests, which lasted one a week over a period of a month. There were people who were totally unprepared, you know, who knew nothing about the experience. I *had* read Huxley's book, but I told them I hadn't, 'cause I really did want to get in on the trip, and what they called psychoto-mimetic drugs. They were interested in seeing what they did to my idio-motor responses; they wanted to see if I was more hypnotic, or could be hypnotized more easily, on the drugs than without them. I don't know if I was or not. I'm not sure what they came up with.

**Relix: Were you confined in one place for that month, or were you allowed to roam free in society in between the tests?**

**Hunter:** Oh yea, right. Eight hours later I was free to go, as long as somebody picked me up. But I tried to escape the first time on acid. I have *never* had better acid than they gave me, or better mescaline, or better psilocybin — boy *they* had the stuff! Here I was — this stuff came on — I, for the first time on this earth of all men, finally realized the *full* truth of just what was going on, you know, the powers of the mind. I had to tell the world and so I tried. I opened my door and looked around and started sneaking down the hall, and this nurse saw me and tried to steer me back into the room — boy, was *she* scared! She thought I was a frothing loony and I was only an enlightened man! I saw how upset she was, and I went back in because I didn't want to upset her anymore. The guy came in and started running the idio-motor tests. He'd come in, draw 5 cc's of blood every two hours or so, and then run these tests on me. I was sitting in the chair and he was running these tests, and suddenly great tears started running down my face. He asked me what was happening, and I explained to him that I wasn't crying; that I was inhabiting the body of this great green Buddha who had a pool in his lap and that the pool was running through my eyes. I brought a typewriter along for those tests, not having such things as cassette machines in those

days, and I wrote down what was happening on my first trips, I have them stashed away somewhere. But after that it was a year or more before I ran into acid on the streets. I couldn't believe it, you know? I thought at the time that if there was any of that lying around I would've scooped it up and put it in my pocket, because it never occured to me that that was ever going to become a popular drug or that I would ever again be allowed to experience those things. And indeed you never do experience the first acid trip again, I guess.

**Relix: I wanted to ask you about Neal Cassady. We never met the man, but from what we've read we understand that he was a pretty heavy dude.**

**Hunter:** Yes he was.

**Relix: Garcia has described him as "The total communicator." What are your ideas?**

**Hunter:** He used to visit me a lot. He paid me the compliment of saying that when he goes to New York he visits Bill Burroughs, and when he comes out here he hangs out at my house. I don't know; he was probably just trying to get some bennies and some camels off me. That's all Neal ever wanted, was a benny and a pack of camels. He would sit there and I'd come in and hand him a microphone or something like that, so I had a lot of that on tape. I subsequently lost those tapes, but he did one tape that I would play, and I'd *swear* that every time I played that tape that there would be a different conversation with me on it. He was flying circles above me. I said "I have a book on that subject." He says "he *would*" — and not in a put-down way, but it was true — I *would,* you know. Listening to that I hear myself kind of bumbling around with what appeared to be a seventy-eyed creature. I was Flakey Foont to his Mr. Natural there. He was Mr. Natural for us. He would say things and if you had him on tape and could listen back, you could hear replies you hadn't heard — multi-faceted replies. The man was phenomenal, a phenomenal brain, yea. He was a *wonderful* guy.

**Relix: Talking to him was like looking in the mirror or something?**

**Hunter:** I tell you, it was hard not to be Neal after he was around. He was such a master of any social situation that you would learn it yourself, and when he was away it would take weeks before you would stop being Neal. This was true of all of us. It was a way of handling a lot of communications. *Sawazzawas I was saying aszwasa say ya wouldn't happenta have a packa camels on ya ha ha hazawaa. . . . . [Slurred]* And you could do it, and it would create the same impression on other people when you were being Neal

as Neal would create on you when he was being himself. Bradley Hodgeman was our best stand-in Neal when Neal wasn't around. He and Ann Murphy would go at it just as though he was Neal. He was such a type that you could get him down; an original. He had a dynamic life, and it was just *packed.* He just enjoyed the *hell* out of it. As long as he could get a pack of camels and a benny he was cool. Never shot any stuff, he was just an all time benny man.

Driving with him was such an experience. Of course you've heard that story a million times, I'm sure. But it was *sooo* frightening because he would depend on his radar, and *I* didn't have that radar and couldn't relax. I finally swore that I'd never drive with that madman again. He'd have your hair standing on end, and destroy your car too! He'd run right through that thing, man.

**Relix: The vision from Electric Koolaide Acid Test, of coming down the mountain.**

**Hunter:** I've been down that mountain with him, coming out of La Honda.

**Relix: Nine mile skid, I guess.**

**Hunter:** Yea, that's a subject you can warm to and talk all day about. That little record that Hank Harrison put into his Dead Book, though, gives you a good idea of his rap. He was like that, except that he was not at his top form on the record except for moments. You'd hand him a book or something if you wanted to talk to him, or a magazine or whatever, and he'd start rapping off current events and whatnot, making all connections.

Photo by Dave Patrick

Artwork by Glenn Harding

**Relix:** Right, that's the key. The key to the rain. Did you write "The Other One?" That was well before Aoxomoxoa. It never says anything specifically on the album, just that it's by the Grateful Dead.

**Hunter:** No. Jerry wrote the parts he sings on that, and Weir wrote the parts he sings.

**Relix:** Was Aoxomoxoa the first album you collaborated on with the Dead?

**Hunter:** Well, the first thing I got credit for. I wrote "Alligator" with them the year before.

**Relix:** That didn't appear as a credit on the album.

**Hunter:** No, surprisingly enough.

**Relix:** Who was the inspiration for "He's Gone?"

**Hunter:** Lenny.

**Relix:** Lenny of Hart? Great. *[laughter]*

**Hunter:** I warned them about him from the beginning. That song just contained more warning: "Rat in a drain ditch out on a limb / You know better than I know him." People thought is was about Pigpen after Pig died, but they didn't think. It was predated and stuff.

**Relix:** It could've been anyone.

**Hunter:** Well, that's just it. There are some times when you can pick out something that gets you to write. But most of my things are *not* sketches of any individual person. I might start off with something in mind, but then the character becomes its own thing in the song and acquires its own attributes. They may be composite attributes, but they're not often about anyone in particular. I'd rather know groups of things. I've got some bitching block, like "Keys to the rain," and I might take half a dozen people, incidents, bummers ("Ship of fools" or something like that) and take a whole bunch of things and put it all into one crashing bummer of a song. I still enjoy doing "Keys to the rain." I don't feel that way anymore, but it's punk you know, and I enjoy it from that point of view.

**Relix: Do you have any formula for writing with Garcia, or is it just one song at a time any way it falls together?**

**Hunter:** I'm starting to get a bunch of scraps together for him now. It's always different. When we lived together in Larkspur, the way we'd write a song was I'd sit upstairs banging away at my three chords for days and days working something out. By the time I had it worked out you know, through the thin walls he'd heard everything I was doing. I'd come down and hand him this sheet of paper, and he'd say "Oh, that's interesting," and he'd play the whole arrangement of it right away, because he'd heard what I was doing and heard where it was going off. I never took any great care to compose very well.

Because I knew he was going to handle that, I got pretty lazy about composition. I've written a few compositions this time for the new album that I think are showing potential. I'm not a good tune writer.

**Relix: Terrapin was a major composition; it seemed like an epic. But I've heard that the major portion was totally deleted. Are you happy with the way it's being done, since it is beautiful work, or do you feel that it was hacked at?**

**Hunter:** I'm dissatisfied in that the symbology in it isn't resolved. It sets up this whole thing and it sets up the symbols that I play with. At the end of it I had Venus rising out of the sea on the back of a mighty Terrapin tossing a coral fan to the beach. In my final image I anthropomorphized my images. It's unsatisfying to me in that it's only the proposition, and the resolution isn't there.

**Relix: You wrote out the resolution, though.**

**Hunter:** Oh yea, I handed them the whole work. I just *wrote* the thing, I had no intention of giving it to *them*. I was just writing this piece, and when I was done with it I said Wow, this would be a good Dead piece that might be just what we're looking for, maybe we should get away from rock n' roll for a while and really do a full piece. And I also asked that it *not* be shortened. But the exigencies of the record business are such that we just really couldn't do a number like that. One side is plenty: two sides of it would've been unacceptable. Jerry set some of the other tunes of it to music already. There just wasn't space enough for it on the album.

**Relix: Which are your favorite songs, the ones you are proudest of?**

**Hunter:** I like "Ripple" a whole lot and "It Must Have Been the Roses," and I like "Cumberland Blues" and "Dupree." "Ramble on Rose" is a particular favorite — there's something funny about that song. I like "Friend of the Devil;" I thought that was the closest we've come to what may be a classic song.

**Relix: It seemed like just before Blues For Allah there was a lull in activity. I sensed it all around the Bay area. Very little new material at all was coming out. I thought that, rather than writing a whole album's worth of songs, you devoted more time to what you did write.**

**Hunter:** I think a lot of the songs on **Blues For Allah** were terribly overworked. From the lyric point of view those were *not* flow easy songs, those were sit down and write it a thousand times, you know, get each line just right. I'm *not* terribly fond of my lyrics for **Blues For Allah.**

**Relix: But you did print the lyrics for the first time on that album. Is this going to continue?**

**Hunter:** Yea, just because so much of it is lost that I'm surprised. A lot of the questions that people ask me show that the lyrics are not getting through. There's no reason to hide them any longer. I used to think that if I printed the lyrics, the band would take the opportunity to mix the vocals down even further. I felt if they didn't print them they would *have* to be on the record. Also, I didn't *want* people to get the whole message right away. I didn't like lyrics on records because I would read them and that was it, I'd hear the music and I'd see the message, and so much for *that* record. I wanted our records so that you had to listen to them a bunch to get it all, so that you were forced to listen to them rather than having it right at your grasp. But that was an egotistical stance, and right now I think it's probably better to go ahead and print them.

I'm going to start doing that with Jerry's new album. I want to publish the lyrics because I've got some real good things this time, stuff that I don't want to go just by the by. People read an amazing amount of stuff into my work, and there's an amazing amount of stuff that they *don't* hear. They hear something else other than the amazing thing I wanted them to hear. Take for example "Might As Well," which nobody even knows was about the Canadian train trip.

Photo by Dave Patrick

Glenn Harding

Photo Credit Lloyd Baldwin

**Relix: About the new Garcia album: I was back in New York for his last tour, and I saw just about all the shows. I wasn't that impressed with the energy level of the performances, but I thought the new stuff was excellent. I thought "Reuben and Cherise" was great.**

**Hunter:** Wouldn't you. That's why I want to print lyrics: I don't want *those* words lost.

**Relix: They're lost because they're flying by with the rhythm in that song. Sounds like a great cosmic fairy tale, but I can't make heads or tails of it.**

**Hunter:** It's the story of Orpheus, and I've added a few little touches, like the singing mandolin which I have after Cherise is carted off to the underworld, and I have Cherise's voice coming from Reuben's painted mandolin while he's playing it to Ruby Claire. When Jerry sings those lines like that (if you can hear them) they make your flesh crawl. It gives me goose bumps; I get chills up my spine; my hairs stand on end. I can only ask that it be *heard,* that's all. We'll print it just in case.

**Relix: Just how much of the new album did you write?**

**Hunter:** I wrote all the lyrics on it, except for the song that Donna sings, that she wrote herself. "Cats under the stars" is something I've been working on for years and years. We've got that one down — a super simplified version which I think is very effective. That came from a scribble I did. I was trying a new art form. You've seen all my Hypnocracy stuff, all those elaborate things. I decided *nuts* with that style, and held my pencil with my fist like

that, and I did these cats. You know, just baby stuff, and that was cats under the stars. Then I wrote a long article on the meaning of cats under the stars that I published in Crawdaddy a couple years back. It was one of those St. Dilbert tales. Then I wrote some changes for it, and even wrote a song about it, and messed with it for a long time. Finally I handed the lyrics over to Jerry after I could go no further with it.

**Relix: I wouldn't think the Dead would work out in advance exactly what they're going to do in a jam. They might have some idea of what's coming next, but it always seems subject to change.**

**Hunter:** Yea. Often Weir will suddenly decide that he wants to do something that's in that same key and he'll start sending signals out, and **wham!** suddently they're into it. If you're hip enough to the Dead you can usually tell a few bars before they do it, if you can hear those signals going back and forth, but you find out about the same time that the band does. It's hard to say how much of that stuff is planned. There still is that vital element of telepathy about the Dead. I wouldn't say it's telepathy exactly, just an absolute understanding of where everyone is about to go next, from playing together for so long.

**Relix: How old were you when you felt that writing might click, when you really believed you might be a writer?**

**Hunter:** I *never* lacked for self confidence in that. I always assumed I was going to be a great writer. Ever since I was a kid my goal was to be a great writer. Not to write, mind you, but to be a great writer. . . .

**Relix: Do you have any plans to publish anything other than lyrics at this point?**

**Hunter:** No, but I think I'm going to put out a book of all the lyrics. It's always a question of waiting for one more record

Photo by Dave Patrick

project to get done, because I want to put *those* lyrics in it too. But it's getting time. I've got probably about 150 lyrics to publish at this point.

**Relix: History looks back. I took my English courses, and we had the complete works of T.S. Elliot . . .**

**Hunter:** There's one who influenced the *hell* out of me, come to think of it.

**Relix: He had his periods, and images he used early in his writing, and he went back in later years and changed them. I'm sure he went through the same trip of "when will I publish." Here's my works through this period, and here's my works for that period. I'm sure that over the years as you progress, you'll gain that acceptance. The faith that you have in yourself I think is well founded.**

**Hunter:** You've got to have it — you get so dejected in this sort of business. I've had the mickey taken out of me by critics to the point where I couldn't write for months at a time. Lester Bangs once called my stuff "non-ending streams of murkily pretentious non-sequeitors." I went . . . *goooolk* . . . . and I couldn't write for six months after that! That guy just came up and threw a bomb in my face. That was a very important phrase to me. It struck home in a lot of ways. Sometimes I'll look at my stuff and say "Is this murkily pretentious non-sequeitor here?" It hurt enough for me to sit up and take notice, for which I thank him, actually. I *don't* develop from people saying nice things about me. You usually develop when somebody slams you and it hurts. When it hurts, it's for a reason. If it's off the target, it's just snottiness, and you dismiss it.

**Relix: Was Saint Stephen anyone specific?**

**Hunter:** No, it was just Saint Stephen.

**Relix: You weren't writing about someone, you were writing about something?**

**Hunter:** Yea, yea. That was a great song to write. I think it took a couple of nights of writing on that, of intense light feeling. It was like I was on to something there, I felt the radiance happening. I'd like to have some of those feelings again, some of those times when the light seems to be in your hands. You follow it along, and some beautiful things just come to you.

**Relix: We seem to have covered most areas.**

**Hunter:** Oh well, it's always a pleasure to sit back and talk about yourself. My old lady won't listen to it anymore.

Glenn Harding

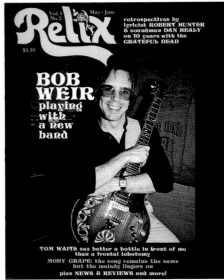

Cover Photo by Dave Patrick      May/June, 1978

Cover Photo Courtesy Grunt Records      Sept./Oct., 1978

Cover Photo by Les D. Kippel      Nov./Dec., 1978

# Editorial: Meditations Ten Years After

## By Jerry Moore

### Easter Sunday 1968

'Twas a day for a walk in the park, a day for celebrating the spring, a day for dreams to be born. Though dawn broke cold the day grew warmer under skies bluer than the eyes of god. Easter morning, and rebirth come again. Even in grey New York City the birds were singing . . . .

. . . . singing despite LBJ, despite Vietnam, despite the national karma hanging heavy over our parents' heads. One nation seemingly without hope; a Nixon roadblock awaiting it six months ahead. How could the birds have known America was a brainwashed dead end?

Central Park spread wide in Easter's dawn, empty save for the handful chanting the sunrise from one of its hilltops. A handful of freaks, a hairy rabble, a human zoo. With beads, feathers, flowers and their many voices, they eased that tired old sun along its way.

Maybe there were 200 there, or more or less. Conviction counts for more than numbers, and nobody there was straight enough to tally heads. It was a weird bunch. For some this might have been a religious experience. For more maybe a trip. For others just a cool thing to do. For the rest an accident? For all it was the start of the Human Be-In.

A party to last from sunup to sundown.

Also an attack on American society.

The longhairs just hung out; they had nothing else to do. Companion souls arrived through the day, to a total of perhaps 20,000. Numbers as well as conviction. No class divisions, no stages. Allen Ginsberg and Phil Ochs were there, just being themselves. The cast of Hair roamed, and Wavy Gravy totally surpassed himself spinning lunatic magic. Richard Farina floated, smile a mile wide.

Emmett Grogan came, to claim the concept "free" couldn't happen. Paul Krassner came too, to call Emmett an asshole.

And nobody was a nobody. The famed freely mingled with the unsung.

With chanting, singing, guitar strumming, portable record players screaming and silence in pockets reigning, the party exploded through the park. From all corners the Airplane and their multiplied west coast cousins made their twelve inch vinyl statements. Joyful chaos ruled.

Fifth Avenue tags Central Park's entire eastern edge: Saint Patrick's Cathederal stands in pompous pride a few blocks from its southeast corner. The Human Be-In shared its special day with the Easter Parade. Straight City.

In the mid morning normal people drifted into the park, from Saint Pat's and her lesser cousins. Dressed in their Easter best, they met the freaks their children had become. Suits and dresses meet body paint. Shades of drabness meet the rainbow. Holy Communion meets LSD. New York meets California (sanity meets madness).

Your parents really saw their offspring for the first time. They were horrified. They didn't understand.

....Lookit George, orange tongues....

....Is it an infection ....hope it isn't contagious.... (It was)

The police didn't understand either They were grossly upset, especially with the clowns who burned the American flag (one of the day's more asinine gestures). Such nonsense aside, the Be-In wasn't a political event.

'Twas instead a day for volleyball, for making love, for playing games. Mind games. America we have come for your daughters, not your wallets.

Society and its freak splinters mixed like oil and water, and the freaks kept playing with matches.

During the day a team of standard model jocks fell into a volleyball game with a motley band of athletically inclined crazies. The jocks had the match locked until the freaks introduced a couple of extra balls to the game, totally confusing the opposition. Normal folk aren't used to seeing triple. They dropped out (unable to cope with madmen) leaving the volleyball net the center of a wild, multi-hued lysergic circus.

Since they refused to take any games seriously, the freaks won all encounters. Society won't play with you if you won't follow the rules.

Bob Fass dashed madly around this carnival, trying to get the whole damn thing on tape. The poor guy was too far gone even to decide which end of his mike to talk into. Somewhere (probably on a dusty shelf at WBAI) is one of the oddest recordings ever made.

Artwork by Glenn Harding

Continues...

# Meditations Ten Years After

## By Jerry Moore   (Continued)

The jubilee had come to New York City . . . .

freedom . . . .

pure joy . . . .

liquid light . . . .

lunacy . . . .

The great spirit walked the park in invisible majesty, and somewhere down the wind Pan faintly played his pipes. Osirus held court by Bethesda Fountain, as Lucifer passed out sugar cubes in the Central Park Zoo. We were all brothers and sisters while party time reeled and rocked along till sunset.

New York met the enemy: the enemy had a wonderful day . . . .

. . . . a glorious day locked into eternity.

**Easter Sunday 1978.**

'Tis a day for sitting indoors with pen and paper, a day for wondering what became of the spring, a day for dreaming of warmer days. This morning's as cold as Easter began ten years back, but holds no promise of warming. Rain beats at my window in sheets: the sky's a shade of grey unlikely to draw a second glance. It's been a foul winter in New York City. If any birds survived they're well hidden.

A rather gloomy day on the face of things. I'd intended to visit Central Park today as many Easters before, but that's not going to happen. No need to drown myself in service to journalism. The day's better spent getting stoned at home, and in contemplation of days ten years removed. Three thousand six hundred and fifty days vanished — where did they all go?

A decade ago this Easter a generation separated from its parents. The world changing, we changed with it. Twenty thousand freaks, mutant children, made a spectacle of themselves in Central Park, birthing the headless wonder known as the Human Be-In.

Critical mass reached . . . .

. . . . enough people had stepped across the line defining madness to make the change permanent. The line was boldly drawn: a counter-culture existed outside California.

In grim New York peace, love and flowers for a day replaced paranoid shackles and chains.

Ten years provides a long perspective. A decade is a seventh of a full human life; more than a third of mine. The kid I was ten years ago is dead; today I'm a long haired dope smoking freak in patched jeans, in many ways like millions of others.

For better or worse, the world changed in the sixties. LBJ and Vietnam are almost forgotten. These days you can walk down Fifth Avenue at lunchtime smoking a joint: even the cops leave you alone. Boredom is a more present problem than paranoia. For ten years we've been so outrageous they've learned to leave us alone. Besides, what once was considered weird is now pretty close to the norm.

The Human Be-In did it, with other rites of passage . . . .

The Gathering of the Tribes . . . .

Chicago . . .

Woodstock . . .

Altamont . . . .

Kent State . . .

The list could roll on through ten years of insanity. Modern times and the counter-culture have combined to warp minds and alter history. Nixon is gone and so are the sixties: there's no turning back.

Easter may be gloomier today than it was ten years ago. No matter. The total picture is a lot brighter. Though outside it's as cold, wet and miserable a day as any I can remember, my spirits remain high. Spring will come again, though not today

It's a good day. ∎

Photo by Dave Patrick

Photo Courtesy Relix Archives

Moritorium Day, Central Park, New York City
October 15, 1969

*Peace Symbols Courtesy Andy Schwartz*

# The Relix Interview: PHIL LESH

## by Karen Kohberger

*Phil Lesh is, beyond a shadow of a doubt, one of the most inventive bassists in rock today. For fifteen years, Lesh has supplied the Grateful Dead's bottom, but unlike most bass players, Lesh doesn't just stick to simple structural bass rifts — he's all over his instrument, providing much of the color and the melodic direction as well.*

*Lesh rarely gives interviews, but **Relix's** Karen Kohberger, with the assistance of Sunburst Studios in Chicago and a pack of Heinekens, managed to spend some time with Lesh and Dead manager Rock Scully while the band was in the Windy City for a set of shows at the Uptown Theater. Their conversation took place late last year and began with a discussion of the then-unfinished new Grateful Dead album.*

**Relix: Are the new songs that the band has been performing live going to be on the new album?**
PL: Oh yeah, and there are two more that we haven't worked out yet. There are eight songs on the album, and all are brand new except one called "Don't Ease Me In," which is an old Jugband tune we used to do.

**Relix: So, the album isn't finished yet, is it?**
PL: Not yet, unfortunately. What we're doing right now is touring the midwest promoting an album that doesn't exist. It's kind of absurd.

**Relix: Who is producing the album?**
PL: Gary Lyons, who has done Foreigner and just finished up Aerosmith.

**Relix: Do all the songs have titles yet?**
PL: Only Bobby's new songs don't have names yet. Even Bobby doesn't know what his tunes are called. There are three of them, of which we now do two. All three are supposed to be related and go together. He composed it that way.

**Relix: Did Robert Hunter write the lyrics?**
PL: No, Bob and John Barlow, his regular guy, wrote them. Gary Lyons and Brent Mydland probably helped, too.
RS: And Matt Kelly, too.
PL: And Jerry has two new songs. One is called "Alabama Getaway" and it's a rock and roll song. The other is "Althea," and that's a spooky blues kind of song. Brent, our new guy, the new kid, ha! He has some,

too. He's damn good. He writes and sings beautifully. He wrote the song that he's been singing in concert, called "Easy To Love You." And there's another one called "Far From Me," which is just as good but we haven't worked out yet.

**Relix: What's the reason you don't sing any more?**
PL: Because I lost my voice and I refuse to have an operation. Bob thinks acupuncture might work.

**Relix: Didn't you work with Francis Ford Coppola on *Apocalypse Now*?**
PL: I worked with Mickey Hart, and Mickey worked with Francis. But when I went to see the movie, there wasn't one thing that I did in the soundtrack. And furthermore, in my opinion, the soundtrack to **Apocalypse Now** is dogshit. The best thing about it is the sound effects. That's what I liked about it. I have a video tape of it at home, and there's no music, except for the Doors. There are only a few moments where there was anything resembling music. The thing about that was that Francis was in traction in the hospital when the final sound editing was going on. And whoever it was that put it together, you couldn't print what I think about it. Francis wanted jungle music and he got plenty of it. But out of all the stuff that Mickey did, I can only hear two minutes worth in the movie. But it's a great movie. It's the best movie I've seen since **2001.** Even though I think Mickey got burned.
RS: He was sure treated well financially.
PL: Yeah, but that's not what he was after.

**Relix: Will the Dead ever play at the Pyramids in Egypt again?**
PL: Thing about Egypt that made it cool for us, morally, was that we didn't go in there and take any money out of the country. They're poor; they're fucking starving. But the other thing is that playing the Pyramids ended up costing us half a million dollars. That was worth it, but we can't afford to do it again. The way it was set up, the tickets went to two different Egyptian charities. Even if we had made a record...well, we won't unfortunately, because the performances weren't that good. The chance of a lifetime and we blew it. You can never push a button and say it's going to come out right.

**Relix: There's a rumor that starting in 1980, the Dead are going to play shows that are only one set.**
PL: Lies! It's possible that we might change our format, though. We've been locked in to this damn format for quite a while now. I think we're the only band that plays as long as we do; correct me if I'm wrong. But that's what the Dead Heads want. One thing is that we haven't even touched on half of our material. Since Brent joined the band, we've only had a certain amount of time to

Photo by Bruce Polonsky

**Reno, Nevada - 1974**

rehearse. And what we needed to do was rehearse the most frequently played stuff, the stuff in our standard repertoire. We try never to repeat. We almost never do a song two nights in a row.

**Relix: Will the Dead ever play acoustic sets again?**
PL: It would be better to ask Jerry that question. I understand that he was asked that question and he said probably not, because of the differences in touch between the acoustic guitar and the electric guitar. One makes you useless on the other. And Jerry has to play electric all the time. I wonder if he ever picks up an acoustic guitar, except for just fucking around.

**Relix: Do you ever play trumpet anymore?**
PL: Not since 1968. I played eight bars in the middle of "Born Cross Eyed."

**Relix: Do you listen to other music besides rock and roll?**
PL: Oh yeah, I was brought up on classical music.

**Relix: Have you ever composed symphonies?**
PL: Sort of. I have a few projects that I have on hold, waiting for the Grateful Dead to die down a little. The only time I have to myself, I'm not much interested in doing work. Sometimes I like to sit around and read science fiction, and watch TV.

**Relix: If you could sum up your feelings about music, what it all means to you, how would you?**
PL: I don't know how to sum up fifteen years of what it all means. Jerry is better at that than I am. He could give it all to you in three sentences. Music is life enhancing. It makes your life worth living a little more, even if you're doing alright, even if you're feeling good. And if you're not, it makes you feel a little better. Music itself is a question. ■

Vol.5
No.3

# Relix

65463

August

$1.50

Photo by L.D. Kippel

# The trail to Cairo   By Monte Dym

From overflowing mounds of second hand information, I've gleaned one certain fact: on the nights of September 14th, 15th and 16th, the Dead indeed played at a place called the Sound and Light Theatre, located near the base of the Great Pyramid in Giza, Egypt. The three shows were arranged as a cooperative effort of the Grateful Dead and the Egyptian Ministry of Culture. The role of the State Department, they say, was kept to a minimum. I suspect that our current administration, given the choice, would be more into exporting Eubie Blake or the Allman Brothers. All proceeds from these shows were to go to Egyptian charities, as well as for the preservation of ancient architecture in that hoary land. Final estimates on production costs ran close to the half million mark. *That* had to make a sizable dent in the band's wallets, but living out this type of rock and roll fantasy couldn't have come cheap.

On each of the three nights, the shows began at 9:30 P.M. with an opening act. Hamza El-Din, a link between San Francisco and the Nile Valley, began the shows, later to be joined by the Dead in a jam session from which they would launch their set. El-Din is noted for his mastery of the oud, an instrument of the middle eastern variety.

And, after Hamza, the Sphinx looked down impassively for three nights at a stage bearing one of the stranger fruits of western civilization, the Grateful Dead. Subjective interpretations of the music played ran the scale from sublime to disappointing, depending on who you talked to. Those let down by the shows had gone there in expectation of musical revelation. Music simply *good* wouldn't have been good enough for *them,* in light of the mystic associations of the concert site. Two things are clear. First, the Dead failed to open the heavens. They found neither the lost chord nor a lost song. Even under eternity in Egypt they've abandoned "Blues For Allah," and there was never a hint of "Dark Star." Song lists say little relevant to musical virtues, but it would have seemed approiapriate had the Dead chosen to play something they'd neglected in recent months. Secondly, and more important than my first point, serious doubts arise concerning the live album some (including the Dead) expected the shows

to produce. They played suspiciously few songs that haven't already appeared on a live album or the two most recent studio albums. *I'd* be into hearing 90 minutes of jamming, but even if this were feasible, I doubt that Arista would be too hip to the idea. The record would have been called something like **Egypt 78;** now it might have to be renamed **No Commercial Potential.**

The audience, as you might have expected, was far from being your typical Deadhead assembly. There were two thousand chairs set up on the site, but considering the endless reaches of desert stretching all around, seeing a show without a ticket would have been no very difficult task. The crowds grew larger as the nights went by but turnout never reached overflow proportions. Those gathered comprised a melting pot of world cultures.

**Gary Kroman**

The Dead played through a sound system shipped down from London, England. The stage was set up in front of the ruins of an ancient building with the Sphinx as a backdrop and with Cheops' tomb, the greatest of the pyramids, standing thirty stories tall just off to the right. At opposite ends of the pyramid's burial chamber were set up a speaker and microphone. Direct sound from the stage was transmitted through the buried speaker, and sent back to the p.a. system by way of the microphone.

Hence an ancient king's monument served the 1978 function of echo chamber. The combination of lighting and sound achieved was described as nothing short of spectacular. The stage, the Sphinx, and several pyramids were all illuminated, to lend an air of universality to the scene. They didn't name it the Sound and *Light* Theatre for nothing.

Though hashish was freely and openly smoked by any who cared to, reports were that the area was somewhat less than heavenly, especially for American women. Perhaps the natives learned about "American foxes" from **Saturday Night Live**. In any case, there were instances where Egyptian men, protected by the language barrier from any clever stateside subtleties, took out in hot pursuit. It was culture shock to the maximum.

In another unrelated but **similarly** annoying cultural clash, we bring you the third night's ferocious flying mosquito attack. It seems that, for the last show, a number **of** nomads who had previously parked and walked found their camels stageside seats before dismounting. The camels brought as guests their hungry hordes of bugs. And so, Grateful Dead music took a back seat to a bunch of scratching Americans.

That night was also different structurally. Where on the two previous nights Hamza had opened the shows at 9:30 or so, on Saturday the Dead began by themselves at nine, and Hamza played before their second set. Actually, the moon opened the show. There was a total lunar eclipse, starting at about 8:30. The Dead began playing just before totality, and their first set lasted for the rest of the eclipse. But the cosmic event sparked no particular return magic from the Dead. Guess Luna will just have to try harder next time. At least the band did their only encore of the three nights. You guessed it. "One More Saturday Night."

The question of whether or not the whole thing was worth it would have to be answered individually, be the questioner, spectator or participating musician. In any case, the Dead richly deserve any gratification they may have garnered in sailing off into the mystic.

---

**Toni's Note:** Though the Dead's material from Egypt was considered to have "no commercial potential," their organization released a CD and DVD set from the journey in 2008, 30 years later.

September/October, 1979

Vol.5
No.6

65464

$2.00

# Relix

## Photo Album

# Part Two — Transitional Evolution

*Relix* went through a major transition at the end of 1978. While the editorial staff had a reprieve with the year-end photo special, they were far from resting.

Editor Jerry Moore made the decision to leave *Relix*, and in came Jeff Tamarkin. Tamarkin had been living in the Bay Area, writing for San Francisco's popular *BAM*. He brought along strong additions to the editorial staff, but loyal readers rallied against the marked change in the publication's direction.

Jeff was musically open-minded, and his vision was to introduce *Relix* to a more diverse audience, adding punk, new wave, heavy metal and the pop music of the day to the original classic rock format. Despite the outcry from readers, the new editor was determined to find his own voice. Bands like Blondie, Cheap Trick, the Cars and the Who graced the covers, and criticism poured in.

Publisher Les Kippel gave Jeff free reign over the editorial content, and the magazine changed quickly and dramatically. Advertising was stimulated, newsstand sales grew, increased freelance contributions came in, and Deadheads were pissed off. But the readership matured and *Relix* went from a grassroots newsletter to a real magazine.

The "Letters" column was deluged with pro and con commentary—Deadheads happy to see new material in the magazine, Deadheads who hated seeing change, and new readers who were just confused by it all. Each issue had lengthy, eloquent editorials by Jeff, and Les had more to say than ever, being called to task to defend the magazine's uncharted direction with the promise that the world of *Relix* would be all right.

It's interesting to reflect on the magazine during the Tamarkin era. The music that was happening at the time (DEVO, the Knack, the Ramones, Elvis Costello, Talking Heads, etc.) was far from what Deadheads were interested in, but many of those artists have become essential while others disappeared entirely.

Jeff was a huge catalyst in the evolution of *Relix*.

—Toni Brown, 2009

Artwork by Gary Kroman

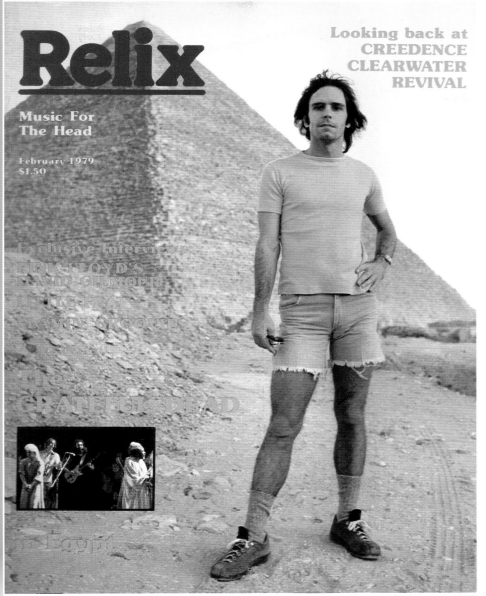

# Relix

**Music For The Head**

February 1979
$1.50

**Looking back at CREEDENCE CLEARWATER REVIVAL**

Exclusive Interviews:
PINK FLOYD'S DAVID GILMOUR
THE DIRT BAND
JAMMIN' GROUPIES

The GRATEFUL DEAD in Egypt

Cover Photo by Adrian Boot/Courtesy Arista Records

January/February, 1979

# Letters

RELIX was originally conceived in September, 1974 as a magazine dedicated to taping and tape collecting, with a print run of 200 copies and a subscription list of 50 [ah yes, I even remember our very first subscriber].

We had difficulty. Taping was not appreciated by the powers that be, so we quietly changed our focus and went with the flow. We wrote about the Grateful Dead. But a strange thing happened. The Grateful Dead went on vacation. So we decided to expand a little more, and started to write about San Francisco and related groups, i.e., Hot Tuna, Cody, Starship. And that worked — for a while.

Naturally, Tuna Freaks complained there wasn't enough Tuna. Starship Freaks complained there wasn't enough Starship. And of course, Grateful Dead Freaks complained that there wasn't enough Grateful Dead.

It is real hard to write about a group while they are not doing anything. If the Grateful Dead are working on an album and are in the studio for two months, and Tuna breaks up, what can you say?

And believe it or not, at the Springsteen show I attended at the Palladium in New York, I saw plenty of die-hard Grateful Dead people there. Also, dare I say that if Jerry Garcia or Bob Weir ever played and performed as hard as Springsteen, and put forth the amount of sheer energy, sweat, and work that Springsteen did, all us Dead people would never think about other music.

The key to all this is that as people who live for and by music, we should see and listen to other music, and that is the purpose and function of RELIX: to be the eyes and ears for our readers, and to report back and show and tell you, our readers what's going on around the music scene WITH AN OPEN MIND and we at RELIX do hope that you, our readers, will have an open mind for music.

Les Kippel, **Publisher**

Artwork by Gary Kroman

Artwork by Gary Kroman

Vol. 6 No. 2 May 1979 $1.50

# Relix

British Invasion 15 years after

## BLUES BROTHERS
### Jake & Elwood's Platinum Blooze

Fab Four get back!

GRATEFUL DEAD on tour

Winterland closes the end of an era

Exclusive Interviews:
THE OUTLAWS
AYNSLEY DUNBAR
Starship's new drummer

The new Folk boom:
STEVE FORBERT
THE ROCHES
& more

Cover Photo by Dave Patrick

Vol. 6 No.3 $1.50

# Relix

Women In Rock

Exclusive Interviews:

Dire Straits
McGuinn, Clark & Hillman
Peter Tosh

Linda Ronstadt
Joni Mitchell
Grace Slick
Donna Godchaux

Chet Helms— Janis' Big Brother

Blondie

One Way Or Another . . .
they're gonna getcha getcha getcha getcha getch

Cover Photo by Joe Kline - Starburst Studios

Vol.6 No.4 $1.75

# Relix

THE TENTH ANNIVERSARY

WOODSTOCK—

The Return Of The Who

CARS
SVT

Jimi & Janis

Exclusive Interview with:
Jefferson Starship's Paul Kantner

Cover Photo by Richard Aaron

photo by Karen Kohberger

# Editorial

*RELIX MAGAZINE is going through changes. Rather than going through a long explanation of how and why these changes came about, we think that our publisher's reply in the letter column sums it up best. But first our new editorial board has a few words of their own:*

Music changes and public taste changes along with it. When we started **Relix,** there was a vacuum in the rock music world. And so, we all became deeply involved with the one band that gave us our highest highs, the Grateful Dead. **Relix** existed for a long time as a tribute to the Dead and everything they represented to us. Most of us lived and breathed the Dead for many years. But as writers, we could only say so much about the same band without becoming redundant and irrelevant, and we began to branch out. From the beginning of our expansion, we were subjected to cries of sell-out by those who wanted **Relix** to remain a fanzine dedicated to the Dead and San Francisco's rock culture. But there was always an even larger group of readers who applauded our growth, and supported us wherever we went.

We still love the Grateful Dead and we'll never forget the incredible times they've given us. But we can no longer justify putting out a magazine that is limited in its scope. We have many interests, and from the feedback we've gotten, so do you. And so, from now on, **Relix** is going to be looking at a wider variety of those interests. We feel that our new expansion will give us an honest reason for putting out this publication, and will justify our existence as rock journalists rather than us being unofficial fan club presidents.

**The Editorial Board — Jeff, Steve, and Clark**

photo by Ed Perlstein

Lowell George, the singer, songwriter and slide guitarist with Little Feat, died of a heart attack on June 29 in Washington, D.C. George had been in the midst of a promotional tour for his solo album, **Thanks, I'll Eat It Here,** and had been receiving encouraging reviews of his first solo tour since the breakup of Little Feat earlier this year.

George formed Little Feat in Los Angeles in 1971, after leaving the Mothers Of Invention. The Feat were considered one of the most tasteful and underrated rock-boogie bands, and George was one of the most respected guitarists in the business by fellow musicians and his legions of dedicated fans. Lowell George was 34.

**Editor's note:** In a somewhat surprising development, **Relix** has learned that Keith and Donna Godchaux have left the Grateful Dead. As we go to press, details are not available, but we did receive confirmation that a difference of opinion as to musical direction was the reason for the split. According to the Dead's publicity agent in New York, the split was amicable. Keith and Donna will pursue individual careers, and the Dead will not be replacing them immediately. The band plans to embark on a college tour of the east coast in early May, and may use guest musicians in addition to the regular five-man crew. The band also plans to record in the late spring, and will also use various sidemen on the record.

Rumors had been circulating for months about the possibility of the Godchauxs leaving, and although the official word is that the pair, who have been with the group since the early '70's, left on their own accord, an Arista Records spokesman did suggest that ''there was a potential there that was never realized, and the band wanted to go ahead in other directions.''

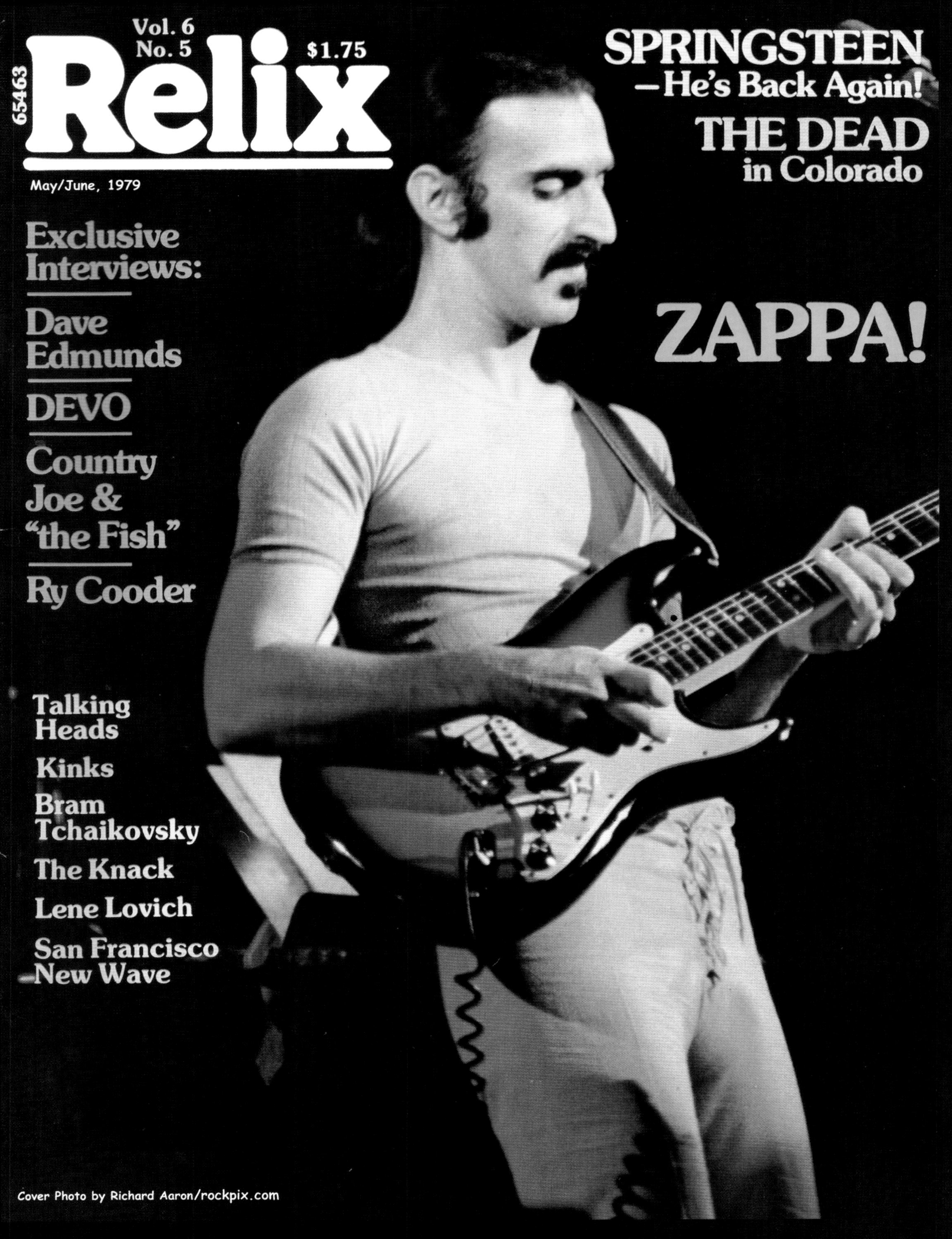
Vol. 6
No. 5
$1.75
65463
Relix
May/June, 1979
SPRINGSTEEN
–He's Back Again!
THE DEAD
in Colorado
Exclusive Interviews:
Dave Edmunds
DEVO
Country Joe & "the Fish"
Ry Cooder
ZAPPA!
Talking Heads
Kinks
Bram Tchaikovsky
The Knack
Lene Lovich
San Francisco New Wave
Cover Photo by Richard Aaron/rockpix.com

**Rolling Stones**

**Bill Kreutzmann, Mickey Hart and Phil Lesh
At The Press Conference Announcing
The Egypt Tour**

# HOT TUNA

Early Hot Tuna

Richard Aaron

Dave Patrick

Dave Patrick

Papa John Creach added a wonderful dimension
to Hot Tuna from 1971 to 1974

Jorma and Jack          Photo by Leslie D. Kippel

Acoustic Jorma - 1978          Photo by Leslie D. Kippel

**Relix** Vol.7•1

*Exclusive Interviews!*
Charlie Daniels
Marshall Tucker Band
Mick Taylor
Southside Johnny
JORMA!
JEAN-LUC PONTY
SHOES
MARTY BALIN

*Plus*
Sex Pistols
Clash
Shoes

*In Concert:*
Dead
Dylan
Fleetwood Mac
Tom Petty
Commander Cody
David Bromberg

The Music of The 70's—
SPRINGSTEEN
PATTI SMITH
THE WHO
ELVIS COSTELLO
MANY MORE

**CHEAP TRICK**
*Interviewed*

Iggy
Ramones
David Byrne
Todd Rundgren
David Johansen
and 10 others
TALK ABOUT DISCO!

FIFTH ANNIVERSARY ISSUE

January/February, 1980

Cover Photo by Kenji Miuri

## FIFTEEN ROCK STARS ANSWER THE QUESTION:
# HOW DO YOU FEEL ABOUT D·I·S·C·O? "
•••••••••••••••
### By Jeff Tamarkin and Clark Peterson

1. **David Byrne**—Guitarist, singer, song-writer of **Talking Heads**:
"We've always been rhythmic but all you have to do is listen to WKTU (a New York disco station) and it's obvious we don't sound like that. To me, disco is separate. It's music that has a particular function. It has guidelines. The reason that people get upset about it is that they're using it for the wrong purpose. Disco isn't music you listen to at home. If you do, you're bound to find it annoying."

2. **David Johansen**—Blue Sky recording artist, singer, songwriter, former member of **New York Dolls**:
"It's dying, I guess. I hope so."

3. **Gary Brooker**—Singer, songwriter, keyboardist, former leader of **Procol Harum**, Chrysalis recording artist:
"It is one of those things you have to put up with. But there are some great disco records made. A disco thing gets across to me when it's a great song as well. Dancing is great; it's fun. And the musicianship on some of it is great. There is a lot more experimentation in disco than it's given credit for, really. Something like the Sister Sledge record, 'He's The Greatest Dancer;' the strings on that one are fantastic."

4. **Elvin Bishop**—Singer, songwriter, guitarist:
"Disco is background music that they play on an exercise show or something. It's fun to dance to, but it has no meaning to me musically, except that it did do one good thing—it made me give up listening to the rock and roll stations. After about the third time through one of those disco tunes, it's torture to listen to anymore. I like to shake my booty but I do it because I take a notion to it at the time or place, not because somebody is exhorting me to, over and over, *ad infinitum, ad nauseum*. I look back at some of the records I bought when I was fifteen or sixteen and I have no right to criticize anyone. You just don't know any better at certain stages of your life."

5. **Michael Cotten**—synthesizer player of **The Tubes**:
'I've been into disco for years because I'm a dancer, but I'm starting not to like it. The lyrics are non-existent. Disco as a generic term will become meaningless, I hope, because it's getting so infused with rock and roll. Dance music is the wave of the future but it's not got anything to do with the term disco as people think of it now. There are a couple of new trends that make it more interesting—Ian Dury, James White and the Blacks, Tubeway Army, B-52's. That's totally happening. The beat in music is here to stay, even though what they call disco is going out."

6. **David Freiberg**—keyboardist, bassist, singer of **Jefferson Starship**:
"Everybody's too busy grunting and sweating to pay much attention to the lyrics. It's the beat that makes the difference. It's easy to dance to. The beat is all the same—120 per minute. The heartbeat is about 72, normally, but when a human being is exercising pretty hard, it's about 120. That's why disco works, I guess."

7. **Greg Kihn**—singer, songwriter, guitarist, Beserkley recording artist:
"It's good for the music business and bad for musicians. I know guys who play guitar in bars and they don't have a gig any more because the guys in bars are playing records. It's good for DJs. The American public wants to dance, and right now if you want to meet people you gotta meet them to disco music. Boy meets girl while move it in, move it out is playing. Hopefully, in about two years, people will be moving to 'Roadrunner' (a song by Jonathan Richman which Kihn has recorded). People's tastes have to change. I'm not down on disco. You have to go out and meet chicks. If you're in high school, where are you gonna meet them, in marching band practice? I met them listening to 'Gloria' at the church coffee house."

8. **Paul Kantner**—Singer, songwriter, guitarist with **Jefferson Starship**:
"The only thing disco is good for is sex, and then only for quickies."

9. **Dave Prater**—Singer in the legendary soul duo, **Sam and Dave**:
"It's no different than the rest of the music. Music is music. I've been doing it for twenty years. I'll still sing even if

Photo Courtesy Elvin Bishop

### Elvin Bishop: "Disco is music for an exercise show."

the music doesn't have a beat. You gotta do what you gotta do to stay alive."

10. **Todd Rundgren**—Singer, songwriter, guitarist, producer, member of the band **Utopia**:
"I don't think of it at all anymore. It's pushed so far in the background of my world that it's almost like Dixieland music. It's that much of a quirk. I never thought it was threatening. As long and as strong as it was, I always considered it a passing phase. I just didn't think it was possible for people to enjoy that music for that long. I don't know that people ever did enjoy the music. It was all background music for a lifestyle. It lasted as long as the lifestyle did. Son of Sam took care of that. He was the biggest blow against disco music."

11. **Iggy Pop**—Singer, songwriter, Arista recording artist, former member of the **Stooges**:
"It was an exciting movement pre-Gamble and Huff, when James Brown was doing some of those funny records like 'Make It Funky.' Then I thought it got even better with Gamble-Huff and that period. After that, I think it degenerated, and I think it's become music for spastics now. It's music for people who have to twitch because they don't know how to dance. I think it's lost it, but as a form I have nothing against it."

12. **Maria Muldaur**—Singer, Warner Brothers recording artist:
"I like to shake my booty and dance, but I think disco is totally formularized, computerized and sounds more like it's made by machines than people. The words are so mindless they make the dumbest rock and roll song seem like a poem by Dylan Thomas. Disco gives the music magnates a very easy way to

## FIFTEEN ROCK STARS ANSWER THE QUESTION:
# HOW DO YOU FEEL ABOUT
# D·I·S·C·O·?
### (CONTINUED)

control, market and co-opt the expression and values of young people. Rock and roll, since its inception, presented a chance to explore alternatives to the straight values of this culture. Disco glorifies the narcissistic, materialistic and escapist tendencies. It distracts people from the important issues."

13. **Craig Chaquico**—Guitarist of **Jefferson Starship**:
"I put disco and punk in the same category: they're both extremes. I wouldn't go out of my way to see either unless my girlfriend wanted to dance. Disco is great to dance to. There is something primitively attractive about the basic rhythm over and over, but I can't see people listening to one disco song after another. It's just so dumb and repetitious that it's got to wear out eventually."

14. **Commander Cody** (George Frayne)—Singer, songwriter, pianist:
"The only people who don't know disco is dead are the bozos who bought the b.s.—the disco clothes and shoes. There's a lot of what we used to call hooples who don't know what is happening and depend on the media to tell them what's cool. The whole social scene is about getting laid. All the foxes went to the discos because they didn't like going to Grateful Dead shows and wearing Levis and no makeup. That's no fun for good-looking girls. Three or four years ago, every town you went into had crummy bars that were Thursday night discos. Now those same places are closed or they're having T-shirt contests and rock and roll bands. Live music is coming back."

15. **The Ramones**—Sire recording group, new wave pioneers, stars of film **Rock 'N' Roll High School**:
Johnny Ramone: It's disgusting.

Johnny Ramone: "Disco is plastic, fabricated music."
**Photo by James Shive**

**Photo by Herb Greene**
**Courtesy**
**Arista Records**

# THE RELIX INTERVIEW:
# Jerry Garcia
# by
# Jeff Tamarkin

Jerry Garcia ambles into the hotel room overlooking New York's Central Park. He appears relaxed, although in four hours, he will be on stage at Nassau Coliseum for the second of a three night stand. But he doesn't seem overly concerned about that or anything else. Garcia appears happy, and if being a major rock star has ever gotten to his head, he doesn't show it. He's as cordial as can be. Does he mind if the photographer shoots a few pics? No, go right ahead. Does he want to do the interview anywhere special? Wherever we want. He's that kind of person, and as an interview subject is a delight, answering every question in detail, in an honest, forthright manner. He seems to enjoy talking about the Dead, himself, the Dead Heads, and the group's mystique as much as the most avid Dead Head does. And for someone in the eye of the hurricane, he has a remarkably acute understanding of its workings.

This is the first of two parts of the **Relix** interview with Jerry Garcia. In this half, he talks about the Dead Heads—how he views them, how they've changed over the years, how they affect the band—and about his relationships with Robert Hunter, the Dead's record company, and drugs in the '80s.

**Relix: I'd like to start off with a general observation and hear any comment you have on it. That is, that most people, after experiencing the Grateful Dead, either love them or hate them. There is no in-between. Someone will either become a Dead Head after hearing or seeing the band, or shrug them off and say ycchh! But they will rarely, if ever, have no opinion.**
**Jerry Garcia:** Well, that seems pretty cut

*'The audience gives us a lot of room. We're not under any pressure to perform the Grateful Dead's greatest hits.'*

and dry (laughs). I'm aware of that phenomenon, I guess. What happens is that someone turns their friends on to us in the same spirit or sense that they would turn their friends on to pot. They turn them on because they have a good experience and they have a good time. It used to be real frustrating. I've talked to fans about this who have said, 'Jesus, I invited 20 of my friends to this and you guys played awful! (laughs). That stuff used to happen to us all the time. We've gotten to be a lot more consistent. Now, those people can bring their friends and at the very worst, they'll get a nice, professional show. But I'm aware of that mechanism. The thing is that it's an ongoing process. Our audience now has a very large number of 15, 16 and 17 year-olds. They're kids who are obviously not from our generation but are every bit as enthusiastic about what we did as any of our audiences have ever been. Our audience is larger now than it's ever been.

**Relix: How do you feel about the hard-core Dead fanatics who follow the band on a 25-city tour? Do you think that's a healthy thing to do?**
JG: Well, it's obviously very important to them. And more than that, it's giving them an adventure. They have stories to tell. Like, 'Remember the time we had to go all the way to Colorado and we had to hitchhike the last 400 miles because the VW broke

Interview Continues next page...

down in Kansas.' or something like that. Y'know what I mean? That's giving them a whole common group of experiences which they can talk about. For a lot of people, going to Grateful Dead concerts is like bumping into a bunch of old friends. There's a vast network of Dead Heads. They're kind of like people who have come to know and recognize each other and it's like support. Sometimes a person can find a ride across the country with a Dead Head, or stay over at somebody's house, or any of that. So, that seems to function pretty well for them.

**Relix: Isn't it possible, though, that some people might put so much of themselves into the Dead experience all the time, that they lose a part of themselves in the process?**

JG: Oh, for sure. I know I have (laughs). So, I'm sure it's possible. But our commitment to the idea is as deep as the most crazed Dead Head's. So I don't feel as though we're burning anybody on that level. We continue to do what we're doing.

**Relix: This is somewhat related. It seems there are two basic types of Dead Heads in a given audience. There's the one who just goes to get high and dance around and have a good time, and the one who goes there to analyze, like by saying, 'Well, that guitar solo wasn't quite as good as the one he did in Boston in '73, but...**

JG: Right, the scholarly approach. The students of Grateful Dead music.

**Relix: If you were a member of the Grateful Dead audience, instead of on the stage, which type do you think you'd be?**

JG: I could go both ways. There was a time in my life when I was one of those guys who toted around a tape recorder. I used to follow bluegrass bands around and record them. I was of the analytical bent. I was a comparer—this show was better than that and blah, blah, blah. But that was sort of a different me. I understand, though, and sympathize. I understand both points of view. I understand the sheer joy of being there, even if the music is not the best possible performance. And also, there are those times when it gets lucky, it gets special. Those are worth waiting around for. Those are the glue that holds us together, our glue-on particle, the possibility that something exceptional will happen musically.

**Relix: How have the audiences changed the most over the years?**

JG: They've gotten bigger, that's for sure. But for us, surprisingly, they haven't chang-

> 'Each human being has things to find out that are inescapable. They'll find them out the easy way or the hard way.'

ed too much. They respond similarly. The Grateful Dead audience is kind of like the Grateful Dead audience no matter what, and no matter where, either. That's another interesting phenomena. European Grateful Dead audiences are not that much different than American Grateful Dead audiences.

**Relix: Or Egyptian Grateful Dead audiences.**

JG: Right! Or Egyptian Grateful Dead audiences. It's an interesting thing.

**Relix: There's always a lot of talk about a certain lifestyle or philosophy based around, or rather, attributed to the Dead. In your opinion, does such a lifestyle exist?**

JG: No. Not in a dogmatic sense. We don't sit around and work out Grateful Dead dogma, or catma if you prefer (laughs). Our trip is that everyone is entitled to believe what they want. There's an old Prankster proverb that goes, 'The mind believes what the mind believes.' Our experience has been the more the merrier. The more possible interpretations ... Like, (Robert) Hunter and I get reports on the contents of our tunes, which include incredibly complex interpretations of what the lyrics *must* mean and all that. And we find, Wow! There's no intention on our part to include those things, but it's lucky that there's that kind of openness, that that kind of range is available.

**Relix: There's a question I was going to ask later on, but since you already brought it up: Do you yourself actually understand all of Hunter's lyrics?**

JG: I edit some of them mercilessly. Sometimes I edit the sense out of them. Sometimes they come to me and they are narrative in intent. But the narration itself will be 90 stanzas. That's a little cumbersome for a song (laughs). Hunter and I have

**Photo by Ralph Hulett**

a trusting working relationship, so he understands when I edit. Sometimes he'll say, 'Well, you've taken all the sense out of the song.' And I say, trust me, man, it'll work out. For me, my own personal preference, because of my background in folk music, is that I always like songs that hint, that hint at either a larger story or something behind the scene, shifting around. Maybe something not quite nameable. So I go for that. The raw lyric might be out front, but what we'll end up with is something slightly more mysterious.

**Relix: Is Hunter aware of this when he writes?**

JG: Yeah, he's real aware of my consciousness. Real aware. He writes songs for me that say what I would have said if I had any kind of agility with language, which I unfortunately don't.

**Relix: Does Hunter usually write a song with the Grateful Dead in mind, or are some of the songs intended only for his own use?**

JG: Oh, sure. You never know. Sometimes we've written songs and just completely forgotten about them because they just can't be used. Sometimes we write them and record them and they turn out to be valueless because they can't be performed. There's no handle that we can get on them. Then, also, there's the thing where a song might go into a dormant period, like we'll record it and maybe forget about it. Then we'll resurrect it in a few years, and start performing it and find that it has something. So, luckily there's a lot of material, there's enough to keep ourselves interested just with the book that we have already. And now everybody is producing (new songs). We have a new guy in the band (keyboardist Brent Mydland) who's writing and has his whole personality. And (Bob) Weir and (John) Barlow have been clicking. So all that is neat. We have more input and more stuff to work with.

**Relix: When you have some spare time, when the band is off the road and not recording, what do you like to do?**

JG: Play music. I study music when I'm not playing music, and film making is something I'm very interested in. That's about it.

**Relix: A lot of Dead Heads probably have some fantasy of what kind of person you are in private. Do you think they'd be disappointed if they knew what your offstage life is like, or would their idea be pretty much on target?**

JG: Uhmm, I have a feeling they probably know as much about me as I know about myself. Maybe more. They may be in a bet-

*Interview Continues...*

ter position to be able to see. I might reveal more than I know. It's difficult for me to know something like that. But when people write us letters I don't get the sense they're missing the mark. They know who they're talking to. So that makes me feel good, since our only tool of communication is our music and what we do. And when they speak to what they conceive of as the Grateful Dead consciousness, they're usually not wrong.

**Relix: I'm sure you get asked this a lot, and must be tired of being associated with the subject, but one more time: What is the role of drugs within the Grateful Dead's existence today, especially as compared to the role they played during the '60s?**

**JG:** Well, for one thing, drugs are much more expensive now. And the quality of drugs is correspondingly lower. I think that's unfortunate. Luckily, there's been great strides in homegrown, and home cultivation. Some people have turned us on to pot that was grown in Iowa that was incredible! Really, just amazing. And there was a time when people would grow pot and take the little leaves off a plant about this high (about six inches from the ground) and roll 'em up and wonder, 'Why can't I get high on this?' Now they understand because the technology of growing has been greatly improved. Now, there's good homegrown in virtually every state we've been in. So that kind of makes up for the commercial problem.

**Relix: In our last issue, Grace Slick said that in the '60s, people took drugs to find things out, whereas in the '70s, people took drugs to get away from things. Do you agree?**

**JG:** I'd say so, yeah. Definitely. That was definitely true in the '60s. She's right about that. In the '60s, we were looking for something and drugs were the tool for helping to look. But as far as I was concerned, psychedelics were the confirmation of that seeking. All of a sudden, here's this experience that goes quite beyond everyday reality, and is certainly very convincing and organized, and there's something there. It's a pity all that has been driven underground, because now we don't know much about the mind as a result. I think a lot could have been found out if it weren't for the fear.

**Relix: You've been playing with the same musicians now for 15 years. Is it still spontaneous every time you get on stage?**
**JG:** It sure is. Totally unpredictable too.

**Relix: Just from playing together so long, you get to know each other person's musical habits. Don't you know when, in a certain jam, Bob is going to do one thing or Phil (Lesh, bassist) is going to do something?**
**JG:** Not really, I never know, really, what Bob's gonna do or what Phil's gonna do. Those guys have an endless capacity for being able to surprise me. It makes it interesting. Plus, everybody keeps changing, too. So everybody keeps growing and keeps changing and the whole thing is dynamic.

Luckily, we don't feel that we've peaked. We feel that we're still on the rise. I have no idea where it's going.

**Relix: You were talking before about the shows being more consistent. Is it still obvious to you when a show is especially good or not so good?**
**JG:** No, it's not so obvious to me anymore. I recognize also that I'm a victim of subjectivity just like we all are in the band. But there's greater agreement now. For instance, if we have a good night, it's more likely that we'll all feel that it's a good night. Rather than one of us having a great night and the rest of us having a lousy night. We're all seeing more of the music all the time, so it's more important how the whole music worked rather than how any one person performed.

**Relix: Do you think the audiences are more objective now?**
**JG:** I think they know. I don't think that anything can be concealed. We can't fool them. If we had a night that didn't quite reach escape velocity, or whatever, they know. And it's nice that they're as patient and they cut us a lot of slack. We have a lot of slack. They give us a lot of room. We aren't under any particular pressure to perform the Grateful Dead's greatest hits, or anything like that. They welcome unfamiliar stuff. And I think any group could have been able to approach their audience in that way. It's really just the matter of us making the assumption that the audience is intelligent. That's worked for us. We have great freedom. We can go out there and play anything, really—all new stuff; stuff that nobody's heard before—and the audience won't go away angry, or disappointed. As long as they understand that we're doing the best that we can and that's our shot.

**Relix: When the band re-introduces a song that hasn't been played in a few years, is that ever because of audience demand? Like, if enough people started shouting out for 'Dark Star,' would you play it again?**
**JG:** Sometimes that happens. But more often, it's because we discover something about the tune that would be fun to do again. It comes from us, from our own personal preference. Then the audience is pleasantly surprised, or maybe unpleasantly surprised. 'Why did they drag that turkey out again?' That can go either way.

**Relix: Are there any particular Dead albums that you look back on and are embarrassed by?**
**Jerry Garcia:** All of them! To some extent. Well, there's moments on all of them that I feel good about and moments that I feel bad about. But by now, I'm so far away from the experience of the albums that I no longer remember what it was that used to annoy me so much about some of the records. Sometimes I have to listen to them again and try to reconstruct it, and then I remember, oh yeah, that's right, I meant to do another guitar solo on that one. I didn't mean to keep that one. Things like that. They're so minor. I never felt that we were a very good recording band. I

think we're just starting to get accomplished at that.

**Relix: About five years ago, there was some talk about just publicly releasing that huge vault of tapes that the collectors would die to get their hands on. Is that at all feasible as an alternative?**
**JG:** Well, maybe, but the problem is that we don't have the time to administrate things like that. We have neither the time nor the manpower to do that. So, it's possible that at some time or another we'll figure out some way to do that. It doesn't pay to make real time copies. It takes too long, for one thing. And it wouldn't work to try to go through an edit thing and make discs and pressings out of them, because they would all have to be kind of limited edition things. So we haven't really figured out a way to handle that, or to deal with it. Nothing that makes any sense. So that remains an archive more than a resource.

**Relix: When you look back at some of the excesses in which the Dead indulged in the mid-'70s—the huge sound system, the stadium concerts, the record company you had —what do you think of all that now?**
**JG:** Well, they were good tries. We had to try. And we certainly learned a lot.

**Relix: Why didn't that all work out?**
**JG:** For a variety of reasons. We didn't have the time or the output. For a record company to work, you have to have accounts going with distributors. In other words, they won't pay you for the records that are coming in. When you send them the new batch of records, they pay you for the ones you already sold. So there's this long credit overlap. And a lot of times they don't pay. A lot of times, they burn you. And we got involved with records with uncannily perfect timing, just the year when polyvinyl chloride went up seven

*Continues...*

*Artwork by Alfred Klosterman*

million percent and oil shortages started to break in heavy. And that same year was the year we got involved. So all of a sudden here we were having to dicker for virgin vinyl, which there is no more.

**Relix: Last year, the music business went through a supposed economic slump. How did that affect the Dead?**

**JG:** It didn't affect us at all. Shit, we're booming. The rest of the world is going to pieces and we're doing fine.

**Relix: Are you influenced by any of the trends that are around? Do you listen to the radio?**

**JG:** Sure. I listen to everything.

**Relix: Anything particular that's turned you on lately?**

**JG:** Just the stuff that's hit everybody. I like **The Wall** a lot. Everybody likes that. I like Elvis Costello. I'm a big Elvis Costello fan. I like Warren Zevon a lot. I mean, I've heard good stuff from almost everybody, just like I've heard bad stuff from almost everybody. I don't think there's anybody who's consistently putting out great stuff, time after time after time. But everybody's got something to say and there's moments in all of this that are real excellent. I go for the moments. I keep listening till I hear something that knocks me out. Dire Straits—I love that band. It's hard not to like that band.

**Relix: A couple of questions for the musicians reading. What kind of guitar are you using now? I know you've used the same one for over a year now.**

**JG:** Yeah, this guitar was built for me by a guy named Doug Irwin, who also built the guitar that I've been playing since about '73. I ordered this guitar from him when he delivered the other guitar. He also built the bass that Phil's playing now. He's kind of retired from instrument making. The work he does is so fine and the instruments he makes are so incredible that there's just no market for them except for a few heavy duty professionals. He's just got an amazing understanding of wood. But above and beyond that, the reason I've gotten guitars from him is because there's something about the feel of his guitars which is really extraordinary. I've played a lot of new guitars by people who are building guitars from scratch, and the thing of knowing about touch is a gift. This guy is one of those guys who's got the gift, apart from amazing craftsmanship.

**Relix: What about amps?**

**JG:** The basic pre-amplifier is an old Fender Twin Reverb that I've been using since '67.

**Relix: Do you use the same equipment on stage and in the studio?**

**JG:** Pretty much. In the studio, I tend to use more of a variety of amps. I have a lot of little old Fender amplifiers. Recording is an illusion. Size and relative volume are an illusion you can create in the studio. An amplifier this big (a foot or two) can sound like a thousand Marshalls. The microphone doesn't hear the way the ear does. So after recording for this long, I've gotten so that I can get what I'm trying to get, in terms of guitar sounds.

**Relix: I'd like to clear up an historical question that's often a matter of dissension among Dead Heads. Did you do any recording before the Dead, not counting the Warlocks single and the record on which you backed (blues singer) Jon Hendricks? Was there anything before that?**

**JG:** I did some various sessions around San Francisco. Demos and stuff like that.

**Relix: In the last few years, the band has been the brunt of a critical backlash. Does it bother you to read someone saying that the Dead have had it, that they're past the peak?**

**JG:** It doesn't bother me. I mean, it doesn't affect us when we get good reviews, either. That isn't what we're doing. We're not fishing for compliments. We're so used to getting bad reviews on our records that we sort of look for them. The worst of 'em are more fun than a good review.

**Relix: OK, one last one. In a thousand years, when it's all gone, what will the music history books say about the Grateful Dead?**

**JG:** Ha! I haven't the slightest idea!

Glenn Harding

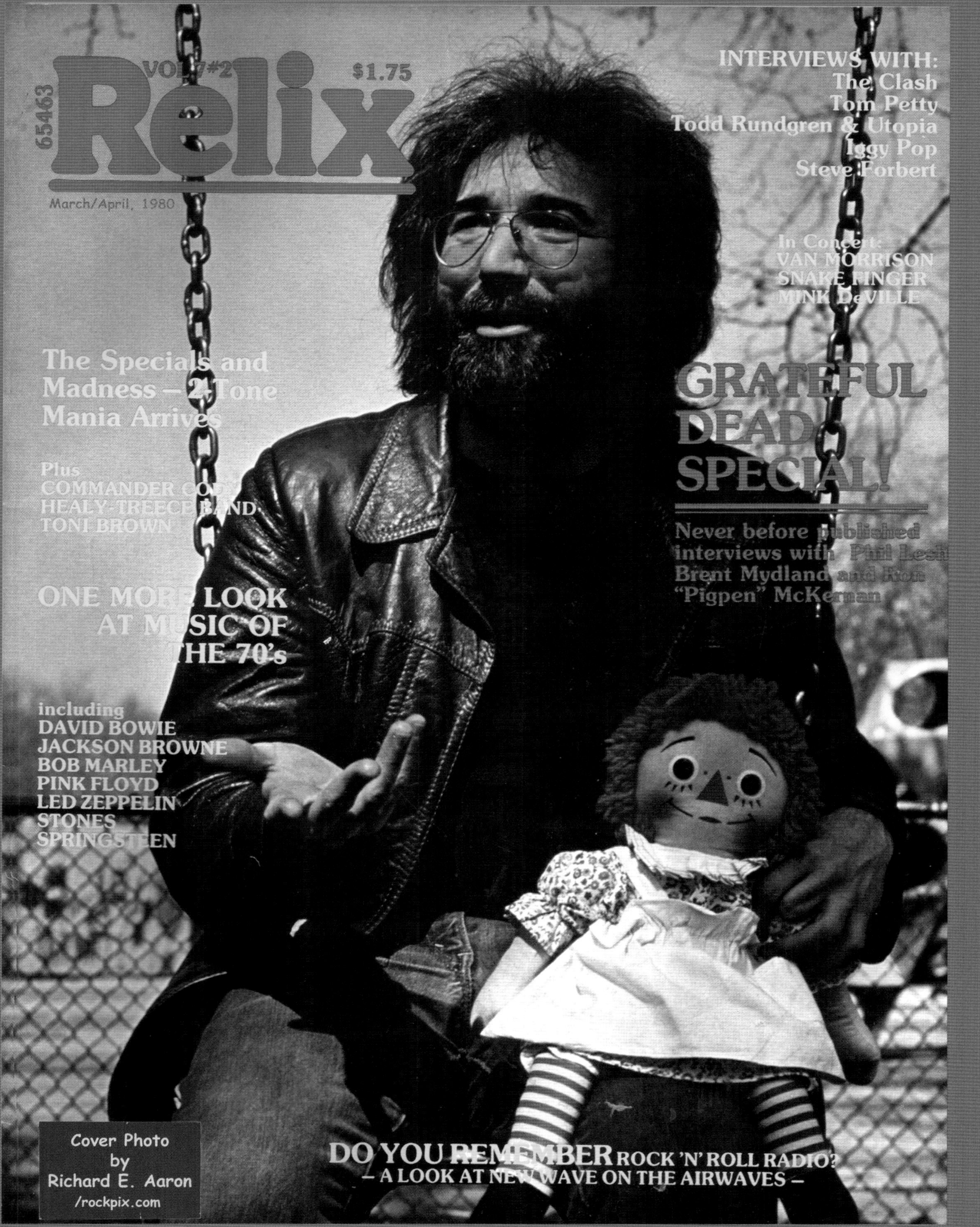
VOL 7 #2
$1.75
65463
Relix
March/April, 1980
INTERVIEWS WITH:
The Clash
Tom Petty
Todd Rundgren & Utopia
Iggy Pop
Steve Forbert
In Concert:
VAN MORRISON
SNAKE FINGER
MINK DeVILLE
The Specials and
Madness – 2-Tone
Mania Arrives
Plus
COMMANDER COD
HEALY-TREECE BAND
TONI BROWN
GRATEFUL
DEAD
SPECIAL!
Never before published
interviews with Phil Lesh
Brent Mydland and Ron
"Pigpen" McKernan
ONE MORE LOOK
AT MUSIC OF
THE 70's
including
DAVID BOWIE
JACKSON BROWNE
BOB MARLEY
PINK FLOYD
LED ZEPPELIN
STONES
SPRINGSTEEN
DO YOU REMEMBER ROCK 'N' ROLL RADIO?
– A LOOK AT NEW WAVE ON THE AIRWAVES –
Cover Photo
by
Richard E. Aaron
/rockpix.com

**Relix** Vol.7 #3 $1.75

May/June, 1980

INTERVIEWS WITH:
The Pretenders, The Jam, The Ramones, The Specials, Brian Eno, PIL's John Lydon

MORE INTERVIEWS:
HEART
GRACE SLICK
LENE LOVICH
RACHEL SWEET

NEW WAVE IS DEAD (EXCEPT IN BOSTON)
HOWIE KLIEN TELLS WHY

GRATEFUL DEAD— NEW ALBUM AND TRIVIA CONTEST

PLUS:
SVT
DIRTY LOOKS
SPEEDIES

PINK FLOYD: BEHIND THE WALL

IN CONCERT:
The CLASH
LINDA RONSTADT
JAMES BROWN
JACK BRUCE
JOE "KING" CARRASCO

TRIBUTE ROCK BANDS: HISTORIANS OR CLONES?

Cover Photo Courtesy Columbia Records

---

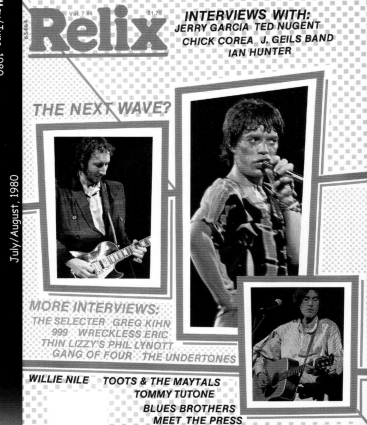

**Relix** Vol. 7 #4 $1.75

July/August, 1980

INTERVIEWS WITH:
JERRY GARCIA  TED NUGENT
CHICK COREA  J. GEILS BAND
IAN HUNTER

THE NEXT WAVE?

MORE INTERVIEWS:
THE SELECTER  GREG KIHN
999  WRECKLESS ERIC
THIN LIZZY'S PHIL LYNOTT
GANG OF FOUR  THE UNDERTONES

WILLIE NILE  TOOTS & THE MAYTALS
TOMMY TUTONE
BLUES BROTHERS
MEET THE PRESS

Cover Photos by Richard Aaron/Thunder Thumbs

---

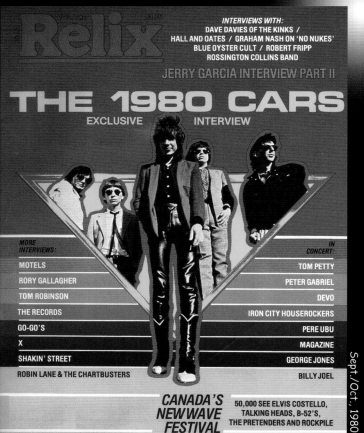

**Relix** Vol. 7 #5 $1.75

Sept./Oct., 1980

INTERVIEWS WITH:
DAVE DAVIES OF THE KINKS /
HALL AND OATES / GRAHAM NASH ON 'NO NUKES'
BLUE OYSTER CULT / ROBERT FRIPP
ROSSINGTON COLLINS BAND

JERRY GARCIA INTERVIEW PART II

# THE 1980 CARS
EXCLUSIVE INTERVIEW

MORE INTERVIEWS:
MOTELS
RORY GALLAGHER
TOM ROBINSON
THE RECORDS
GO-GO'S
X
SHAKIN' STREET
ROBIN LANE & THE CHARTBUSTERS

IN CONCERT:
TOM PETTY
PETER GABRIEL
DEVO
IRON CITY HOUSEROCKERS
PERE UBU
MAGAZINE
GEORGE JONES
BILLY JOEL

CANADA'S NEW WAVE FESTIVAL
50,000 SEE ELVIS COSTELLO, TALKING HEADS, B-52'S, THE PRETENDERS AND ROCKPILE

Cover Photo: The Cars/Elektra Records

---

**Relix** Vol. 7 No. 6 $2.50
PHOTO ALBUM

Nov./Dec., 1980

GRATEFUL DEAD
THE ROLLING STONES
THE WHO
THE BEATLES

EXCLUSIVE PHOTOS!
PAUL McCARTNEY
LED ZEPPELIN
FRANK ZAPPA
JANIS JOPLIN
DAVID BOWIE
SEX PISTOLS
TOM PETTY
BLONDIE

SPRINGSTEEN

PAT BENATAR
CLASH
RAMONES
B-52'S
MADNESS
PETER TOSH
MEAT LOAF

Cover Photo by Bob Sorce

# John Lennon

## A REMEMBERANCE  *by Karen Funk Blocher*

Two people committed suicide. Others walked around in a daze, attending candlelight vigils, sharing their grief. Condolences were sent to Yoko Ono, fifteen sacks' worth.

Yoko issued a touching statement about 5-year-old Sean's reaction when she tried to explain to him about his daddy s murder. Sean and his father were "buddies," the statement said.

The three people she called when she returned from the hospital were Julian Lennon, John's 17-year-old son from his marriage to Cynthia Powell; Mimi Smith, John's Aunt who raised him, and Paul McCartney.

Of the other ex-Beatles, only Ringo came to see Yoko and Sean, surrounded by bodyguards as he plowed through hundreds of mourning fans who reached out to touch him.

There was no public funeral. Yoko did not want a circus. The public mourning outside the Dakota, where the murder took place, and around the world, was "getting out of hand," she said.

And through it all the parents of the Beatles and Lennon fans, the Sinatra generation, wondered at the fuss. The candlelight services, one such parent said, were "quasi-religious" ceremonies for a generation to whom Christianity had no meaning. Lennon was still "more popular than Jesus." Why?

The answer is that for many, the Beatles, more than any other band, more even than most politicians, had a major and direct influence on daily life. The now-legendary Ed Sullivan appearances introduced British music to America for the first time, a new kind of rock and roll even Leonard Bernstein could appreciate. The Beatles opened the door through which other British groups came to the U.S. —The Rolling Stones, the Who, the Kinks, and hundreds of lesser names.

**T**HE Beatles made rock and roll respectable, with their neat Anglo-Saxon appearance, with their even-tempered wit at press conferences, with their music, which parents soon discovered was actually hummable. In the process, the Beatles affected hairstyles, clothing, attitudes towards drugs and other subjects, most of all, music. Rock songs no longer had to be about adolescent love, played with guitars and drums with an occasional keyboard thrown in. The Beatles introduced string quartets and other orchestral instruments, and were early users of synthesizers and Indian instruments as well.

Of the songs credited to Lennon-McCartney, Lennon's songs were generally the ones on which he sang lead, and tended to be first-person expressions of feeling. "And I Love Her" and "I Want You (She's So Heavy)" are not so different in approach from the primal pain of

**A** *MURDER* on December 8th affected a whole generation. "Where were you when Kennedy was shot?" a childhood memory brought forth from that generation. Now adults, they ask, "Where were you when you heard about John Lennon?"

January/February, 1981

Springsteen Photo by Leslie D. Kippel

Cover Photo by Ross Gadye

Garcia Photo by Jim Shive

"Mother" and the love songs in *Double Fantasy*. It would be a mistake to shortchange the other Beatles in the rush to appreciate Lennon after his death. It was, after all, Paul who wrote "Yesterday," and George and Ringo contributed their share. But John's songs hold up well, as melodic as McCartney's but more self-centeredly personal in approach.

And it was John who wrote the books filled with tremendous wordplay, John whose relationship to Yoko is a classic love story of our time. It was John and Yoko who appeared nude

on an album cover, who spent their honeymoon talking to reporters about peace.

And it was John who came to America with Yoko and fought to stay here, who raised a son here, who made it possible to meet an ex-Beatle on the streets of New York. Many fans made the pilgrimage over the years, hoping to meet him. One of them brought a gun. ∎

Artwork by Glenn Harding

# fragments

## by Toni A. Brown

**W**ARREN Zevon sings about "Lawyers, Guns, and Money," and this month's Fragments is filled with just that.

The Grateful Dead have certainly livened things up for New York City's Radio City Music Hall. If you can remember back to October, 1980. the Dead played a sold-out eight concert stint at the New York landmark. The performances, which thrilled the attending Dead Heads,have infuriated the Hall's management.

It seems that the management at Radio City has taken exception to the Dead's on-stage antics and off-stage business enterprises. Radio City was especially bothered by the group's posters. which were to be sold as souvenirs of the event. The posters featured two skeletons, familiar trademarks of the Dead, lounging against the Radio City Music Hall's marquee. Radio City denied ever granting permission for the use of their logo. and promptly brought the Dead to court.

The Radio City suit claims that the posters "damage the plaintiff's image. suggests the Music Hall's impending death. and is unpatriotic." The Radio City suit is aimed against the band-members, road manager,promoter John Scher, and Arista Records. If successful in court, Radio City will have halted or at least postponed a cable T.V. special filmed at the concerts, a live album featuring the questionable artwork used on the poster, and a videodisk.

Radio City is looking to collect $1.25 million in damages. The Dead have not remained stiff during all this legal havoc. Scher has filed a formal complaint with the American Federation of Musicians. He claims that the band has not yet been paid for the shows, which ended on Halloween and was simulcast in theatres nationally. No pay, now that's not much of a treat!

So, how are all these hassles going to be solved? Both sides have agreed to a federal court appointed consent decree. The live LP and the cable shows might be able to roll ahead, but noticeable changes would have to be made. Final results are still murky, but one thing is certain, *The Grateful Dead Movie* won't be on the roster of upcoming events at the Hall.

What a long, strange trip it's been! The hotly awaited legal confrontation between Radio City lawyers and The Dead has simmered down out of court. Radio City has dropped its $1.5 million suit. and The Dead have agreed to behave like good, decent American boys. The Dead have stopped the distribution of the "offensive" posters, and have cancelled plans to release a videotape of the 8 night concert stint.

Due out in the spring is an acoustic LP from the Radio City sets. The album's artwork will feature a cyclops with crossed-bones. The honor of Radio City has been preserved. Their logo will not be depicted.

Artwork by Alfred Klosterman

**Relix** Vol. 8 #2 $1.75

Interviews: LEON RUSSELL
REO SPEEDWAGON
TOM ROBINSON

SAN FRANCISCO

MEMORABILIA

GRATEFUL DEAD
COLLECTIBLES
BEATLES
FLEA MARKETS
POSTERS
TAPES

In concert:
ELVIS COSTELLO
GRATEFUL DEAD
BOOMTOWN RATS

Cover Art by Gary Kroman    March/April, 1981

**Relix** Vol. 8 #3 $1.75

JIM MORRISON:
A Recollective Interview

in concert:
ADAM AND THE ANTS
GARY "U.S." BONDS
DEAD KENNEDYS
JORMA
U2

MORE ON BEATLE
COLLECTIBLES
VIDEO WARS

GRATEFUL DEAD
A BRIEF HISTORY

interviews
GARLAND JEFFREYS
LENNY KAYE
JAN & DEAN

Cover Photo by Gloria Stavers    May/June, 1981

**Relix** Vol. 8 #4 $1.75
music for the mind

THE WHO'S
JOHN ENTWISTLE

In Concert:
BOB DYLAN
THE CLASH
ROBERT GORDON
JOE WALSH
WILLIE NILE
and more!

SPRINGSTEEN!

Special Interviews:
RONNIE SPECTOR
BLACK UHURU
JIMMY CLIFF

SPECIAL INTERVIEWS:
PSYCHEDELIC ARTISTS—
KELLEY, MOUSE, GRIFFIN AND SINGER

Cover Photo by Leslie D. Kippel    July/August, 1981

**Relix** Vol. 8 #5 $1.75
music for the mind

Exclusive interviews:
PETER TOSH
ROBERT HUNTER
PAT BENATAR

THE
ROLLING STONES
AGAIN!

in concert:
MOODY BLUES
IAN HUNTER
ICEHOUSE
REGGAE SUNSPLASH 1981

interviews
MARTY BALIN
THE TUBES
BIG BROTHER'S
DAVID GETZ

NEW GRATEFUL DEAD
SONG TITLE CENTERFOLD

Photo by Leslie D. Kippel    September/October, 1981

# BAM ARCHIVES:
## THE PACK RAT
## OF ROCK By Clark Peterson

**B**AM is not only the sound made when Batman thrusts his fist into the Penguin's mouth, it's also the name for an archive devoted to preserving music and memorabilia, especially when it concerns the San Francisco area. It is the BAM Archives' task to act as a zoo for music, saving rare species from extinction

Located at The Automatt recording studios, in space donated by producer David Rubinson, the Bay Area Music Archives (BAMA) feature a complete collection of *Rolling Stone*, 2,500 books, posters, handbills, ticket stubs, T-shirts, buttons—you-name-it. About 6,500 records were donated by the estate of the late John L. Wasserman, a former *San Francisco Chronicle* columnist killed in a car crash. Another 17,000 records, located at Fantasy Records across the bay in Berkeley, were donated by KSAN when the famous radio station converted to country and western programming last year.

Perhaps the rarest item in the Archives is a tape of Janis Joplin singing with a Dixieland band in Port Arthur, Texas, in 1964. It was discovered in the closet of a photographer living in San Francisco.

According to general manager Paul Grushkin, other prized items include such magazines as the *Oracle*, *KYA Beat* and *Night Times*, ticket stubs for concerts at San Jose Civic Auditorium by the Byrds in 1966 and the Yardbirds in 1967, and portraits of Jimi Hendrix painted by Nona Hatay. But the best stuff might be the KSAN collection of 3,000 tapes.

"If a group was big and played in San Francisco in the 70's," says Grushkin, "the chances are good KSAN broadcast them and kept the tapes."

When it comes to posters, the Archives contain the best of the late 60's when Kelley and Mouse, Rick Griffin, Victor Moscoso, Randy Tuten, Bob Fried and others were cranking out beautiful concert art. Many of the posters feature the Dead. These posters are now very rare and *very* collectible.

"We've got the first Dead fan poster," says Grushkin. "Well before the Deadheads became official with the Skull and Roses album, there was the original Dead fan club in San Francisco. This poster advertises the first Pigpen T-shirt, which was the first official Dead T-shirt of any type. It's a Kelley-Mouse design from about 1967 with a striking image—very dark and brooding."

"We also have the poster from the Dead's Radio City shows last October. None of them got sold in New York because the Radio City management objected to the design. They don't understand Dead symbology and thought

two skeletons leaning over Radio City meant death and destruction. I've even heard from the Dead office that the cover design of the upcoming Dead album had to be changed because it has material from the Radio City shows."

The Archives can boast about having a poster for a 3-day festival that never took place. Called the Wild West, the Kezar Stadium shows were to feature the Dead, Joplin, Quicksilver, Country Joe and the Fish, Airplane, Santana and others (such unlikely acts as Turk Murphy, the Edwin Hawkins Singers and the obscure Fourth Way) in August of 1968 (give or take a year).

"It was a king's ransom of entertainment for only $3," says Gushkin. "Rock Skully, the Dead and others wanted this to be a big showcase for San Francisco 2 to 3 years after the great human be-ins, but the city scotched it. There were reports from Eastern festivals of violence and drug-taking, so the city said *no* to giving tacit approval."

One rare concert that did take place was the Dead at a Black Panther benefit at Oakland Auditorium on March 5, 1971. The poster proclaims a Revolutionary Intercommunal Day of Solidarity for Bobby Seale, including a post birthday party for Huey P. Newton following his release from jail. Gushkin was at the show, rubbing shoulders with Angela Davis et al.

"The Dead's music paled in significance to the politics of the event," he says. "They did their best to keep their music stern and uplifting and not too degenerate."

As you can see, most of the best mementoes in the Archives date back to the late 60's to early 70's, when San Francisco experienced a renaissance in music and the many other creative arts.

"Very little has been thrown away," he says. "Most rock and roll stuff is in private hands."

So, start collecting!

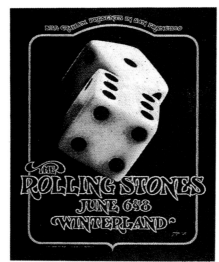

**Paul Grushkin - General Manager of Bay Area Music Archives - 1981**

Photo by Chester Simpson

**Toni's Note:** Paul Grushkin wrote *The Official Book of the Dead Heads* as well as other collector-based books. Ironically, soon after this article ran, *Relix* publisher Les Kippel discovered he and Grushkin were cousins when Les's mother saw Paul's pictures in the magazine.

Artwork by Gary Kroman

# Morrison's
## CELEBRATION OF THE LIZARD

A RELIX interview with Danny Fields by Toni A. Brown and Leslie D. Kippel

**D**ANNY Fields is a very popular figure in the music industry today. He has been a part of many young musicians' lives, and seen many of them through success and failure. His involvement continues as he guides many a new-comer over the pitfalls of the business. This interview is a brief recollection into his relationship with Jim Morrison and The Doors.

**RELIX:** How did you first meet James Douglas Morrison?

**FIELDS:** I was an independent publicist at the time, and I had promised to return a favor for a friend of mine in L.A. I was to do some publicity for a band coming east called 'The Doors.' When they arrived, they were booked to play Ondines, a small rock and roll club in mid-town, NYC. I remember how impressed I was by the band—especially the lead singer. A song called "Light My Fire" kept spinning through my mind. It was a very catchy number.

The next day, I walked into the offices of Elektra Records and told them I was the publicist for the Doors. The folks at Elektra were thrilled, and immediately accepted me! The music business was so loose in those days!!! At that time Elektra had just chosen the Doors' first single, "Break On Through" b/w "End Of The Night." That was January, '67.

After that first Elektra meeting, I went down to the club where the Doors were rehearsing and introduced myself to them. I gave them a brief run-down on some of my ideas for promotion. I asked if I could talk with each of them individually. That was when I first met Jim.

**RELIX:** How did Jim act at that first meeting and what was your first impression of him?

**FIELDS:** He was trying to be dramatic. It was one of the many moods and theatrical performances I was to observe throughout my relationship with him. I found him to be as charismatic off the stage as he came across on the stage.

**Relix:** When was your peak period of involvement with Jim and The Doors?

**Fields:** That probably was when Jac Holzman of Elektra had me start up the Publicity Dept. of his record company. The week I started, "Light My Fire" hit the number one spot on the charts. That was May, 1967.

Up until that time there really hadn't been too much promotion for the Doors, so it was time to get things in motion. The first thing I did was approach Howard Smith of the Village Voice and tell him about a new musical sex symbol. Howard got a copy of that Joel Brodsky photo of Jim, the one of him bare chested, wearing the string of beads. It was extremely flattering and sensual. Once that photo appeared in the Voice, the media began to recognize Jim as a sex symbol. [In later years, Jim admitted to resenting that picture. It was too good, and he felt he never looked as good as the picture made him appear. He always felt he had to live up to this image the picture seemed to portray.]

Later that summer, in my continuing publicity campaign for the band, I had arranged a telephone interview from L.A. to N.Y. with Gloria Stavers of the trendy 16 Magazine.

The only way of guaranteeing that the interview would take place according to plan was for me to fly out to L.A., and at a pre-arranged time, get Jim to a phone and hook the two togethr for this major interview.

Jim and I were staying at a place that everyone called the Castle. After finishing the interview, which went somewhat poorly, he ws supposed to follow me in his car. Naturally, Jim had to be difficult. He was the worst person to have follow you! He would stay just out of sight so you had to keep slowing down and waiting, and pulling over to the side of the road for him to catch up. Finally, arriving at our destination, Jim was ready to party.

**RELIX:** What sort of girls did Jim hang out with?

**FIELDS:** That was one of the things that annoyed me about Jim. He always had these trolls—druggies and groupies all around him. He always made himself available to them. I felt that as his publicity agent, I should try to do something about it.

Two lady friends of mine were at the Castle—Nico and Dee-Dee Sedgwick. Nico was one of the Warhol girls and had been a cover girl in her native Germany. She sang with the Velvet Underground and she loved to drink, as did Morrison. Nico adored dressing in black leather, something else I found her to have in common with Jim. She had long silver-blond hair that accentuated her ageless beauty. I thought Nico and Jim would make a great combination. My plan was to get them together and, hopefully, elevate his taste in women.

When I introduced the two of them, all they did was stare at each other. Just stared—did not speak a word! They never stopped looking at each other or at the same things. They were like two cats. They watched each other's movements, followed each other around the house, but did not say one word at all!

That night, Jim wanted to get a little high, so he smoked about 1/4 ounce of hash I'd had, swallowed my entire stash of ups, dropped a few hits of LSD, and downed it all with 2 quarts of Vodka. I saw him do all of this, and he was still going strong!

**RELIX:** Was all of this natural for Jim, or was he trying to shock everyone?

**FIELDS:** Oh no!! He was just trying to get high! He got so stoned that I started to get nervous. I was worried that he was going to decide to go for a ride, so I went down to the car and hid the keys. I'm glad I did. No sooner had done this, when Jim decided that he wanted to leave. So, he went down to his car but couldn't find the keys. We were isolated and didn't have a phone, so he couldn't call for a cab either. But by then it didn't matter, he was really off in his own world.

**RELIX:** How did the rest of the evening go?

**FIELDS:** Well, it was pretty quiet until about 3 A.M. I was in my room, when I looked out of my window into the Spanish style courtyard. couldn't believe what I was seeing! Jim and Nico were standing there under the full moon in the middle of the fountain. Jim was pulling Nico's hair, and she was screaming. He never said anything, he just kept on pulling her hair Suddenly, he ran into the house, and Nico, in her deep voice, just stood there in the water sobbing.

I had just recovered from that scene, when glanced up, and there was Jim—stark naked—

dancing along the edge of the parapet. I watched him until he bopped out of sight. Well, somehow we survived the night

But that was how Jim did things. He had to be the center of attention. Like the very next day, we went over to a friend's house who had a pool. When Jim hit the water, everyone got out. He was an incredible swimmer and truly beautiful to watch. He actually took up the entire pool with his presence.

**RELIX**: About some of the shows the Doors did, are there any events that really stand out in your mind?

**FIELDS**: Boy!!! I remember that show in Forest Hills, N.Y. when the Doors played with The Who. The Who opened the show, and after their set Pete Townshend told me that the audience was real tense and ready to explode. So I thought I should tell Jim about it. Jim responded with, "How can *you* tell?"—and he walked away. Well, the show ended with a riot and about 20 people were taken to hospitals.

Another night, the Doors were opening for Simon and Garfunkel. After the opening, Jim walked off of the stage in a slump. I asked him what was wrong, and he said, "They hated it, they *laughed* at me!"

**RELIX**: Did you notice any changes in Jim as the Doors became more popular?

**FIELDS**: Well, one night we went to Max's in New York for dinner—Jim didn't say a word all night. He even pointed out his order to the waitress. He was acting like a 6 year old, making everyone feel uncomfortable.

**RELIX**: Morrison seemed to like dangling people from his own self-styled parapet. Do you think this was his favorite form of self indulgence and amusement?

**FIELDS**: Oh yes! There was another night at Max's—we were sitting around the table and he was too stoned to go to the bathroom, so he took an empty wine bottle and pissed into it. He kept doing it all night. At the end of the evening, Jim was smiling and in good spirits. The waitress was cleaning the table and he told her that since he couldn't finish the wine, she should take it home and enjoy it. The waitress was so thankful—Jim Morrison gave her something!

**RELIX**: Boy, that bottle would probably be worth a fortune today!!!!! How did things actually go on the Ed Sullivan Show?

**FIELDS**: Not *that* bad really, aside from tearing down the whole set—and after promising not to use the line about getting much higher, singing it anyway. The sponsors went wild.

**RELIX**: Was he really enjoying himself?

**FIELDS**: Oh, he loved everything! He loved singing. He loved acting. He loved keeping everyone guessing. He *loved* being difficult.

**RELIX**: Did you find the other members of the Doors resenting Jim?

**FIELDS**: No. They knew which side their bread was buttered on. I think they thanked the Lord for Jim Morrison. They all knew he possessed a magnetism that they lacked. They also knew that their music was unique and that Jim was a major influence on their music. None of them would have wanted to take his place.

**RELIX**: Did Jim have to be watched on the day of a performance to insure he would arrive on time?

**FIELDS**: They hired Bobby Neuwirth to be his drinking partner, an alcohol companion that would guarantee getting Jim to the gigs. Bob said that he understood heavy drinkers and that he could handle the job. He used to boast about his long time relationship with Dylan, and having seen Janis Joplin and other heavies through the alcohol scene. Well, for a few months, Bob did his job—but after awhile, he had to give up. He just couldn't handle Morrison and he quit.

**RELIX**: Any other stories that come to mind? How about that legendary night at "The Scene" in New York?

**FIELDS**: Ah yes. I remember—the night when Jimi Hendrix was performing there. Jim was *very* drunk. Hendrix was jamming and it was quite late. I noticed some commotion way up front at the stage, and there was Jim crawling across the floor toward Hendrix. When he finally reached him, he wrapped his arms around Hendrix's knees and started screaming "I wanna suck your cock!" He was very loud and Hendrix was still attempting to play. But Morrison wouldn't let go. It was a tasteless exhibition of scene stealing—something Morrison was really into. To top it all off, Janis Joplin, who had been sitting in the back of the room, suddenly appeared at the edge of the stage with a bottle in one hand and her drink in the other. She had a *strong* dislike for Morrison, whom she referred to as "that asshole." She stepped in and hit Jim over the head with the bottle—then she poured her drink over him! That started the three of them grappling and rolling all over the floor in a writhing heap of angry hysteria. Naturally, it ended up in all three of them being carried out. Morrison was the most seriously hurt. His bodyguards were summoned and he was driven away. I'd heard that earlier in the evening, Jim had knocked a table full of drinks into Janis' lap.

**RELIX**: What was the relationship between Joplin and Morrison prior to this?

**FIELDS**: They had met at a party and got very drunk together. Jim suddenly became rowdy and grabbed Janis by the hair, pulling her head to his crotch. She broke free, and when he left, she ran after him, trying to hit him with a bottle. They both frequented Barney's Beanery, and I'm sure they'd see each other there often. Before Janis died, they had both made some amends for which Jim was grateful.

**RELIX**: Did Jim ever get together musically with any of the San Francisco bands?

**FIELDS**: No. He hated them. He considered himself a "New York-L.A." person. This dislike arose when the Doors weren't invited to play at Monterey. They were very upset about it. They just weren't accepted. One night Jim went to the Fillmore East to see the Airplane. The audience was heckling the band, and Grace Slick remarked sarcastically. "Oh, I see Jim Morrison is here tonight—you must be Doors fans." This only increased Morrison's dislike for the Bay area musicians.

**RELIX**: Do you think the myth of the man, Jim Morrison, is probably greater than it would have been had he lived?

**FIELDS**: Yes. I think Jim did the right thing by dying at the age of 27. But seriously, I think he did what he was happy doing and that he believed he'd lived a good life.

**RELIX**: Jim and Pamela Courson retained a relationship of sorts for a long period of time, prior to his fame until his death. Do you think Jim was capable of a serious, giving and loving relationship?

**FIELDS**: Not for any period of time. Jim could be violent at times, often with a woman he didn't know very well. But his relationship with Pamela was pretty positive.

**RELIX**: How did Pamela react to Jim's death?

**FIELDS**: She'd found his body in the bathtub in Paris where they lived then. When she returned home to California, I flew out there to be with her. She was living in a little house in Sausalito with Sage, her golden retriever. Pamela was obviously quite despairing, and she was all of the proof there was that Jim had actually died. So, there was Pamela with her dog. Every time the dog would make a sound, she would kneel beside him, and in a soft voice would ask, "Yes, Jim? What are you trying to tell me?" She *truly* believed that Jim's spirit had certainly returned in the dog.

Artwork by Alfred Klosterman

# Mom's A Deadhead

## by Emily Rosen

HEY listen folks! I may not be a certifiable "Deadhead" but I do have some credentials. Radio City in '80, Lunt-Fontanne in '87 and now the New York summit — Madison Square Garden in '88, complete with T-shirt and jeans. So I'm about to run for Deadhead Mother of the Tour.

My 32 year old son has already gotten his picture in the local paper, (headline: "Living With The Dead") for the monumental accomplishment of being a quintessential "Deadhead," and I figure that some of the fame fallout might accrue to me.

It's "prep" time. We are "setting up" in the taper's section, surrounded by a forest of ten foot Sennheiser mic stands (looks like Antenna City) and a bunch of Sony D-5s, and D-6s, and the more elite German-made Uher tape decks. Plenty of headsets. Everyone is an expert in sound technology here.

"Whose got extra duct tape?" The mic stands need to be stabilized.

"One a-you guys got some double A batteries?"

What's yours is mine. Deadheads share. Pass the beer. Pass the joints. Your seat. My seat. What's the difference, we stand in the aisles anyway.

We are awash in T-shirt technicolor, a mass of sayings and designs. Not many duplicates in Ts. Somehow there's enough variety to go around.

"Hey you guys. This is Mom," my son points. They come from all over the taper's section to say hello to this 'ole' lady. "Glad to meetcha. Isn't this fun?"

I'm really getting into it now. Different from Radio City eight years ago. I was a novice Deadhead then, too busy feeling out of place, wondering why I wasn't in Lincoln Center watching and listening to Lenny Bernstein. Different from Lunt-Fontanne last year. The intimacy is gone. This is the vast indoors where everything seems miniaturized by distance. From where I am sitting, the band is not identifiable (or is it just my old eyes?) except by shape. They are one big blur.

There go the lights. Up comes the roar. Like a symphonic crescendo, the bodies rise to the occasion hailing their gods. Buddha Jerry and lean Bobby merely appear. Billy, Mickey, Phil, Brent — they all wander in as if to ask, "Is this the place?" No fanfares, no waves, no introductions, no announcements. Just: Here we are, and let's go!

"Little Red Rooster" yay! And the crowd pulsates with the rhythm of the guitar. Bodies are revving up for the gyrations.

Don't ask me how great the music was. I squeeled for "Frankeeeee" when Sinatra was at the Paramount in the great stone age. My idea of music is Harry James and Glenn Miller. Michael Feinstein is my current cult hero. (What? You've never heard of him? He's about 30 years old and sings Gershwin and Porter and those guys, caberet style, the darling of the geriatric set.) Just give me an evening with George Shearing and Mel Torme and — to coin a phrase — all my troubles melt away. So where do I come off talking about the music of the Dead?

Considering that it's the music of the 60s, it seems to me there is still an urgent pandemonium quality that carries it legitimately into the 80s. And yet for contrast, I hear Segovia somewhere in the background every once in a while. The spontaneity of jamming, Jerry Garcia's or Louis Armstrong's, fine-tunes the listener the same way a good mystery glues us to the seat of our pants. We get involved. How's it going to turn out?

This is a festival of sound. A Kreutzmann and Hart drum set beats into my guts with shivers and trembles and wakes up dead passions right down to my toes.

There is a modicum of restraint in the taper's section. We don't bounce with fervor, for fear of loosening the legs of the mic stands, and introducing extraneous sounds onto the tape. And the wooden platforms in the Garden have a fragile shakey quality that command repect. So some folks exit onto the floor and perform expressions of worship, moving with the rhythm and the beat, building up to a healthy ecstasy. Serious tapers quietly rock in place, beaming flashlights or fumbling at an assortment of dials and knobs, while being transported to some netherworld by Dire Wolf or Far From Me or Queen Jane. Some sink into hillbilly heaven with Tennessee Jed.

Last year, the music sounded to me like plates breaking, cans banging, fire erupting, thunder and earthquakes. Last year I yawned out loud, and no one heard me. But recently I traveled cross-country with a young Deadhead friend, and our musical agreement was: "Driver's Choice." She drove 3600 of the 4000 miles, so I am well primed for this concert.

Now I hear the music. I screen out the noise, trying to catch a lyric, trying to discern a melody, trying not to be distracted by the show around me, even finding recognition. I am feeling loose, and I am going with the flow. There is an intuitive bond on that stage, an unspoken signal of energy that fuses six people into one. Are they dispensing music — or love — or both?

They bow out with The Mighty Quinn and a roar from the crowd.

The tapers dismantle and are already talking about tomorrow's concert. I look around and try to figure out what makes a Deadhead. But wait! That's beginning to sound serious. My new Deadhead friends are closing in on me. "Hey Mom, wasn't that fun?"

Fun! I guess that's the password. But please don't breathe a word of this to my stodgy friends at Lincoln Center. ∎

**Artwork by Alfred Klosterman**

65464

# Relix

## PHOTO ALBUM

Vol. 8
No. 6

$2.50

**ROLLING STONES 1981 TOUR**
**GRATEFUL DEAD**
**SPRINGSTEEN**

## MORE EXCLUSIVE PHOTOS

**GARCIA**
**OZZY OSBOURNE**
**PAT BENATAR**
**TOM PETTY**
**ADAM & THE ANTS**
**FRANK ZAPPA**
**THE CLASH**
**ROBERT GORDON**
**DEVO**

## JIMI HENDRIX

Cover Photo
Courtesy
Reprise Records
November/December, 1981

Photo by Les Kippel

# Death Don't Have No Mercy

# Pigpen, Ten Years Gone

## by
## Jeff Tamarkin

ONE day in February 1973, Ron "Pigpen" McKernan got out of bed in his apartment in Corte Madera, California, where he'd recently been spending most of his time, and walked over to his piano. He pushed the record button on his tape recorder and started playing a slow, bluesy dirge. His voice was shot, withered away like the rest of him. He sang:

*"Look over yonder, tell me what do you see?*
*Ten thousand people lookin' after me.*
*I may be famous or I may be no one,*
*But in the end all our races are run.*
*Don't make my race run in vain."*

He threw in a couple of fills on the keyboard and continued:

*"Seems like there's no tomorrow,*
*Seems like all my yesterdays were filled with pain.*
*There's nothin' but darkness tomorrow."*

It was the saddest song he had ever sung. Although Pigpen's thing was the blues, his was never the blues of death and loneliness, but the blues of whiskey and women. He lived them both too much for his own good. In the end, it was the whiskey and women that did him in. He continued:

*"Don't make me live in this pain no longer.*
*You know I'm getting weaker, not stronger."*

It was actually a song for a girl that had walked out on him, but it was also Pig's goodbye song to himself.

*"I'll get by somehow.*
*Maybe not tomorrow, but somehow . . .*
*I didn't realize what was happenin'*
*To my life . . .*
*I'm gone,*
*Goodbye, so long."*

Goodbye, so long, it was to be. Pigpen didn't get by, not tomorrow, not ever. On March 8, 1973, a month after he put down that song—one of a number of tunes he'd been writing for a solo album that was never to be on tape, Ron "Pigpen" McKernan got up out of that same bed, walked a few feet and died. He put his yesterdays filled with pain behind him.

Pigpen's race was run, but today, 10 years after the Grateful Dead lost their soul man, we have to wonder: *did* Pigpen run his race in vain?

There are times that it would seem so. The name McKernan does not get mentioned in the same breath as Morrison, Hendrix, Joplin, Presley, Holly, or Lennon when we talk about the rock and roll greats that have left us. But perhaps it should be. Pigpen should not have died in vain, and his contributions should be recognized. Pigpen was not just the best blues singer to come out of the San Francisco scene, he was one of the best white blues singers rock and roll has ever known. Whereas Eric Clapton, Mike Bloomfield, Steve Winwood, Steve Miller, John Mayall and the rest had to study the blues, to figure out what the black man meant in his music, Pigpen only had to live it—and he did. Pig was more than just a singer in a band—he was one of the most fascinating personalities ever to find his way into the rock and roll history books. And the fact that he sang with the Grateful Dead is another whole story in itself—Pigpen gave that band an element of coolness they never would've had without him. It is debatable whether there would even have been a Grateful Dead without him. But then again, it made absolutely perfect sense that he should be a part of the Dead. Who else would have taken him? Who else would've understood him? Who else would've let him get away with being the way he was?

The Grateful Dead, with Pigpen singing, comprised the perfect American band for the late '60s and early '70s. Think about it: with Pig up front, you had a blues singing country boy fronting a rocking folk band with jazz sensibilities. Can you get more American than that?

Pigpen brought the music of black America to the Dead. Whereas Jerry Garcia brought folk and bluegrass, Bob Weir brought pure angry teenaged rock and roll, Phil Lesh brought electronics, jazz and wierdness, and Bill Kreutzmann brought incredibly flowing, sharp rhythms (doubley incredible when Mickey Hart was around), Pigpen brought James Brown, Lightnin' Hopkins, the Coasters, Elmore James, Jimmy Reed, Wilson Pickett, John Lee Hooker, Howlin' Wolf, Otis Redding, Bobby "Blue" Bland, Sonny Boy Williamson, Muddy Waters, the Olympics, Willie Dixon, Chuck Willis and Chuck Berry. It was often said that Pigpen *was* a black man in white man's skin, and it was not a lie; this wasn't another case of white man's guilt—Pigpen was simply a blues-breathing kind of guy.

Ron McKernan was born either in 1945 or 1946, depending on which account you read—in either case, it was apparently on September 8. His father was a rhythm and blues disc jockey and the boy, who lived in the industrial area in and around San Bruno, California, south of San Francisco, took an early liking to the kind of grits his papa was laying down on the turntable. He picked up the harmonica and learned to play it the same way those cats did.

He learned to play the piano and the organ. He learned to play the guitar. He learned to go by feeling in his singing and not technique; he learned to project and to incite a crowd. Ron was playing acoustic and electric solo guitar in the coffee houses near the colleges in his area. He became sort of a local hero, this white kid who could play and sing black. Folk music was enjoying a revival in the early '60s and the blues was a part of it; college types dug that down-to-earth pure American sound the same way they dug the bluegrass music that local groups like the Sleepy Hollow Hog Stompers and later, Mother McCree's Uptown Jug Champions—both featuring a young banjoist in his early 20s named Jerry Garcia—were playing.

It wasn't long before this teenaged blues junkie with the slicked back hair and the thin mustache and the voice that totally ignored key and pitch was discovered by Garcia and his friends, and they let him sit in and do a blues every so often. Pigpen, as the young McKernan kid had become known, didn't mind; for him it was a chance to play his Leadbelly tunes to someone other than the old black dudes that would hang out in the sleazy bars where he used to play. And the bluegrass guys didn't mind; for them it was a chance to have a bona fide oddball conversation piece adding some guts to their all-American, wholesome kind of hillbilly sound.

It was 1962 or '63 when they met, and by 1964 the whole thing had blossomed into a full-grown scene. Pig's friend Jorma Kaukonen was around, playing his blues. Guys like David Freiberg and Robert Hunter were around, as were David Nelson, Peter Albin and an accomplished musician named Phil Lesh. They played every place from clubs like the Boar's Head and the Tangent to local Jewish Community Centers, in various configurations. And they began attracting a weird bunch of people: literary types like Ken Kesey; Hell's Angels; a kid guitar player named Bob Weir. Somethin' was happenin'. Dope became less of a secret and more of a lifestyle. And there was this new shit called LSD. Everybody started taking it and talking about its mystical, "mind-expanding" properties. It became a way of life for Kesey and his crowd. Garcia was a big fan of the drug. It seemed everyone was getting stoneder and stoneder. Except Pigpen, that is. The blues kid didn't need nothin' but his guitar and harp and a bottle of cheap rotgut wine.

1965 was the year of electricity. Garcia, Lesh, Weir, Kreutzmann and Pigpen—a bunch of misfits if there ever was one—picked up electric instruments and started jamming around the peninsula, playing a weird conglomerate of go-go pop, electric folk-rock, excruciating noise and interminably long blues tunes. They all became phenomenal musicians, 'cept Pig, whose Farfisa playing was kind of circus music-like, but cool. They became the musical accompaniment for Kesey's tripping parties. the Acid Tests. They got weirder and weirder. Then, before they knew what had hit them. they got bigger and bigger. They changed their name, not, as Garcia had suggested, to the Mythical Ethical Icicle Tricycle, but to the Grateful Dead, pulled out of a dictionary by Lesh. The misfits signed a recording contract, became famous, toured the U.S.

By 1968-'69, they had become the kings of San Fran psychedelia. But by then Pig's position in the band became insecure. He wasn't interested in their expanded trip music unless it was blues-based, and it was becoming less so. The Dead relegated Pig to congas and occasional vocals. Tom Constanten took over on the organ, playing an ethereal, classically-rooted sound Pig didn't know from and didn't care to know. The band was way out there (witness the *Aoxomoxoa* album) and Pig was out of place. He threatened to quit. Then, they changed their minds, and came back heavier than ever. Pig played his Hammond organ and loved it.

Pigpen fronting the Dead around 1970 was an experience beyond description. Standing at stage center in his cowboy hat, denims, black fuzz growing around his mouth—top, bottom, sides and down into a point below his chin—with his harmonica in his hands, Pigpen commanded attention. And he got it. No one in a hall sat when Pigpen walked out from the wings—sometimes eagerly, sometimes damning the others for calling him away from his comfortable backstage perch—and launched into one of his soul grooves. Whether it was a hell-raiser like Otis' "Hard To Handle," or the Rascal's "Good Lovin' " or a stone soul hard blues like "Smokestack Lightnin' " or James Brown's "It's A Man's Man's Man's World," or a slow, cool blues like Slim Harpo's "King Bee" or an acoustic version of Lightnin's "She's Mine," Pigpen was the focus of attention. He knew how to grab an audience and he did so in this band by providing an element of funkiness that the others didn't have. His earthiness and their spaceness was the perfect combination—heaven and hell. Pigpen got away with being raunchy and by doing so he added street-tough to the various images projected by the Dead.

And he inspired the band, did he ever. The nature of his music by itself forced the group to play a different way. Blues and soul are more disciplined linear musics than the free-form music the Dead engaged in during "St. Stephen," "Dark Star," "Cold, Rain And Snow," "The Other One," etc. The blues demanded that Garcia play more pronounced, solid, lyrical, chunkier lines on his guitar, almost taking the place of a horn section. It put Weir in the position of having to skip his usual flourishes and stick with strict rhythms. The drummers were forced almost to be stiff. And Phil Lesh, though he did what he could with the bass rhythms, was put in the all-important position of having to lay the path that the singer would follow. This they all did rather admirably, and their reward came during the breaks, when Pig stepped aside to let them "ride awhile." Pig would sometimes play along with them on organ or harp, and although no one ever accused him of being a good musician, he played soulfully. But his playing *was* rudimentary in comparison. The jams that came out of Pigpen's songs however, were often nothing less than physically and spiritually draining. Once let loose after a few minutes of actually backing a vocalist, these improv-hungry musicians took off like a rocket. The jams that could be found in the mid-section of a "Good Morning, Little Schoolgirl," "Easy Wind," "Hard To Handle," "Smokestack Lightnin' " or, the *tour-de-force* of Pigpen/Dead-dom, "Turn On Your Lovelight," were easily some of the most sensational exhibitions of raw improvisational musicianship ever to emanate from a band working within a rock and roll framework. Pigpen made them work hard and they did .

Pig was also the clown prince of the Grateful Dead. He was a wise-ass and a showman in a band that purposely practiced anti-showbiz attitudes. It was Pigpen who would get pissed off at a lousy sound system and tell the sound man that if he didn't get the sound in shape real soon, Pig would proceed to "cut off your head and shit in it." It was hardly a line one might expect from Jerry Garcia.

Or how about the immortal version of "Lovelight" from the Fillmore East in Arpil 1971? Pig was fond of extending the song by inserting an ever-changing rap into the loose body of the tune. He would usually invite the guys in the audience to clap their hands, to "take your hands out of your pockets and stop playing pocket pool." He liked to get people in the audience to act together and get it on together—Pig was a firm believer in sex and more sex, the nastier the better—and was known to suggest to audiences (for instance at Stonybrook, NY in October '70) that they should "turn to your neighbor and say, 'Let's fuck.' " But in that April '71 gig, the same one at which the Beach Boys walked out of nowhere and joined the Dead onsage for awhile, Pig did it up for real. He pulled two people out of the crowd and invited them onstage. He introduced them, and then he sent them off together. "Chris and Marcia have just made it!" he announced proudly, mission accomplished. And it wouldn't be surprising if Chris and Marcia were still together today: such was Pigpen's charisma.

It was around the time of those closing gigs at the Fillmores, however, that Pig's life started taking a turn for the worse. I remember that the first and only time I ever met him was while waiting on line one afternoon for a front spot at a general admission Dead concert—at the Manhattan Center in New York. About four in the afternoon, Pig came strolling by. "anybody know where the nearest bar is?" he drawled in that not-quite-Southern accent that you shouldn't have if you're from California unless you're a white black man. We pointed across the street and he went in that direction, accompanied by his black girlfriend of the time. About two hours later Pig came strolling back, obviously stewed. A few of us talked to him for awhile about the latest Dead news: about the New Riders, about Mickey Hart's recent departure from the band and about wine—he was an expert on cheap wine and he liked to talk about it as much as he liked to drink it. Then he walked into the theater. But I remember some people on line commenting that he didn't look well.

A few weeks later, at the aforementioned Fillmore gigs, we waited around one night after the show for the band to leave. Pigpen came out first. He was still acting as wild as he had been an hour ago as he brought the show to an end with one of his rave-up show-closing bashes. he had his black girl on one arm and a white one on the other. His cowboy hat was pulled down almost over his eyes—was he cross-eyed or was it the booze that made them look so screwed up?—and started walking quickly down Sixth Street toward Second Avenue. Suddenly he howled at the top of his lungs in his own inimitable outlaw-on-the-run style. It was light out and we—audience members—were ready to pass out for a few days: *we* were drained of energy. But Pig was still on the go. After the howl he shouted halfway down the block for a taxi, which stopped in its tracks to pick up this less-than-harmless-looking trio. And he was gone. That was the last time New York ever saw Pigpen in tip-top shape. He missed a good part of the East Coast tour in the fall of that year and didn't sound up to par at the shows he did make. The reason the band gave for his absence was that Pig was sick but he'd be back soon.

He was back in March 1972 to play the Academy of Music shows, one of them featuring the Dead serving as a backup band for legendary rocker Bo Diddley. And he made it to Europe the next month, against his doc's advice. He played his last gig with the Dead in June '72 at the Hollywood Bowl. After that, there were few excuses the band could make. Although he had seemed well enough on the European tour in the spring, Pigpen McKernan was losing his grip on life. The doctors told him what he needed wasn't good lovin' but a lot of rest, no booze and lots of protein to put his decaying liver back together. He couldn't do it, lost his will to live, and in March '73 we got the news that Pigpen had died.

Photo by L.D. Kippel

It didn't seem all that much of a surprise when someone came ringing my doorbell that spring day to tell me what had happened. When this non-Dead Head friend casually mentioned that "A guy in the Grateful Dead died," it didn't trigger a mad dash for the radio to find out who it was. I knew who it was, and although I was a hardcore Dead Head at the time I wasn't shocked. It was only a matter of time: most of the hardcores had long ago come to terms with the fact that we were probably never going to see Pig alive again.

And many of us knew that we'd never see the Grateful Dead quite as alive again, either, that the band which had given us the highest musical heights we'd ever known was going to lose a lot of its soul—and heart. Although Keith and Donna Godchaux had already been added to the band by the time Pig died, giving them a new direction, the experience of getting off on the Grateful Dead dropped a few levels in terms of the bliss factor when the group's official mascot took the next Easy Wind out of town for good. No longer could we expect to be awakened from the psychedelic haze at their shows by the cowboy riding in for another shot of rhythm and blues, putting a smile on our faces while making our feet dance crazy rhythms. Pigpen was a big guy in life, but by listening to his work with the Dead, and recalling what he was like, he seems, 10 years after his liver gave in, even bigger in death. There will never be another one like him.

Vol.9
No.1

$1.75

# Relix

### music for the mind

65463

January/February, 1982

STONES - 1981
GRATEFUL DEAD
EUROPE - 1981

SPECIAL
GRATEFUL DEAD
ISSUE!

Cover Photo by Dennis Callahan

54

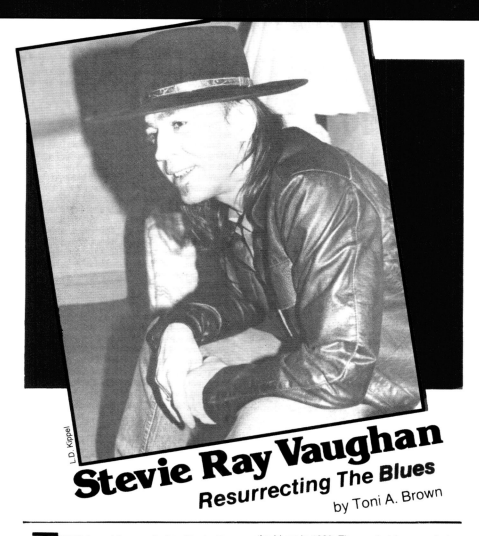

L.D. Kippel

# Stevie Ray Vaughan
## Resurrecting The Blues
by Toni A. Brown

TEXAS born blues guitarist, Stevie Ray Vaughan, is finally garnering some attention after 20 years of playing the blues. After so much time spent paying his dues, Stevie looks back and says there were good times and fun, and none of it was too bad.

Stevie Ray Vaughan doesn't seem to be the type to let success go to his head. He is a quiet and reserved man, but at the same time, an inner fire burns. He has obviously gone the route of many blues musicians before him, but instead of slipping into obscurity, something clicked. Word of his ability spread before he got off the club circuit. He has since been blowing everybody off of the stage! By the time he was scheduled to open up for a past Moody Blues tour, more people were buying tickets to see this guitar wizard than to see the legendary Moody Blues. But justifiably so. Stevie Ray is being compared to some of the best guitarists, including Jimi Hendrix and Jeff Beck. When we asked him how he felt about these comparisons, he patiently replied, "I figure that people need to use comparisons just to explain what they're talking about.

"Jimi Hendrix was a big influence on my music. What he was doing with his music and why, the soul he projected. But there was only one Hendrix and there'll never be another," explains Stevie Ray Vaughan. "I guess I've been influenced by everything I've ever heard. But I'd have to say my brother Jimmie was my biggest influence. He's in the Fabulous Thunderbirds now."

Stevie Ray Vaughan and Double Trouble are responsible for single-handedly resurrecting

the blues in 1983. They ended the year playing to a sold-out house at New York's Beacon Theatre. Among the crowd of blues devotees was one of Stevie's earliest fans, Mick Jagger, who actually ventured out into the audience to watch Stevie's guitar pyrotechnics! After being thoroughly dazzled, Mick attempted to regain admittance backstage but was stopped by a security guard who demanded identification. Luckily Mick didn't leave home without his American Express card, because that was what he used.

1983 also saw the release of Stevie's critically acclaimed album, *Texas Flood*, which recently won honors as "Best Guitar Album" in the 1983 Guitar Player Readers Poll—the first

blues album to ever win that category; additionally, Stevie was voted "Best New Talent" and "Best Electric Guitarist."

Considering the fact that Stevie Ray Vaughan is a "new" artist, and the "types" of music that usually find success, we asked Stevie if he was surprised at the success of *Texas Flood*. "I was surprised at the great response we got. But I also figured that one of the strongest selling points was that it wasn't synthesized. It sticks out, it's completely different from anything on the commercial market."

Stevie Ray Vaughan and Double Trouble (Chris Layton and Tommy Shannon)

We asked Stevie if he had studied music. "I took music in school once, and for the first six weeks, I passed. Then I flunked for the rest of the time. I think people who can't handle formal training get stuck just having a piece of paper in front of them. But it doesn't hurt to know those in-betweens."

Stevie Ray Vaughan is very loyal to his band, Double Trouble. We wondered how they got together. "I met Tommy Shannon (bass) in Dallas around '68. We've been playing together off and on ever since. Chris Layton (drums) and I are together about 5 years. I met him in Austin. Actually, when I met him, he had his drums set up in his kitchen. He had headphones on and he was banging away for about 5 minutes and didn't even know I was there. When he finished, I just asked him if he wanted to change his gig."

A new album has just been recorded and should be released sometime in April, 1984. Stevie anticipates doing some video work around it, but isn't sure of what songs will be used. But he does promise some surprises on the album.

Stevie Ray and Relix's Toni

**Toni's Note:** In 1982, David Gans called and asked if we were interested in an interview with Ozzy Osbourne, who was very popular at the time. I knew David's roots and suggested he write from a Deadhead perspective. Instead, he presented a very good but very "Ozzy-esque" interview that we decided to run.

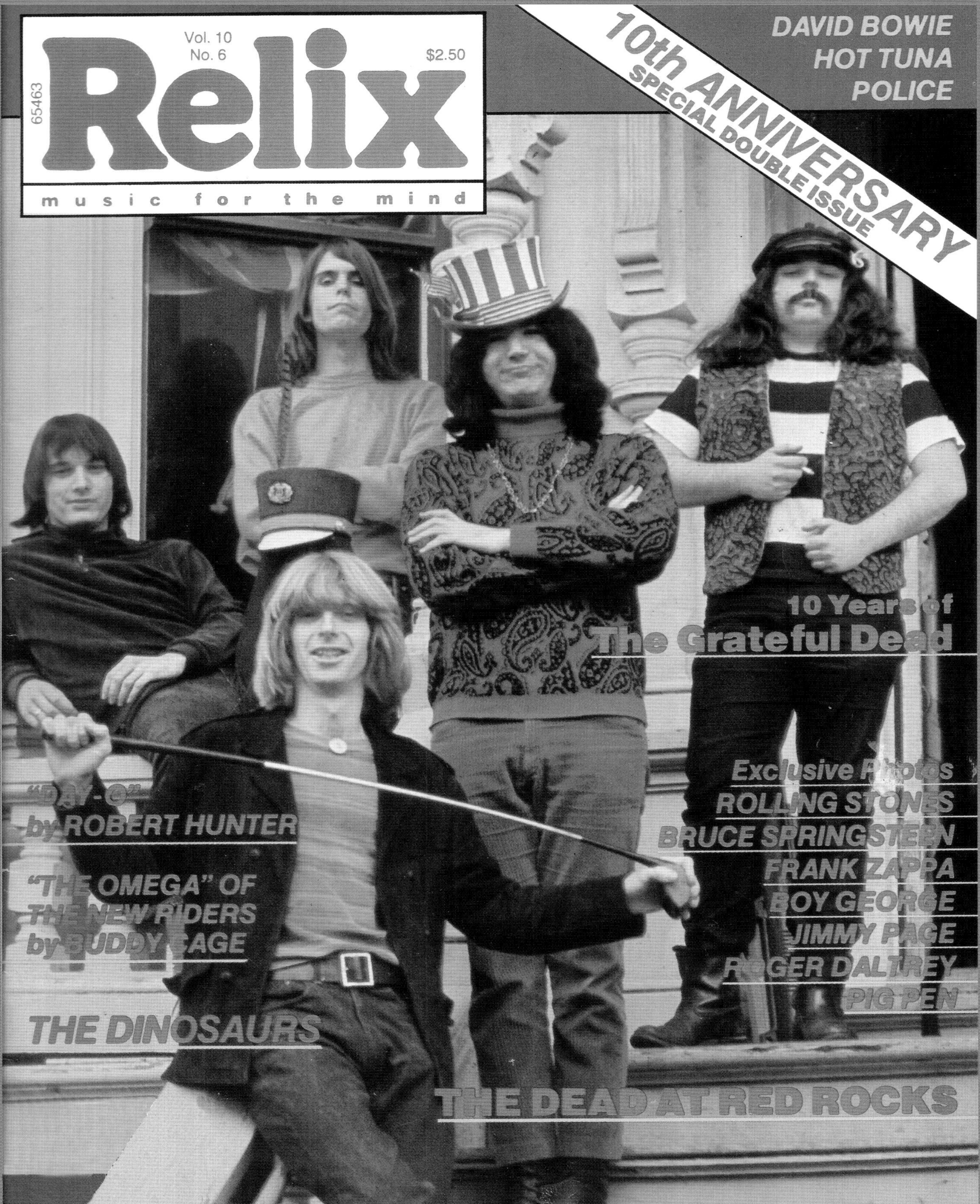
Vol. 10
No. 6
$2.50
65463
Relix
music for the mind
10th ANNIVERSARY
SPECIAL DOUBLE ISSUE
DAVID BOWIE
HOT TUNA
POLICE
10 Years of
The Grateful Dead
Exclusive Photos
ROLLING STONES
BRUCE SPRINGSTEEN
FRANK ZAPPA
BOY GEORGE
JIMMY PAGE
ROGER DALTREY
PIG PEN
"DAY-O"
by ROBERT HUNTER
"THE OMEGA" OF
THE NEW RIDERS
by BUDDY CAGE
THE DINOSAURS
THE DEAD AT RED ROCKS
Cover Photo by Gene Anthony

Photo by Ed Perlstein

## An Interview with
# Mickey Hart
### By Toni A. Brown

FOLLOWING their most recent East Coast tour, Relix had the opportunity to meet with Mickey Hart, Grateful Dead percussionist extraordinaire. Over a late breakfast and the rattle of dishes, we set into conversation. We discussed his life and love of percussion, and his two newly released solo albums, *Dafos* and *Yamantaka*.

*RELIX:* There are many people out there who put on your solo albums and don't get what they expect of them. How do you feel about those people?

*HART:* I don't think of those people. I don't know what they expect. I try to sound like what I feel. This is what I do, I play music and I would hope that someone would like it. If they don't, that would be their misfortune and mine, but I couldn't play to their tastes—whatever they may be.

*RELIX:* Did your Egypt experiences help you transcend the traditional percussive boundaries?

*HART:* It started before Egypt. When I went there, I had learned the instruments of Egypt so I wouldn't be a gringo—a stranger in a strange land. I learned their language, their customs and their instruments. They knew I took the time to share their culture. I've been into other percussion in other worlds for years. I knew that the world of percussion didn't end with a bass and snare drum. I was always attracted to it because I like sounds.

*RELIX:* On *Rolling Thunder*, your first solo effort, you used a variety of unusual sounds —rain, marimbas, a water pump . . .

*HART:* That's what "The Greatest Story" started with, my water pump. I live in an old place, and the pump brought the water out of the well. Those were early experiments, because everything was sound. In my life, the early Grateful Dead life, let's say, everyone was taking acid and smoking pot and doing all kinds of weird and crazy things. Everything started having their own individual meanings. It was time to think about things, to hear things other than the normal waking everyday sounds. I'd say we were more aware of our surroundings, so we used our surroundings in the music.

*RELIX:* What were your earliest influences, and what drew you to expand beyond tradition and consider yourself a percussionist, as opposed to being a drummer?

*HART:* I don't think I tried to *become* a percussionist. It just happened. I never realized the difference.

*RELIX:* But you don't stay within any confines, as most drummers do.

*HART:* Oh no! There are no rules for me. The only rules are what I want to sound like and the inspiration I have to go to an instrument. When an instrument comes into my path, I have to find out if I can feel for it. I usually pick it up and it will mean something to me. And if I have a feeling for it, then I'll sit down with it.

*RELIX:* Do you find it easy to pick up a new instrument?

*HART:* Sometimes. If it's an instrument I should be playing. For some reason, you're better suited to certain percussion instruments. I'm talking about devoting time to an instrument. I'm not talking about picking it up and playing it for an hour. I'm talking about bringing it into your home, like a child or a friend. My home is filled with these instruments, and one by one, I pick them up and I go around playing them. Some of them wind up way in the back of the barn. Some wind up right in my bedroom, hanging from the walls. Those are the instruments that are dear to me.

*RELIX:* Do you use the same timing and rhythms with the Grateful Dead as you do with solo efforts?

*HART:* It's really all the same thing. But I do use different instruments.

*RELIX:* What is the strangest instrument you've ever played?

*HART:* The human skull. Living human. His name is Steve Parish. I played him in L.A. when we were making *Terrapin Station*. I got him into the studio, put a couple of mikes on his skull, used a giant beater, put it through some processing, and played a human skull!

*RELIX:* Are you constantly making additions to the Beast?

*HART:* All the time! I added a new one this last time around. It's called the Ballaphone from Kenya. It's a marimba. All the bars have been tapped electronically. So now it's an electric ballaphone. It's the first of its kind. A new breed is born.

Photo by Rob Cohn

*RELIX:* On the *Apocalypse Now Sessions*, were you given a set of circumstances to work within, or were you given artistic freedom?

*HART:* Artistic freedom, I'd call it. Frances (Coppola) wanted a performance of Apocalypse and I assembled the instruments and myself, Airto, Billy (Kreutzmann), and we played the movie. He just said, "make it happen," and we did.

*RELIX:* Is there still a Diga Rhythm Band?

*HART:* Oh no. Diga was just a whole group of people. But that was then. We couldn't keep that band together. I think there were 15 of us. That lasted for just a little while. That was a *band*, a percussion orchestra.

*RELIX:* Let's talk about your newest release, *Dafos*. I sense some jazz overtones. Were the songs pre-arranged and rehearsed, or somewhat improvised?

*HART:* Somewhat improvised. We assembled certain instruments to play, and described it before hand and talked about it, then played it. It isn't overly composed music. Yes, it has a jazzy flavor because it just turned out that light. Instead of the Marshall drums, this is a more musical drum. This is more tune percussion. It's really clean. Then there are Airto, Flora Purim and Bobby Vega, the bass player. These people are really accomplished musicians, they really play. So, it's percussion, but it's also got what people call music because it's got melody in it. It's easily digested.

*RELIX:* Whose idea was it to bring this particular group of musicians together?

*HART:* My idea. But the idea isn't as important as the result. I've had a lot of ideas that were good, but this *sounds* good. This situation just turned out to be ideal. The production was done really well. The people at Reference Recordings are real good people. The production was flawless. We had an easy time with a lot of people. Bill Graham let us use the Kabuki Theatre in San Francisco. We moved in there. There was a real large stage, so we were able to set up the Beast and all the instruments of Batucaje, the Brazilian Players and Keith Johnson, a recordist. He built his own 3 track. machine—2 channel stereo, then he has a bass track in the middle. He's a great remote recordist. He was able to capture and phase correctly the ambiance of the Kabuki Theatre without sacrificing any of the transient responses. It is quite accurate. And he has an 8 track mike remote unit. It's analog, but it's so clean, almost digitally clean. So the percussion was able to live in this environment and sound good in it. This record travels at 45RPM. That's to enhance the groove depth, or the fidelity. You remember the 45's and how they sounded so robust coming off the machine. That was because of the depth of the groove. This record shares that. It's an LP, but it revolves at 45 because of the extreme highs and lows put on this record. This record was made as an audiophile record, that means that it was pressed on virgin vinyl using extremely high tech techniques. A lot of care was taken for quality. It's an expensive record. Each stage of this record was cared after. It wasn't something you throw down to the mastering lab and it's over. So what you'll hear is the imagery. It's just beautiful. You can really see the whole band there.

*RELIX:* It's a very exciting record, some very up moments.

*HART:* It has moments of up, down and sideways. I wanted it to be both soft and hard at the same time, quiet and loud. Sort of a Zen record. I won't do another record like it for awhile. The package is also beautiful. The photo on the cover is by John Werner. He developed a special process. Multi-track photography. He never advances the film and keeps shooting the same frame. It took him three days to do it.

*RELIX:* Is there a special audience you'd like to reach with this album that you haven't necessarily reached before?

*HART:* The audiophile people. The people who have really fine equipment and appreciate frequency response, sonic quality. Some Deadheads, I imagine, are audiophiles, or will become audiophiles.

This record was made by listening to the playbacks on really fine equipment so you could hear the extreme lows, the extreme highs. There's nothing like a percussion album to let you know what your system really sounds like. But it's not a bunch of drummers making sound effects.

*RELIX:* When you begin to put an album together, are you concerned with commercial success?

*HART:* I'm concerned to the point that I'd like the record to make enough money to pay for itself. The record company should be able to make their money, at least. This is the record business. Me, it's another record. I'm in the Grateful Dead and I play live music. That's how *we* make a living. We don't make our livings selling records. It's part of it, though not a major part. But if a record could make enough money to enable us to make another record, then that would be commercially successful. But we'll go on anyway because we have to make our music. Some records are just more successful than others. Now, *Dafos* is getting incredible reviews and I didn't expect people to like it as much as they do. It's my music, and it's a very personal thing with me. But there's some easiness about listening to this album.

*RELIX:* You have another new release entitled *Yamantaka.* I haven't heard much about it.

*HART:* Yes, that's another audiophile record. It just happens that *Dafos* and *Yamantaka* were released at the same time. I didn't *do* them at the same time. Sometimes it takes a long time to get a record right. This one was done on Teldec vinyl and they were having trouble with the process, so it took a long time to come out. This is a record with no membranes. There are *no* drums used. Henry Wolf and myself, he's the Tibetan bell player, we struck things, metal things, and we rubbed things. We did so many different things but we didn't hit any membranes. So this is more of a music record. Twenty-first century kind of music. You won't hear anything you'd recognize on this record. It's lighter percussion. You can meditate to this album. It's really out there.

*RELIX:* You're stepping out of boundaries again.

*HART:* This is just another part of me, another dream. This is what the dream sounded like. This wasn't made for great commercial acceptance. I don't know what people think of this one yet. It was released by Celestial Harmonies.

*RELIX:* What does *Dafos* mean?

*HART:* *Dafos* is a place—Airto and I are into collective consciousness—this is a fantasyland where this record lives. We painted a picture of a place where things happen, like the "Dry

**Mickey Hart**  Photo by Bruce Polonsky

Sands of the Desert," "The Gates of Dafos." Those are physical representations of this land our imagination takes us to. We sit around and talk about other places, other worlds, other levels of consciousness, and how they would act. how their music would be. It's just our imagination running away with us—us having a good time with our imagination. That's what *Dafos* is. It's not like anything else, it doesn't sound like anything. It's just a place.

*RELIX:* Are you still into hypnosis?

*HART:* Oh yes. Self hypnosis. I use it all the time.

*RELIX:* A form of concentration . . .

*HART:* Sure. And sometimes I have to do some superhuman thing, like climb over a building. I use it if I'm tired, if I have to be sharper, or if I have to remember something. I use hypnosis in that way in my music.

*RELIX:* Where do you see yourself going in terms of future solo projects, film sound tracks . . .

*HART:* I do have a lot of things coming up, but it's really hard to talk about them because they're all in the works. Some will happen and some won't. I've worked on a film, "The Whales

Weep Not," shot off the coast of Sri Lanka. It's a whole family of sperm whales playing under the water. We'll be working on another one by the same people. I'm doing some of the microphoning of the whales. I'm going to mount some contact mikes in their mouths to analyze their sounds and put them through the computer and see what their frequency response is. I'm doing underwater recording, digital remote recording. I'm going out on the week-ends and recording everything in sight. I stay active in the recording world all the time just by recording things.

I've also written a play with Barry Melton about humans and insects. I'd like to see it brought to the stage.

*RELIX:* Where do you see yourself going with regard to the Grateful Dead?

*HART:* Upward and onward. We're just coming into our own. Really feeling good. It takes a long time to really play good music. I'm enjoying it.

*RELIX:* You played St. Stephen on your last tour. That was a thrill!

*HART:* Yes. It really was. It's a good song. What great words. Robert Hunter is always with me with those words. "Writing 'what for?' across the morning sky . . ."

# Part Three
## Put The Dead Back In Relix!

There was a lot of controversy over what music should be covered in *Relix*. After a short yet sensational two-year tenure, editor Jeff Tamarkin left. His departure put the magazine in my lap, although I had no professional skills. I had worked with Jeff briefly, and he passed on quite a bit in that short time, but I was left to sort it out organically.

In 1980, Les and I got married. We were a partnership in a variety of ways, but didn't always see eye-to-eye. *Relix* magazine, Rockin' Relix, Relix Records and a number of other projects took our undivided attention, and we put in as many hours a day as was necessary, often working around the clock.

It occurred to me that the magazine was floundering, and I wanted to take it in a direction that I could relate to. Les slowly relinquished the reins as I struggled to include more Deadhead-friendly material.

It was David Gans who, in a unique way, helped me find my direction. He called and asked if we were interested in an interview with Ozzy Osbourne, who was very popular at the time. I knew David's roots and suggested he write from a Deadhead's perspective. Instead, he presented a very good, but "serious" interview that we decided to run. We had quite a reaction from our readers with that issue.

I was pregnant with our son, Philip (1982), and by the time the dust settled on Ozzy, I was forced to take a little time off. Against my wishes, Les put Joan Jett on the cover that followed the Ozzy issue. We had a huge revolt from our readers, and I gave Les the ultimatum to allow me to focus on our core readership's demands and my own instincts. It was time to put the Dead back in *Relix*!

In an effort to show a commitment to our readers, we did so literally, by placing the word "Dead" back in the magazine's title. I also took over as publisher, taking full responsibility for *Relix*'s future.

---Toni Brown, 2009

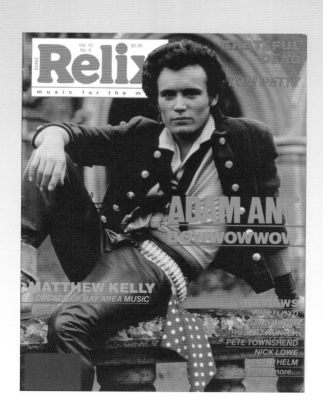

**DEAD**

# Relix
65463    Vol. 11 No. 4    $2.00

music for the mind

**GRATEFUL DEAD**
**SPIRIT**
**NRBQ**
**DIRE STRAITS**

Reviews
COMMANDER CODY
BIG BROTHER AND
    THE HOLDING CO.
FLORA & AIRTO
DAVID GILMOUR
STEEL PULSE
FREELANCE VANDALS
and so much more . . .

SPRINGSTEEN

EXCLUSIVE
THE DEADHEAD'S GUIDE
TO SAN FRANCISCO

Cover Photo
by
Dan Dunn

# Relix
65463    Vol. 11 No. 1    $2.00

music for the mind

**ARMS BENEFIT**
**VANILLA FUDGE**
**88-40**

PAGE, CLAPTON,
BECK, COCKER,
WATTS, WOOD,
WYMAN
and others!

DYLAN
DOORS
TALKING HEADS
STONES
STEVIE RAY VAUGHN
B52s

**THE POLICE**

Exclusive Interviews
THE GRATEFUL DEAD'S
MICKEY HART

HOT TUNA'S
JORMA

NICKSILVER'S
CIPPOLINA & GRAVANITES

Plus:
ADAM ANT, CULTURE CLUB, THE BEAT,
JAM, MERL SAUNDERS, HENDRIX,
and more!!

Cover Photo
Courtesy
A&M Records

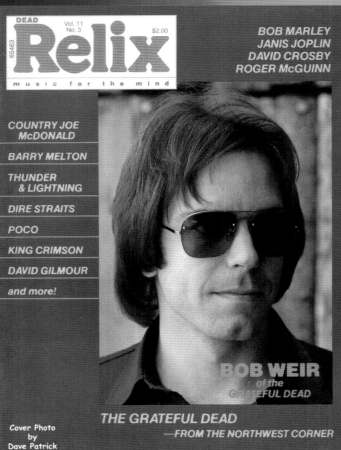

**DEAD**

# Relix
65463    Vol. 11 No. 3    $2.00

music for the mind

**BOB MARLEY**
**JANIS JOPLIN**
**DAVID CROSBY**
**ROGER McGUINN**

COUNTRY JOE
McDONALD

BARRY MELTON

THUNDER
& LIGHTNING

DIRE STRAITS

POCO

KING CRIMSON

DAVID GILMOUR

and more!

BOB WEIR
of the
GRATEFUL DEAD

THE GRATEFUL DEAD
—FROM THE NORTHWEST CORNER

Cover Photo
by
Dave Patrick

# Relix
65463    Vol. 11 No. 2    $2.00

music for the mind

**GRATEFUL DEAD**
**BEATLEMANIA**

Exclusive Interviews
ROBERT HUNTER—
  on Amagamalin St.

STEVIE RAY VAUGHAN—
  Resurrecting the Blues

THE BAND—
  Danko, Helm, Manuel & Hudson

RICHARD THOMPSON

**BOB MARLEY**

Reviews
STRAY CATS
JOHN LENNON
MOBY GRAPE
GRACE SLICK
and more!

Bob Marley
Photo
Courtesy
Island Records

THE FESTIVAL EXPRESS
The First Rock Railroad by Buddy Cage

# JERRY GARCIA

Artwork by Clay DuVal

# The Festival Express

## The first Trans-Canadian R & R Railroad

### by Buddy Cage

Artwork by Gary Kroman

My Dad worked for the Canadian National Railway for 40 odd years. He rose to the gravely responsible position of Yardmaster. He has the peptic ulcers to prove it. The job could be compared to that of an air traffic controller. He would take trains coming into his yard, disassemble them, have each car checked for destination, and then reassemble them into their proper eastbound or westbound packages. No mean feat. Certainly on a day to day basis, fewer human lives at stake, but an error in judgement could be grievously expensive and even near catastrophic. As in the case of a derailment in Mississanga, Ontario about three years ago where some 250,000 persons were evacuated from their homes. The derailment caused the explosion of two liquid propane tanker cars and the potential melt down of one filled with chlorine gas. The person responsible for this rather unfortunate set of circumstances was a Yardmaster. He had put the three tanker cars next to each other instead of spacing them safely with a dozen or so harmless flats or box cars. The blockhead!

Trains carry highly toxic, explosive, corrosive and other weird, volatile and dangerous materials that are restricted by law from being transported by any other popular methods. Such a train was assembled in July, 1970. The railroads waybill indicated that the commodity was "Entertainers," the American Federation of Musicians knew it officially, as the "Festival Express." We, the cargo, had a few other affectionate, unprintable epithets for it.

Two wealthy Canadian entrepreneurs, Thor Eaton and John Bassett carried off an adventure. A rock n'roll adventure with unusual trappings. They had leased an entire railroad passenger train to carry a virtual cornucopia of demented and very talented minstrels from Montreal to Toronto to Winnipeg to Calgary to Vancouver. Across Canada with grand style! Trains can be the best possible way to travel, if it's the right train. This was!

Amtrak, to the old-timer, is a profanity. It's the microwave version. The only comparison with the authentic old trains is that they run on the same tracks, but shouldn't. The old trainman knows. The traditional passenger trains have class, style, real kitchens with real chefs. The railroad that carried us was the Canadian Pacific, an ultra-conservative Canadian firm and it takes a kicked-back soul to appreciate it. Airplanes are great at 30,000 ft., and ocean liners offer no view really but endless sea and the occasional port.

I was born in Canada as were Ian and Sylvia Tyson, the members of the Band (Danko, Robertson, Hudson, Manuel), with the exception of Levon, two members of Janis' Full Tilt Boogie Band (Ricky Bell and John Till.) I wouldn't use any of the aforementioned as sterling examples of Canadian Conservatism, but as a rule the country operates with a far less wide open attitude than does the U.S. I've heard Canadians described as English folks dressed in American clothes. Don't use that comparison on a Canadian nationalist, he'll probably throw an empty beer bottle your way. Never, a full one, beer in Canada is sacred.

The idea of a train odyssey reflects the Canadian ideal of good manners, a sense of order, decency, neatness, of environmental appreciation—peace. A time to stop and smell the Dogwoods, trilliums. Fleurs des lis, and Douglas Firs. I wax poetic at the mere thought. When scores of musical maniacs are thrown together with the "old guard," we might anticipate friction. That train crew, with my experience, qualifies as the "old guard." Remember this was 1970 and people like us were considered radicals by the establishment. No joke.

The star diplomat on board was Janis Joplin. My God, she was persuasive. She went up to the engine and boogied with the engineer, smoked a joint with the straight, old bugger, demanded that he slow the train down—make it last a little longer—(he did). She had the whole crew rockin'. Thinking back on my Dad and his railroad cronies, I was amazed. The crew had such a good time from Montreal to Winnipeg, so much so, that they tried to 'sign on' for the rest of the tour. Unfortunately, they

were prevented from staying on by virtue of their own union regulations. A new crew was assigned in Winnipeg and Janis had no alternative but to initiate the 'new guys'.

At the time I was working with Ian and Sylvia Tyson, the finest folk duo to come out of Canada. Our own personal tour schedule kept us from joining the passenger list from Montreal to Toronto to Winnipeg. In retrospect, I know I had missed a great deal. In any event we played the Festival concert at a football stadium in Toronto, took off to play some other engagement whilst the train bounced along to Winnipeg. We flew into Winnipeg and took a cab to the railroad siding where the train was parked. Ian, Amos, Garrett (our guitar player) and I stumbled around the train, just checking it out. Sylvia was busy hauling her gear into their compartment. The train seemed deserted so when we found the first bar car we settled down for a beer.

Presently Janis joined us and during the next several rounds, filled us in on the segments we'd missed. From Montreal to Toronto is only 340 miles but the biggie had to be the trip from Toronto to Winnipeg coming in at 1,300 miles. Oh, boy!

Before going off to the stadium, I took the opportunity to check out my lodging. My cabin was about 4 feet by 7 feet, featuring a wonderful comfy sofa-seat, which faced forward. Opposite the chair was a hide-a-way sink and a head, mirror, A.C. outlet, picture window (with drapes), my own little world. A handle on the wall above the sofa-seat turned the entire wall down into a bed. Miniature luxury! A minor inconvenience was the use of the head after the bed was down, I had to get out into the aisle and let the bed back up. Nocturnal use of the head is the curse of the dedicated beer drinker.

People who travel constantly can appreciate the importance, yea, the necessity of having comfort and privacy in their living quarters. Small, seemingly unimportant details can have a dramatic effect. This little cubicle suited me to a Tee. If life, at any moment on the train, got too busy for me, I could retire to my cocoon, close my door, open my window drapes and gaze privately at the Canadian Landscape.

After the days performance, a lot of us hit the bar car yakety-yak, yakety-yak. The most popular topic of conversation was about the amazing opportunity we all had been afforded in being able to fraternize with each other so casually. Road bands run into each other usually only when they're playing the same bill. And even then your schedules don't really permit any serious gooning-out together.

So, there we were sittin' around quoffing the local libation (Canadian beer comes in at 5% alcohol, kids) and telling each other lies and every hour or so our numbers were increased by the members of other bands returning from their performances. Now, this train was *not* moving. In fact, the only thing moving was the horseshit we were trading conversationally. Our departure was at seven the next morning.

I took leave of my colleagues and prepared to bed down. I was awakened by a visitor. It turned out to be this guy I knew from Toronto who had, with three other folks, driven his car to every gig. He'd been to the shows in Toronto and Winnipeg and I'd given him guest passes. He asked for tickets to the Calgary gig and I promised him he would have them. In appreciation, he tossed a bag of grass into my compartment and we said goodnight.

Next morning—movement—looking out my window, we're pulling away from Portage La Prairie. Relax! Sure would be neat if I had a joint to smoke. Hey! I scrambled around through my bed sheets for that stupid bag. Ah—here we are, here we have it! Just dandy—smoked one laying in bed. Check that scenery! Well, I'm feeling great—totally in command. Time to get ship-shape or whatever the hell the railroad equivalent is. Put away the bed, wash-up—yeah, looking good and feelin' soooo—fine! One fat joint left—might as well. Sittin' in my "smokin'-chair," stoned out of my skull with the Canadian Prairies movie running past my window. Simply outstanding! The click-clack of the train wheels on the track was hypnotically enhancing that beautiful, safe, insular feeling. Womb vibes.

After a couple of hours in the zone, I got the hungries. I thought I'd just nosey on down to the dining car for some breakfast. Easier said than done. Positively ripped. I made my way carefully down the aisle and then cautiously between the cars (Oh, Christ, this is the place where they eighty-six the nefarious types in mystery novels—Orient Express). The dining car—I made it. Nuts! It's packed to the tits with diners. Oh, God, I wish I hadn't left my little nest. But before I could turn around to make a hasty departure a loud, verbal order came my way at about 100 decibels. It was Janis. She'd noticed my predicament and was offering the seat opposite her. The only vacancy in the car.

"You must be starved man," she said. I nodded. It was all I could do. Hey, John, (her road manager), get this poor baby a drink—looks like he needs one! What're ya drinkin 'man? "Screwdriver." "Hey, John, make it a double!" That good ol' gal saved my butt. Damn, she had presence.

She let on that it was all true about the first leg of the trip. Yeah, she got the engineer stoned, even had him agreeing that we'd never relinquish control of the train when the trip was over. If push came to shove when the C.P.R. tried to take their railroad train back we'd hi-jack the mother and drive it straight into the Pacific Ocean. In fact, everyone was talking up the idea of continuing this train tour throughout the

United States. Maybe a month or two. How grand!

By the afternoon, things aboard were pretty mellow and Garcia was playing some acoustic guitar in the box car. I really don't know who started it—might've been Danko—but someone started singing "Cane on this Brazas," the old Leadbelly tune. Before long, harmonies were added. Ian and Sylvia, Danko, Janis, Delaney and Bonnie Bramlett, Eric Anderson and Jerry on guitar. When things like this were happening, the film crew came out of the walls.

Did I forget to mention the constant filming of all this? The promoters intended to shoot the entire adventure, presumably for release in North America. To my knowledge it never made the theaters, but I do recall seeing some footage of it. I can't remember where.

A suggestion was made to set up two steel guitars, mine and Garcia's. We played around for a while and took note of the new counter rhythm being insinuated into our music by the motion of the train. Every note played on or about the fifth beat was jolted by the train wheels against the track separations. The beauty of it being that everyone in the jam was affected simultaneously, so that the overall effect created was a bizarre neo-time signature. Nobody had any power to prevent the metrical abberation, so as transmuters, we simply worked within it. It went something like this:

Dee-dee-dah-doo-BLAP! widdy-widdy-ZOTTFRIPP! lah-dee-dum-dee-BLOPP! Shazza-skoo-de-RUPP! Innovative.

Late afternoon poured into evening, and I *do* mean poured. That is until the well ran dry. Our two Canadian promoters observed that, as we were approaching Saskatoon, Saskatachewan we would be saved. In that province, package stores stayed open 'til midnight and with a collective effort we could be bathing in the bubbly in no time at all. Dollars were tossed into the kitty and the train was stopped. Our booze crusaders took off on their misison. They returned

with a ton of beer and whiskey. But the Holy Grail of this pilgrimage was a mammoth bottle of Canadian Club, somewhere in the neighborhood of 133-½ ounces. It was a long way to Calgary. The train started to roll again and so did the party.

There's some confusion over how I got the N.R.P.S. gig. Some say the idea came from Garcia during this tour. Nelson told me that when he heard me play at the Toronto show he was convinced I was the guy. Both may be correct. But I know that there was more to it. Bob Weir's old lady, Frankie, took a personal interest and did her own lobbying. She gave me a lot of support during the first year of transition. Frankie went out of her way to make sure I felt accepted and important in my role, over and above Gar's reputation. Well, on the Festival Express, if there was a counterpart of Janis in helping that train move along, it was Frankie. I'm sure that everybody who met her felt the same. A natural catlyst with a huge heart.

News came that Calgary was going to be the last stop. The mayor of Vancouver in his infinite wisdom had cancelled our concert there. The prick. I guess it being 1970, he thought we might bring a whole world of trouble to his city. Avoid riots in the street, etc. Bummer was, we all missed the final leg of the journey, the one where Western Canada really gets spectacular! Lake Louise, the Rockies, forget it! His Honor, the mayor had done a real bad thing. We, on the train were miserable about it.

The Calgary concert was the only one I personally saw from start to finish and it was a monster. I saw it with my motorist friends from Toronto. We sat right in front of the stage just short of the security fence. This area was provided to give the entertainers their own frontal view of the concert.

Blues Image from Chicago "blue-blew" me away! Rick Derringer (I can't remember with what group) played his ass off. All the early acts were super. I'd played real early, around 11:00

Artwork by Gary Kroman

a.m. or noon and just kicked back out front to watch and listen to the rest of the circus.

Sha-Na-Na was a different band then, not anywhere as commercial as they are now on television. Today, they entertain the kiddies but their early stuff was heavy. Even scary. The announcer introduced them, "Now, Ladies & Gentlemen, the epitome of refinement—Sha-na-na—watch 'em carefully—they're fast". Au contraire. It took them about 10 minutes to, one by one, assemble into playing position. A snail's pace. God, they were funny! Their guitar player was busted on some musical technicality by the leader of the band, and in defiance he spit in his face. You don't see that on T.V.

The Band, of course, playing like the Band, performed the stuff which would become standard. Buddy Guy, during a seemingly endless guitar solo, climbed the P.A. staging, like some 20-30 feet in the air. Mountain played Mississippi Queen, the Dead-Riders played their three-part set. First, the acoustic bluegrass set with Jerry on banjo and guitar, followed by an electric country set with steel and finished by a pure G.D. set. At the time I thought it was unusual for Kreutzmann, a rock n'roll drummer to be trying to settle down to a straight country—bluegrass thing. My error. He knew exactly what he was doing. Very tasty, Bill. I hadn't done my homework on Kreutzmann.

Janis and the Full Tilt Boogie Band closed the show around midnight. The band started by playing one of those R & B intros. Fast! You know, like the Otis Redding or James Brown thing, to introduce the star. About 96 bars worth Janis walked on nodding "howdy" to her band, took a pull on some Southern Comfort and WHAM! She exploded! One powerful chick for sure. She electrified about thirty-four thousand people for the next 9 minutes.

On the final number, Tyson cued me for the ride back to the hotel. I reminded him that I had my steel and would he give me a couple minutes to heave it into the trunk of the rental car. We were staying at a hotel in Calgary—no more train—so I was in no hurry. I was sitting in the rear seat with our drummer, N.D. Smart (his real name) and a Grateful Dead roadie, Sonnie Heard, Ian and Sylvia were up front. A few peaceful miles passed going into town. At every stoplight we kept getting harassed by this carload of Calgary toughs. These young dudes were making rather obscene innuendos directed at Sylvia. Now, she could toss that shit off easily, but Ian is a real ass-kicker and I could tell he was getting hot.

I think everybody in our car intuitively knew what was going to happen next. Tyson held himself in check until we reached the hotel, so as to let Sylvia have immediate protection. I guess those young cowboys were just looking for a good ol' Saturday Night brawl but unfortunately for them, they had picked the wrong people to mess with. N.D. was a martial arts student and Sonny Heard was as big as a house. And, Ian—can be one rough dude—and how.

Now, normally, I'm no threat, but I had my mind on one of my guitar legs in the trunk. It can pack a wallop. Everything, after we pulled to the curb, went like a coordinated stunt in a Hollywood film. Sylvia jumped out and ran for the hotel—Tyson snapped off the ignition. I said, "Gimme the keys!" He tossed them over his shoulder, to me, into the rear seat. Ian, N.D. and Sonny were out of the car and then me. I had the trunk open in a matter of seconds, with one of my guitar legs in hand. You have to eyeball one of those legs to know how brutal they could be. I got a real good purchase on it, and

jumped into the fracas swinging. Too late—no cigar. It was all over. There were 3 bodies on the sidewalk and one in the gutter, cowboy hats laying around. Theirs, not ours.

Sylvia had called the police and with perfect timing they picked up the young dudes and hauled 'em away. I'm told that the Calgary City Jail is a notch below Yuma Prison. Just like a goddamned movie, a hell of a way to end the train tour—a good thing for them that they didn't get a good taste of my steel. "Just passin' through town, Sheriff. Thought I'd just stop long enough to settle the dust in my throat. Much obliged!"

Ian broke his hand, the other two caught a couple of bruises, if that—ME? Not a scratch! Where was that fuckin' film crew? Probably back at the site, shooting the equipment pack-up. They missed a piece of rock n' roll history that only a direct participant can experience. Such is video.

Next day in the hotel lobby groups were in the process of being checked out. Folks were in and out of the hotel bar saying goodbyes. Man, that's one tough job, saying goodbye. You just spent some of the happiest days together ever, and what can you say? Goodbye? Good Luck? Oh yeah, all of those—But, how about, I love you, and I'll miss you and that goddamned train. Let's do it again.

Note: As records of this event are unavailable, it is difficult to give a full account of the people that were present. We have spoken to several artists, and others who were in attendance were Seatrain with Peter Rowan, and Robert Hunter.

We have tried to contact the promoters of the Festival Express, but have, as yet, been unsuccessful.                                              —ed.

Photo by Brian Gold

SEBASTIEN Faure said "whoever denies authority and fights against it is an anarchist." By that definition, I've never met anyone in rock music who wasn't an anarchist.

When asked by the illustrious editor of this periodical to write a short literary piece of my choosing, I was in somewhat of a quandry: Interviews are easy; the interviewer provides the outline of discussion and the interviewee merely fills in the spaces. But what to do with no direction whatever??? DENY AUTHORITY AND FIGHT AGAINST IT!!!

The roots of anarchism can be traced to the earliest yearnings of mankind and its traces found in the works of Lao-Tse, Aristipus and Zeno, including entire religious movements like the Anabaptists, Hussites, Doukhobors and Essenes. And who could forget Rabelais, who said "DO WHAT YOU WILL."

Yet these roots of the anarchist *idea* are not the roots of the anarchist *movement* and it is the earliest chapter of the movement, a movement that I would assert every rock musician and fan is a part of, that I seek to explore more fully in this article.

So, return with me now to those thrilling days of yesteryear, when civil war was raging in England during the middle 17th century. From the struggle that arose within Cromwell's ranks, two radical movements emerged: The Levellers and the Diggers.

The Levellers will not be dealt with here; in brief, the Levellers were not unlike the Democrats of today and in their time espoused a doctrine of universal suffrage and political equality with the officers in the New Model Army who commanded them.

It is the Diggers, whose movement was given voice by Gerrard Winstanley, who formed the basis, heart and soul of the modern anarchist movement and are the historical antecedents of all who pride themselves as being part of any movement which denies authority and fights against it.

The Diggers began in 1648 and their movement of ideas soon became an example. In April, 1649, the thirty or forty people who comprised the Diggers claimed St. George's Hill near Walton-on-Thames. They espoused a doctrine of community that among its features included no leaders, sharing of resources and non-violence. They dug the hill and planted wheat and vegetables; and although they predicted their movement would grow, they were beaten by paid thugs, fined by the courts, their houses were burned and their crops destroyed.

They were taken in front of General Fairfax and refused to be intimidated when troops were sent out to investigate them and through it all, they maintained their non-violent philosophy.

*Photo by Amy Bursten*

# The Roots of Rock
# The Beginning of the Modern Anarchist Movement

by Barry Melton
( c 1984 Seaford Music)

We have very little left of the Diggers—their movement was all but destroyed within three years after it began. We do have some of the pamphlets by Gerrard Winstanley that they published during their short existance, most notably the *"New Law of Righteousness,"* first published in January, 1649. Here are a few examples of passages from the pamphlet:

"Every one that gets an authority into his hands tyrannizes over others; as many husbands, parents, masters, magistrates, that live after the flesh do carry themselves like opressing lords over such as are under them, not knowing that their wives, children, servants, subjects are their fellow creatures, and hath an equal privilege to share in the blessings of liberty."

"The influence over government must be shared among the people. If every individual which comprises their mass participates in the ultimate authority, the government will be safe."

"And let all men say what they will, so long as such are rulers as call the land theirs, upholding this particular property of mine and thine, the common people shall never have their liberty, nor the land be freed from troubles, opressions and complainings."

My mind is on these thoughts in this 1984 election year. I don't think the Diggers would do much better in America today than they did in 17th century England.

Paine and Jefferson had good ideas when this country began—they probably read Winstanley, but Winstanley caved in to pressure. Jefferson was made a chief executive and Paine died of terminal disappointment.

I'm disappointed, too, and pray that it's not terminal. The Diggers failed to change the 17th century much, and rock music may not change the 20th century, but it falls on us to keep the idea alive that change is possible and preserve the tradition so that it may become reality in the future.

DENY AUTHORITY AND FIGHT AGAINST IT!!!

*Alfred Klosterman*

KLOSTERMAN 93

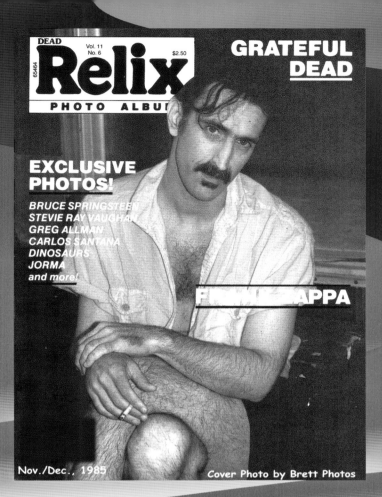

**DEAD** 65464 Vol. 11 No. 6 $2.50
# Relix
## PHOTO ALBUM

**GRATEFUL DEAD**

## EXCLUSIVE PHOTOS!

*BRUCE SPRINGSTEEN*
*STEVIE RAY VAUGHAN*
*GREG ALLMAN*
*CARLOS SANTANA*
*DINOSAURS*
*JORMA*
*and more!*

**FRANK ZAPPA**

Nov./Dec., 1985

Cover Photo by Brett Photos

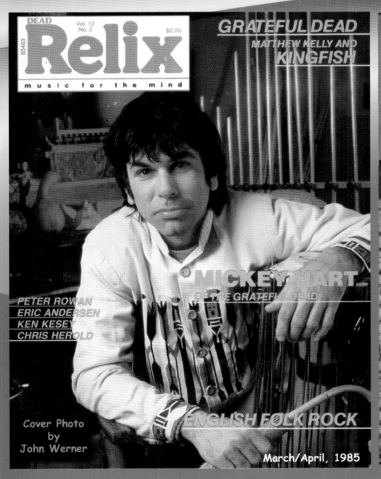

**DEAD** 65463 Vol. 12 No. 2 $2.00
# Relix
## music for the mind

**GRATEFUL DEAD**
*MATTHEW KELLY AND*
**KINGFISH**

**MICKEY HART**
OF THE GRATEFUL DEAD

PETER ROWAN
ERIC ANDERSEN
KEN KESEY
CHRIS HEROLD

Cover Photo by John Werner

**ENGLISH FOLK ROCK**

**March/April, 1985**

**DEAD** 65463 Vol. 12 No. 1 $2.00
# Relix
## music for the mind

**GRATEFUL DEAD**
**BLUES PROJECT**

WURLiTZER

**JORMA KAUKONEN**

THE FIRST AGE ROCK & ROLL CONVENTION
THE ALBIN BENEFIT CONCERT

Cover Photo by L.D. Kippel
January/February, 1985

JERRY GARCIA, TOM CONSTANTEN
BOB DYLAN, THE WHO, DEEP PURPLE, KINKS

# John Barlow
## IN OTHER WORDS
## by Ken Hunt

**Photo Courtesy John Barlow**

*J*OHN Perry Barlow is, after Robert Hunter, the second most important lyricist working with the Grateful Dead. Like Bob Hunter, Jerry Garcia's usual writing sidekick and the Dead's most prolific wordsmith over the years, John Barlow has been involved with the group since its nascency, because of his connections with Bobby Weir; theirs has become the second great songwriting partnership within the circle, although Barlow's professional relationship with Weir as a lyricist only dates from around 1971. His lyrics emerged for the first time on Bob Weir's Ace and in the intervening years his songs have graced both Weir's and the Grateful Dead's subsequent works. In the process they have built up an impressive body of work, although their collaborations lag well behind those of the 'old frim' of Hunter & Garcia.

*Perhaps before continuing with John Barlow's tale, it is worth mentioning that in stark contrast to the lives and lifestyles of the Californian chaps based around San Francisco, John Barlow's life centers around ranching in the natural splendours of Wyoming, a far, far cry from the citified ways of San Francisco. Several of the band's members have been involved with ranches over the years, but for Barlow ranching in Wyoming is his livelihood and a way of life.*

*Against this backdrop Barlow's lyrics take on a greater significance quite often and it should come as no big surprise to discover that his environment and background are reflected in those words of his.*

**Relix:** When I was researching a possible interview with you, one thing that stood out was the lack of information available about you.

**Barlow:** Most of the interviews that I've done have been in connection with other areas in my life, like politics and ranching and that sort of thing. I've kept a reasonably low profile. Not that many people know where I am, and I don't spend a lot of time on the road with the band. Weir and I have done some infamous radio interviews, but fortunately nobody ever bothered to set them in print; I'm not sure they could have been printed. It was amazing they were broadcast.

**Relix:** Bob Weir described you as "born, raised and lives in Wyoming." Beyond that I know relatively little about your background, so could you fill in some of that missing background?

**Barlow:** This is at least sixteen of the eighteen volumes. I was born in Jackson, Wyoming. I was raised here until I got into a fair amount of trouble when I was about fourteen. My father was in politics and I'd been an exemplary kid up until that point. And something just clicked. I quit the Mormon Church, in which I had been quite serious, quit Boy Scouts, got a motorcycle along with about six other kids. . . The boy scout troop turned into. . . well, we were very enamoured with the idea of being like James

Dean at the age of fourteen. It was real dumb. So we did a lot of destruction and my father was told it was best to get me sent away if he wanted to go on running for office, which is how I got sent to the school where I met Weir. The school funcitoned largely for kids with behavioural difficulties, not in a clinical sense, but it was a pretty openminded place.

I was a hick kid and hick kids hate hick towns, especially if they've got a lot of big ideas about themselves. I went to college and I travelled a lot, lived in New York for a while, wrote a novel, wrote some articles and was on my way to become an apprentice TV scriptwriter for Warner Brothers in Los Angeles. I stopped here and I've been here for the last thirteen years. This is what I do. I do lyrics maybe two weeks out of the year. I ranch and I do a lot of the things connected with ranching.

The only way I feel OK about taking a vacation from here is if I feel I'm involved in work. It's important for me to get away from this and so the songwriting has been really helpful in that regard. Kept me from getting stale. I do it mostly because I'm real fond of Weir: that's why I started doing it and that's why I still do it.

**Relix:** Bearing in mind Weir's comments about your Wyoming life and upbringing, and what you've already said, how did you come to run into him?

**Barlow:** Well, as I said, we did meet in a prep. school in Colorado Springs, place called Fountain Valley, a real good school, but, as I said, patterned to misfits. Weir and I actually managed to be the biggest misfits in this school. The upper classmen singled us out for particular hell. It made us very fond of each other. That was a long time ago.

**Relix:** Had you kept in touch in the intervening years since school? For example, had you been listening to the Grateful Dead's music or was it a far less tenuous friendship?

**Barlow:** Bobby got kicked out of Fountain Valley and then he came to work for the ranch that haying. Then he went to this place called Pacific High School which was very outrageous. Actually Pacific High School had a lot of the elements that became the Haight Ashbury in its faculty and they were already breaking out. I was in touch with him during that period because I'd originally thought of going there with him. I didn't, but we were writing and that sort of thing, keeping in touch. Then Bobby took acid—about the same time as I did—but it rendered him totally incapable of communication and he dropped out of my sight. He re-emerged right at the point when the Grateful Dead was coming together; that was the first time I saw him. Which was in '66. Then from that time on we've been together a lot, pretty continuously. He's my closest friend.

**Relix:** The first time that your two names appeared on credits was on *Ace*, released in 1972. Is there any particular reason for there having been no earlier evidence of your collaborations?

**Barlow:** Weir just started writing songs. That was all. He started coming out of the zone that he'd been in from the time of the Acid Tests, during which time he played the guitar and did very little else. He started having creative impulses and tried to work with Hunter. Hunter found it very hard to work with him, well, probably for the same reasons that I do. I'd been a college poet. I discovered at a certain point that I could read my poetry at Mount Holyoke College and get laid, and had worked it over pretty good with that in mind. It was better than being the captain of the football team. It led to some very rewarding relationships, but I wasn't real serious about poetry—I'd learned how to write it and that was about it. Weir figured that since I was a poet I ought to be able to write lyrics and he decided to see. And he did see. We started around 1971, early '71. I'd finished my novel, I'd gone to India and I was kinda adrift. Farrar,

Straus & Giroux were trying to decide whether they were going to print it; I was on hold. I was living in New York. Weir approached me and I wrote some lyrics, "Mexicali Blues." I wrote "Black Throated Wind" when I was in India—I always thought that was kinda weirdly set. In any case this was right at the point when Bobby was thinking about doing a solo record, and so we started to work.

**Relix:** On *Ace* there are five songs of yours: "Black Throated Wind," "Walk In The Sunshine," "Looks Like Rain," "Mexicali Blues" and "Cassidy." Were these the first fruits of the partnership or had there been earlier, abandoned or subsequently used songs?

**Barlow:** There had been one earlier, abandoned effort, which had just been strictly a pilot for the series and which Weir keeps talking about doing. It was really that good. I wrote "Mexicali Blues" and "Black Throated Wind" and then he set them to music. Then he got a contract for this solo album which was in many respects that year's Grateful Dead studio album and was treated as such by him, Warner Brothers and, well, the Grateful Dead. We just started writing the songs after he went into the studio, after those two. He had "One More Saturday Night," which I'd contributed a little to, and "Playing In The Band," which Hunter had written. That was their last collaboration.

**Relix:** Bob Hunter, talking to me about the emergence of the 'newcomers' spoke of, in his eyes, his "stranglehold" being broken which was something that he didn't exactly welcome. During LPs like *Wake Of The Flood* and *Blues For Allah* while your partnership with Weir was being established, how did you feel the listeners were reacting to the changes? In a sense you (and the other collaborators) were usurping the tried and tested Garcia/Hunter firm.

**Barlow:** First I've got to say that my favorite Grateful Dead songs are still Hunter/Garcia songs. They're just *better* than we are, but on the other hand Bobby wanted to write and I felt like, whether it was a matter of our being capable of writing as well, I knew he had a different kind of voice that deserved a hearing. And so did I. So we did it. I did it because Bobby wanted to do it and I wanted him to. What the Hell! *I've* enjoyed it. It's given me the opportunity to have some experiences that I certainly wouldn't have had in Cora, Wyoming!

**Relix:** Presumably some sort of natural balance has been struck amongst the Dead's various songwriters, as the flow of composer credits seems pretty even and stable now. Could you elaborate upon that relationship?

**Barlow:** It doesn't seem even and stable to me. I don't have the luxury of looking at it in some kind of long-term perspective. It's always just what's happening right now. I know that in my case it seems to be kind of random whether we're actually coming up with stuff or not. It has as much as anything to do with our relationship with each other and also, obviously, with ourselves. I haven't the slightest idea how Hunter/Garcia work: they're a mystery to me.

**Relix:** Presumably your relationship with Bob Weir is firmly cemented. Have you collaborated or do you have plans to collaborate with anyone else?

**Barlow:** I've done a little. I did some stuff with the New Riders of the Purple Sage and I did one song on the Midnites album with Al Johnson. At one point I was going to work with Warren Zevon, or it appeared that I was, but it seemed his writer's block cured. I haven't really sought out any songwriting in any other con-

text, because I didn't do it to be songwriting. I did it to songwrite with Weir pretty much. I occasionally give Garcia songs which he has so far politely declined. Usually they're more like messages to Garcia. I *don't* have any burning desire to expand the field.

Every once in a while I hear country and western music and I think, "Goddamn it, I wish I could write something that sweet and that corny and that obvious!" Or I hear something by a very political group and I think how nice it would be to indulge rhetoric a little more often, but it's just not something that's done in this particular *métier*. So I don't do it.

**Relix:** To what degree does Bob Weir alter your lyrics and to what degree do you collaborate on the words?

**Barlow:** He *does* often change things and I can respect his reasons for doing so, because he has to get up in front of a whole bunch of people and sing them. If they're not something he can sing, he's gonna look like an asshole and *feel* like one more importantly. I have to say that one of the hardest things about collaborating is having somebody hold the continuing capacity to change what you have written, but I think that it's probably good in terms of my long-term progress towards humility to work with somebody on that level.

**Relix:** What do you look for in a song? For instance, on "Bye and Bye" on the first Kingfish album you're using a traditional song as a basis for the arrangement, so that may be an interest of yours, but I also wondered which writers' work appeals to you.

**Barlow:** Oh boy! There are an awful lot of songwriters whose work I admire and it's a shifting pantheon, depending on what they've done recently in a lot of cases. Some people everybody admires obviously: like Dylan, whom I've continued to admire even through his Bible-thumping phases. Randy Newman, Jackson Browne, Tom Petty I like a lot, Bob Seger, Jagger & Richards . . . Mostly straight out rock and rollers. But I listen to a lot of different kinds of music; I listen to some new wave music; I listen to a lot of music that doesn't have lyrics because it's classical music; listen to a lot of country and western music. I find things in all those forms that attract and delight me. I'm often saying that I would have given some part of my anatomy to have written *that*. I could rattle off a very long list of the people who have made me say that.

**Relix:** Bob Hunter said that he felt that his style of imagery and language hadn't clicked with Bob and that yours was far better suited to his tastes. What do you think is the attraction of your words as far as Bob Weir is concerned? Has he offered any views on that?

**Barlow:** He has not offered any view on that . . . It has to do with the fact that Hunter is a *real* poet. He's the genuine article. It's as difficult for Hunter to write in a literal vein as it would have been for Wallace Stevens or T.S. Elliot. And Bobby likes his imagery concrete. He wants everybody out there to understand it; they don't, of course. But that's what he's shooting for a lot of the time, so he rebels when I try to slip in something that's a little vaporous, which I personally would prefer to do more often because, while I'm not the poet that Hunter is, I would rather have my songs be poetry. But there can be poetry in the obvious.

**Relix:** Do you play any instrument?

**Barlow:** No.

**Relix:** Have you ever been fired by the desire to play?

**Barlow:** So fired by the desire that it turned into a huge block! Which is the reason why I don't play an instrument. I love music, a surprisingly large percentage of my friends are musicians, I've spent a long time immersed in the music business, but I don't play an instrument: it's really one of the few things about my life that I really regret.

**Relix:** Having established the precedent, are you going to continue occasional collaborations with Brent Mydland? Or is the arrangement one of catch as catch can? Did you work together on Brent's solo album?

**Barlow:** No, we did not work together on Brent's solo album. Brent is himself a perfectly competent songwriter who needs no help. He writes good songs. They are pretty commercial; they're not what you'd call "artsy," but I think they're solid. The reason that I collaborated with him on *Go To Heaven* was that the president of Arista Records, a scumsucking pig named Clive Davis, had decided that Brent's songs were not real Grateful Dead material. Well, his line was "Couldn't there be something in here about pyramids or something?"!! (*Laughter*.) Because Brent, paradoxically enough, sounded *commercial* to him; he wanted the Grateful Dead to sound like the Grateful Dead, so at least the Dead Heads would buy them, and to that end I was conscripted to write his lyrics. I felt bad about doing it. The same thing happened with Alphonso Johnson on the *Bobby & The Midnites* record: there was a displeasure with the style of Alphonso's lyrics, but I thought they were just fine. They were not in keeping with the style of the rest of the record but I couldn't see that that was a problem. So I wrote a whole set of them that Weir sang without having the goodness to inform Alphonso. But I felt like an assassin actually.

**Relix:** Do you have any particular favorites amongst the songs that you've written? Or ones that you're especially proud of and, if so, which and why?

**Barlow:** The *only* one that I am proud of is "Cassidy," which I think is fine. The rest of them don't seem like they made it. They aren't as good as they could have been either because the words weren't as good, the combination of the words and the music wasn't as good, the music wasn't as good .. there's just always been something wrong.

**Relix:** Do you feel that applies on the album as well as in concert? Or do they differ?

Interview Continues...

# John Barlow
## IN OTHER WORDS
### (continued)...

**Barlow:** Those songs, when I hear them in concert, I'm usually quite proud of them. Of course, it could be because I'm jazzed up myself and full of this strange, mystic aura of the Grateful Dead. I'm not sure I'd feel that way about them if I heard the tapes of the gig. But they do develop a lot and one of the mistakes that we made in the past is that they were done so close to the time of the release of the album, and for that specific purpose, that they were never done on stage, so nobody had learned all the nuances that lay in the song. Recently I think that's changing and I can't help but think that's going to be a change for the better.

I don't like Grateful Dead records very much. I haven't liked any Grateful Dead records since *American Beauty*; I'm not sure that anybody in the band has either, I don't know. Everybody is kind of high on them at the time, but three weeks later the same gloom sets in with regards to studio work. But then on a good night they're the best live rock 'n' roll band in the world. They do something that nobody else does: they create mass hysteria of a *very benign* sort which makes people hear and see things that cannot be heard and should not be seen. Everybody gets carried away, gets transported and that applies to the band, I think, as well as the people in the audience. Indeed it depends on both sides getting transported each by the other. But they're a very disorganized group in the sense that they are a genuine democracy; democracy is a clumsy tool. I've always thought of music as being the space between the notes, the silence that the notes frame, and when you've got a democracy and six guys who want to stuff notes in, there isn't much of that space. Somehow on stage, in that kind of time, it works. But on a record album, it sounds cluttered and muddy to me. So, I don't like the way that most of our songs have come out. "Cassidy" I like, mostly because it is so spare. There is not much to it. There was a depth of feeling on both our parts, but very little ornamentation. I don't like ornamentation very much.

But I go on doing it, in the same way that I go on ranching, with the idea that someday this time it's going to be different, and there are enough near misses so that it continues to be encouraging. I think that my attitude towards whether we've been successful or not is healthy from the standpoint that at least I'm not resting on my laurels. I don't feel that I have any to rest on yet: there's still better work to be done.

**Toni's Note:** John Perry Barlow has made himself a name in more circles than just the Deadhead community. He was the first person to apply the name "cyberspace" to the "place" it now describes, and is cofounder of the Electronic Frontier Foundation. He is a recognized commentator on cyber liberties, virtual community, privacy, and the social, cultural, and legal conditions forming in cyberspace. A 2008 appearance on the *Colbert Report* was enlightening, but his affiliation with the Grateful Dead never came up.

You can learn more on Barlow's many achievements and interests at http://homes.eff.org/~barlow.

Relix $3.00

## 20 YEARS OF ROCK+ROLL

## GRATEFUL DEAD

Cover Artwork by Gary Kroman — May/June, 1985

Artwork by Gary Kroman

Artwork by Gary Kroman

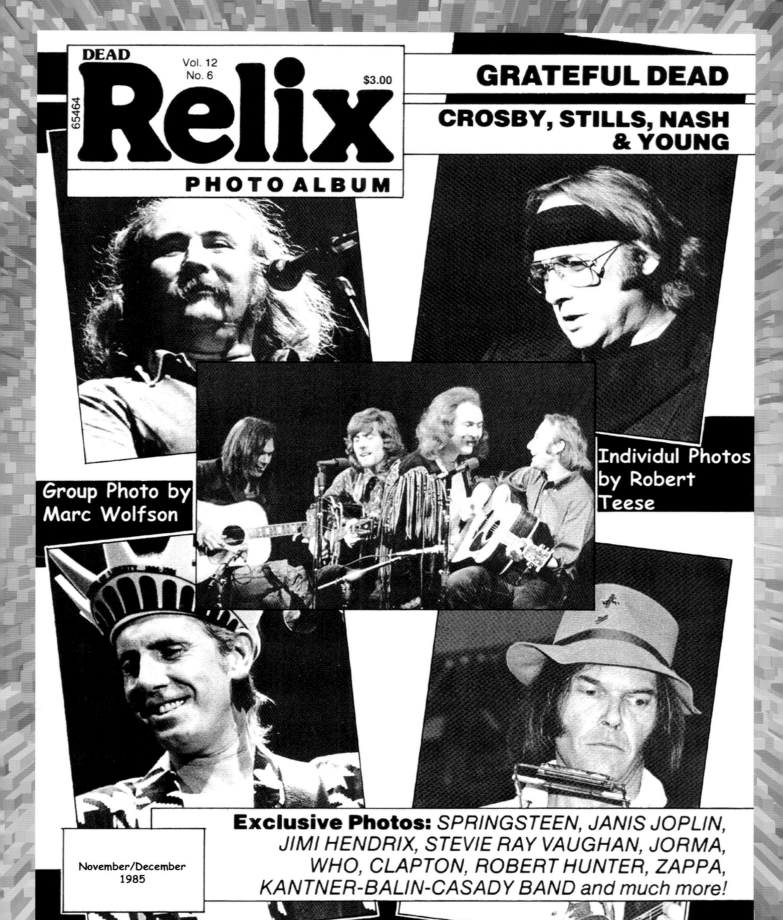

# DEAD
# Relix

Vol. 12
No. 6

65464

$3.00

**PHOTO ALBUM**

**GRATEFUL DEAD**

**CROSBY, STILLS, NASH & YOUNG**

Individul Photos by Robert Teese

Group Photo by Marc Wolfson

November/December 1985

**Exclusive Photos:** *SPRINGSTEEN, JANIS JOPLIN, JIMI HENDRIX, STEVIE RAY VAUGHAN, JORMA, WHO, CLAPTON, ROBERT HUNTER, ZAPPA, KANTNER-BALIN-CASADY BAND and much more!*

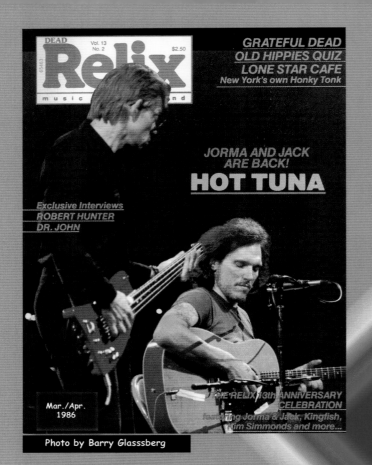

Photo by Barry Glasssberg

Artwork by Gary Kroman

Artwork by Gary Kroman

## 100 SONG TITLE POSTER
### HOW MANY CAN YOU FIND?

Artwork by Robert Bryson

Artwork by Glenn Harding

"THE EARTH IS OUR MOTHER.
EMBRACE HER, DON'T
SQUEEZE HER."

# The Greatest Stories Never Told:
# Robert Hunter Talks About The Dead's "Greatest Hits"

## by Jeff Tamarkin

Photo by Maureen Hunter
Courtesy Robert Hunter

Y OU'VE heard them a million and one times, but do you know where they came from? Strange as it seems, in its decade-plus of covering the Grateful Dead, *Relix* has never before asked the band's main lyricist, Robert Hunter, just how he wrote the Dead's most popular songs. Without further ado, the solution to that problem.

**Truckin'**—"I wrote that in several different cities, starting off in San Francisco. I finished it up in Florida. I was on the road with the band and writing different verses in different cities, and when we were in Florida I went outside and everybody was sitting around the swimming pool. I had finally finished the lyrics, so I brought them down and the boys picked up their guitars, sat down and wrote some rock 'n' roll changes behind it. The bust in New Orleans which I wrote about had happened about a year earlier.

"There was no lyrical change when the song got to the band. It was fed to Bobby a line at a time when we got to the studio, with me telling him how to pronounce it. He'd go in and put a line down, then go back in and work out how to pronounce the next line. That's the one and only time such a thing has happened. The music was always like a Chuck Berry thing; they did it a little differently than I wrote it, put a different accent to it. The 'Sometimes the lights all shinin' on me' part is definitely Grateful Dead."

**Casey Jones**—"I was working on songs for the *Workingman's Dead* album, and I had written down in my notebook: 'Drivin' that train, high on cocaine, Casey Jones you'd better watch your speed.' I thought that was very, very funny. I didn't think of it as a song or anything else, and just went on writing other songs.

Some time later I came back to it, and thought there might be a song there.

"We were working it out, playing it for Stills and Crosby, just jamming on it, and then we decided to record it. Then there came up the question of the word cocaine. This was a time when this was still a very risky word, as was goddamn in 'Uncle John's Band.' I said, 'Give me some time to think about it,' and I tried to write other concepts. I wrote 'Drivin' that train, whippin' that chain.' No. 'Luggin' propane.' No. I tried any way to get away from it and there just was no way. That was the line for the song, and it had to go in."

**Dark Star**—"That was the first song I wrote with the Grateful Dead. We were down in Rio Nido [California] and I heard them playing it in the hall they were going to play [author's note: This would be September 1967]. I just started scratching paper and got the 'Dark star crashes, pouring its light into ashes' part, and I said, 'Why don't you try this with it?' It worked well and then they wanted more verses. I finished up the second set of verses back in San Francisco. I got up—I was staying at 710 Ashbury—one morning fairly early, about 10:30 or 11, and stumbled over to the Panhandle at Golden Gate Park. I was sitting there, getting stuck on a verse, when along came a hippie who handed me a joint. He asked me what I was doing and I said I was writing a song called 'Dark Star.' He said 'Oh.' That's pretty much the story."

**St. Stephen**—"I had been working on this a long time before I gave it to the Grateful Dead, before I took off to New Mexico, which is where I originally sent them the lyrics from. I don't know what to say about this song except that it was very important to me. It seemed to be saying oodles. It's still one of my favorites. I didn't know who the real St. Stephen was until after I wrote it. He turned out to be the first Christian monk or something."

**Uncle John's Band**—"The band had already been working on the music and they asked be to score it. The first thing I came up with was 'Goddamn, Uncle John's Band,' but I thought I could come up with something more universal than that. It eventually worked out to become 'Uncle John's Band.'"

**Friend Of The Devil**—I was playing bass with the New Riders, although I never did actually get to the stage with them. We were sitting around practicing one night and I had 'Friend Of The Devil' more or less already written. I said 'Try this out,' and David Nelson and John Dawson helped by smoothing out some of the rough changes. I still have the recording of that evening and it's not that much different.

"Then we went down to get some coffee and Marmaduke said, 'It's a real good song but it has that one repeating line.' The line was, 'It looks like water but it tastes like wine,' and he asked me if I coud get anything punchier. I said, 'I got it' and came out with 'A friend of the devil is a friend of mine.' He said, 'You got it, that's it.' So I took the tape back to the Larkspur house where the Riders were staying and got up the next morning, and I heard Garcia listen-

ing to the tape. He had that funny look in his eye. The next thing you know he'd written a bridge for it, the 'Ann Marie' part. Before that it was the same melody all the way through. The next thing I knew, the Grateful Dead had snapped it up, much to the New Riders' dismay."

**Dire Wolf**—"The imagery occured to me in a dream. I woke up and grabbed a pencil, before I was entirely awake, and wrote the whole song down. I think I managed to capture the quality of the dream by writing it down before I was wide awake."

**Playing In The Band**—"That was written the same day as 'Greatest Story Ever Told,' which was written to the sound of a pump, by the way. Mickey had a beat for it and laid down some rhythm tracks, then asked me to write some lyrics for it. I wrote the lyrics, then Weir came around and wrote a guitar part for it. I wasn't certain it was going to be a Grateful Dead song; I just thought it would end up on Mickey's *Rolling Thunder* album [where it's called "The Main Ten"—author]."

**Cosmic Charlie**—"That was done during a burst of songwriting when we were actually sitting down together saying, 'OK, let's write some songs.' It's very psychedelic."

**Box of Rain**—"Phil was going through a hard time at that point because his father was dying. He had written a set of changes out and wanted me to get the lyrics done quickly so he could sing it for his father. That was one of the rare times I wrote a song in one sitting; I wrote it in about half an hour and didn't go back to scratch out a line or anything. The melody couldn't be improved on, as far as I'm concerned. That is just about my favorite song I've written for the Dead."

**U.S. Blues**—"I originally wrote it for the song which became Weir's 'One More Saturday Night.' He took the lyrics and wrote some rock 'n' roll changes behind them, and then he decided to rewrite the lyrics. This was well and fine, but then he asked me if he could use the title 'United States Blues.' I said, 'No, man, that's mine.' So he called his song 'One More Saturday Night' and I took the title 'United States Blues' and rewrote it again. And I gave it to Jerry this time."

Artwork by Glenn Harding

74

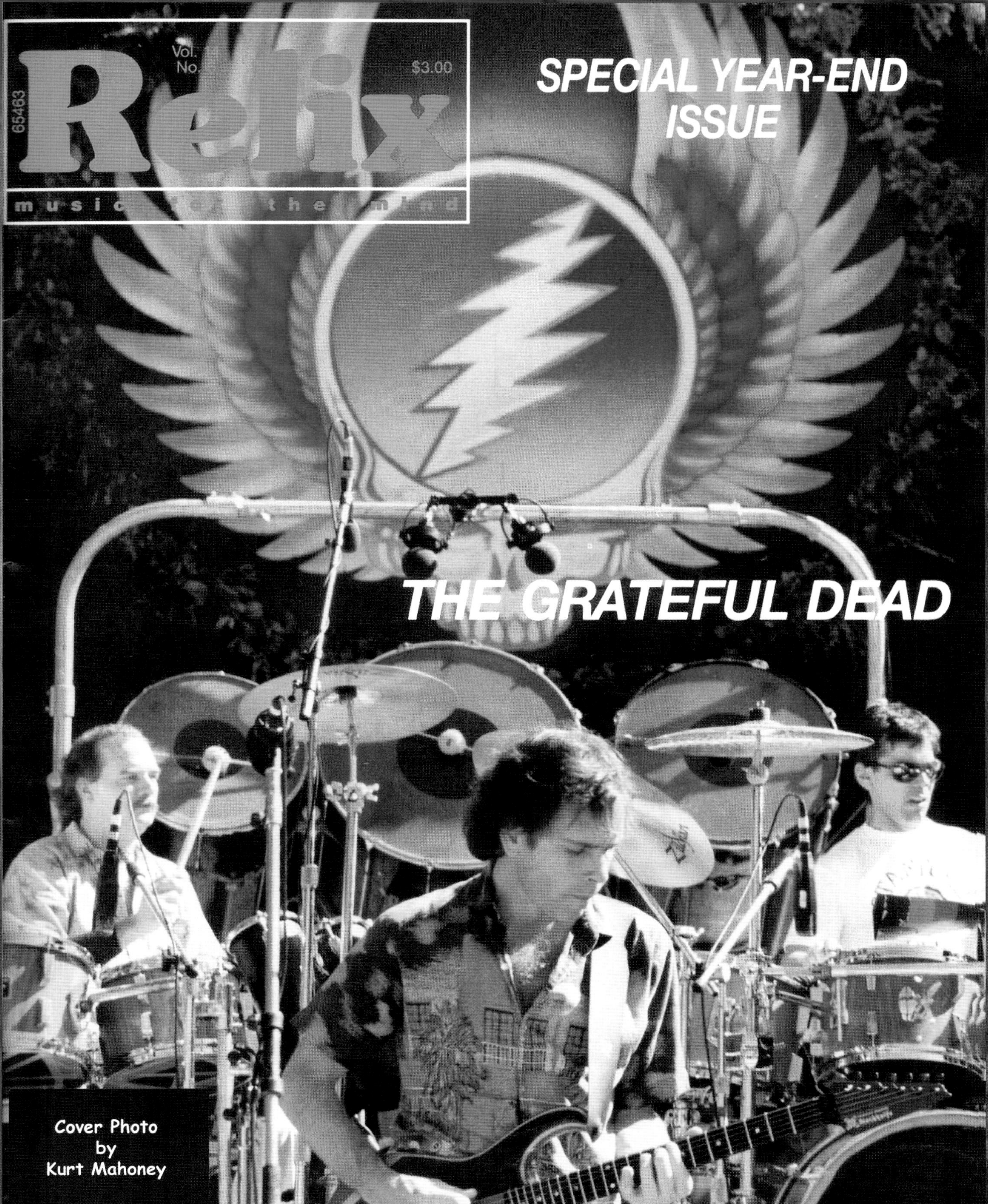

Vol.
No.
$3.00
65463

# Relix
music for the mind

THE GRATEFUL DEAD

Cover Photo
by
Kurt Mahoney

# THE GREAT RECORD PLANT SHOOT-OUT

### A BEDTIME STORY

## BY BUDDY CAGE

THESE days, Sausalito, California is a charming little tourist town on San Francisco Bay, just over the Golden Gate Bridge, North of the City. Of course, 30 years ago it was probably an awful lot more charming. The Record Plant recording studio was built there and I suppose became a more attractive place to record because of its Sausalito location and its proximity to San Francisco's treasure-box.

The Plant has character. Inside, it's Northern California chic wood, wood and more wood, the walls, ceilings and floors are made out of hand-cut woods. Different types of wood indigenous to northern California and placed in exotic patterns, mandalas for instance, and Byzantine type arches and domes. When there is an absence of wood, there's padded multi-colonial cloth design. On a wall inside Studio H, there's a mirror in the shape of the uprighted top of a grand piano and a mirror figure beside it in the form of a 10th Century concert pianist, playing in obvious musical ecstasy. When a real grand piano is placed against that, with its mirror accoutrements, it looks like the dimensional musician is actually playing the three dimensional keyboard. I've gazed at that image for hours on end and it still gives me a chuckle. it must be a trip for a piano player to be doing a session in that position.

There's a glass walled jacuzzi room, a couple of "quiet" rooms, and an amusement room with a jukebox, video games and a Coke machine that dispenses bottles of ice-cold Coors beer. Two studios only, are featured, A & B. This seems to cut down on the traffic inside the Record Plant, but in the circular lobby in between the 2 studios, there's enough interesting action going on from time to time to brighten up your day. Over my years spent there, your counterparts in the opposite studio can vary in styles, considerably.

For example, when I was working on the New Riders album for A&M, Rick James was next door, and *that* was fun. Another time, a rock band from L.A. called the L.A. Jets was next door. But Joe Cocker, that was *not* fun.

I got a call from my producer, Bob Johnston, to mosey on down to the Record Plant and pick up a tape from him. I was to take the tape home, listen to it, get familiar with it, and gear up to put down some overdubs in a couple of weeks. Bob was in Studio A with the L.A. Jets when I got there and they were in the final stages of recording, which is to say that they were mainly just listening back to hitherto recorded material and making some critical mixing decisions.

I had been in the control room with them for about 15 minutes when I quietly excused myself to run to the coke machine and grab a beer. Be right back! To get from the control room or studio to the lobby, one must negotiate two heavy soundproof doors. There's an air space of about 14 inches in between the two doors to help deaden extraneous noise. As the one door closed on me and the other opened, a sawed-off shotgun was stuck in my face from outside. On the other end was a Sausalito town cop. He eased the door open for me with his left hip and with his free hand, grabbed my wrist. His verbal instructions were "Just shut the fuck-up and do everything I say—quietly." That was my intention, at that moment. This cop was shaking, visibly nervous, the shotgun was cocked.

He led me into the lobby and placed me face-first into the carved wooden door to the studio. He was bringing my ams around behind me so as to perform the ancient art of hand-cuffing. I still had a lighted cigarette in my mouth and started to mention this to him and it was burning S.O.S. signals in the door. He shoved the shotgun up against the back of my head and I simply ran out of things to say. No sudden moves.

At that time, someone came out of studio B, a guitar player with Cocker. He was immediately treated to the same official welcome that I had been afforded. He and I were hand-cuffed together back to back and were laid down on the lobby floor. That's okay. I was familiar with the lobby floor anyway.

The reason for all this fuss started over in Berkeley, in the east bay. There had been a police set-up to catch a couple of cocaine dealers and it had gone sour. The culprits made off with their coke, the dollars, and in trying to make their escape had apparently tried to run down a police officer with their van. Dealing is one thing, but the attempted murder of a police officer is quite another. The fugitives beat a path across the San Rafael-Richmond Bridge and fled down Hwy 101 to the "saftey" of the Record Plant. These two kids were not thinking too clearly at this point, for sure. The cops had followed them to the studio and proceeded to contain anybody inside whose face they didn't

**Artwork by Michael Wysochanski**

recognize. I'd walked right into their bust.

Cocker then came halfway out of the studio and instantly grokked all the hardware and started to shake and mumble. I don't know what he was on, but he looked pretty gone. A cop said. "Hey. I know you. Aren't you that English singer?" Crockett? (Or something?) Joe nodded vigorously. Yes indeed, he was Joe Crockett. English. Yup. The cop went on. "All right, you're clear, now get the hell back in the room and don't come out again!" Joe vanished.

When the police had rounded up all the visible bodies. they took us into the amusement room. Presumably for some amusement. When they searched my wallet they found a couple of fifty dollar bills and since that was the denomination of the narc money, they decided to keep me for awhile. Like about 2½ hours.

About the time the handcuffs had finally succeeded in "arresting" the circulation in my arms. the Record Plant attorney showed up, demanded and got my release. I went directly to the coke machine for my Coors, then back to the Studio. Bob Johnston looked at me and the beer I was holding. "Goddamit Buddy. how long does it take you to get a bottle of beer?" Haw-Haw. "Bob. you wouldn't believe me if I told you. but it has something to do with a 20 gauge shotgun."

**Artwork by Michael Wysochanski**

DEAD
**Relix**
Vol. 13
No. 5
$2.50
65463
music for the mind

BOB DYLAN
GRATEFUL DEAD
STARSHIP
ROBERT HUNTER

FRANK ZAPPA

FREDA

FEATURES:
**FLYING BURRITO BROS.**
**RADIATORS**
**KIM SIMMONDS-**
**SAVOY BROWN**

Cover Art by
Tony Freda/Redline
Sept./Oct., 1986

REVIEWS:
KREUTZMANN-MARGEN BAND, VENTURA '86,
THE PIER-NYC, NEIL YOUNG and much more!

*Tire on the Highway*
(to the tune of "Fire on the Mountain")

Long distance driver, on his way to the tour,
Got up, got out, got out of his door,
He was playing Dead music on his stereo,
But now he's just sitting, with no place to go,
He hit a big pothole and he heard his wheel
    blow
Doesn't have a spare one, can't get to the show
CHORUS:
Tire, tire on the highway. . . .

Long distance driver, walking the highway's
    side,
Sticks out his thumb, but can't get a ride,
Made a sign saying "need a lift please,"
But three hours of walking and he's down on his
    knees,
Then a deadhead drives by him and stops up
    the road,
Now it looks like the driver's gonna get to the
    show
CHORUS:

Long distance driver, well he got to the show,
Heard for the first time a hot "Jack-A-Roe,"
Bob closed the first set with a great "Let it
    Grow,"
Jerry opened the next set with "Cold Rain and
    Snow,"
After the concert, he realized the fact
That he was stuck at the Dead show, he had no
    way to get back
CHORUS: (repeat)

by David Mlodinoff

Artwork by Mark Tuchman

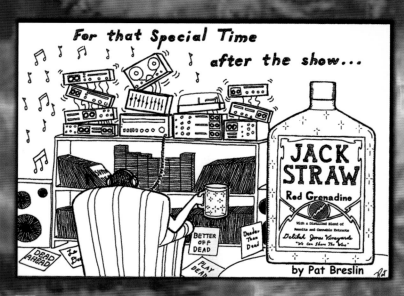

For that Special Time after the show...

JACK STRAW
Red Grenadine

by Pat Breslin

Cover Artwork by Gary Kroman

DEAD
Relix
Vol. 13
No. 6
65464
$3.00
music is the mind

SPECIAL
YEAR-END
ISSUE

Featuring
PHOTOS
ARTWORK
COMICS
PUZZLES

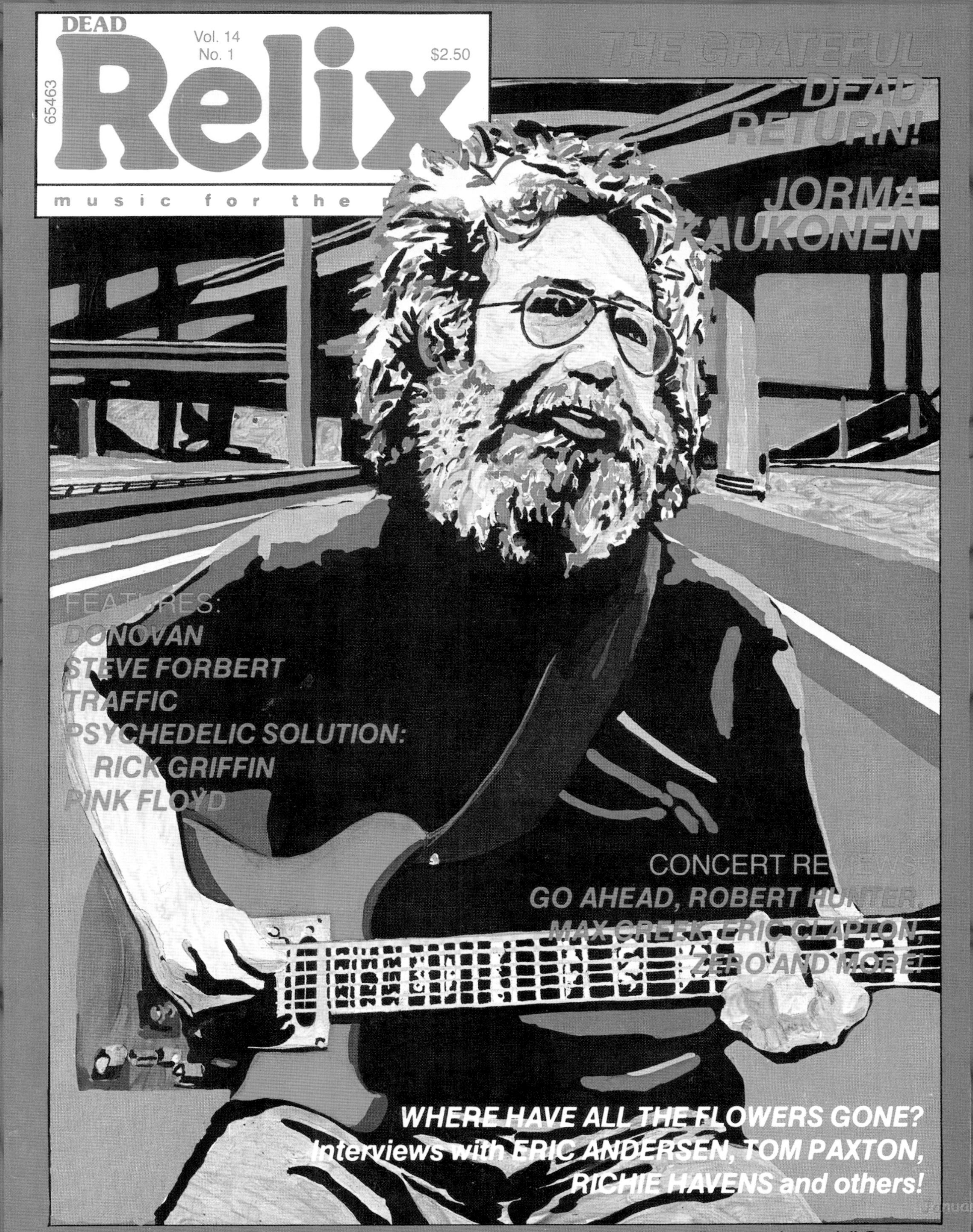

DEAD

# Relix

Vol. 14
No. 1

$2.50

65463

music for the m

THE GRATEFUL
DEAD
RETURN!

JORMA
KAUKONEN

FEATURES:
DONOVAN
STEVE FORBERT
TRAFFIC
PSYCHEDELIC SOLUTION:
   RICK GRIFFIN
PINK FLOYD

CONCERT REVIEWS
GO AHEAD, ROBERT HUNTER,
MAX CREEK, ERIC CLAPTON,
ZERO AND MORE!

WHERE HAVE ALL THE FLOWERS GONE?
Interviews with ERIC ANDERSEN, TOM PAXTON,
RICHIE HAVENS and others!

January/Fe

www.CommanderCody.com          Cover Artwork by George "Commander Cody" Frayne

THE FIRST ICE CREAM FLAVOR
NAMED AFTER A MUSICAL LEGEND
Vanilla Ice Cream with Bing Cherries & Chocolate Flakes

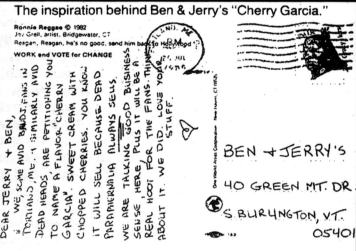

The inspiration behind Ben & Jerry's "Cherry Garcia."

Ronnie Reggae © 1982
Jay Grell, artist, Bridgewater, CT
Reagan, Reagan, he's no good, send him back to Hollywood

WORK and VOTE for CHANGE

DEAR JERRY + BEN,
WE, SOME AVID BAND J. FANS IN PORTLAND, ME, ( SIMILARLY AVID DEAD HEADS, ARE PETITIONING YOU TO NAME A FLAVOR "CHERRY GARCIA", SWEET CREAM WITH CHOPPED CHERRIES. YOU KNOW IT WILL SELL BECAUSE DEAD PARAPHERNALIA ALWAYS SELLS.
WE ARE TALKING GOOD BUSINESS SENSE, HERE, PLUS IT WILL BE A REAL HOOT FOR THE FANS. THINK ABOUT IT. WE DID. LOVE YOUR STUFF.

BEN + JERRY'S
40 GREEN MT. DR
S. BURLINGTON, V.T.
05401

# Cherry Garcia Forever
## by
## Rosina Lida Rubin

THE events that would soon lead to a five-alarm ice cream attack began when my phone rang on Friday, February 6, at about twenty minutes before noon. "I can't talk to you now, but listen to the noon news on WNEW," Toni said.

I turned on the radio and heard the voice of Mr. Marty "The Rock 'N Roll Smarty" Martinez reporting that a new flavor of Ben & Jerry's ice cream had been created, in honor of the Grateful Dead's upcoming East Coast tour. The confection was named *Cherry Garcia*.

*Cherry Garcia*. Even the name sounded delicious. And the description—vanilla ice cream with bing cherries and chocolate slivers—to die from. The first pints were arriving in supermarkets now, according to Ben, who was being interviewed live in the studio by Dave Herman.

In the background was the sound of ice cream being devoured—by the reporter, the dj, and assorted station staffers, all of whom were undeniably loving every mouthful to the FCC limits. It sounded like they were having a religious experience.

A combination of two of my favorite ice cream flavors—cherry vanilla and vanilla chocolate chip. Made by a company that puts as much soul into their ice cream as the Grateful Dead put into their music. I wanted some bad, real bad. The feeling was bordering on lust. But roaming the streets in search of ice cream is not exactly the kind of behavior that someone on a diet should be proud of, so I restrained myself.

Four days later, the folks at WNEW were still singing the praises of *Cherry Garcia*. It was time to give in and stalk the city until I found a pint. Surely the Food Emporium would have some.

There it was in the dairy freezer, just waiting to come home with me. I silently vowed to save it for the weekend, make my first experience with *Cherry Garcia* a special event. Who was I kidding? Maybe I'd just take a little taste, but the notion of that kind of discipline when faced with such a delicacy was foolhardy.

Beyond the lid emblazoned with Grateful Dead-style lettering was a mixture pinkish in color, the cherry juice flowing ever so subtly into the vanilla ice cream base. The real fruit pieces were ample and succulent. The chocolate slivers were substantial, rich and flavorful. The total impact of the sweet sensation was out of this world.

Yes, I had tasted the joys of ice cream heaven. Not a drop of *Cherry Garcia* would be forced to spend a cold, lonely night in my freezer.

# 1967:
## A Vinyl Retrospective by Mick Skidmore

THE 60's was certainly a radical decade that saw many changes in terms of people's philosophies, social awareness, as well as seeing immense political and cultural change.

It was also a time of great musical innovation. In fact, music took on a new seriousness in the middle of the decade when it assimilated some of these radical changes. The music became looser and freer. It was music to dance to, music to trip to and through the social and political messages of the lyrics, music to listen to on a different level than ever before.

Rock music became the voicepiece for the youth of America. If one had to pick out the high point of the '60s, it would be easy to make a favorable argument for the summer of 1967, the summer which became affectionately termed "The Summer of Love."

The Summer of Love saw the peak of an era that spawned hippies, LSD, communes, free love, sexual freedom, be-ins, light shows, flower power and all manner of other revolutionary ideas and ideals. By 1967 San Francisco was a veritable hot-bed of musical and cultural activity. It had become for America what Liverpool had been for England earlier in the decade.

It's true, now that we can look back at the innocence or naivety of the times, to argue that maybe the cultural revolution never really got off the ground.

Nonetheless, musically it was an exciting time and the freeness and openness of the sounds that emanated from the San Francisco area had a great impact on what we hear today.

Now, 20 years later, it's interesting to look at some of the albums that made that year so special. Jefferson Airplane was the first of the big-name San Francisco bands to make it nationally on a commercial level. They did so with their second album, *Surrealistic Pillow* (released in February 1967). Musically it may not be their strongest or most exciting album, but it's wonderful mixture of folk, rock, pop, jazz and blues make it one of the most enduring rock albums ever.

Grace Slick, who arrived in the group in late '66 (she replaced original vocalist Signe Anderson), not only added her stunning visual appearance and high-piercing powerful vocals, but a couple of superb songs. She brought "Somebody to Love," a searing rocker written by her then husband Darby Slick, and her own "White Rabbit." Both songs were to be hits during the summer of '67.

"White Rabbit" had Grace and the Airplane bringing a drug song to the airwaves and homes of middle America, while "Somebody To Love," captures the power and intensity of the Airplane in a tight three-minute rock song.

"She Has Funny Cars," "3/5's of a Mile in 10 Seconds," and "Plastic Fantastic Lover" all found the band in overdrive with Jack Casady's thunderous bass and Spencer Dryden's jazzy drumming propelling Jorma Kaukonen's shimmering acid-rock guitar lines, while the vocalists Marty Balin, Grace Slick and Paul Kantner complemented each other perfectly."

"Today," and "Comin' Back To Me," were delightful ballads that found Balin in superb form. The Grateful Dead's Jerry Garcia even added some delicate guitar to the latter.

Jorma Kaukonen's instrumental "Embryonic Journey still sounds as fresh and inventive today as it did 20 years ago. It's one minute fifty one seconds of acoustic guitar magic.

Moby Grape was a group that consisted of former Airplane drummer, Skip Spence (by now playing guitar,) bassist Bob Moseley, drummer Don Stevenson, lead guitarist Jerry Miller and Peter Lewis on guitar. The entire band wrote and sang.

Their eponymously titled debut album (released in May 1967) is one of rock's most neglected classics. Columbia, the group's label, tried to cash in on every aspect of the hippie scene with elaborate publicity stunts (they even released 10 of the albums 11 songs as five singles simultaneously with the release of the album).

Moby Grape mixed folk, blues, soul and country rock with tight four and five piece harmonies and slight psychedelic undertones. Songs like the wistful "8:05" with its delicate complex vocals and melodic jazzy "Someday," and the equally melodic jazzy "Someday," were hightpoints of the album, while "Hey Grandma," "Omaha," "Changes" and "Indifference" caught the group, with its three guitarists, in a flood of electricity. A classic album that stands the test of time remarkably well.

If any group embodied all the cultural and musical aspects of the spychedelic '60s more than any other it was the Grateful Dead. In 1967 the Dead released their first album, simply titled the Grateful Dead. There is no denying that the record was rough in places, and far from musically perfect, but it does have a certain ambience that adequately captures the period. Surprisingly the music (and the group itself) have endured better than any other from the period. Songs like "New New Minglewood Blues," and "Beat it on Down the Line" still appear occasionally in Dead sets.

Highpoints were the psychedelic influenced blues of "Good Morning Little Schoolgirl," and the lenghty "Viola Lee Blues," as well as the charming "Golden Road (To Unlimited Devotion.)" Not by any means a great album, but an influential one of immense proportions.

No retrospective review of 1967 would be complete without mentioning Country Joe and the Fish. This band that hailed from Berkeley, which was led by former folk singe/activist Joe McDonald, made what is undeniably the greatest psychedelic album in *Electric Music For The Mind and Body*. The album with its drug oriented songs, "Flying High," and "Bass Strings," its imaginative instrumentals full of mysticism and hypnotic riffs, "Section 43," "Masked Marauder," and the political satire "Superbird," was by far the most provocative and exciting, not to mention the most musically accomplished of all the Bay Area bands.

Barry Melton's flickering lead guitar and David Cohen's gloomy, dirge-like organ were the perfect backdrop for McDonald's ethereal, sultry vocals and stunning lyrics.

Songs like the bouncy "Porpoise Mouth," with its sexual connotations, and the complex vocal patterns of "Sad and Lonely Times" were stunning and way ahead of their time, but no songs better captured the trippy nature and magnificence of Country Joe and the Fish better than the atmospheric "Not So Sweet Martha Lorraine" and the lengthy ode to Grace Slick, "Grace."

Truly, *Electric Music for the Mind and Body*, was an album without a bad track, and the epitome of the term acid rock.

All the albums mentioned here are still available in one form or another and should be in the collection of every self-respecting Relix reader. Sure, there are plenty of great albums out there, and plenty of other classics from 1967, but none that capture so many of the unique aspects of "The Summer of Love" so well, and which in essence portray what Relix is all about. Here's to the next 20 years. It sure has been a long strange trip, but what an interesting one!

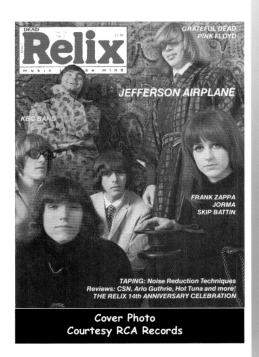

Cover Photo
Courtesy RCA Records

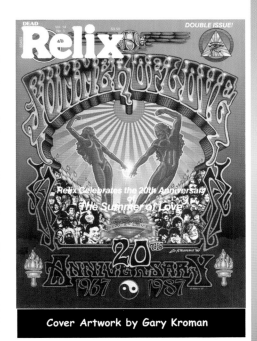

Cover Artwork by Gary Kroman

## "MY WIFE WAS A TEENAGE DEADHEAD"

by: Steve Barancik

### by Steve Barancik

MY wife was a teenage Deadhead. But now she's twenty.

Last night the phone rang at 4:30 in the morning. My wife pulled all the sheets and blankets off of me—her way of saying I should answer it. Just like with any late night phone call I was filled with a feeling of dread. "Hello." I said.

"Is Laura there?"

"I think she's sleeping. Who's calling?"

"This is Gwen. Is this her husband?"

"Yes."

"Hi. Please tell her that Bob's dog died."

"Bob's dog?"

"Yeah. Bob's dog. She'll want to know. I'd talk but I've still got twelve other calls to make. Bye."

This is typical. I don't know whether she intentionally hid it from me, or if I was just blinded with love, but I had no idea my wife was a Deadhead until after we got married. The time was last June. She had just graduated high school, and I had just graduated college. The world was our oyster. We moved to San Francisco. At the time I thought the decision had been mine, but now I know better.

My wife had told me that decorating our new home would be a cinch, that she had lots of art. I think this was my first clue. When we put her "art" up I discovered that it was all Dead, and being in San Francisco her art collection grows constantly. Every time I open a door or drawer, (yes, she lines our draws with it ), I never know what I'll see. She feels that Dead art must be "circulated" in order to feel its full effect, so every couple days she takes everything down and puts it up someplace else. We spent twenty-five bucks on masking tape last week.

And of course there's the music. Now don't get me wrong—I don't dislike the music. But I can only stand so much of it. Back in October I think it was, I put my foot down—and lifted the needle up.

"No more Dead on the stereo," I said.

My wife looked at me as if I'd outlawed oxygen. "You're kidding," she said hopefully.

"Uh-uh," I said. "You can play it if I'm not around."

"If I got a Walkman, could I play it on that?"

"I'd have no objections," I said, but I should have known better. She was out and back in fifteen minutes with her new Walkman. I heard her before she got within twenty feet of the door. Have I mentioned that my wife has the worse voice in the known universe? Imagine Joan Rivers after sucking on helium. She was singing Casey Jones, "...Hits River Junction at seventeen to-o-o...," when I realized that the stereo had been on my side all along, drowning her out. I bought the Walkman from her the second she walked in, (she insisted on making a profit for her trouble,) and ever since then I play my Soothing Environmental Sounds tape on the Walkman, full blast, when she has the stereo on. The Mount St. Helens cut works best.

I'll never forget when I saw our first phone bill. There were two numbers on it that repeated every day, during peak calling hours, and I didn't recognize either of them. I had the usual jealous husband reaction combined with the usual "I'm not made of money" reaction and confronted her with it. "What's this number?" I asked, pointing to the first of the two.

"That's the West Coast Deadhead Hotline," she said innocently.

I wasn't ready for that. "Huh," I finally said.

"Jerry's sick," she said, as if that explained everything.

"Who?"

"Jerry Garcia," she said rolling her eyes like she was talking to her father, not her husband. "He could be dying. I call every day to see how he's doing."

"Well, what's this number?" I demanded, seizing the offensive.

"The East Coast Deadhead Hotline." I suppose I should have been ready for that one.

I'll never forget what happened when Jerry got well and the band started playing here in town. It was a night in December, I think. I went to bed at the regular time, but my wife said she was going to stay up a little later. The next morning my alarm went off, and a very unfamiliar male voice, right next to me, said, "Hey, man, do you think you could turn that off." I went off in search of my wife, stepping over bodies and rolling them over if they looked like her from behind. I found her under the coffee table.

I shook her awake. "Laura," I said, "What the hell is going on here?"

She looked slightly irritated that I had awakened her. "A couple of heads needed a place to crash," she said. I counted "heads," roughly seventy, but I hadn't checked the bathroom yet.

So I did. The bathroom, it seems, was off limits for "crashing." But in the shower were three heads of at least two different sexes, with the water running, two standing and one lying down looking up. I ducked back out and decided against a shower. I reached into the cabinet below the sink for my toothbrush, toothpaste and hairbrush and another strange voice said, "Let's do it in here, man." I decided that for one day I could forego personal hygiene before work. I went to the refrigerator for some nourishment, opened it and twenty-two cubic feet of popped popcorn fell at my feet. So much for breakfast. Our front door was blocked by one very large deadhead who was snoring at the top of his lungs, standing up, so I escaped through the window, relieved that we lived on only the third floor.

I called home from work later that morning to ask that everyone leave. The conversation went something like this.

"I'd like to speak to Laura."

"Who's this?"

"This is the man who owns the apartment you're in."

"You're out of hot water, man." He sounded like he thought I should know.

"Could I speak to Laura?"

"What does she look like?"

"She's the lady who lives there."

"We all live here, man."

When I got home from work, Laura was on her way out the door. "Where are you going?" I asked.

"Shopping," she said. She was holding a list in her hand. I took it and looked at it. There were about a hundred items, each of them in different writing. The first one was "Twinkies." The second was "More Twinkies."

I could go on: The Steal Your Face tie for my first day at work, the famous "I'm in favor of it" comment when we had my boss over for dinner and he sought her opinion on the acid rain issue, or, God forbid, the trick or treat fiasco —but our lawyer has advised us not to comment on that until the judge reaches his verdict. But what's the point? I love my wife and she loves me—though I've a sneaking suspicion that she'd trade me and a blank for an early acid-test tape.

Photo by Gene Anthony

The Charlatans with Jerry Garcia

# THE DEPTH OF THE SOUNDS OF SAN FRANCISCO

## A Look at some of the "Other Bands"
### by Charles P. Lamey

1967. Has it really been twenty years? It's easy to grow misty-eyed nostalgic about the twentieth anniversary of the Summer of Love. It was an era when people could express themselves freely, both in their lifestyles as well as in their music. The rules of existing weren't nearly as rigid, encouraging people to do whatever they felt like, as long as no one else was hurt by their actions. Drugs were used as a tool to break down barriers and acquire knowledge, not as a decadent instrument of wasting brain cells. Free love was a way of communicating, not the act of sexual conquest. Now with bad drugs and life theatening social diseases attacking us from every direction, it would be virtually impossible for those elements to crop up again. But, at least, the good music from San Francisco's Summer of Love still exists. We were right about the music because it never faded.

Doubt that? Well, walk into any record store and check out some recent releases. You'll find albums by The Steve Miller Band, Starship, KBC Band, Santana, Quicksilver, Jorma Kaukonen, John Fogerty, et al. Add to that regular tours by The Dead (with a new Arista album due this summer), Hot Tuna, Kingfish, and John Cipollina in a half dozen bands, and older albums by the likes of Big Brother & The Holding Company and Jefferson Airplane, which outsell a lot of current product, it's easy to see the Summer of Love's musical impact lives on twenty years after the national media exploited it and tossed it aside.

This article's intention is to mention some of those one-time popular bands that were headliner status, but, are now forgotten. The reasons for this are numerous, ranging from poor management, too many drugs, changing trends, lack of record company support, or just dumb mistakes, but rarely was the quality of music the issue. Some continue to attempt comebacks, while others are content to live with their memories. No matter, the following bands were equally as important to the San Francisco music community, as those still making records today, and their importance should not be understated. These thumbnail sketches are, by no means, the whole story. All the following deserve features of their own.

### BLUE CHEER

Blue Cheer were the black sheep of the San Francisco music scene. Their punkish attitude put them at odds with the love and peace of their fellow performers. They hung out with the Hell's Angels, had the longest hair, and used the biggest amps. Blue Cheer weren't messing around, they meant business. Their first album, *Vincebus Eruptum* (Philips, 1968) spawned the hit cover of Eddie Cochran's "Summertime Blues," and their second, *Outside Inside* (Philips, 1968), was in part, cut outside on a pier because recording studios couldn't capture their sound. Both were closer to what would be later thought of as heavy metal than what the other bands were doing. Still, mixed in with the hard driving rhythms, simplistic riffs, and power chords, were some cool psychedelic production tricks and enough hippie jargon to grab some fringe credibility. After all, hadn't Dickie Peterson (bass/vocals/songwriter), Leigh Stephens (guitar), and Paul Whaley (drums) taken their name from a type of L.S.D.?

With Blue Cheer's third album, *New Improved* (1969), the band members and the music were changing. Randy Holden, Bruce Stephens, and Gary Yoder all took turns in the lead guitar spot, and this, along with the next three albums, were more attuned to what was going on in the city. All four of these long-players compare favorably to what other groups were doing. Each change made Blue Cheer stronger, though it alienated them from their original fans, who didn't fancy their more mellow attitude. Unfortunately, it was too late to win over those who were turned off by their first two albums. Blue Cheer called it quits in the early seventies only to reform in 1985. The resulting album, *Beast Is Back* (Megaforce), was the original power trio with guitarist Tony Rainier filling in for Leigh Stephens. They hit the road looking for a heavy metal audience, which they never found.

### COLD BLOOD

Cold Blood were a popular R&B horn band that often played The Fillmore. Their main strength lay in the vocals of Lydia Pense. Like Janis Joplin, Pense was comfortable singing blues/R&B, and her vocals were always a treat. It's unfortunate the band's horn charts lacked the fire of her performances, as they would have probably been able to break out of the Bay area. Their albums for the San Francisco and Reprise labels are nice, if not exceptional. Cold Blood can be seen performing in the documentary of the closing of the Fillmore. From viewing this, it's safe to say, Cold Blood were more at ease on a stage than in a studio.

### COUNTRY JOE & THE FISH

Maybe the most psychedelic outfit of all, Country Joe & The Fish began as a folk duo of Joe McDonald (Country Joe) and Barry Melton (the Fish), but quickly became a real rock and roll band adding drummer Chicken Hirsh, guitarist/organist David Cohen, and bassist Bruce Barthol. Being based in Berkeley rather than San Francisco, the band always had political leanings their contemporaries lacked. But Country Joe & The Fish never let it spoil the fun.

Their debut, *Electric Music For The Mind & Body* (Vanguard, 1967) was truly a cosmic listening experience with swirling organs, Eastern guitar leads, "trippy" melodies, and spacey lyrics. Its follow-up, *I Feel Like I'm Fixin' To Die* (1967), continued in this tradition with strong material and the band growing a lot tighter. This also included their legendary "Fish Cheer," which made them famous through its use in the *Woodstock* movie. If anyone wants to get an understanding of what was going on at this time, these two albums are good examples.

Their third album, *Together* (1968) was anything but, as the band was rapidly losing its cohesive feel. It's okay, with a few standout tracks, like "Rock & Soul Music," "Streets Of Your Town," and "Waltzing In The Moonlight," but the Fish were losing their sense of direction. They split and a revamped Fish (with only Joe and Melton retained from the originals) did *Here We Go Again* (1969). Once more, there were a few nice tunes but little magic. *C.J. Fish* (1970) was their final effort with yet another line-up. These guys were real pros and this was the band that played Woodstock. They split after its release. Barry Melton made some solo albums, led a couple of bands, and today he's a member of the, thus far, recordless Dinosaurs and a lawyer. Joe McDonald is still active in political issues and has issued numerous solo albums for Vanguard, Fantasy, and his own Rag Baby label. David Cohen has made instructional records/tapes for both piano and guitar.

In 1977, the original Country Joe and The Fish cut *Reunion* and they nearly recaptured the aura of the first two albums. In the end, though, it was a nostalgia trip for their original fans. From the cover art to the music in the grooves, Country Joe & The Fish's albums are true period pieces, but they still sound fresh thanks to honest performances.

### THE CHARLATANS

The Charlatans were, quite possibly, the most influential San Francisco band and not just because they were one of the first. This group showed tightness wasn't a prerequisite to get one's message across, and that rock and roll wasn't just mindless teenage music but a potent force. A lot of San Francisco folkies would have probably remained on the coffee-house circuit if they hadn't come under the influence of The Charlatans.

The group came into existence during the summer of 1964 when San Francisco State student George Hunter decided to put together a band that would be America's answer to the British pop invasion. To him, it didn't matter that he barely knew how to play an autoharp or bang a tamborine in time. Nor had Hunter any stage experience as a vocalist. He just wanted to make an artistic statement, and forming a rock band seemed the best way. He quickly recruited friends Mike Wilhelm (guitar), Richard Olsen (bass), and Sam Linde (drums). Shortly after their formation, they added pianist Mike Ferguson, who also had the distinction of having one of the first second hand/antique stores in Haight Ashbury. Surrounded by Ferguson's vintage artifacts, Hunter, the art student, hit upon The Charlatans dressing in

*Continues...*

old clothes, hence their fascination with being thought of as Edwardian cowboys. Bizarre, yet always colorful, even before playing a note in public, The Charlatans were a sensation. After only a few rehearsals, Linde was replaced on drums by Dan Hicks.

At first The Charlatans played white boy R&B/classic fifties tunes, but then they evolved into more of a folk-rock territory. Unlike most other bands, The Charlatans were closer in spirit to The Lovin' Spoonful than The Byrds. They made their debut in Virginia City, Nevada, playing for hippies and college students, building on their western mystique by toying with vintage firearms. Mentally, The Charlatans were living in the Old West, while physically they were breaking new ground with each set they played. Back home, people talked of The Charlatans in reverent tones. When they returned to San Francisco, The Charlatans were as tight as they were going to get.

Producer Erik Jackobson was turned onto The Charlatans, liked what he heard and signed them to Kama Sutra for one album. Nine tracks were cut, but the label balked at The Charlatans wanting to issue Buffy St. Marie's "Codeine" as a single. Eventually, they put out "32-20" on the Kapp label and the relationship was severed. Years later, France's Eva label reissued these sides, which are rough but still enjoyable. It's easy to detect what made The Charlatans so important to the scene, but it's also just as easy to understand why they would quickly be left far behind. Compared to the "more mature" work of The Jefferson Airplane, Quicksilver, Grateful Dead, and Moby Grape, The Charlatans seemed overly simple and old fashioned. In fact, for all their importance, The Charlatans couldn't get a stronghold in the ballroom scene. They were usually to be found in small clubs. The scene quickly passed them by.

An album was eventually released (1969), but Ferguson and Hicks were gone. Hicks formed his Hot Licks, which, through a series of albums found a large cult following. Ferguson ended up in Tongue And Groove with vocalist Lynne Hughes, who often sang and recorded with The Charlatans. The resulting album was nice, but a bit sloppy, yet worthy of being bought because of Mike Wilhelm's tasty playing. Since then, Wilhelm fronted the promising Loose Gravel, joined The Flamin' Groovies for a few albums and tours, and made a couple of fine solo albums. George Hunter is a designer. Mike Ferguson died of diabetes in 1979. Dan Hicks plays solo, and Richard Olsen still performs.

### GREAT SOCIETY

Regarded solely for giving us Grace Slick and the original versions of both "White Rabbit" and "Somebody To Love," The Great Society aren't mentioned as being a good band. They were, at times, really hot. Their two-record set for Columbia consists of primitive live recordings, yet one can feel a dynamic band itching for acclaim. Had they stuck it out, we might be listening to the Society today instead of the Starship. Grace Slick is raw and passionate on these sides, and although it's unfortunate The Great Society never got to make an official album, these sides are entertaining. The Great Society are an important footnote in San Francisco's Summer of Love.

### IT'S A BEAUTIFUL DAY

Arriving late on the scene, It's A Beautiful Day epitomized all the good feelings that went into the San Francisco Sound. Their music was warm, vibrant, and instantly memorable. Some also thought it to be slick, since there was lots of violin, courtesy of leader David LaFlamme's classical training. But, in truth, he propelled them into being a vital band, and his singing, along with Patti Santos', produced glowing results. Their self-titled 1969 debut was an instant FM favorite, thanks, in large part, to the incredible "White Bird." But, with the exception of some excess, the whole album was worth hearing. Their second, Marrying Maiden, was nearly as good, with excellent originals like "Don & Dewey," along with a stunning cover of Fred Neil's "The Dolphins." After that, the rot set in with uneven records being the result of an unstable line-up. David LaFlamme later made two solid solo albums and is now back on the road with a revamped It's A Beautiful Day.

### MAD RIVER

After releasing their own EP, Wind Chimes, Mad River joined Quicksilver, Sons Of Champlin, and Steve Miller at Capitol, but, through no fault of their own, their two albums were lost amongst the many classic releases of the day. Their music was colorfully arranged, making fine use of psychedelic guitar leads. Their self-titled debut (1968) was more consistent, but its follow-up, Paradise Bar & Grill, isn't far behind, bringing in a healthy country influence to go along with the acid jams.

### LEE MICHAELS

Multi-instrumentalist Lee Michaels started in Los Angeles, but came into his own after moving North to San Francisco. Never quite a star, in spite of a few minor hits, Michaels did make numerous albums which varied from interesting to boring. Though capable of playing a variety of instruments, most of Michaels' music was just Hammond organ and drums, played by, first Frosty and later Keith Knudsen, who, eventually joined The Doobie Brothers. A regular in the ballrooms, and, because of his limited use of guitars, a true original. At times self-indulgent, Lee Michaels was also capable of making quality music, too. This dichotomy was probably the reason Lee Michaels couldn't sustain his career.

### SONS OF CHAMPLIN

One of the Bay area's first bands, the Sons were gigging as early as 1965, even though their debut album, Loosen Up Naturally for Capitol wasn't issued until 1969. Actually, they cut an album for Verve in 1966, which except for a single, never came out. It's rumored the tapes were destroyed so we'll never get to hear The Sons in their infancy.

The Sons of Champlin by 1969 were an exciting band that used horn arrangements that ranged from funky R&B patterns to free form jazz. Throughout, Terry Haggerty can be heard playing some blistering guitar lines, and Bill Champlin always sang with plenty of soul. Never stilted, the Sons were probably too loose to score hits, but they did fit in nicely with the hippie community, and, for a short while, that was more important than radio smashes. The

Sons' three albums for Capitol are essential. Welcome To The Dance (Columbia, 1971) is a bit uneven, but still worth picking up, and their Ariola albums are more commercial, trying after roughly a decade, to crack top-forty. Today, after a couple of solo albums, Bill Champlin got his wish as a member of Chicago. Terry Haggerty released a wonderful solo album and now has a new tape. Both are close to the spirit of early Sons Of Champlin, and Haggerty, who is better than ever as a guitarist, freely uses the talents of his ex-bandmates. This makes the possibility of a Sons reunion seem somewhat likely.

### SOPWITH CAMEL

Ah, the curse of AM radio. The Sopwith Camel were a delightful old-timey band not unlike The Charlatans and Lovin' Spoonful. In fact, the likeness to the latter was responsible for them being signed to Kama Sutra and producing the hit "Hello Hello." Lazy vocals, simple guitar breaks, and minimalistic drumming gave their debut a goodtime feelin', and promised great things. Too bad the hipper locals wrote them off as a teenybopper band when they scored their hit, because they deserved a better fate. They tried again in 1973 with The Miraculous Hump Returns From The Moon (Warners), but things didn't gel. The album is okay, more in tune with the so-called hipper element, but now they seemed to be behind the pack instead of leading it. Peter Kraemer's vocals were similar to John Sebastian's and no less appealing, indicating a great deal of potential that was suffocated by their lack of acceptance.

These bands, along with familiar names such as Jefferson Airplane, Steve Miller Band, Grateful Dead, Big Brother & The Holding Company with Janis Joplin, and Quicksilver helped to give the San Francisco music community depth. But there were plenty more. Groups like Aum, Oxford Circle, Crome Syrcus, Notes From The Underground, Flamin' Groovies, and Mystery Trend were also kicking up a fuss, as were the transplanted bands like Electric Flag, Buddy Miles Express, Linn County, Charlie Musslewhite, Youngbloods, Mother Earth, and H.P. Lovecraft, who might not have originally been from San Francisco, but certainly contributed once they moved there. Then, there were acts like Daily Flash, P.H. Factor, The Other Half, 13th Floor Elevators, and The Sons Of Adam, who performed in the Ballrooms so often many thought they were locals.

The story is long and complicated, but, from glancing at the charts, watching MTV, checking the club scene, and looking at the dollar value of out-of-print San Francisco bands' records, one thing is certain, the Summer of Love is still going on twenty years after the fact. Maybe the lifestyles and times changed, but the sounds these performers created was good enough to last long after it was declared dead by the media.

*Artwork by Glenn Harding*

Photo by J.P. Niehuser

# EUROPEAN DEADHEADS
## by Mick Skidmore

TRY and imagine what it would be like to the most diehard U.S. Deadhead to *never* hear a Dead song on the radio, rarely see an article in the music press, let alone a positive one, and get to see their favorite band about once every five to ten years! Hard to take? Well, the answer is don't move to Europe, because that's what the Deadheads over there are faced with.

Yet, surprisingly enough the fans in Europe are incredibly loyal, and seem particularly well informed on the bands activities and other Dead related happenings. The reason for this is there is a whole blossoming network of Dead

related organizations and fanzines, most of which seem to be picking up momentum at present despite the Dead's six year absence from European shores.

Although there are Dead fans scattered throughout Europe, in countries like Switzerland, France, Italy, Holland, and Sweden, the main strongholds are West Germany and the United Kingdom.

Taking Germany first I have to thank Uli Tuete, an avid and knowledgable German Deadhead.

Tuete states, "As in the US, most German Deadheads tend to be generally connected with "hippie" ideals. They are mostly between 20 and 30, and tend to be academics. There are, of course, the old die-hard's in their 30's."

Tuete further breaks down German "Deadheads" into three categories. First there are what he labels *Tape Heads*. "There are some excellent collectors who specialize in vintage Dead (66-72) while some others are into special years like 1976 or 1980 and have complete collections." He added that obviously due to the lack of live shows in their country these collectors are primarily archivists but have extensive collections and sophisticated lists."

Secondly, we have what Tuete calls *Jet Heads*. "Instead of spending three or four weeks at a Spanish beach in the sun, a number of German Deadheads spend their vacations in the U.S. following the group from show to show."

Lastly we have *Rockpalast Heads*. These are the younger fans that first found exposure to the music of the Dead via their March 1981 TV/FM broadcast from Essen on the Rockpalast show. The show which lasted five hours (with the Who opening for the Dead) went out to nine different European countries, and was viewed by millions despite being shown at a late hour. (It began at midnight and lasted until the early hours of the morning.)

As far as publications go in Germany there are none at present (to my knowledge) that deal exclusively with the Dead. However, there used to be several that were West Coast-oriented. There was the now defunct, "West Coast Society," Starcluster Infos (which later changed into Music Unlimited,) and Taxim.

Starcluster used to regularly feature a Dead column, often written by Tuete. Starcluster also put out a book-sized edition devoted entirely to the Grateful Dead and offshoot bands.

Also, out in Germany is *Dead Lyrics*, a book that contains in English, the lyrics to Dead songs. The publication, I believe, is still available .

As far as national press the Dead get very little in the way of mentions, generally. However, there are a couple of organizations for fans. K.I.T. (Keep In Touch) is located in Cologne, and offers copies of newspaper articles, a newsletter, and helps find Dead related items for the fans. Tuete says, "including Relix records which are not always easy to find in Germany except for the mail order system."

Deadheads in Hamburg host an annual meeting (they've had four so far ) showing videos (still hard to come by in Germany) and sharing tapes.

Italy, while not exactly a Grateful Dead stronghold, does have some good magazines that occasionally give the Dead good ink. L'ultimo Busadero mentions them once in a while, and also carried an interview with Weir in 1981. Il Mucchio Selvaggio has also carried

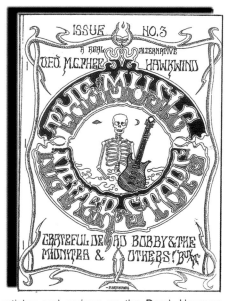

articles and reviews on the Dead. However, both magazines are exclusively in Italian.

Britain is the Dead's main stronghold in Europe, and the place the Dead have visited more than any other, with dates in 1970, 1972, 1974, and 1981.

Back in the late 60's and early 70's there was a whole plethora of magazines that were heavily into West Coast music. There was Zig Zag, Fat Angel, Hot Wacks, Dark Star and Comestock Lode. However, with the advent of new wave a lot of these publications disappeared. During the last few years a whole new generation have appeared including Swing 51, Spiral Light and The Music Never Stopped.

*Continues...*

# EUROPEAN DEADHEADS
## (Continued...)

Swing 51 has its main roots in British folk and US bluegrass, but has covered the Grateful Dead on a number of occasions, with interviews with Garcia, and Hunter as well as Weir's writing partner John Barlow.

Perhaps the most dedicated Dead organization in England is D.I.E., (Deadheads In Europe). They run the publication Spiral Light, which deals exclusively with The Grateful Dead and offshoot bands. It's well written and well put together and really is about as up to the minute as a publication of this ilk could be. They have reviews, tour dates, set lists and general historical articles as well as news.

Editor Ken Ingham explains, "The magazine goes out to nearly 450 subscribers in all parts of the UK and most European countries. We also have members working in China, Africa and Thailand, as well as a few discerning U.S. Deadheads."

As I have already mentioned, European fans seem rather loyal despite the lack of attention the Dead themselves pay to them. Ingham tries to shed some light on this extra dedication. "I think that the lack of live shows is an important point. If we were able to see the Dead every week or so, we could become blase about it all and some of the magic could perhaps be lost."

Like German fans, tape collecting is an important factor with Spiral Light readers. "It all helps to fill the gaps between shows and whet our appetities, but it sure as hell is not the real thing. We tend to congregate in small groups and listen to the latest shows to substitute for the lack of concerts," says Ingham adding "This lack of intimacy with the band also lends itself to keep the mysticism alive."

Ingham, like many, but not all European Deadheads I have spoken to seems a little concerned at the Dead's trend towards larger stadiums and general commerialistic aspects.

"The band seems to be growing away from their original ideals," although he is not totally unrealistic when he adds, "It's something they've not had too much control over. In the 80's there aren't too many places they can play free concerts. To me they have on the whole become more of an institution than a band, and as such have generated some of the problems that transition acquires."

Ingham also had this to say about a lot of U.K. Dead fans and himself. "I have seen 13 Dead shows in 14 years—I couldn't tell you the track list of any of them, but I know they were all amazing—just as I know the next one will be, where ever that may be! The British festival scene is still alive and flourishing (although Thatcher and her merry Police force) put an end to Stonehenge, a particularly special event. We would love to see the Dead over here at a festival of some sort, and hope that day will come to pass."

As to who the Spiral Light readers are Ingham says, "They tend to be varied. Obviously there are a whole bunch of old hippies like me who first saw the Dead at Bickershaw or Wembley in 1972. Some are still taking drugs regularly and dreaming of the halcyon days of the 60's, and then there are the younger fans who either saw them at the Rainbow in 1981 or in some cases have yet to see them. These tend to be psychedelic collectors in general, having reacted adversely

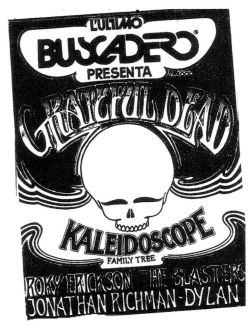

to the punk explosion of the late 70's, and decided to take a further look backwards."

Simon Hart, director of Terrapin Trucking Co., an organization that is a distributor of Grateful Dead product (magazines, posters, badges, books, etc.) in the UK and Europe, further explains some of Ingham's last remarks by talking about the growing interest in the Grateful Dead.

"Since starting the company a couple of years ago, and with the help of some Grateful Dead fans, we now have a lot of interest in the Dead. They are not written about in the weekly papers, except mockingly. Although the London Evening Standard has a columnist named Peter Holt who mentions them once in a while because he actually likes them. In England there's something of a psychedelic revival or West Coast revival. A lot of this is through people like Demon, who are reissuing albums like Spirit's *Family That Plays Together*, the first Quicksilver album and records by Moby Grape, Janis Joplin, The Flying Burrito Brothers and others.

'I think there's always going to be an interest in the older music. Some of it's to do with the hippie syndrome, because there is still a strong hippie community in England, but a lot of it has to do with nostalgia. A lot of old artists have been making comebacks, and a lot of people are backtracking to see what made the 60's and early 70's the kind of era's they were. We are finding a lot of interest from younger people. If I put a Grateful Dead album on in the shop someone, usually a younger person, says 'That's really good' and often ends up buying the record.' The music speaks for itself. The interest is there. I have had people coming down from the North of England for the day just to visit the shop. They'll end up spending 200 or 250 pounds on Grateful Dead posters, books, t-shirts, because there is so little in England, and the band hasn't been here in over five years, so the fans want all they can get."

Giving another perspective of UK fans and their attitudes is Alasdair MacDonald, who runs another fanzine type publication called The

*Music Never Stopped*. MacDonald is one of the newer generation of Dead fans being only 23 years old. He proudly states, "When the Dead first played in England I was only 7 years old." He later recalls seeing odd snippets about them in magazines like New Musical Express and Sounds, especially the famous Grateful Dead/Beach Boys shows at Wembley that never materialized. His first introduction to the Dead was at school by an American exchange student who played him some tapes, and then the 1981 Rainbow Theatre shows. "I had no idea what I was letting myself in for. My consciousness of the Grateful Dead was zero and a lot of Dead fans I have met since have expressed the same feeling. You can't comprehend what the Dead are like until you have listened to a whole tape or seen a whole concert. One person I met at the Rainbow in March 1981 couldn't understand why the show was starting at 7:30. He thought we'd all be home by 9 or ten o'clock."

Unlike some of the older fans, readers of *The Music Never Stopped* tend to be less elitist in nature, judging from comments by MacDonald.

First off, *The Music Never Stopped* carries articles on lots of other bands despite being strongly into the Dead. "A lot of UK Deadheads listen to what is . . ."Hippie-type" music, groups like Hawkwind, The Pink Fairies and Syd Barret. I also listen to a lot of reggae and hip-hop music."

The magazine's readers cover a wide range of ages from new fans through to old hippies. Again, MacDonald, like nearly all the European fans I contacted, put taping as a priority. "Most of the Dead Heads that I know are through letters and through trading tapes. The taping is really important. Every year we have another 60 or so shows to try and collect. Most of us now have pretty healthy collections and collectors with 1000's of hours worth of tapes can find things on our lists of interest. Because of the lack of live shows in this country, a lot of energy goes into trading tapes."

What does MacDonald consider important factors about Deadheads and the Grateful Dead? "The fact that the Dead play so many different styles is important, but the thing is if you find a Deadhead in this country, it's not because the media pushes it at them, it's not because all their friends are Dead Heads and they want to be one. It's most likely that they searched them out and discovered that this is amazing or whatever their own personal feelings were. That's got to be the main sort of difference in environment over here. Being a Deadhead is not forced on you because there is no one to do it."

MacDonald further emphasizes the Dead's underground status in Britain by adding, "To be honest it's off putting if everyone else likes something—you have to be a little suspicious if everyone likes something, because it's likely too nice or bland. All I can say is thank god the Dead don't get good press over here. The last thing we want is for them to become a fashion thing like so many other forms of music. I got into the Dead for their music and for the music's sake. I am quite happy to disagree with them on any topic unrelated to music, or even on musical matters."

Perhaps MacDonald's most important remark was when he summed up his feelings as to why the UK Deadheads are so loyal. "If you could take a list of all the Deadheads and

*Continues...*

# EUROPEAN DEADHEADS
## (Continued...)

take say the top ten percent, then you'd have the Deadheads we have, the only Deadheads we have, would be of that ilk! I don't mean to sound trite, but that's it. These fans live pretty much on the tapes and the perpetual rumors. The Dead have almost made it over on a number of occasions, and there are always rumors, and that kind of stuff helps keep people's enthusiasm and interest going whereas otherwise it might flag."

As far as his own personal feelings go, MacDonald puts political things as his main priority, but says, "My liking of the Grateful Dead is subordinate to my thinking about the world in general, although I think I'd pay some sort of credit to the Dead music for opening my ears in musical terms...the Dead have never shaped my overall political views, because that is something I have shaped myself, but it compliments it all. The Grateful Dead's music is not patronizing in the least, nor is it sexist or politically offensive."

If there was one thing that ran through my communications with European Dead Head's it was the hope for more shows in the near future. How about it? These guys take the stuff pretty seriously and deserve a little more attention.

TETE ROCK, GRACEFUL DEAL ET CABARET NOMADE
PRESENTENT:
**CAPTAIN TRIPS FESTIVAL**

Informations et réservations: Hot Brass (1) 42 00 14 14

K.C.O.H. G.R.F.X.

COME ON ALL    OR GO ALONE!

**THE DEAD HEADS, GRATEFUL DEAD MUSIC,
EYES OF THE WORLD LIGHT SHOW & SURPRISE GUESTS**
Locations: FNAC, Virgin, Gibert, Carrefour
**JAN. 14 1996    HOT BRASS**
de 16h à 1h du matin    Parc de la Villette
ENTREE: 70 FF    75019 PARIS
A GATHERING OF THE TRIBES

"In The Dark"
Platinum Record Award
Presentation

Photo
by
Bob Leafe/Courtesy
Arista Records

by Scott Boldt

**Relix**

Vol. 15 No. 5 $3.00

music for the

*GRATEFUL DEAD*
*ROBERT HUNTER*
*ALLMAN BROTHERS*

*JACK...*
*BOB DYLAN...*

JOHNNY WINTER

Cover Photo by L.D. Kippel

*Little Feat*
*Living Earth*
*Peace Walk*

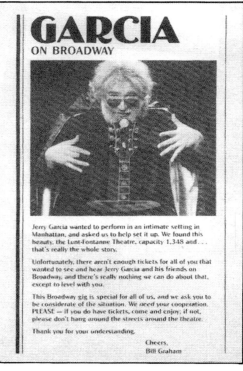

Artwork by Mike Zmuda

## A Notice from Grateful Dead Productions

*The following notice was distributed with Grateful Dead Mailorder tickets, and we feel the information should be passed along to everyone.*

Dear Deadheads,

Here we are sitting on top of the world: big record, open doors and lots of steaming plans. This raises the question of who we are — the answer is: partly us, partly you. Our part is to provide the music and logistics of the Grateful Dead experience; your part is to have one hell of a good time without anyone getting hurt or sore, which is what this trip is mostly about.

Our current situation demands that we provide our part to growing numbers who are beginning to catch on to what you knew all along.

There is no blanket solution to the problems caused by increasing demand and there is no turning back. We are now the biggest "draw" in the history of rock and roll. That's not a self congratulatory statement, rather a bald fact showing the seriousness of our logistical problem. The good old days when we were your personal minstrels have been overshadowed by a new reality which *must* be addressed. We are not a political, religious nor a grass roots movement; not a counter culture, drug culture nor the latest big shakes snatch and run glamor

act — we are a symbiotic fun machine designed to get 10,000 or more heads straight at a pop.

We don't want to be consigned to doing only stadium gigs but, in order to play smaller venues, our friends must heed our pleas to not attend certain shows without tickets. Otherwise, cities will simply not rent us their facilities and that will be that.

Many doors have been closed to us in the last several months due to the trash and boogie behavior of new fans who have no regard for the way the Dead do things.

Environments as large as those which we are called upon to provide must be controlled or we will be responsible for the ensuing Pandemonium.

Some of the charges we are making are for our benefit, others are for yours. Frankly, we don't intend to hand over a big portion of the bread we need to run this operation to organized crime. This is no joke, there are some big time heavies muscling in. Follow the cigar smoke! Hence we are forced into a tighter structuring of merchandising. What began as a spontaneous vagabond marketplace has devolved into a competitive and obnoxious full scale illegal rip off, squeezing out the gypsy Deadheads and offering violence to rival merchandisers. We intend to step on it — hard!

Wherever venues allow it, good people will still be allowed to make road money dealing artifacts — all you gotta do is ask for permission. You keep what you make, or give us a cut

if you deal our trademarks. Fair and simple.

Tapers, as you may know by now, are assigned certain sections because they are so touchy. We let you tape for free and love when you exchange tapes. But if anybody asks for more than the price of the blank tape, they are playing a different game.

If you can keep your sense of proportion and understand that we are doing what must be done to ensure our rights and yours, we gratefully invite you to experience this unexpected era of Mega Dead-dom. Take it with the grain of salt it deserves and enjoy watching the ripples as our personal tributary begins mingling with larger currents. It's just as weird for us as it is for you, but, after all, this wasn't meant to be a private party!

Robert Hunter
for Grateful Dead Productions, Inc.

**Counterfeit Ticket Warning**

Over the last year the counterfeit ticket problem has gotten much worse, culminating with the New Years Eve concert at which over 350 bogus tickets were stopped at the door. These 350-plus people did not get in, and learned a very expensive lesson.

Only buy tickets from authorized ticket agencies, do not buy tickets on the street!! They will most likely be counterfeit and you will not get in!!

If you don't have a ticket, please don't come to the concert. Thank you.

65463

# Relix

Vol. 15
No. 2

$3.00

music for the mind

GRATEFUL DEAD
THE BAND'S
LAST WALTZ
JOHN CIPOLLINA

NEW RIDERS PURPLE SAGE

JOHN DAWSON • DAVE NELSON • BUDDY CAGE

Cover Art by David Nelson
David Nelson Band
www.nelsonband.com
New Riders of the Purple Sage
www.nrpsmusic.com

OLATUNJI
KITARO
UNDERGROUND COMIX
CONCERT AND RECORD REVIEWS

Zero: Greg Anton, Steve Kimock, John Farey, John Cipollina, Bobby Vega and Martin Fierro

# Independents Daze by Mick Skidmore

IF the introductions to this column were as interesting as the music, I'd ramble on a bit more, but as they're not, on to the music. And where better to start than with *Here Goes Nothin'*, the long-awaited debut album from Zero on none other than Relix Records.

Anyone who has seen this wonderful musical ensemble live should know what to expect, and rest assured Messrs. Kimock, Anton, Cipollina and company deliver the goods. They play with flair and imagination from the opening funk-filled jazz of "Golden Road," to the powerful closing blues/rock strains of "Goin' Down."

However, it is in the jazzier improvisational instrumentals like "Straight Jackets," "Girls Drums" and "Tear Tags Off Mattresses," that they really show their musical prowess. Simply the most adventurous album put out by Relix to date. Check out the CD version which also includes "Showboat," an extra track with Donna Jean Godchaux-Mackay on lead vocals. Need I say more!

Robert Hunter also shines with his latest Relix album, *Liberty*. This is Hunter's most commercial record to date and should serve to widen his audience considerably.

As usual, Hunter waxes lyrical in his own inimitable fashion, but what makes the record so appealing is the uptempo arrangements and alluring melodies. Backing him is a really tight band of bassist Michael White, drummer Dave Mann, keyboardist/vocalist Rick Meyers and Jerry Garcia on guitar.

Hunter, whose vocal range is still limited, seems more comfortable as a singer, and has obviously spent a lot of time on the arrangements. This is best exemplified in the title cut, the fast paced "Bone Alley," and the stomping "Come And Get It." Also impressive is the lengthy "Cry Down the Years," which features a nice solo from Garcia. A very satisfying album.

NRBQ has finally gotten around to releasing a live album, *God Bless Us All* (Rounder). Recorded in one set at Lupo's Heartbreak Hotel in Providence on April 18, 1987, this record captures the spontaneity and versatility of the group's music better than any of their other albums.

There's some great rockers like "Crazy Like A Fox," "Me and the Boys," and "12 Bar Blues," some hot funky jazz like "Mouthwaterin'" and "Down At The Zoo," as well as some odd endearing ditties like the title cut and the infectious "Every Boy, Every Girl." This record captures the true essence of rock and roll in its least pretentious form.

Following hot on the heels of their two Relix releases comes a new album from Savoy Brown, *Make Me Sweat* (GNP/Crescendo.) It's a solid effort of hard hitting, boogie-based, bluesy rock that the band is known for.

Kim Simmonds proves to be in fine form throughout, providing some exciting guitar work, while vocalist Dave Walker injects plenty of energy into the songs with his gutsy style.

Best cuts are the rollicking "Limousine Boogie (Hey Hey Mama)," "Hard Way To Go," and the bluesier "Good Time Lover."

If *Road To Bayamon* (Philo), the lastest album from the Tom Russell band, gets half the attention that it deserves, it will be hailed as a country rock classic. Russell is one of the best contemporary writers around. His songs are full of rich lyrical imagery and his vocals have an earthy quality that brings out the best in his seductive melodies. Add to that a dynamic band that's as adept at playing tex-mex, rock and roll and country, and you have one hell of an album. The title cut with its accordian driven beat and Russell's poignant ode to Gram Parsons' "Joshua Tree " are standouts, but really each song is a well-crafted masterpiece.

Poet/songwriter, multi-instrumentalist John Kruth (a contributor to Relix I might add) has his debut album, *Midnight Snack*, out on Hopewell Records.

It contains 12 highly original songs that are just a little bizarre. Sort of a cross between Loudon Wainwright and Christine Lavin, but with more unusual musical twists than either of those two provide.

"Stretch Marks and Hairlines" is a humorous mid-60s sounding song, while "Atomic Mama" is a wonderfully whimsical number about nuclear power. But best of all is "Ugly Mood," which starts with Kruth's mandolin dueting with

an accordian before erupting in a rush of electric guitar work.

Helping out Kruth are The Violent Femmes and keyboard ace Sigmund Snopek III among others.

Hawkwind is a British band that has always been deeply involved in the hippie underground of that country and is the band that crops up most frequently as the favorite of British Deadheads. If you want to check out what your UK counterparts listen to aside from the Dead, give *Live Chronicles* (GWR/Profile) a listen, but beware as there are no similarities in style. It's a specially priced ($12.98) two-record set recorded live during Hawkwind's 1985 tour.

Having personally never given the band much time in the past, I found this a pleasant surprise. Most of the songs segue into one another via spacey instrumental segments or spoken passages. The music itself is a brash mix of psychedelia, science fiction and fantasy filled lyrics laced with metalic guitar riffs and electronics. Most impressive is the instrumental "Shade Gate," and the dynamic rocker "Master Of The Universe." ∎

## woodstock maze

**Maze by John Lucchese**

# TOO NEW TO BE KNOWN

**by Mick Skidmore**

**Photo Courtesy Phish**

IT never ceases to amaze me how many great unsigned bands there are out there.

**Phish,** a four-piece that hails from Burlington, Vermont, is one such band. It consists of Trey Anastasio on guitar (he also writes most of the music), Page McConnell on keyboards, Jon (Phish) Fishman on drums and trombone, and Mike Gordon on bass.

Phish has a strong base of highly original material that it liberally laces with jazz, rock, funk, calypso, and blues elements, as well as some truly bizarre lyrics that would do Frank Zappa proud.

The band has been playing the New England club and college scene for the past five years to ever-increasing audiences, and on the strength of their self-produced cassette release, *Junta*, it's easy to see why.

The tape is superbly recorded and shows the band possesses a musical flair almost beyond belief. Sure, the songs are a little odd, especially the whimsical "Contact," a love song to a car, and the poetic "Ester," but the underlying strength of all the material is the virtuoso musicianship and wry sense of humor that runs through it. Guitarist Anastasio's playing is of a highly exploratory nature and ranges from jazzy runs through melodic phrases to daring improvisations. Keyboardist McConnell embellishes the sound with some intricate playing, while the rest of the band creates a complex mesh of syncopated and polyrhythmic sounds. This is most notable on the lengthy, mainly instrumental "David Bowie" (the only lyrics are the title and UB40 repeated!), and the equally exciting "The Divided Sky" and "You Enjoy Myself."

According to a spokesperson for the band, the tape only reflects a small part of their complex repertoire of originals. They even have an entire suite that runs an hour and a half! I hope we get a chance to hear more from these extremely talented musicians in the not too distant future. Meanwhile, this tape comes highly recommended.

**Toni's Note:** Mick Skidmore was the first person to review Phish after hearing an unreleased copy of *Junta*. It wasn't long before the band exploded, becoming one of the most successful touring bands in jamband history! Skidmore continues to uncover musical gems as a freelance writer.

Artwork by Alfred Klosterman

Artwork by Alfred Klosterman

Photo by L.D. Kippel

Artwork by Mike Swartzbeck

# On Line With
# The Grateful Dead

## by Evan Rudowski

THE Grateful Dead community never stays in one place for long. It packs up and moves from town to town like a traveling carnival.

Deadheads can't wait for those times when the carnival pulls into their town. Sometimes they'll even make a special trip to be there. But what about those times when the Dead just aren't around?

Thanks to the computer age, there's now a way to bring that carnival right into your home. In growing numbers, Deadheads are finding that it's easy to stay in touch by calling one of the several Grateful Dead computer "bulletin boards" that have sprouted in various parts of the country.

A computer bulletin board is a place that people can "visit" electronically to talk or get information fast. With the help of a "modem," a computer can connect with the telephone line and dial into any other modem-equipped computer. Bulletin boards are computers that are always ready to take calls and offer information that callers can use.

These Grateful Dead bulletin boards are a goldmine of information for Deadheads. They can be updated instantly and easily, so that they can offer the song list for last night's show, or let you know who wants to trade two Fridays for two Saturdays. You can visit them to find out how Jerry sounded last night, or that Bobby jammed last week at the Lone Star.

"I thought it would be a great way to spread information," said Klaus Bender, who, with his wife, Gretchen, runs the Dead Board in Biglerville, Pennsylvania (717-677-9573). "It's generally just fun for us. Getting the song lists after every show is a pretty neat thing."

"It's been six months since I've seen a Dead show, but it seems like I've been in a parking lot every day," said James Scofield, who runs Terrapin Station in Darien, Connecticut (203-656-0134). "I can't wait to see what my board looks like a year from now. I'm just going to sit back on the bus and enjoy the ride."

It's "the kind of stuff that Deadheads talk about all the time," says David Gans, who helps run a Grateful Dead bulletin board on a California system called the Whole Earth 'Lectronic Link (The WELL — 415-332-6106). "It's really just a hangout."

"Hanging out" is accomplished by sending electronic mail. Users can send messages to each other or to everyone on the system. Callers can choose a CB-radio-style handle, or use their real names.

Deadheads who call these boards have recently discussed such topics as the Spring tour, Robert Hunter's new video and the low-power FM broadcasts emanating from the soundboard.

Callers have also been able to get complete ticket-ordering information, including on-sale dates and instructions for sending in their orders. Hotline busy signals are a thing of the past for Deadheads who are on the on-line "bus."

The information available on these bulletin boards is usually reliable, although the boards are not officially affiliated with the Grateful Dead. However, since so many Deadheads call and respond to what they see, "ugly rumors" are usually corrected quickly by people who have better information.

The Deadheads who run these boards are simply people who learned about the technology and saw how it could work in our scene. All of these system operators — or sysops — have day jobs. None of them profit from their efforts, except by making friends and helping to broaden the Grateful Dead universe.

Klaus Bender works for the federal government, and Gretchen Bender is a proofreader. Scofield — whose handle is Captain Trips — grooms show horses. Gans hosts the syndicated "Deadhead Hour" radio show and also has co-authored a book with the band. Mary Eisenhart and Bennett Falk also help run the Dead conference on the WELL.

The WELL also offers "Deadventure," an interactive computer game. Players find themselves at the site of a Dead concert, but without a ticket. The object of the game is to piece together the clues and make it into the show and backstage to meet the band. Deadventure, developed by Robert Diamond, may also be played by calling (201) 846-2460 and typing "DEAD" at the "login" prompt.

Computers are still freaky to many people, and one might think they'd be especially freaky to Deadheads. But the Heads who are already on-line think it's a natural.

"I don't think it's strange at all for Deadheads to be into high tech equipment," said Dead Board user Mark Israel. "We may enjoy some of the simple pleasures in life, but we are not simple people."

Steve Stein of Acton, Massachusetts, who uses the handle "Sunshine Daydream," says that bulletin boards can help bring the Dead scene closer together. "With the advent of bulletin boards, Heads can get more organized," he said. "They can get to know each other even if they are geographically distant, and they can organize meetings and parties around concerts."

Stein already has met other users, including one who was "a lot like me." Klaus and Gretchen Bender also regularly get together with some Heads they've met through their Dead Board. During the past spring tour, a bunch of on-line Deadheads met in Boston on the day between the Hartford and Worcester shows.

The Dead may be bigger than ever but, as always, Deadheads have found a way to adapt to this strange new world and make it their own. Bulletin boards are playing their part by bringing the Dead scene out of the concert hall and onto the table top.

## THE TECHNICAL SIDE . . .

There are a few things you must do before you can call a bulletin board with your personal computer. You need the right hardware and software, and you need to know how to use that software.

In the hardware department, you'll need a telephone line before you do anything else. An ordinary modular wall jack — like the kind your phone is plugged into now — will do fine. You can even disconnect your phone and just plug in your computer.

Next, you'll need a modem. Modems convert your computer's data into a signal that can be carried through the phone line. The computer on the other end uses a modem to convert the signal back to normal.

# LYRIC HISTORY

## by David Kopel

Ship of Fools

Artwork by Gary Kroman

FROM the Texas swing of *Mama Tried* to the African rhythm of *Throwing Stones* to the Bulgarian folk cadence of *Uncle John's Band*, the Dead draw their musical inspiration from the whole world's musical culture. Like their music, the Dead's lyrics draw on the full richness of our cultural heritage.

For example, the diverse imagery of *Ramble on Rose* takes us from the 1920's all the way back to the Old Testament. We all know the line "just like Billy Sunday, in a shotgun ragtime band," but who was Billy Sunday? The greatest preacher of the early 20th century, Billy Sunday shouted the gospel to a total audience of 100 million people. With the support of the Ku Klux Klan, he railed against the teaching of evolution and for the prohibition of liquor.

While Billy Sunday was a social conservative, Mary Shelley (as in "Just like Mary Shelley, just like Frankenstein") was just the opposite. She and her husband, the poet Percy Bysshe Shelley, traveled throughout Europe and cavorted with the great Romantic writers of the early 19th century — including Keats and Byron. It was at Byron's Swiss castle where she began composing *Frankenstein*, inspired by a nightmare that followed an evening of ghost stories by candlelight.

*Ramble on Rose* continues: "Just like New York City, just like Jericho, pace the halls and climb the walls and get out when they blow." In the Old Testament, as the Hebrews fought to conquer the Promised Land of Israel, they ran into Jericho, whose tall, sturdy walls made it seemingly impregnable.

At the Lord's command, Joshua, the Hebrew leader, ordered seven priests — each carrying a ram's horn trumpet — to march around Jericho for six days. On the seventh day, they marched around seven times. When the priests blew the horns for the seventh time, the Hebrews shouted in unison, and "the wall fell down flat."

While there is no single "right" way to interpret Dead lyrics, understanding their historical roots opens up new meanings. Like Billy Sunday, the Dead at times represent rural, traditional, community-oriented values. Billy Sunday and the Dead preach against the false security of a New York City or a Jericho — the idea that

technological prowess can make one invulnerable. Like Mary Shelley and Dr. Frankenstein, the band members have created a huge, strange creature — the Grateful Dead — that at times threatens to destroy its creator.

In *Uncle John's Band*, Jerry sings, "Goddamn well I declare, have you seen the like? Their walls are built of cannonballs, their motto is 'Don't tread on me.' " Whose motto? The Americans who fought the War for Independence. They carried flags that showed a snake (representing America) warning "Don't tread on me." For a while, the "Don't tread on me" flag was the official battle flag of New York State's troops.

While British Deadheads haven't had much to cheer about since the 1981 tour, they can at least consider how many Dead songs involve British culture. *Scarlet Begonias* starts off in London, with Jerry "walking round Grosvenor Square," a fashionable residential section of London.

Later, "the wind in the willows plays tea for two." *The Wind in the Willows*, of course, is the famous children's story by Kenneth Grahame. It details the adventures of Mole, Water Rat, and Toad on a river in rural England.

Jack Straw hails from Wichita, but the first Jack Straw came from rural Britain. In 1381, Jack Straw and Wat Tyler led an unsuccessful peasant and labor rebellion against Britain's King Richard II. Jackstraw later came to mean a man without property, worth, or influence.

Also harking back to very olde England is *Sugaree*, which begins: "When they come to take you down, when they bring that wagon round, when they come to call on you, and drag your poor body down..."

The lyric evokes the medieval practice of hauling dead bodies away in a wagon. (Remember the beginning of *Monty Python and the Holy Grail*, when a man directing a wagon shouts "Bring out your dead.")

Another medieval image is The Ship of Fools. A common figure in religious paintings, the Ship of Fools reproached people who thought of sailing only as an end in itself, rather than a means to reach a port — people who cared only for the earthly pleasures, and forgot the goal of salvation.

Next time your parent/teacher/boss/ authority figure tells you that "In the Dark"

is destroying your mind, explain that you consider the album a sort of history lesson. For example, in *Hell in Bucket* Bob mocks his former sex partner: "You might be the reincarnation of the infamous Catherine the Great." Empress of Russia in the late 18th century, Catherine the Great really deserved her infamy. By conquest and diplomacy, she vastly expanded Russian power in Europe, the Middle East, and the Far East. Under her reign, many once free peasants were enslaved as serfs. Up until her death at age 67, she had sex with a huge variety of (mostly young) men, including her great Field Marshall Potemkin. Her sexual appetites reportedly extended to sado-masochism and beastiality. Although she actually died of natural causes, rumors persist that she was killed while lying in bed, waiting for a stallion to be lowered onto her; the winch broke, and she was crushed by the weight of the horse.

You can explain that you're listening to the new album because of your interest in early European cartography. "Here there may be tigers," we are warned in *When Push Comes to Shove*. That line comes from an old map of Asia, drawn by a European explorer; the map includes a vague drawing of India, and the warning "Here there may be tygers."

History won't get you far with *China Cat*. Nobody's ever seen a "Copper dome bodhi drip a silver kimono." The "bodhi," though, is short for "Bodhisattva." In Buddhism (one of the major religions in Asia), a bodhisattva is a being who compassionately does not enter Nirvana, so he can stay on lower (earthly) planes and help others.

One of Robert Hunter's greatest strengths as a lyricist is how his words carry so many levels of meaning, each reinforcing the other. For example, the proclamation "you are the eyes of the world" is a strong and upbeat message reminding people that they have special gifts to offer. The line is reminiscent of the Sermon on the Mount, where Jesus made the same point: "You are the light of the world." Similarly, "The heart has its seasons, its evenin's and songs of its own" seem inspired by the 17th century French philosopher Pascal's saying: "The heart has its reasons which reason does not understand." (Pascal was explaining why he could accept Christianity on the basis of faith, rather than reason.)

In one sense then, the song places itself in the Christian tradition. Yet while Hunter restates an element of Jesus' message, Hunter's lyrics later seem to reject the idea of a Jesus (or anyone else) as a permanent source of inspiration: "There comes a redeemer and he slowly too fades away." Hunter's point is that all things — including the most cosmic — participate in the cycle of birth and death: "Seeds that were silent all burst into bloom and decay. Night comes so quiet, it's close on the heels of the day."

But immediately after Hunter delivers the "evening" message that nothing is permanent, he brings the song around to the refrain's "morning" message: "Wake up to find out that you are the eyes of the world." By paraphrasing the words Jesus said two millenia ago — and Pascal's affirmation of the words 1600 years later — the song acknowledges that some things may endure through all time.

*Eyes* contains both a direct idea (everything grows and then decays), and an anti-idea (some things, like the words in the Sermon, may survive forever). By uniting two contradictory ideas, the song imitates the world it describes, where life and death — two opposites — become part of a greater whole, and where the conflict between permanence and decay is never fully resolved.

In *Touch of Grey*, Hunter's borrowings strengthen one of that song's major themes. "Light a candle, curse the glare," is an ironic variation of the Chinese proverb: "It is better to light a single candle than to curse the darkness." While lighting a candle in the darkness (a good act in a bad time) is a positive event, even that good act has a negative side — the candle's glare. The chorus repeats the same theme; every dark cloud, as the saying goes, has a silver lining, but "every silver lining's got a touch of grey."

In *Don't Ease Me In*, Jerry is "Standing on the corner, talking to Miss Brown." This seems to be about the same thing as "going down by minglewood," since "Miss Brown" is 18th-19th century British slang for female genitals.

There are other meanings in the songs that Hunter did not intend. Although St. Stephen was the first Christian martyr, Hunter says he did not write the song with the historical figure in mind.

Nevertheless, much of the song's imagery is consistent with a martyr's story. Images in the song such as Stephen's rose (a martyr's emblem) and the "babe in scarlet colors" easily work as Christian symbols. Following a conviction of blasphemy, St. Stephen was stoned (!) to death by a crowd — "wherever he goes the people all complain." The historical St. Stephen grappled with ultimate questions, and eventually decided he was ready to die to defend the answers. The character in Hunter's song asks his own big questions, and wonders what the importance of the answers will be.

One of the great aspects of the Dead experience is that it is not just a one-way message from musicians to audience, but a reciprocal experience, in which the audi-

St. Stephen/Ramble On Rose

*Artwork by Gary Kroman*

ence helps create the meaning. The songs acquire a life of their own, partly independent of their author's intentions.

On "Live Dead," *St. Stephen* segues into *The Eleven*, another song influenced by what Ken Kesey called the "messianic" LSD culture. The song carries out a numerical countdown, reminiscent of *The Twelve Days of Christmas*. The "six proud walkers on the jingle bell rainbow," remind the listener of another Christmas carol. The "five men writing with fingers of gold" parallels the "five gold rings" from *The Twelve Days*. The "Four men tracking down the great white sperm" are Captain Ahab and his crew in their obsessive, epic quest for Moby Dick, the great white whale.

The song concludes: "William Tell has stretched his bow till it won't stretch no furthermore and/or it may require a change that hasn't come before." In legend, William Tell was the brilliant archer who, after shooting an apple off his son's head, assassinated the Austrian dictator of Switzerland, precipitating the revolution that changed Switzerland into an independent nation.

Bible imagery abounds in Grateful Dead lyrics — not because the Dead necessarily agree with everything Billy Sunday said — but simply because the book is the world's most influential work of literature.

For instance, the first book of the Bible, Genesis, gets a thorough treatment. *Greatest Story*'s main characters are Abraham and Isaac ("sittin' on a fence"). Abraham is the man that God picked to father the Jewish nation, and Issac is his son.

Isaac's two children were Jacob and his twin brother Esau. Older by a few minutes, Esau was a rough, burly hunter, and his father Isaac's favorite. ("Our father favored Esau . . . ") Isaac's wife Rebekah, though, preferred Jacob, who was quiet, shrewd, and lived at home.

As the oldest son, Esau was entitled to Issaac's final blessing (an event of legal and financial importance). As Isaac, nearly blind, lay dying, Jacob went to him, and pretended to be Esau. Disguising himself as the hairy Esau, Jacob covered his arms with goatskins. Unable to see, Isaac felt the goatskins, thought they were Esau's hairy arms, and gave Jacob the blessing intended for Esau.

Jacob's mother knew that Esau would kill Jacob when Esau found out about the trick, so she sent Jacob away on a 500 mile journey. On the trip, Jacob lay down by the side of the road to sleep, and used a stone for his pillow. (Remember the line from *Black Muddy River*, "when I can't tell my pillow from a stone.") Jacob dreams of a ladder which reaches from earth to heaven. At the top of the ladder is the Lord, who promises Jacob he will protect him, and that Jacob's numerous descendants shall be a blessing to all people of the Earth. Thus the lines: "Before the killing was done, his inheritance was mine . . . Sometimes at night I dream he's still that hairy man, shadow-boxing the apocalypse, and wandering the land."

Conflict between brothers also appears in *Mississippi Half-Step*, where "they say that Cain caught Abel, rolling loaded dice." In Genesis, Cain and Abel were the children of Adam and Eve; Cain killed Abel because the Lord liked Abel better.

Thinking about the Dead's historical and literary roots does help a person understand them on some new levels. What's most important about the Dead, however, is an experience that transcends culture, history, and even language.

John Barlow expresses this thought in *Let It Grow*, with a reference to one of man's sillier attempts to apply reason to the things that are beyond reason. During the middle ages, religious scholars had debated how many angels could fit on the head of a pin. (Possible answers: one, since a pin is so small; three, for the holy Trinity; or an infinite number, because angels don't take up any space.) Barlow asks, "What shall we say, shall we call it by a name? As well to count the angels dancing on a pin."

When God appeared to Moses in a burning bush, Moses asked God his name, and God replied, "I AM WHO I AM." Instead of trying to name the unnameable, Barlow suggests we look at the "Water bright as the sky from which it came. And the name is on the earth that takes it in, will not speak but stand inside the rain, and listen to the thunder shout 'I AM, I AM, I AM, I AM!' "

Inside the Grateful Dead, we can all shout "I AM." We can find out that we are the eyes of the world, and by looking through and beyond the Dead's lyrics and the Dead experience, open ourselves to the world's possibilities ∎

Samson & Delilah    **Artwork by Gary Kroman**

May/June, 1988

Vol. 15
No. 3

$3.00

65463

# Relix

music for the ~~head~~

**GRATEFUL DEAD
LYNYRD SKYNYRD
COUNTRY
JOE McDONALD**

# THE DINOSAURS

*Peter Albin, Barry Melton,
Merl Saunders, Spencer Dryden,
John Cipollina*

*HOT TUNA
WAVY GRAVY*

Cover Photo
by
Chris Fallo

*Zero, Living Earth,
Frank Zappa and more. . .*

*Photo Courtesy Sumertone Records*

# Merl Saunders

## by Jeff Tamarkin

**M**ERL Saunders might be the newest member of the Dinosaurs — he joined a few years ago when Robert Hunter opted to leave — but he's no latecomer to the San Francisco music scene itself. Although most Dinosaurs fans probably got their first taste of Saunders' jazz-influenced keyboard work in the early '70s, when he teamed up with Jerry Garcia in the first of a series of club bands that would keep them working hard whenever Garcia wasn't on the road with the Grateful Dead, Saunders had already been a professional musician for some 15 years by that time. Long before bands like the Jefferson Airplane, Big Brother and the Holding Company, Quicksilver Messenger Service, Country Joe and the Fish and the Grateful Dead were formed, Saunders was learning his craft and applying it in working jazz and rhythm and blues groups. With the exception of Spencer Dryden — whose career stretches back as far as Saunders' — the other Dinos were still in high school when Saunders was already on the road.

And even after three decades Saunders has no intentions of resting on his laurels. His lengthy career has already found him working not only with Garcia and the Dinosaurs but with everyone from Miles Davis to Muhammad Ali, as well as scoring television programs and directing the music for stage shows. But Saunders prefers to look forward, not behind him. "I'll be a Dinosaur for awhile," he says, "but I still have the urge to do my own music.

Saunders grew up in San Francisco's Haight-Ashbury district, where he listened to the early rock 'n' roll of the '50s and took an interest in the organ, particularly in the then-uncommon sound of jazz organ. It was in the mid-1950s that Saunders heard the musician whose style would come to influence him permanently, jazz organist Jimmy Smith. "The first time I ever heard of him," Saunders recalls, "I was in Europe and I heard him on the radio in Paris. I'd always dreamed of playing organ and when I heard him I said this is the guy of my dreams. I came back to the U.S. in 1957 and one of my friends told me there

was this organ player in L.A. named Jimmy Smith and I jumped up and down."

Saunders went to L.A. to hear Smith play and met up with him after the gig. A month later, Saunders was taking organ lessons from Smith. "He showed me how to sit at the organ, how to relax, how to breathe and how to use my hands and feet, how to listen to the bass pedals." It wasn't long before Saunders was earning money himself as a jazz organist — even if he was only taking home $9 a night.

Saunders spent the mid-'60s touring Europe and the Far East with an R&B band. When he returned to San Francisco in 1968, his old neighborhood just wasn't looking the same at all. "It used to be a nice little district," he says with a laugh, "with old ladies and their shopping carts. I was still doing my jazz trio thing, wearing a silk suit. Meanwhile, in the Panhandle [of Golden Gate Park], where my parents lived, there were these rock bands playing loud music. My mom wanted to call the police but I said, 'Don't do that, mom, because I'm going to be down there with them. I'm one of *them* now, mom.' "

In 1968 Saunders started working as the musical director for a play called *Big Time Buck White*, which eventually landed in New York on Broadway — starring Muhammad Ali. Saunders has fond memories of the production, especially of some of the musicians with whom he worked. "I got a 12-piece band together and I wanted to use a particular drummer," he says. "But they wanted to send over this young guy. I said okay, and asked the guy to play a 12-bar blues with me. He played four bars and I told him he was hired. His name was Billy Cobham."

One major fan of the play was Miles Davis, the jazz trumpet great. "He was there every night," Saunders recalls, "and after the show closed he asked me to open for him at the Village Gate [in New York]. Then I got called to do a Harry Belafonte-Lena Horne special out in Las Vegas. I did a couple of albums with Harry Belafonte."

*Photo Courtesy Sumertone Records*

Merl Saunders and Jerry Garcia

Photo Courtesy Fantasy Records

Merl Saunders and Aunt Monk

Photo Courtesy Sumertone Records

Still, Saunders was looking for something more challenging, and he returned to the Bay Area, where he began doing a lot of studio work with blues singer-producer Nick Gravenites. Through Gravenites he met bass player John Kahn and guitarist Mike Bloomfield. And through them, another guitarist, Jerry Garcia. "Jerry was playing some dates at the Matrix in San Francisco and he said to come down and hang out with him — there was already an organ there. That's how it all started. But in the middle of all that, John Kahn got a call from Paul Butterfield in Woodstock asking him to grab Merl Saunders and bring him to Woodstock. That lasted about six months before I got tired of it and moved back. I formed the Merl Saunders Band and Jerry joined it."

With Kahn, former Creedence Clearwater Revival guitarist Tom Fogerty and drummer Bill Vitt (who had worked with the Sons of Champlin), the Saunders-Garcia Band began gigging regularly in Bay Area clubs. "I remember at first there were 15 people at the gig," says Saunders. "Then there'd be 115. Then 215. The next thing I knew some guy would be saying he came from Boston to see us, and I just went 'What!' People started coming from all over the country to hear us play and we just decided to go out on tour."

They also went into the studio. Saunders had had a record contract with Fantasy Records — he recorded a jazz album called Soul Groovin' in 1967, soon to be reissued — and, with Fogerty producing the quintet, they recorded Heavy Turbulence in 1972 (Saunders also contributed to two Fogerty LPs during this period). They cut Saunders originals as well as the Band's "The Night They Drove Old Dixie Down" and John Lennon's "Imagine" and followed that up early the following year with Fire Up, which again combined Saunders' soul-jazz compositions with band workouts on rock classics, this time including J.J. Cale's "After Midnight" and the Soul Survivors' "Expressway (To Your Heart)."

By mid-'73 the band had built up a considerable reputation as a live band and was not only packing clubs in the Bay Area but larger halls back east. The double LP Live At Keystone, recorded in July of that year (by which time Fogerty had left), captured the band at its performing peak at its home base in Berkeley. It also put Garcia in the forefront with Saunders, and some of the guitarist's best improvisational work outside of the Dead can be found on this record.

Featuring such jams as Dylan's "Positively 4th Street" and "It Takes A Lot To Laugh, It Takes A Train To Cry," the Rodgers and Hart standard "My Funny Valentine," the Arthur Crudup-by-way-of-Elvis rockabilly-blues classic "That's All Right, Mama" and the Byrds' "It's No Use," the LP has long been out of print. Until now, that is — Fantasy has just reissued it on vinyl and CD. And even better news: two new volumes from the same sessions, Keystone Encores Volume 1 and 2, have joined them in the racks. Now for the first time, those who don't already own the tapes can hear how the group handled Smokey Robinson's "I Second That Emotion," Marvin Gaye's "How Sweet It Is" and six more blues and soul tunes, reworked into Saunders-Garcia excursions.

The Saunders-Garcia bands went through numerous changes in the next few years, even taking on a few different names (Legion Of Mary, Aunt Monk, Reconstruction). Vitt left and was replaced by Elvis Presley's drummer, Ron Tutt, and at one point they even worked with a horn section. But eventually it was time to move on and the Garcia-Saunders collaboration ran its course. Those who attended the 1975 S.N.A.C.K. benefit concert in San Francisco did get one special treat during this period, however, when Saunders played onstage with the full Grateful Dead for one all-too-brief appearance (playing "Blues For Allah").

Since then Saunders has been keeping busier than ever on a number of diverse projects. He's recorded a few albums on his own and has moved into television work, scoring children's programs and working with the Dead on the music for the revived Twilight Zone. He even toured Europe with folk singer Buffy Sainte Marie — along with his sons Tony and Merl Jr.

He was working with Dead lyricist Robert Hunter on the Twilight Zone project when Hunter mentioned he was going to be leaving the band he had been playing with, the Dinosaurs. "The next day," says Saunders, "the Dinosaurs called and asked me to replace Hunter. It was a big joke between Hunter and I but I said I was going to try it because I liked working with John Cipollina and the guys. I'd played with Country Joe and Barry Melton on some benefits and I'd done some jamming with the Dinosaurs so I started playing with them for awhile. I was going to quit because I had other things I was working on, but they said they'd limit the playing to two or three times a month, and I've been with them ever since."

It was early this year when the Dinosaurs finally ventured to the East Coast, to play a concert at the Saint — in the building that once housed the Fillmore East. Days later, Saunders is discussing the show. He's saying that he was surprised at the audience's reaction. "It was kind of reserved," he says. "We're used to seeing people dance, and seeing two or three thousand people staring at you kind of overwhelmed me. They couldn't believe us and we couldn't believe them."

But why not? It's been a long time since Dinosaurs have ruled the earth. ∎

**Artwork by Mike Zmuda**

# Editorial

From Volume 15, Number 6
December, 1988

THE most crucial topic of our day is not how to act at a Dead show (although this is a matter of concern that touches close to home), but what is becoming of our environment. Thanks to the Grateful Dead, we have become more aware of the devastation in store for us with the destruction of the rainforests. Yet, there are so many other ways that we are being affected through shear neglect and stupidity.

It would be easy to sit back and say, "What can I possibly do that will matter in the scheme of things?", and do nothing. There is so much we can each do as individuals. It all starts at home. The easiest part is to just become aware. Some of the little things we can do could make a big difference.

When you get your garbage together after a day, do you ever wonder where it's going? This can become an obsessing horror, but with a little forethought, you'd be amazed at how much less waste you create when you face the end result. Recycle bottles and jars — if they're deposit bottles, return them. If they're disposable, don't dump them, re-use them! Re-use your plastic containers as well. Plastics are not biodegradable, and plastic bags are creating some unique dumping problems. They have recently begun making plastic bags out of cornstarch. These are biodegradable, so ask for them in local stores. I am searching out the manufacturer and will pass this on in a future issue.

Other environmental hazards are a little less obvious. Styrofoam is made with the use of flourocarbons which is the biggest culprit destroying our ozone layer. Fast food restaurants insist on using styrofoam containers to this day, even with this clear threat to our planet! Keep your car together. Automobile fumes are a major polluting factor. And what about cigarette smoking? Think about the number of cigarettes smoked each day — that much tobacco smoke must be doing something towards increasing our environmental problems, not to mention what it is doing to you and me. Parents who smoke in their homes increase the chances of respiratory ailments in their children by about 80%, so if you won't stop for yourselves, think of their health.

Don't buy exotic woods (like teak or mahogany). Much of this is taken from the rainforests. Fast food beef is in large part grazed on land that was once a rainforest. And to make matters worse, that land can only be used for grazing for eight years before if becomes useless even for that. A rainforest can't grow back. Not only does the rainforest account for much or all of the air we breathe, it is believed that the cures for our most dreaded diseases will one day be found there. Many current remedies were discovered in rainforests. Moreover, rainforests capture, store and recycle rain, thus preventing floods, drought and soil erosion. They also serve to regulate local and global climates. And what about the creatures living there? It is said that if you spent one day in a rainforest, you would discover a previously undocumented species of life. Rainforests are the traditional home of hundreds of thousands of indigenous tribal people. These unique cultures depend on the rainforests for food and shelter.

This might all seem a bit heavy, but the situation has gotten progressively worse and it just can't be ignored any longer. In order for us to celebrate many new years, take warning. Take part. It's up to you. Education is our best defense. By learning all you can and passing the word, we can't avoid helping the situation. It's up to us to help the ignorant abusers as well as ourselves.

In the late sixties, there was so much consciousness raising, and our environment was of major concern. Somewhere along the line, the issue was put aside (not forgotten, as I'm sure it lurked in the back of many minds, just scratching the surface of reason). But here it is, we are now faced with a problem that has grown twenty years worse. And it affects us all, including our children and their childrn.

It is a proven statistic that at the rate we are destroying our environment, there won't be a habitable place on earth within one hundred years!

Sincerely,
Toni A. Brown

Hey Now! I have just sent off my letters to 4 organizations asking for info on the rainforests. Your editorial certanly "gave my ass a kick." I love the Dead, and with their help and by helping myself I have learned to love this world. I was very saddened by your editorial, but I know that you are telling the truth. I attend a small, conservative Catholic (I'm not Catholic, but what the hell?) University so hopefully I will find ways to inform people there. I would like to be a teacher so I may continue to keep people informed and I want to make the world a better place for everyone.

Jennifer Hipple
West Chester, PA

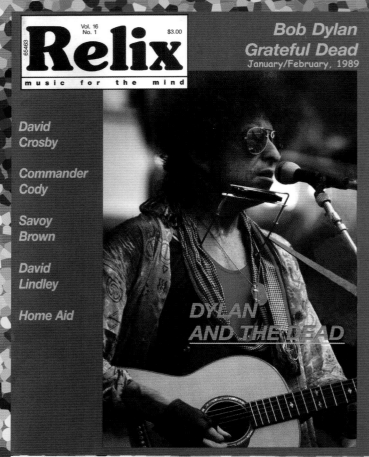

**Relix** Vol. 16 No. 1 $3.00
65463
*music for the mind*

Bob Dylan
Grateful Dead
*January/February, 1989*

David
Crosby

Commander
Cody

Savoy
Brown

David
Lindley

Home Aid

DYLAN
AND THE DEAD

Cover Photo by Tommy Noonan/Artist Publ.

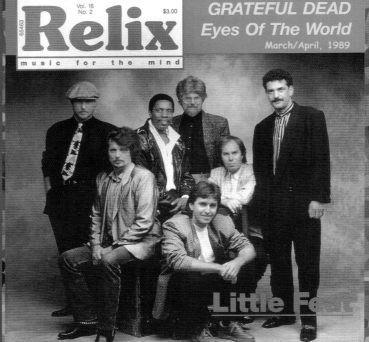

**Relix** Vol. 16 No. 2 $3.00
65463
*music for the mind*

GRATEFUL DEAD
Eyes Of The World
*March/April, 1989*

Little Fear

Interviews with *Frank Zappa*
*Mickey Hart* on World Music
*Henry Kaiser*
*and much, much more!*

Cover Photo Courtesy Warner Brothers Reords

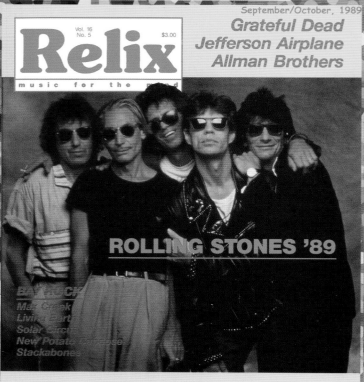

**Relix** Vol. 16 No. 5 $3.00
*music for the mind*

*September/October, 1989*
Grateful Dead
Jefferson Airplane
Allman Brothers

ROLLING STONES '89

BAY ROCK
Max Creek
Living Earth
Solar Circus
New Potato Caboose
Stackabones

Also: Underground Comix Artists
S.F. Poster Artists
World Music
and more!

Cover Photo Courtesy CBS Records by Dimo Safari

**Relix** Vol. 16 No. 3 $3.00
65463
*music for the mind*

*May/June, 1989*
GRATEFUL DEAD
SPRING TOUR

SUMMER '89
QUICKSILVER
RADIATORS
DICKEY BETTS

Cover Artwork by Patrick Moran

Comic by Stephen Martin

Artwork by M. Wysochanski

## FROM THE FRONT

Some friends and I attended the Sept. 30 and Oct.1 Dead shows at the Shoreline Amphitheatre in Mountain View, CA. with Saturday's show even better than Friday's (we hadn't planned to stay). Also, the Deadheads were a beautiful experience in themselves: dancing, hugging, filled with love.

So here's my complaint: The personnel at Shoreline were beyond rude; more than just unfriendly. They were just plain mean! One girl in a blue jacket (these stormtroopers wore blue or yellow jackets) was screaming hysterically "Go home! Get out of here!" We were none of us idiots, we understood there was no overnight camping, but they seemed to expect 40,000 people to be gone in 2 minutes. I saw 3 staff gang up on a lone deadhead. The staff had told him to leave, to "go someplace you can take a shower." Another staff member asked us to "walk in the road, you F'in' druggies, so the cars can hit you."

I have been mistreated and insulted before, but never like at this show. I can't believe the Dead accept or condone this behavior. I would only put up with it for a Dead show. As a journalist, I was outraged. As a customer, I was indignant. As a Deadhead, I was saddened. Please let the world know of this outrageous behavior. I know I'm not the only one who feels compelled to tell the story.

Robert Blacksmith
Davis, CA

I am writing this letter in an attempt to find some kind of solution to an age old dilemma. I was at the Landover show and in one day a boy was trampled by a police horse (the policeman left him there without so much as asking if he needed help), and another boy was beaten by 3 policemen and 1 policewoman. He didn't strike back once, and even tried to get in a car and leave, but he was dragged back by the police and beaten some more. I realize I do not know all of the circumstances, but if what this boy did was that bad, why didn't they arrest him? They didn't. We keep getting letters from the Dead telling us to be cool, and I whole heartedly agree, we do need to be cool. There has been too much trouble and trashing by some "heads." But I've seen kids handcuffed for saying something to a cop. I fully sympathize with that, knowing these cops are intimidated by 10,000 "freaky" kids. But is this reason for being beaten?

Come, wash the night time clean
Come, grow this scorched ground green
Donna Jean McGuigan
Hbg., PA

After reading some of these incredible, insulting and ugly letters from some of my fellow "Deadheads," I am compelled to write. It's all about this "problem" that the Grateful Dead have. Well, boys and girls, I'm here to tell you the problem isn't with the band, it's with the sad ignorant people who feel that they have to consume 19 beers on the way to the concert, 19 beers in the parking lot, 19 beers after the show, then proceed to trash the concert area, puking, pushing, screaming, stealing, passing out, and in general, looking, acting and smelling like a complete asshole! Don't get me wrong, I'm all for partying, but haven't you people ever heard of the word moderation?

August West
Newport, NH

I went to all three shows at Laguna Seca and I'd like to thank the Grateful Dead once again for a great time.

I was one of the thirty or so people who saw that note and decided to stay after the third show to clean up the place. I personally stayed inside until 9:45 pm, as several others did, filling trashbags and helping out. It was really great to look back around and see what was a real dirty scene looking so immaculate. I know the people there were happy.

When I left the inside, I spent another six hours or so (hey, I was on a roll) picking up trash outside. The other heads were all very supportive and lots of people joined in with help and/or encouragement. The Laguna Seca people kept seeing me and they all expressed some good feelings too.

When my ride woke up around dawn to take me back to Berkeley I felt great. Still, upon leaving I noticed that the outskirts of the show (from the lot to about 2 miles out) looked filthy. It's a shame more of us didn't take time to clean up after ourselves. Maybe more trashbags should have been handed out in those areas.

I will help out the cleanup efforts in the future (the winter shows will probably be my next) and I hope more people get into it so that those of us who do won't wake up sore!

Daisy Rainwolf-Roberts
Plainfield, VT

At the Cap. Centre shows in Landover, I saw my worst nightmare. No, it wasn't ruthless scalpers selling tickets for $75 a piece, although I saw that too. No, it was what I believe to be an even lower form of life — a guy selling bootlegs. I had heard about this practice before, but being naive and trusting, I never believed anyone would actually do such a thing.

This is a plea for all Deadheads to put an end to this type of practice. This guy, and others like him, obviously care nothing about the Dead and Deadheads and what we stand for. I don't know of anyone who would deny a fellow Deadhead access to his or her tape collection. No one should have to pay for what the Dead allow us to have for free! They are generous enough to allow taping sections for all their shows — something no other group allows. People like this bootlegger may force them to take this privilege away from us — if we don't put him out of business first. PLEASE boycott bootleggers and scalpers — they are a disease amongst us that threatens the whole Grateful Dead community.

Anne Riddle
Denver, CO

I am amazed at the number of animals I see at shows lately, especially dogs. I have nothing against animals, I'm an ardent animal lover. But the majority of animals I see at the shows are unleashed and very confused. The number of people who ask me if I've seen Rover or Spot blows my mind. At Landover this year I saw a dog get hit by a car in the parking lot. At Philly, I spoke to a girl who had with her an 8-week old puppy. While she was in the show, she was leaving the puppy locked inside a car. I don't know if anyone realized, but that is illegal, inhumane, and it was pretty cold outside.

It seems to be some sort of cool to bring an animal to a show. Please, if you love your pet, leave it home. These animals cannot fend for themselves, they aren't civilized enough to stay out of traffic, and don't know enough to meet you back at the car after the show. In essence, when you bring an animal to a show, you bring an infant. Heads, think twice about it, show your animal love and respect and leave it safe at home. We all need to look out for one another, some living creatures need a little more help.

Denise
Maryland State DH

I have just returned from the frontlines — the ticket lines that is — and I'm pleased to report that the news is primarily peaceful and good, at least from the Big Apple.

Even the early bird may not get the worm when it comes to tickets these days. Luck plays a larger and larger role and folks are at the mercy of whether or not a ticket machine feels like functioning. I got to my local Ticketmaster at noon the day before tickets went on sale and found myself 4th in line. The day and night went by enjoyably and the only discomfort I experienced beside the hard pavement was the weird sensation I got from being the oldest person on line by a good fifteen years. I guess most Deadheads of my vintage have come to the realization that sleeping on the sidewalk is crazy. Tickets went on sale at 9 am on the dot after a minor hassle with some scalpers who had to be shown the end of the line. I was able to get my tickets, but it may be time for me to step aside and let the kids have their fun. Never again....until the next time.

Ted Bowen

I am writing about something of great concern to me and to (I hope) the whole family of Deadheads. Having been a Deadhead for a few years now I had grown to expect a certain level of open-mindedness, tolerance and personal politics from Deadheads, a state of mind quite different from what you normally find among more mainstream kinds of people. Let me also add that I am a Deadhead of color and I am politically active in issues concerning people of color.

Considering all of this, I was surprised, hurt and offended when I went to see Jerry on Halloween at the Kaiser (a miraculous show for me, incidentally) and saw several white guys in blackface with fake dreadlocks on. I don't know how many folks were dressed this way — I stopped counting at 4 or 5 because I was having such a good time and didn't want to ruin my evening by dwelling on it just then.

To those guys (I didn't see any women costumed like this) who were dressed this way: Please understand that I am not attacking you. I hope you will be open-minded enough to consider that perhaps you acted out of certain misunderstandings — a misunderstanding of what it means to be Black or Rastafarian, a misunderstanding of what it means to be any person of color, whether Asian or Latino or Native American. Growing up in a racist society, we have all internalized racial misunderstanding. Nobody is exempt. The only thing we can do is try to overcome that internalized racism. Speaking as an Asian American, I realized later that it would not have been nearly so easy for me to ignore it if I had seen even one white person costumed as an Asian person.

I urge all Deadheads to take the personal responsibility to educate themselves on racial/ethnic issues. It does take some effort, but it's too important not to make that extra effort. Take an ethnic studies class if you're in school. Read Invisible Man (Ellison) or This Bridge Called My Back (eds. Moraga & Anzaldua). Look inside yourself and around you. We are living in an increasingly multicultural, multiracial society (especially here in California) and it is everyone's responsibility to work towards a greater understanding of all the implications of such a wonderful mix of peoples and cultures. This includes discovering and appreciating your own roots culture, whether it be Irish, French, Jewish or whatever. (Are those Jews for Jerry buttons still around?)

A Concerned Sister Of Color

Letter To A Scoundrel:
Thanks A Heap For:
1) Breaking into my truck while it was parked outside of the Landover shows.
2) Stealing all of my photography equipment.
3) Stealing my trash bags I intended to hand out. (Why?)
4) Stealing my portfolio which contained 10 years worth of my published writing.
5) Effectively nipping my writing career in the bud.
6) Bumming my head after a particularly magical show, which doesn't seem to come around too often these days.
7) Making my life miserable.

I know you're not reading this but I feel better. Let a Being higher than I forgive you.

Rick Passaro
Hampton, VA

# John Cipollina Remembered

## JOHN CIPOLLINA GOES HOME:
### Notes From A Roadie's Briefcase
### by Kevyn Clark

**Photo by Ed Perlstein**

John wanted me to write this. The last time I saw him sitting backstage at the Catalyst Club in Santa Cruz he and Spencer Dryden were chuckling to themselves about how John had suckered me into helping the other roadies change his broken guitar string. "You'll always be a roadie," he told me, "Unless you get your book done and really retire from this crap." He was talking about 'True Tales From The Next To Last Tour,' a book he helped inspire during several short jaunts and a couple of longer stays out in America, walking the rock 'n' roll beast on tour.

I met John long before I started working for him. I was hustling a tape for some band I knew and gave him a copy at some Dead show. Two years later, he still bugged me about it because I used to give his roadies a hard time when the Dinosaurs were first cranking up, and we didn't see eye to eye. "Are you still pushing disco music?" he would ask. I usually countered with "So, you still trying to play guitar?" I was, in his words, "A monkey on [his] back." Only after he saw that I wasn't going to give in, did he finally accept me. I still bugged him about it though, asking who his favorite monkey was every time he walked out on stage to play.

John seemed to be afraid at times. Not scared, Cipollina wasn't scared of anything, but he was leery of the people that worked for him. Too many prized guitars or amps had disappeared after roadies or friends decided the equipment was worth more to them than John. Nothing pissed him off more. At his studio, he would tell me stories about the guitars and other equipment lying around, then shake his head sadly and whisper, "There used to be a hell of a lot more."

John was also saddened by the fact that his fans sometimes missed the point he was trying or not trying to make at any given time. After gigs, sitting around in hotel rooms, we'd talk about how hard it was doing and being the way people expected you to be. "I'd rather trade fucking recipes than talk about the good old days with Quicksilver sometimes." He was put off too by the rumors and remarks passed along by his so-called adoring fans. Too many times some kid would ask if John remembered some off-the-wall time and place where the two of them allegedly did some inhuman amount of drugs or re-wrote sexual history, and John would answer by saying "No, but I'm sure you do." I remember when the demands, favors, and questions overpowered him and he would ask me to keep him away from the crowd. "Tell them to leave me alone." It seemed to me that too many people knew John, or had a piece of him that he wanted back but couldn't afford to buy. Sometimes he just seemed tired of it all. "These people want to see John Cipollina, not me." It wasn't that he didn't give; when he

played, he did it for those who came to listen. But still, he sometimes felt that the point was missed, misconstrued. The show was always important, but there was always something more. He used to joke about how badly he wanted to walk out on stage one night and do a puppet show while wearing a clown suit. He gave me a red rubber nose one night and told me to wear it at the appropriate time.

I let John down a few times during our relationship. Usually when things got too heavy for me, I'd split, leaving some dork (Dr. Waldo and some others excluded) holding the bag for the Dinosaurs. When I'd return, John would tear into me about leaving him with some idiot who couldn't tune his guitars or fix his amps. I'm sorry, John, you know how it is sometimes.

I came out of retirement the other night and attended a memorial gig at The Chi-Chi club in San Francisco. I was curious to see what would happen, and came away thinking that John would have been laughing. Not because he was cruel and saw humor in peoples' sorrow, but more so because no one could seem to grasp the reason for being there. Yes, to pay homage; sure, to relive the good times, but still, why?

John is dead. I know he's happy. I'm sure he got back the $15.00 he'd loaned Hendrix all those years ago, but I'm positive he'd want everyone to lighten up; things ain't that serious. Put on those big floppy shoes and red rubber noses, man. I'm wearing the one John gave me. I'm sure he'd ask the same of you.

## JOHN CIPOLLINA
### 1943–1989
### by Greg Anton

When John checked into a hotel room where he'd be staying for more than a few days, the first thing he'd do was carefully remove the thin white paper band that was stretched across the toilet seat and deftly place it in an empty drawer, out of harms way.

Just before he checked out he would expertly replace the strip and wait around for the maid or someone to notice. Chances are, the maid, still off balance from the unused toilet, would flick on the unused T.V. and the picture tube would be upside down.

John had those extra long, ultra-thin, guitar calloused fingers. Musicians' hands. Delicate instruments that he loved taking to their limit performing delicacies like the toilet seat caper

John would chuckle about something like that for days. And talk about it for years. He loved to talk. He loved fun. He revered quality. And he hated sushi.

He cared deeply about people and what they cared about, and exhibited an abiding kindness towards everyone around him. He had a profound respect for his audience and was adamant about being truthfully represented.

At John's funeral, a priest said that everyone who knew him had a unique and different relationship with him. Everyone fortunate enough to have that relationship truly cherished it.

J.C. Triple Virgo. The Quintessential Rock and Roll Gentleman: guns, girls, guitars, ganja. Lucky Strikes, and a lifetime subscription to the National Enquirer.

He worshipped bats, drove a bloodmobile, and filed his teeth.

He played guitar with Jimi Hendrix, Pete Townshend, Charles Manson, Groucho Marx, and the Governor of New Jersey.

Totally nocturnal, nighttime was John's habitat. Going by waking hours, John was 100 when he died. He never wanted to miss anything. "I'll sleep when I'm dead," he said.

He'd been known to fall asleep with his fingerpicks on.

John Cipollina was one of the finest people that has ever lived. Everyone who knew him knows that.

*(Greg Anton, drummer with Zero, has recorded six albums with John and performed with him for the past 15 years.)*

**Comic by Stephen Martin**

July/August, 1989
Vol. 16
No. 4
$4.00
65463
Relix
music for
WOODSTOCK
JIMI HENDRIX
JOHNNY WINTER
JANIS
BACK BY POPULAR DEMAND
ANNIVERSARY
'89
Robert Bryson 89

# PART FOUR

# GRATEFUL DEAD

# IN THE DARK

e stars were aligned for *In the Dark*. It was played on the radio . . . often! That hadn't
pened with a Grateful Dead record before. It was apparent that something was
ferent even before the album was released. Videos were planned, and there was actua
motion being done by Arista Records, unlike other Grateful Dead releases that had
ne and gone with little fanfare.

The Dead were doing well at the time, playing the biggest venues they could, selling
every show. But no one anticipated the surge that would follow because there was no
nt of reference for the signs of "success."

"Touch of Grey," the first Grateful Dead single to hit the charts, sparked the
lective media's attention. Add to that the colorful story of the traveling circus known
Deadheads, and the culture became the biggest buzz of its time. The media blitz fueled
already problematical scene, provoking friction amongst the band's veteran fans and
newcomers. Tickets became scarce, blatant drug use increased, the ticketless throng
w, and more episodes of violence emerged. Many venues closed their doors to us, the
king lot scene was suspended, and, most significantly, Deadheads became targeted by

# Grateful Dead
# Spring Tour
## 1989

by Steve Clark and John Grady

**S**PRING 1989 found the Grateful Dead bringing musical magic back down to Dixie. For 16 nights spread over three and a half weeks, the spontaneous San Francisco six-some rocked and rolled across the land.

Ever-growing numbers of fans shook, bopped and danced to the inspiring sounds of the Dead in large halls and arenas, many of which the band hadn't been back to in more than 15 years.

This year's version of the annual springtime Dead outing opened with two dates, March 27 and 28, Atlanta, Georgia. Touring through Southeast cities, the band made its way out west to Ann Arbor, Michigan and Milwaukee, Wisconsin, ending on April 17 in Minneapolis, Minnesota.

While thousands of fans on the tour were enjoying the "Good Lovin'" of the Dead, many fans in the Northeast were surprised and disappointed to find out that the closest city their favorite band would play in during this 1989 spring tour was Pittsburgh, Penn.

But with the track record of past spring tours, changing concert locations was a necessary and logical move.

During the past few years the number of Grateful Dead fans and followers has wildly increased. More and more vendors and campers, following the band from city to city, are creating problems. These range from simple parking and congestion to serious altercations with police and security.

Because of this, Dead Heads are no longer welcome in Hartford, Conn., Worcester, Mass., and Portland, Me.—all stops on previous spring Grateful Dead tours.

With the band still growing in popularity, the "sunny side of the street may be dark" (to paraphrase "Shakedown Street").

Mixed reports from the band's Southern tour prove Dead-mania is still spreading and, while there are hopeful signs developing within the explosion, a few "Dead-enders," with their irresponsible behavior in some places, are giving a bad name to all Dead Heads. These black sheep within the GD family may accomplish what time has not: take the band off the road.

On Sunday night, April Fool's Day, at the first of the two shows in Pittsburgh, lax security led to a large rush of the gates.

The next night, police tightened up and increased their ranks only to be engaged in a fracas with more than 500 unruly gate-crashers. Bottle throwing was responded to with Mace, billy clubs and many arrests. Bad news travels fast and the "riots" were highlighted on MTV.

At a news conference the next day, Pittsburgh mayor Sophie Masloff said "I don't want those 'Dead-enders' ever back again. The band is fine, but those people who follow them around are not."

Pull another welcome mat out from under the dancing skeletons and bears.

Arrests, violence, complaints, theft, drug abuse and more continue to cancel out places that the Dead can perform.

Dennis McNally, author and longtime publicist of the Grateful Dead recently said, "Vending and camping are killing the Grateful Dead. . . we are in danger of going up in flames from our own success."

What he is referring to is not vending and camping per se, but their effect on Grateful Dead concert logistics.

Since the band's beginning, artists and craftspeople selling their wares have always been part of the GD phenomenon. However, since 1985 the ranks of vendors have increased dramatically.

At the same time, so have the legions of Dead Heads. Thousands of people will show up at concerts without tickets knowing that, if they can't get a ticket on the street, they can at least party in the adjacent marketplace.

Most venues are not prepared, and are unable to understand and deal with this type of impromptu street party. Very few, if any, other rock groups today draw more concertgoers than tickets sold. This situation is unique to the Dead.

But new models for success on the latest tour, such as the smooth and relaxed Louisville, Ky. show—where everyone was happy and the city made money—are offering hopeful signs amid the confusion. And after years of taking a free ride on the Grateful Dead train, there are signs that the vendors themselves may try and take over some of the responsibility for their own activities.

Promoters this year have been trying to make arrangements for the legions of Dead Heads who follow the tour. These efforts have resulted in mixed degrees of success. The disaster in Pittsburgh was followed by the overwhelming success of Louisville. Most Dead shows are run well, with about as much impact as a normal stadium-sized sports event will have. As always, it is the small splinters that grab attention and cause the most pain.

In Greensboro, N.C., promoters worked with Coliseum officials to set up campgrounds in one of the parking lots. However, to use the campground you needed a ticket to one of the shows. According to Bailey Hobgood, director of public relations for the Coliseum, a lot of the "ticketless" just slept out in the surrounding, fairly middle-class neighborhood.

Hobgood was quoted as saying, "We did the right thing for the ticket holders and we thought they did right by us. We got nothing but good reports from the people they had contact with in stores and restaurants. They kept commenting on how gracious and polite the Dead Heads were."

But, according to Hobgood, the 1000 or so ticketless urban campers that came along for the ride, created problems and complaints from the citizens in the neighborhood. Once again, it's those who show up for concerts without tickets who are spoiling it for the rest.

At the next stop on the tour, Pittsburgh, the problems got worse—much worse. These concerts were the closest ones to the Northeast, the hottest bed of Dead-Headism.

The back-to-back shows were the first to sell out and attracted the largest crowds. As many as 5,000 people showed up without tickets to either show.

Many of these so-called Dead Heads have taken to gate crashing as a sanctioned activity at sold-out concerts. There should be no question in any Dead Head's mind about gate-crashing (see Dead Ethics sidebar). It is and always has been taboo. Those who instigate such behavior should be run out of town on a rail.

It seems that a lot of Dead Heads think nothing of driving hundreds of miles in hopes of scoring a ticket. Isn't anyone listening to the

Photo by John Rottet

Greensboro

band's pleas? How many times do they have to buy radio air time and implore fans to stay home if you don't have a ticket?

The Dead were halfway through the tour as they rolled down Highway 75 for two consecutive one night stands in Cincinnati and Louisville, respectively.

As the vendors filtered into Cincinnati in search of a location for their tie-dye bazaar, they were met with some confusion on the part of officials who bounced them around like pinballs from one parking lot to another in a cold rain. They finally settled at the Union terminal parking lot—the city approved camp ground.

The Cincinnati officials had done their homework by contacting Pittsburgh authorities. In spite of the problems there, Cincinnati police were told to expect a crowd that is basically non-violent but "into partying."

Security who doubled at the Riverfront Coliseum where, ever since the 1979 Who concert debacle when 11 concert fans were crushed to death while trying to get inside, crowd control has been an utmost priority.

A handful of undercover detectives posing as Dead Heads filtered through the crowd making numerous drug-related arrests. More than 40 persons were arrested and most were charged with drug trafficking or possession.

Sgt. Larry Hale, second shift supervisor at the Intake Section of the Hamilton County Justice Center was quoted as saying, "This is the largest number of arrests I can remember within such a short span of time at any concert here."

Prior to showtime, hundreds of people hung out, looking for their "miracle" tickets, holding up signs and fingers. Word was out that bogus tickets were abundant and scalpers wanted $125 a ticket.

Meanwhile, after its shaky opening, the tie-dye marketplace was booming at Union Terminal. The vendors had set up on the bottom floor of the multi-leveled parking lot and were protected from the damp, raw weather outside.

Well after the show began, a few thousand people milled about, checking out the various concessions or bouncing to the impromptu and endless percussion sessions.

Enter Louisville! Formula for Success.

Louisville is a city that's used to crowds. Every spring the city hosts two weeks of "Derby Days" prior to the Kentucky Derby. Anyone who is familiar with horse racing can tell you. Derby Heads can party down with the best of them.

The Kentucky Fairgrounds and Exposition Center are on the outskirts of the city. Its huge parking lots are separated by large areas of green (or is it blue) grass.

The city's Mayor Abrahmson is noted for his liberal attitudes toward accommodating ideas that will stimulate the local economy. The city of Louisville owns and operates the Fairgrounds on which sits Freedom Hall—an 18,000 seat basketball arena.

Promoters and fairground officials worked hard and well together to prepare for the arrival of the GD entourage.

Beginning at midnight after the Cincinnati show (about 90 minutes away from Louisville), the fairgrounds opened a parking lot and grassy camping area, complete with a clean water supply and 30 porta-potties. A $10 entry fee per vehicle allowed its occupants to stay till 10 a.m., the day following the show. No tickets were required to gain entry to the fair grounds or camping area.

The media had done an exceptional job as well in preparing the local citizens and businesses on what to expect. The Louisville Courier-Journal had sent two staff members to the Greensboro concert for photographs and reports on Dead Head behavior.

So when the 18,000 fans rolled into Louisville on Sunday morning and afternoon, the stage had been set.

The vendors found exceptionally good conditions. Many took advantage of the camping opportunity to arrive early and stake out their turf.

By 2 p.m., the parking lots were full and the tie-dye bazaar was a sea of faces. The weather was cool but sunny and a fresh wind was blowing. Although official Fairground rules prohibit alcohol on the premises, no attempt was made to enforce them. Buck a beer concessions popped up out of car trunks like mushrooms.

Back at central police command, a casually dressed undercover detective offered his opinion. "This is a well-behaved crowd," he said. "We expect very few problems."

The Courier Journal reported the next day that only 17 people had been arrested, mostly on public intoxication or drug charges.

Access to Freedom Hall, unfortunately, was limited to two gates, making it a major ordeal to pass through the doors. There is no doubt that this measure was taken to prevent gate crashing. There was some confusion because mail order tickets and those from Ticketron were being checked separately. An unusually large amount of bogus GDTS mail-order tickets had surfaced on this tour.

Once inside, the security was strict, with ushers at every entry and aisle. Cautious and helpful, they insured that concertgoers found their seats.

The show started only a few minutes late and ended around 11:30 p.m. As the throngs of happy faces floated back out to the parking lot everything was peaceful. The noticeable absence of fireworks, rowdy hoots and howls was perhaps related to the band's soulful but mellow performance. But one cannot deny the influence of an entire day of cooperation within the Dead Head community itself.

That night, Al Caldwell, vice president of fairgrounds operations, told the Courier Journal, "I'll tell you right now, I'd do this show again. I'd do it tomorrow."

Of a half dozen vendors interviewed in Cincinnati, all felt there were a lot more people selling wares this spring than on last summer's tour. All were feeling new and heavier competition.

Erin Murphy, from San Francisco, has been selling tie-dyes in the wake of the band for five years. On Saturday night in Cincinnati, she stood shivering beside her wide range of rainbow-spiraled clothing layed out carefully on a blanket on the damp pavement of Union Terminal.

"I'm not sure it's worth it," she said. "We're encountering more and more hassles. Today we bounced back and forth four times between two parking lots—paying each time we entered—before we were finally allowed to set up shop.

Murphy agreed that the ranks of vendors were larger than ever. She mentioned that some of the larger concessions would resort to unfair and perhaps even underhanded tactics in securing the best locations for their stands.

She said there was talk among some of the fulltime touring concessions of organizing somehow. "We talked about having a concession representative precede the vendors' arrival into any particular town or city."

By working with local officials this rep could secure both camping and vending facilities for the associated concessions. Of equal importance, the rep could secure any permits which are often necessary for sidewalk salespeople.

The logistics of setting a person up in this position would obviously be complicated. Not to mention that he or she would, most likely, need to be paid.

However, in the past five years, these resourceful merchandisers have been riding the coattails of the GD. They have taken little if any responsibility for their collective actions. They have relied on promoters and GDP to accommodate their needs in each city. Now they are in danger of striking down the skeletons with their own lightning bolts.

"Jerry Garcia does not want to be the de-facto mayor of a small, traveling city," says Grateful Dead publicist Dennis McNally.

"The musicians in the Grateful Dead should spend their time on the road practicing their art and making people happy. They shouldn't have to be worried about young fans crashed out in the streets or ending up in jail."

**Brent Mydland**  Photo by Rob Cohn

I'm Uncle Sam, that's who I am! Been hidin' out in a rock & roll band! Shake the hand that shook the hand Of Ferdinand Marcos & the Shah of Iran!

"DEAD GIVE-AWAY" (KODAK 35MM.)

with apologies to ROBERT HUNTER

O.K. FREEZE! KEEP YOUR HANDS WHERE I CAN SEE 'EM!!

HEY, NOW... LET'S SEE WHAT WE GOT HERE...

HEY! THERE'S NOTHIN' IN HERE BUT **FILM!** That's right...

MIND-FUCKED

THAT'S NOT FAIR...

MIKE SWARTZBECK '87 Dedicated to KEVIN CLARK & the heroic Heads of Nassau County

DEAD Vol. 16 No. 6

65464

$3.50

# Relix

music for the mind

## Year-End Issue

# Built To Last:
## An Exclusive Interview with Jerry Garcia

by Steve Peters

Photo by Rob Cohn/DeadImages.com

**W**ITH the release of Built To Last, the Grateful Dead have reached another pivotal point in their career. The new album is the band's first studio effort since 1987's In The Dark, the record that spawned the group's first Top Ten single and finally brought them beyond the realm of devoted Deadheads and into the pop mainstream. While this crossover success garnered the Dead the recognition their fans always knew they deserved, it also brought some unexpected problems. With the band's 25th anniversary just around the corner, some of the venues that have hosted the Dead for years are refusing to invite them back to perform, the result of a number of isolated incidents surrounding certain shows. And with another potential wave of new attention seemingly imminent, there's no telling what the future might hold.

But Jerry Garcia seems to be taking it all in stride. The Grateful Dead has undoubtedly had their share of ups and downs over the past two-and-a-half decades, and their recent surge in popularity is simply the latest excursion in what has indeed been a long, strange trip. With Built To Last, Garcia feels the band has inched closer towards their notion of a record that properly represents what the Dead is all about. "Foolish Heart," a Garcia/Hunter song that is being released as the LP's first single, is an upbeat, irresistible tune that explores the unpredictability of romance. The album also marks the emergence of keyboardist Brent Mydland as one of the Dead's key songwriters, from the tough and rousing "Blow Away" to the tender and affectionate

*"I Will Take You Home." With tentative plans to play in Europe and possibly Russia in 1990, the band is clearly looking forward.*

*The following interview took place in an all-purpose space that the Dead have occupied for almost 15 years, located just across the road from the hotel that is depicted on the cover of the band's* Shakedown Street *album. It was two days after a weekend-long stint at the Shoreline Amphitheater in Mountain View, California, during which the Dead performed "Death Don't Have No Mercy" for the first time since 1970, and exactly four weeks before the new album's Halloween release date.*

**Tell me about what's happened with the band in the two-and-a-half years since** *In The Dark* **was released…**
Oh, I see — you're just going to throw the door open! Well, let's see…we started working on another record about a year-and-a-half ago. We'd been more or less working on this project, but in reality we didn't really start focusing on the record that we finished until about April of this year. We took some stabs at it, 'cause we thought "Well, the last approach that we tried, the *In The Dark* approach, worked really well…"

**Do you mean recording the album live?**
More or less live. So we thought "Well, what we'll do is we'll use that approach again because that seemed to work," but it really didn't work at all. We *tried* it again — we tried at the Marin County Civic Center, and then we did the stretch up at Skywalker Ranch, and what we started to discover was that our material was saying something else about itself and that approach was not going to work on this record, and that we're really looking for something else entirely different. So we screwed around there for about a year, a year-and-a-half, and then right around April we started to get serious and sort of focus in on the record. The material shifted a lot, too. We had a whole bunch of tunes that didn't go on this record, so the whole thing mutated while we were working on it and we ended up with what did come out — which is a good Grateful Dead record.

**A lot of people will probably be surprised to see that Brent has four songs on the record, as opposed to three by you and a pair by Bob…**
You always go with whatever your strong suit is, and in this case it was Brent that had the good songs — I mean, more of 'em. Actually, he had three or four other songs that didn't go on the record, so he had more of everything, generally. These songs are really good. The other ones are actually pretty good, too, the ones that didn't go on. But I think it's more the thing of Brent's getting to be more comfortable with the band. He sees it being as much his band as everybody else's. So it's just the thing of getting over the "new guy" thing.

**Which took about ten years…**
Ten years, right (*laughs*). He's been pretty conservative about getting comfortable in it, but now — I mean this record, it's nice to be able to show off what he can do on a lot of different levels. And his contribution to this record is really outstanding all over. Not just his tunes and vocals, but everything else — all the keyboard parts, and just ideas and general stuff.

**Do you personally find it more difficult to come up with new material these days?**
I've never been a very hot writer, you know? I tend to go in little fits and starts. I mean, if I do three songs a year, that's pretty good for me. I'm not a songwriter. I'm really a guitar player,

sort of, so writing music is not my forte. I'm a default songwriter. I write because you've gotta have new material, and that's one of those things — that's an axiom from back in the '60s, "You have to have original material," and so it sort of fell on me to do it. It's a default position, not something that I actually choose to do. I have never been particularly in love with my own inventions, for one thing. But over the years, working with Hunter, I've sort of gotten to where I'm getting a handle on the craft of songwriting. I don't think I'm a real brilliant songwriter but I get off a couple of good ones occasionally. By good I mean they have enough of whatever a song needs for me to be able to perform them and not feel awfully uncomfortable about it, and that in itself is a big thing.

**Do you write songs with the consideration of how they might work in a live setting?**
No. Sometimes I have a kind of a notion where I sort of imagine the band playing and I sort of imagine the song and the kind of effect that I hope it will have. But usually the idea that I have at the inception of a song is very different from the way the tune turns out. For me, the song that took the most turns on this record was "Foolish Heart." I originally had a sort of Pete Townshend, acoustic guitar kind of rhythm, open strumming…you know, something along those lines as the setting for it. But the way it came out is completely different. It came out something uniquely Grateful Dead-ish. So a lot of times my sense of how a song is supposed to work or how it's supposed to function, even in the live setting — just how it's supposed to work — has no bearing on its ultimate evolution, so I've learned to disregard my own ideas along those lines.

**Has the increase in popularity that occurred when** *In The Dark* **was released leveled out at all?**
Not very much, no. We haven't come to the end of whatever our growth spurt is.

Photo by Kurt Mahoney

**Your popularity has caused some problems, such as ticket demand exceeding supply and not being asked to return to certain venues. Have you come up with any solutions?**

We don't have any solutions. The thing is that by the time they get to us they're ultimatums. They're no longer possibilities, they're *lack* of possibilities. By the time we hear about something — say, the town of Hartford says, "Absolutely not. You can't play here," and we say, "Why not?" "Because of the camping and the vending," and that kind of stuff. We're getting that same rap from nearly everywhere now. There's very few places that welcome the way the shows, the way the audience and so forth, has defined itself previously. It used to be kind of a nice thing, but I guess now it scares people or something. I'm not sure what the objection is, but the point is that there's somebody out there who objects seriously to the way the crowd is. And this is *not* behavioral. I don't know what it is exactly that they don't like. I don't know what they're offended by so badly, but whatever it is it's very offensive to somebody because they're not letting us come back to places. This puts us in a weird situation where now we have to start to try to control the outside world, which is like hey, c'mon. Nobody can do that. The police can't do it — why do we have to do it? It's one of those kind of situations. I really feel that our audience is getting a bad rap that it doesn't deserve. I think probably the only reason that we have problems is because we play more than one night at a place. I mean sporting events, the audiences are way worse. Any professional football game, the audience is way rowdier. So it isn't just the behavior of the audience. I guess it must be the thing of being there for two or three days or whatever. We try to communicate with Deadheads: "Look, we're scaring them. We either have to do this, clean up, behave yourself, park out of town," I don't know what. We can offer suggestions and open up the subject for discussion and hope for some helpful suggestions, and hope that Deadheads will find some other way to define themselves in some other context, though I'm not exactly sure how.

**Next year marks your 25th anniversary. Do you have anything special planned?**
We don't have anything specific planned, except that we know we're going into our 25th year — well, actually, our 26th year. As far as are we going to do anything special, hopefully everything we do is special!

**Besides the** *Dylan And The Dead* **LP, you haven't released a live record in some time. Are there any plans for one soon?**
We recorded the summer and we're recording this autumn tour, so we may cough up a live album. That may be a good 25th anniversary project.

**Can you give me an example of a recent performance that you felt was particularly strong?**
No, not really. Well, Sunday night I kind of liked, down here at Shoreline was pretty neat. And the third night at the Greek Theater that we did not too long ago, that was a good night.

**That's interesting, because I preferred the second night. Goes to show you how subjective it all is…**
Absolutely subjective. I mean, I'm talking about it from my point of view. I have to do it, like — when I go out onstage, I think of it as kind of like being up to bat, you know, what your batting average is. So for me, I judge it from a batting average point of view. "How many times did I try for something and have it work out kind of nice and invisibly?" And when *that* happens, nobody appreciates it but me. 'Cause it sounds like I mean it. It sounds like "Hey, this guy is just

playing competently, he's not playing great." But if you go from the point of view where it starts off from absolutely nothing and I'm inventing it as I go along, if it works out right — if the i's are dotted and the t's are crossed and it's punctuated correctly — it's like a miracle. So from my point of view this stuff is miraculous, but nobody else is able to appreciate how really miraculous it is 'cause nobody is inside me when I'm playing.

**How in touch are you with the Deadheads themselves? Is there any interaction beyond getting onstage and playing?**
Yeah, a certain amount. I don't have meetings with Deadheads on a regular basis, but people do talk to me, and people write to us endlessly. People make known what their feelings are.

**Are the rigors of constant touring taking more of a toll on you as you get older?**
No, it's getting easier in some ways! And we also make every effort to make it as humane as possible, too. I mean, we've already done our tough tours. We had those during the '70s. It's pretty easy to survive it now.

**Are you feeling healthy these days?**
Yeah, pretty good.

**Did you have to find substitutes to replace your previous habits?**
Not really, no. It's kind of like when you've had enough you've had enough, really. For me, it was one of those things that was not that difficult. It was easier than I thought it was going to be. On the other hand, I have no idea how much drug-taking or any of that had to do with my subsequent breakdown. But it's ironic that after I cleaned up, *then* I broke down! (*laughs*) That was weird. It was like "Hey, maybe I was better off on drugs! At least I wasn't dying!" But I'm okay now.

**I wanted to ask you what kind of music you're currently listening to. Do you keep abreast of new things?**
No, I don't keep abreast, but I do listen to new stuff. I've been listening to some interesting music from Martinique, which is a French-speaking island, and this stuff is recorded in France. It's

got some of that Afro-Cuban intensity, but some of that kind of Brazilian sophistication harmonically. It's something in between those two worlds. It's very engaging music, really pretty stuff, and also has a great drive. Other stuff, too — there's some interesting African guitarists, a kind of finger-picking thing with African music that's interesting. I keep up with the bluegrass world some, and I kind of listen to whatever's going on. I spend a lot of time going back and listening to stuff, too. I always go back and listen to Art Tatum and Django Reinhardt, and Miles' [Davis] stuff I listen to all the way through, his whole career. John Coltrane. Ornette Coleman. Mostly it's one of those things where you stumble from one thing to another, and somebody says, "Hey, listen to this. This is really great." Musicians turn you on to stuff.

**The collaborations you did with Ornette on his last album were great. It was really a pleasure to hear you in that kind of setting...**
Yeah, it was interesting to do. I'd love to do more stuff like that.

Artwork by A.R. Klosterman

Continues...

Photo by John Rottet

**Do you have any outside projects in the works? Before we started the interview, you mentioned Edie Brickell...**

Well, it's a trios thing. Rob Wasserman is doing a trios album. His last one was *Duets*. Now he's doing a trios one, and he wants me to do a thing with Edie Brickell. I would love to do it. It would be interesting and fun to do. I like to stay open for things like that. I'm doing some stuff for Merl Saunders, and I did some stuff with Warren Zevon. You know, whenever these things come up, if the time is there — I owe Country Joe McDonald a record, too. I'm supposed to produce one of his records, and if I ever get the time I'd love to do it. I'd love to do more producing if I could. Time is the killer for me. There's not enough time to do all the stuff I want to do.

**It seems like whenever there's down time between Dead gigs, the Jerry Garcia Band pops up. Do you get stir crazy if you're not performing?**

Yeah, I sure do. I like to keep playing.

**How do you relax when you do have time off?**

I go scuba-diving.

**Around here?**

No, in Hawaii usually. That's what I like to do.

**During the Shoreline shows, I thought I noticed some onstage tension between you and Bob, and it made me realize that all of the other so-called "huge" bands — the Stones, the Who — have been forced apart at one time or another by a monumental rift. How has the Dead managed to avoid that? Do tempers ever flare?**

Nah. What's the point? Well, sure, they flare all the time. But it never amounts to anything.

**How do you keep that in check?**

I don't think we could put up with anybody else, to tell you the truth! It's gone past family. It's gone past blood. We've been together and so intimate for so long that it's beyond any other kind of relationship. There's just nothing that quite compares to it. It's who we are, really.

**Does it bother you that sometimes in the straight press, the element of drugs at the shows sometimes overshadows the music?**

No. It's always something. The press is always

**Greensboro Coliseum
North Carolina - March 30, 1989**

looking for a handle other than what it is that you do. If it wasn't drugs — it used to be stuff like the Hell's Angels. They've always had some way to characterize us that didn't have anything to do with our playing. They've always done it, so there's no reason to imagine that it would stop now, or that they would suddenly become fair-minded out of the clear blue sky. But that's the nature of news. You do look for other handles on stuff.

**Do you think the band is getting more respect now as opposed to ten or 15 years ago?**

Yeah, in a way. On some levels, yeah, but I'm sure that'll disappear. It comes and goes in waves. Sometimes it's fashionable to be a

Grateful Dead basher for a couple of years, but we've seen this stuff come and go several times already. It seems to me that there's times when the press approves of us and times when they don't. It kind of goes like that.

**If you had to pick a song that the band currently performs that you could take or leave, what would it be?**

That I could take or leave? You mean preferably leave?

**Yeah.**

You mean a song that I really am tired of? I would say it'd have to be probably — I'm starting to get tired of [some of] the Dylan tunes, but I still love 'em. I think — "Minglewood Blues" probably. We've done that more than is fair and right, you know? I try to get Bob to start doing more of his regular tunes from the past. And he keeps saying, "Well, I'm gonna rewrite the words on this or rewrite the words on that" or something like that, but he never does.

**Out of Bob's songs, are there any that leap to mind as tunes you really enjoy playing?**

Most of his tunes are at least challenging to play. I love "Estimated Prophet." I think that's a wonderful tune. He's really a truly interesting songwriter, Weir is, and his songs are really interesting, too.

**Do you have any final comments about the Grateful Dead in the '90s?**

Well, I hope we get through them the way we did the '80s. Or maybe better. ∎

MOONBEAM IN THE 21ST CENTURY "DEAD DESERT"

DAVID SPORRONG ©1997

# DARK STAR CT 3500 →

## we are everywhere!

DUCKBURG NEWS 1928

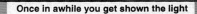

Once in awhile you get shown the light

Toni visits Duckburg News to get the latest publishing tips – Disneyworld '93

Eric with a spectacular find

Brian Gold

Dancin' with Jerry

Monica Young's 14th

BANBURY KING FISH
TEL. 4648
KEBABS BURGERS PIES GRILLS

England

Gerry O'Neill

The Bear Essentials in classwork

Miller Smyth

John Rottet

116

By Pamela Kolb

THANK YOU JERRY

CIVIC

BXO'RAIN

# we are everywhere

Steven Brandon

Jack Straw Farm

TEXAS
AIKO-1
MAY 92

Peace Through Music

John Rottet

In the land of the dark
the ship of the sun
is driven by THE GRATEFUL DEAD
— Egyptian Book of the Dead

David's 21st Birthday

Chuck Jenkins

GARCIA
Kentucky

DEAD FOR LIFE

We don't get a lot of snow in North Carolina, so we go a little crazy when we do

John Rottet

117

Mt. Everest, Nepal

# Sitting on Top of the World

## by Michael Fasman

**M**ISSING all those Dead shows is probably the only thing wrong with traveling around the world for a year. Keeping the spirit alive Down Under, through Asia, the Middle East and Europe wasn't always easy, but once in a while you can get shown a Deadhead in the strangest of places if you look for them right!

After the Tempe August '87 show I headed West. From the beaches of Bali to the Himalayas, there were many times I was reminded of, and missed, the band.

The subject would often come up when travellers commented on the ten tapes accompanying my Walkman: all Dead concerts. "Don't you like other types of music?" they'd ask. "Sure, but everyone else has all the other music, no one has Live Dead!" It's hard enough explaining "our kind" to American non-believers, let alone Europeans with limited English. Being abroad is exciting, but there are countless hours spent on buses or trains, or waiting in bus and train depots. The live tapes made these times go by easier, and often enhanced the setting. "Long Beach 12-13-80" with Flora Purim and Airto accompanying the Rythm Devils was the perfect soundtrack to the jungles of Fiji.

I met my first Head on New Zealand's Routeburn Trail, a three day mountain "tramp," as they call hiking, past countless waterfalls overlooking snow capped peaks. It was easy spotting Nancy from Seattle in her skull-and-roses tie-die, and we spent a rainy night in a Park Service hut talking shows and tapes. She'd been traveling for over six months and hadn't heard much gossip, especially regarding Jerry's health. While my friends occasionally wrote letters and sent tapes and Relix, as my trip went on I found myself eager for Dead news from "Yanks" that had just seen shows in the good ol' U.S. of A.

For three months I didn't meet any Heads, so aside from a few Australians who'd heard of "In The Dark" it was just me, my walkman and the tapes. An amber Indonesian sunset off the northern beaches of Bali was greatly enhanced by "Playing>Terrapin."

March: Walking through the streets of Kathmandu, Nepal, one realizes the influence of the 60's, when this medieval city was a haven for hippies who flocked here for the legal hashish, opium and the Himalayas' energy. While the drugs are now illegal the lure of the world's greatest mountains still attracts thousands of tourists. In the Thamel section, popular with backpackers, inns, cafes and trekking shops line the narrow, crowded streets. A favorite souvenir is silk embroidered t-shirts from closet sized tailor shops. Among the Mt. Everest and Annapurna artwork are dozens of Dead shirts! Each hand sewn, steal-your-face in silk rivals anything found for sale at the shows. In one store a tailor was looking at a photo of Jerry some American had given her, and faithfully reproduced His Grey-ness in thread! At 125 rupiah ($5) each they made fine gifts for my friends back home.

Cut to the Himalayan mountains. It was the 14th day of hard trekking towards the Everest Base Camp, elevation 18,300 feet. I arrived at the day's lodging, a two room stone inn in the five building village of Dole, 13,500 feet. The air is thin and crisp in this white landscape surrounded by majestic snow-capped peaks.

There was already half a dozen trekkers there, sitting by the hearth eating sampa, a Tibetian oat porridge, and drinking chung, a home brewed rice beer. The conversation came around to music, and I mentioned something about the Dead. The couple in the corner joined in "yea, there's nothing like a Grateful Dead concert!" Dave Coots and Tara Granger of Boulder started talking shows and tapes, thoroughly confusing the other trekkers. We tried to explain the Dead phenomenon, but the Swedes and Germans only shook their heads, thinking "some more crazy Yanks."

After another week of trekking Mt. Everest rose directly overhead, perhaps the grandest sight I've ever seen. On the way back I visited a Buddist Monastery. I set my pack down in the guest dorm. Thomas of Germany noticed the skull-and-lighting patch and exclaimed "I luff za Grate-vul Ded!" He had never seen them, or even heard bootleg tapes, but had all their albums. He was returning to Germany to sell all his worldly possessions and live in the forest. When we parted I gave him a tape. He decided he'd keep his walkman but sell everything else!

Back in Kathmandu I met up again with Dave and Tara. We had a fun night munching on pizza and normal beer at the "San Francisco Pizza Parlor," which had photos of Jerry on the walls and was playing live-Dead on the stereo.

My back was hurting from a poor fitting pack so I went to a highly recommended local massuese. Ramjoy was a thin Indian man who had been fasting for two weeks, living only on herb tea and cigarettes! With some reluctance I went ahead with the massage. He combined strange chanting and odd smelling incense with surprisingly strong hands, and despite the bizarreness I felt great afterward. He asked if I'd like to rest awhile and listen to some music. His large tape collection contained over a dozen live Dead tapes. Asking him how he got them he told me he had visited California and given massages to the band! He was too knowledgeable, and too weird, for it to be untrue. Maybe.

After six physically exhausting weeks of

A t-shirt shop in Kathmandu, Nepal

Author and Jim in Dali, China

Fiji

Visiting Egypt

trekking, plus a bout of dysentry, the beaches of Thailand were the ultimate in rest and relaxation. I stayed on Chaweng Beach on Koh Samui Island, off the southeast coast. My private bungalow was large and comfortable, with a king size bed, ceiling fan, western bathroom (one gets real tired of squatting) and a porch overlooking the warm South China Sea, just 10 steps away. It was one of the more expensive places to stay, at $6 a night. The days passed blissfully, listening to tapes, watching half naked Danish girls frolic in the surf and drinking Mekong, the local whiskey. It was fun spreading the "Dead gospel" by playing tunes out of my little Walkman speakers. Most Europeans have never heard of the band, and some really enjoyed the music. Peter Clabbers, the guitar player in the popular Dutch band "The Mix," was especially amazed by Garcia's virtuosity. We wiled away many happy hours in the sand as he learned the tunes.

I met some other Deadheads in Thailand, including American Kurt who hadn't been back to the States for ten years. He used to live in a bus, selling bracelets and such as he followed the tours, and now was selling bracelets as he meandered around the Third World. His last show was Winterland in '78, but he still appreciated the music and enjoyed listening to *In the Dark* and some "recent" concerts.

Well, the Dead never showed up in China as they were supposed to, but I was there in May waiting for a show. After spending some time with the "Reds" I realized the bureacratic and logistic nightmare that would face a rock band entering this massive, backward country. It was not uncommon to wait three or four days for a train ticket to the next town. I found Beijing oppressive and unfriendly, but the South was scenic and sociable.

The small town of Dali in Southwest China is renowned as a backpackers-only retreat, as regular tourists won't brave the grueling 12 hour bus ride through back roads. Situated in the mountains, Dali is cool in the summer and has a lovely lake and an interesting ethnic mix of people, including hill tribes and Burmese refugees.

One afternoon I sat sipping Coca-Cola in the "Peace Cafe" with the owner Jim, a young local who spoke surprisingly good English. With an English menu that featured pizza (sort of) and french fries (kinda), the Peace Cafe was a favorite hang out for us foreign white devils. His stereo was off so I slipped in a tape. Suddenly another patron turned and exclaimed "DEAD!" Kent Rooney of Wisconsin had been studying in China for a year and was starved for new tapes. Ross Blaufarb of Los Altos, CA soon turned up, guitar in hand. We proceeded to take

Kent Rooney with Bai woman in Dali, China

over, blasting bootlegs and serenading other visitors with "Uncle John's" into "Playing." Later that night Jim left but let us keep the place open. Along with a couple of wild English girls we carried all the furniture out to the street and formed Dali's first, and only, Disco Night. A dozen international partiers boogied to the Dead, Talking Heads, soundtrack from "The Big Chill" and German and Scandanavian rock. The locals at first were greatly amused, but by two AM were decidedly unhappy and called the militia. The People's Army were friendly but firm, ending the night's fun. Our gang hung out together for a week drinking the horrendous local beer, which tasted like warm flat Bud the morning after the night before.

While I didn't meet any Heads in Egypt it was fun visiting the sites of the Dead's '78 tour. The ancient country has many magical places, and now I listen to Hamza El-Din's October '78 Winterland appearances with visions of pyramids and Sphinxes.

The trip was winding down, summer's come and gone, my oh my. I had to do Europe quickly as a week in Paris costs as much as a month in Asia. Europe is full of Americans, so I met quite a few Dead-fans. Got briefly excited by an 'ugly rumor' there was going to be a Fall Europe tour. In Holland I stayed with Peter for nearly two weeks. Amsterdam is still full of hippies. You can even buy Dead t-shirts in this wild town!

Finally, on October 1 the skyline of Boston came into view as the plane landed back on American soil. It was good to be back after such a long, strange trip. I knew I was REALLY back Home on December 9 as "Scarlet/Fire" filled the Long Beach Civic Center. Now, if only the good ol' Grateful Dead would do a Europe '90 tour so I can both travel AND see the band! ■

# The History Of Taping

## *Through The Eyes Of One Deadhead*

### BY LES KIPPEL

IT'S a night on tour in 1990. The tapers are setting up in Taper's City. The mike stands are permitted to rise to six feet, and the music is about to begin.

Almost the last thing any taper is thinking about is, "Why am I doing this?" And what about the history of taping? When did it start, who were the first, and how did it become what it is today? With literally every Deadhead admitting to owning at least one live tape, there must be one heck of a good story!

As the person who started *Dead Relix,* which became *Relix* magazine as we currently know it, I can offer my own version of the story. Back in 1969, I was attending Pace College, in my final year, and living in Staten Island. The set of events happening then is important. Nixon was in office, and the Viet Nam war was in full swing. Americans were getting killed for reasons a lot of people didn't understand. Riots between construction workers and "hippies" were happening on a daily basis. Marches on Wall Street and on Whitehall Street, where the major induction center for the draft was, were a daily happening.

And here I was, in Pace College, taking a course called "Rock In Contemporary Society." Sounded easy for a senior only taking three classes, the other two being Spanish (repeated for the third time) and English.

The professor had us play rock music and talk about it. My term assignment was the Doors' *Soft Parade.* Explain it and talk about it. No written papers, please. One of the extra-credit assignments was a field trip to the Fillmore East to see a band called the Grateful Dead. Extra credit. Well, there was much more happening in Staten Island at the time (or so I thought), and it was a big trip, so I passed it up.

A few brief months later, my friend Steve Kraye came up with a pair of tickets to see the Grateful Dead at the Fillmore. Even though the tickets were in Row F, upper balcony, why not check them out this time? Our friend Bob Terrella said, "Hey man, this is the most different group around. Ya gotta see 'em."

So, Steve and I prepared for the all-night event that these Dead shows were rumored to be. When we got to the Fillmore, we sat down to check out the scene; all the folks around seemed friendly. The first act came on stage. They played a kind of country, with a bearded guy on pedal steel, and the lead singer, this Marmaduke guy, made this joke about the stage being painted purple in their honor. He said something like "The New Riders of the Purple Stage." Couldn't figure that one out no how.

The New Riders ended their set and everyone piled into the lobby to hang out. Then, all of a sudden, like magic, we started meeting people we knew. Before we could count, we must have met over 50 friends. The weirdest thing was, no one had any idea that any of these other people would be at this show! A gathering of tribes.

A group of people had seats in the 18th row (Row R) that they bought from a Fillmore ticket outlet in a local clothing store. (This was before Ticketron and computers and that stuff, of course.) They gave me a ticket stub, and I made my way to Row R.

Boy, did things look different now. What were all those tie-dye boxes onstage? What were all those boxes with guitars plugged in with lights on them, and what was that long line of gongs going from very small to gigantic doing there?

As the lights dimmed, some guy came out, and announced something like, "Ladies and gentleman, the Grateful Dead, Scene Two, Act Two."

They played a lot of country kind of songs, nothing that was really amazing to me, but I was having a thrill being in the 18th row with my friends. Unfortunately, poor Steve was upstairs.

After the next intermission, there was another introduction, "Ladies and Gentlemen, the Grateful Dead, Scene Three, Act Three." Then it hit me: this band all of a sudden got serious. Whatever they did for the first two "scenes" in no way prepared anyone for what was now taking place. All those guitars and lights—who was that guy with the flame thrower onstage? The volume and intensity of the music made me realize that something special was happening here, something that I had never seen before.

I remember the anticipation of the audience for every song, as though there was some sort of non-verbal communication between the band and the audience. I remember that bearded guy, looking at the audience, playing one note, and the entire audience screaming, "Yes," in approval. I think the band then played "Dark Star."

The audience and band seemed as one, there seemed no separation. The next few songs went by, with the two drummers smashing away, and that Pigpen guy blew me away! Then they started playing a song called "Morning Dew." I wondered, "Are they telling us that morning is approaching, and is it time to go?" And then, that drummer, hitting those gongs.

The next thing I remember were the exit doors being opened, and it was light outside, but no one was leaving. Finally, the band came back and all stood around one mike and sang a song that said, "And we bid you goodnight." It seemed like the perfect thank you from them to us, for coming and sharing this perfect evening with them.

But it didn't end there. I was living in Staten Island, which meant getting from the East Village, where the Fillmore was, down to the Staten Island Ferry. Don't ask me how I did it, I don't remember. Waiting for the ferry, there must have been about 50 or so of the very same people who I had shared that special evening with. Whether they remember now, who knows. Along with the others on that ferry ride, with the sun rising from the east, I saw a cruise ship entering the harbor, and passengers on the deck taking in the sight of arriving at the break of dawn in New York harbor, with the sun shining on the Statue of Liberty and this ferry boat treading its way across the water from New York City to Staten Island.

I knew that the energy that I experienced that night had to be caught, and that I had to become part of the energy.

The next time the Grateful Dead played at the Fillmore, I got my own 18th row seat. Also, at about the same time, the Japanese were coming out with these portable tape machines that were small enough to be brought into a concert hall without raising much suspicion. I smuggled one in and gave it to my old Row R friends, who had now moved up to the first row, and asked them to record the show for me. I

was thrilled: I was going to get a Grateful Dead tape so that I could remember the experience.

Much to my surprise, these people really didn't think about pointing the microphone at the stage; all that was heard on the tape were things like "Hey, man, pass the wine sack!"

I realized that the only way to do it was to do it myself, and I started to record shows. Responsibilities for smuggling in extra batteries, extra microphones, and extra tapes were split between my friends and me. Soon, my friend R.T. joined me in taping, and then a short while later, at a Garcia show, I ran into Jim from New Jersey.

Jim had about the same number of shows on tape that we had, and we decided we should trade and get a club together for the purpose of collecting and trading tapes. Naturally, all the same questions that are still here today were the ones that we had to deal with first: should there be a charge to copy a tape, who should get a tape, why should one person get a tape and another person not?

We finally decided that all exchanges should be FREE, and that we should call ourselves "THE FIRST FREE UNDERGROUND GRATEFUL DEAD TAPE EXCHANGE." We also decided to promote the idea, and get other people to start their own exchanges. Within months, there must have been 30 or so exchanges, with business cards to boot!

Naturally, some members of the Grateful Dead family really got a kick out of this phenomenon, while others freaked beyond compare.

One of the funnier stories concerned the Grateful Dead Woodstock tapes! It seems that at Woodstock, the Grateful Dead were scheduled to go on hours later, and were really laying back enjoying the scene, when they were given five minutes notice to play! They were not ready! Not only that, but people in those days forgot about things like grounding microphones and keeping them out of water. All the Grateful Dead gear was not grounded, and in the ensuing downpour, whenever one of them tried to sing into a microphone or touch his guitar, he got a major jolt of electricity! These Woodstock tapes found their way out of the Warner Brothers archives and into the hands of the First Free Underground Grateful Dead Tape Exchange around the time the Grateful Dead headed to Florida in 1974. Word got to Phil Lesh that this tape was around, and he made a bee-line to the room of the person who had the tape. He sat there transfixed, not moving, and then became animated and couldn't control his excitement. He turned to the people in the room and said, "I must have a copy of this tape." Naturally, everyone was thrilled. "But," he continued, "don't bother recording the music. I only want the talking!"

I started recording in earnest in 1971, but until 1974, when Sony came out with the 152 and the ECM-99 stereo microphones, the quality didn't shape up. I feel that the '74 shows from Roosevelt Stadium, New Jersey, the Spectrum in Philadelphia, the Miami, Florida, shows, and Providence, Rhode Island, were the premium ones made. Some of those might have already been replaced by soundboards, but even if not, look for them.

I believed in trading with everyone, and tried to maintain an open door policy, whether people had tapes or not. Eventually, I found that people didn't want to bother recording shows themselves, but just wanted to copy tapes. I came to realize that recording took away from the

enjoyment of the shows, and I wanted others to get involved.

During 1973, I took a break from recording in an attempt to get tape collectors to realize that they had to share the responsibility of getting tapes for people to collect. It was in 1973 that I was hanging out with some friends and came up with an idea to let myself step aside and let people get together without my involvement to collect and trade tapes. I decided to start some form of newsletter, sort of like a fanzine, where articles about taping could be printed, and people could advertise tape trading for free. (After all, the entire point of the Free Underground Tape Exchange was the key word: FREE). Jim McGurn, an old friend, said, "Well Les, what are you going to call this thing?" We thought, they are DEAD tapes, sort of like relics, so why not DEAD RELICS? So, the name was created. From that point, we started to get the first issue out, naturally, dedicated to the trickiest taper of all times—Richard Nixon!

At one time, we had a meeting with the Grateful Dead and made a proposal to them for a "Connoisseurs Club" of tape collectors, a proposal which said that they should open up their vaults and make copies of all their shows available to their fans at a reasonable fee.

Ron Rakow, then their record company president, reviewed our 93-page proposal and turned it down. The latest we hear is that the Grateful Dead have now decided to cull their tapes and start to issue their old shows in CD format, 18 years after we proposed the idea!

It's definitely been a long strange trip for taping. From small Panasonic machines and batteries that lasted 15 minutes to DAT machines, tapes and nicad batteries that last for hours. And through it all, one thing has remained the same, Deadheads are still recording the shows, trying to catch that magic that the Grateful Dead have been putting out for 25 years! ∎

**Artwork by Scott Boldt**

May/June, 1990

Vol. 17
No. 3

# Relix

## music for the mind

$4.00 U.S.
$5.00 Can.
£4.50 U.K.

SUMMER SPECIAL

GR TEFL
DE D

SILVER
ANNIVERSARY
ISSUE

# NED LAGIN

## AN INTERVIEW BY MICK SKIDMORE

Ned Lagin's electronic album *Seastones*, originally released on the Grateful Dead's Round record label in 1975 and prominently featuring Dead bassist Phil Lesh, is one of the most oblique and esoteric side projects with which any Grateful Dead member has been involved. The album, long a collector's item, has recently been reissued on CD.

Since the original release, Lagin has kept a low profile, but through the years the subject of reissuing the album has come up periodically. In 1990, Lagin was approached by Rykodisc to reissue the album. After several months of negotiations, it was agreed that they would put it out along with a previously unreleased, shorter version of the piece. The newer version is closer in content to the live versions that were performed by Lagin and Lesh during the summer of 1975.

The album should be of interest to Deadheads, given the participation of Jerry Garcia, Mickey Hart, and Phil Lesh, as well as David Crosby, Grace Slick, David Freiberg, and Spencer Dryden. But don't expect to hear a soaring solo from Jerry or Slick's shrill voice. All the music is processed through Lagin's complex network of computers.

Lagin's background is quite diverse. At the age of six, he began playing piano. He then took classical lessons, which led to playing Broadway show music. By age 12 or 13, he got into jazz. As the avant-garde jazz scene evolved, he was an avid listener, taking in the sounds of John Coltrane and Archie Shepp. He later studied jazz piano greats such as his hero Bill Evans. In 1966, he went to Boston and studied science at MIT, jazz at the Berklee School of Music, and orchestration and composition at Harvard, as well as playing in various jazz ensembles. It was during this period that Lagin's musical tastes and penchant for experimentation developed.

At the time, he says, "I wasn't really into rock 'n' roll very much. I was really a jazz musician and part of the art-jazz scene in Boston and New York." It wasn't until some friends who'd heard Lagin's music insisted he listen to the Grateful Dead that Lagin paid attention to rock. In October, 1969, he recalls, "I went to a Grateful Dead concert. I was still in my jazz world. I was in a corduroy jacket with patches, a turtle-neck sweater; very academic. I saw them at the Boston Tea Party. It held about 400 people, and there were only about 100 or 200 people there. They came on about three hours late. And I was tremendously impressed."

The same year, Lagin had written a complex experimental composition for eight speakers, to be performed at the MIT chapel. The speakers were arranged in a circle, and people sat in the middle. The music was designed specifically for that space, taking into account the acoustics of the building.

Friends convinced Lagin he should convey his musical ideas to the Grateful Dead. He wrote a letter to Jerry Garica and received no reply, although the letter actually had a profound effect on both Garcia and Lesh. In fact, when the Dead came to play at MIT (a concert that was organized by Lagin and other friends of his in the anti-war movement) in May, 1970, they sought out Lagin and a friendship was struck up. The Dead heard Lagin's composition at the MIT chapel, were suitably impressed, and duly invited him to come out to California and mess with a 16-track recorder.

Later that summer he did just that, eventually spending a lot of time at both Phil's and Jerry's houses learning Dead tunes. Lagin recalls his first day in San Francisco: "I got off of the Greyhound bus and walked a couple of blocks to a studio I had never heard of, Wally Heider's, and there were three studios. One had the Grateful Dead in it, and only Garcia was there. He was early, and I was early, and he said 'Good, you can play on our record,' which was *American Beauty*. In another studio was the Airplane, and part of the time in the third was Santana and part of the time was David Crosby. That was when everybody was one big happy family. If you weren't playing on one album, you ran around the corner to the other studios and played on another album or just jammed."

During the summer of 1970, Lagin contributed to *American Beauty* and sat in at various gigs through the fall of the year, generally contributing to such songs as "Dark Star" and "That's It For The Other One."

Lagin made a brief return to the East Coast to finish his education before moving full-time to the West Coast, where he began working on compositions that would eventually become *Seastones*. In fact, the work was written and recorded over a four-year period.

When initially released, the album met with a wide range of responses. As Lagin remembers, "People either thought I was God or they absolutely hated me." The new recording is more accessible, but it is still way out there in left field. Despite the listing of musician credits, it's impossible to figure out who appears at a given point, so Lagin is asked to give a fuller explanation of the newer piece.

"Recording each of the musicians for each of the sections we used a score, and there was verbal guidance, and in some cases I played with them," he responds. "In only one or two sections did the whole group ever get together to play the sections. In other words the thing was layered together. It was impossible, due to other recording and travel commitments, to get all those people together, or for that matter to have enough time with those people to explain the music and what was trying to be achieved.

"I spent the most time with Jerry and Crosby, even though later on Phil and I went out and performed some of this music. Most of the music that's recorded was with David [Crosby] and Jerry. From each of the versions, I can give you a little bit of an idea. For example, in the newer version, the first section is obviously just myself and Phil for the first half and then myself for the second half. It's basically Phil's new quadrophonic bass and my quadrophonic synthesizer, and the lines that we are playing start out as very separate lines and become one line, and that one line is metamorphosed into a very tonal string sounding orchestral conclusion. The third section is multi-layered live and studio performances. It includes, myself, Phil, Jerry, David, and Spencer Dryden, and several of the layers date from after the first *Seastones* release. The next section after that, section four, is myself, Jerry, David, and Spencer, and is the same ensemble playing that occurred in the earlier version. The fifth section, which is a very short section and sounds like percussion, gongs, or drums, is actually prepared piano. It is synthesized piano, just me solo. The final section, the 13-minute section, which is somewhat colored differently in the two versions and shows very different dimensions of part of the piece, starts out with about five minutes of just Ned and Phil going into about another five minutes of Ned and David. The synthesizer stays the same, but the bass becomes voice. In the final three minutes or so the voice also becomes synthesizer. That section took a long time, even though it's one of the most minimal sections."

Lagin is asked if he has any future plans to release more electronic works or to work with members of the Grateful Dead again. "Between '75 and January, '82, I did a lot of music, some with Phil and those guys," he says. "There's a lot of that period that I have that we are thinking of releasing. In 1981, I started a second album. It didn't include Phil or any of those guys, because it never got that far, but it did include some basics. I did some things with Terry Haggerty from the Sons of Champlin. I have been talking to Phil this year about releasing some more material. Phil has committed to two weeks in October or November of this year to record some other compositions of mine. There were three or four compositions that we performed in 1975 that I am thinking of resurrecting. I hope to include some of the music I did outside of the *Seastones* genre, the more jazz, rock, and orchestral things. I also have plans, and I am only in the preliminary stages, for doing an animated CD ROM for Macintosh for parts of *Seastones,* so it would come out on CD and would be played on a Macintosh and have an interactive score on the screen and people would be provided with compositional tools and could be more involved in putting their own versions of *Seastones* together."

In the meantime, the new version of *Seastones* is available for the more adventurous souls out there. Even the original version sounds considerably different in its CD format. Lagin's atmospheric computer-based sounds may not be everyone's choice, but there's no doubt that he's an innovator. ∎

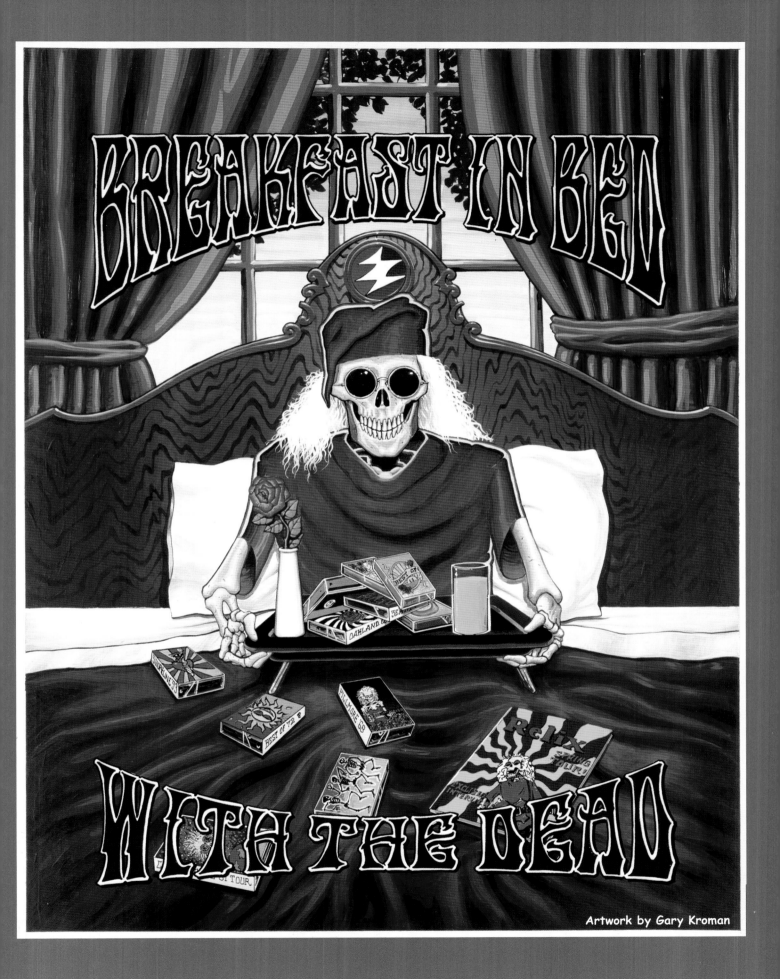

Artwork by Gary Kroman

John Rottet

## we are everywhere!

Give me liberty, or give me Dead
Stephanie & Sharon at the Liberty Bell

John Rottet

Nancy Slawson

Store in Greenville, NC called Blt's

Cafe in
Hilo,
Hawaii

Arthur West

John Rottet

We are Everywhere

Paul Kimpel

Patrick
Johnson
in the
Mojave
Desert

Artwork by Glenn Harding

January/February, 1991

Vol. 18
No. 1

$3.50 U.S.
$4.50 Can.
£4.00 U.K.

# Relix

## music for the mind

**LED ZEPPELIN
BYRDS**

★ ★ ★ ★ ★ ★ ★ ★ ★ ★ ★ ★ ★ ★ ★

# GRATEFUL DEAD
## european tour

U·S OF A

·EUROPE·

Cover Artwork by Gary Kroman

# Dan Healy

## FROM THE VAULTS TO THE PYRAMIDS
### THE GRATEFUL DEAD'S SOUNDMAN SPEAKS

### BY
### TONI A. BROWN

*FOR many, the availability of the Grateful Dead's live concert archives in soundboard quality would be a dream come true. After two decades of sending out set lists and making taping contacts, tape collectors may soon have the material at their fingertips, and the entire taping scene as we know it may become obsolete.*

*In the following interview, Dan Healy discusses the Grateful Dead's latest effort, One From The Vaults, released through their own Grateful Dead Merchandising. We delve even further into his views on the taping section, some obscure locations relating to sound, and what the future holds for that most innovative of bands, the Grateful Dead.*

Susana Millman

**Dan Healy**

*Relix:* Where did the idea to go into the vaults come from?

*Healy:* Since day one, we've tried to record as much of our shows as we possibly could. In early days, like the '60s, the tape recorder technology was not as advanced. It was before the days of portable equipment and cassettes. If you were to record something with any kind of quality, it was a big ordeal. So the tapes are somewhat sketchy, but by 1969 we were able to maintain a good quality standard collection of shows.

Some of the old stuff has fallen out from sitting on the shelves because the earlier formulas that tapes were made of, it was before the days of plastics that don't ever go away, so while it's bad for the environment it's good for tapes. But at any rate, because the old tapes are starting to get flaky, we decided that it was time to go through our entire collection of tapes and convert them to digital tapes and restore them on modern format and modern media. At the same time, there's been requests for years from our audience, from fans wanting us to pull out favorite old shows and release them. We know that this has been coming for a long time, but it's also true that the technology up until

recently was such that it would have been diminishing returns to try and master some of this older material.

We're now on a monumental project because there's 80-some-odd shows a year average for 25 years, so that gives you an idea of the wad of tapes we have. We've got three rooms, and each room is about 20 x 20, and it's full to the door with tapes. It's a really ambitious task to do it, but modern technology being the whole digital format provides us with the means of retrieving the old tapes and restoring them in a much longer lasting format in such a way that the audio quality will be enhanced or at least not [degraded]. As long as we're going through the tapes and we're going to update them all, we figured while we're there doing it we can also select various shows from the past and make them available to our audience through our own merchandising at a lower price than sort of the record company/record store version of studio releases and stuff like that. The object

is to get the music to our fans, while at the same time we're developing a database, and we're going through and updating all of our old tapes.

*Relix:* Are your tapes chronologically by date?

*Healy:* Pretty much. We're in the mid-'80s now, so we've gotten that far. What we're doing is, we are developing a computer database that has all the shows and each tape listed individually, various comments about the tape and notes about what formats they're on and so on and so forth. We've recently constructed a new part of our studio rehearsal complex in so far as we've built a room that is strictly for listening, editing, and dubbing tapes. It has the computer in it that's doing the database of all the tapes, but it also has other computers in it that [are] converting the analog tapes to digital. Plus, it has all the format machines of the past years that can play the various formats of the tapes because our tapes exist on every known tape format, like cassettes, multi-tracks, two tracks, even some of them are old monaural tapes and stuff like that. So this little room is like the work center where we're going through the vault, noting what we've got and retrieving it and converting it to digital stuff.

*Relix:* Some Deadheads have actually been collecting reel-to-reel tapes over the years, which is almost an obsolete format at this point.

*Healy:* We've certainly got our share of those!

*Relix:* They've stocked away extra equipment because they know at some point they're not going to be able to get the machines anymore.

*Healy:* I still have a machine from 1967 that we did *Anthem of the Sun* on. It was a machine that was a radical format not compatible with any other machines, but we built it because we wanted to have a four-channel tape recorder, which in those days was big news, but it also needed to be portable. So it's a 1/4" four-track. The tape is really strange in the terms of its format, so I packed away the machine, and now I have it. I actually have a number of machines. There was a period of time when we had three-track tapes and I saved the old three-track tape machine, too. I'm glad I did now, because I go through hell trying to play back some of these old tapes.

*Relix:* How far back do the archives date?

*Healy:* They date back to the very beginning, clear back to the Warlocks days in sketchy forms. It's fairly sketchy until about '68-'69. First of all, you have to realize that in the early days none of us realized that the Grateful Dead was going to become what it has become.

[The decision of what tapes will be released] is to sort of mix between the from-day-one concept and from the most-noted-event concept and try and use those as a vehicle to get to the meat of what's going on. I try to receive as much input from fans and friends. One of the things I discovered is that for everybody you talk to there's a different opinion.

I listen to and keep track of everything everybody says. I obviously have to figure out some way of making a decision because that's a situation that would have wound up going nowhere. So I took all of that that I described to you to this point, and I also wanted the first attempt at the releasing of the vault to be a significant event.

Just the task of making a record and releasing it in itself is a whole job. So rather than pick something that had really poor audio quality from maybe an obscure earlier show and add the amount of effort trying to retrieve that and make something cogent out of it, along with all the business of putting together a release and doing all the release aspects of it and the record, CD, and cassette manufacturing and stuff was an impractical large thing to do. So, I decided instead to make the first one, at least draw from it, takes that I knew were fairly well recorded, that were cogent in quality and cogent in event significance. So, while the next one might not be something like that, I might go back and apply something closer to the day-one theory without that much emphasis on audio quality and stuff. I arrived at this because it was the most viable version to attempt to release.

*Relix:* Your first *From The Vault* release was from a significant year, considering that the Grateful Dead hadn't really been touring.

*Healy:* That was part of it. We recorded the *Blues For Allah* album at Bobby Weir's house, where he has a recording studio. We hadn't played for almost a year, and we were anxious to play with each other. We took the year off because when we developed our Wall of Sound system, which was really a magnificent thing, it

was also very complicated, very time consuming, and very costly. We were working 11 months of the year and we were broke all the time supporting the sound. So, when the nation's economy went out the window with the gas crisis and all that, it took an already difficult situation and sort of made it prohibitive. So, it was no longer feasible to carry around the Wall of Sound and to tour with it. So, we retired that. But we were also fried ourselves, and it wasn't a statement of, "We don't wanna be a band anymore," it was more a statement of, "Man, I'm tired, I've gotta take a break." So we kinda laid back for almost a year, but during that time we recorded the *Blues For Allah* album, and we were all very busy together as the Grateful Dead, it was just that we weren't doing tours and stuff. So, it looked from the

outside like we weren't doing anything, but actually I probably did more Grateful Dead stuff that year than I do in a touring year, because we did the Grateful Dead movie and things like that. So, I didn't have a single day off that whole year, and I think that's true for most of us. At any rate, when we finished the *Blues For Allah* album, it was also the first album on our own record company, which was another celebration and another event that happened. So, we were very anxious to play together, and we wanted to celebrate the completion of *Blues For Allah,* and we also wanted to celebrate the announcement of our own record company. So, we decided that at the end of the recording of the studio album that we would pick up all of our equipment, and we chose the Great American Music Hall. We had retired the Wall of Sound and we really didn't have a large sound system because we hadn't played in a while. We didn't really want to get involved in a large-scale gig, but we figured this would be a good way to get to play together and to sort of start back up playing again and also celebrate all the other aspects of it. So, we made up announcements, and it was by invitation only, and it was directed mostly towards the media and record companies. So, it was kind of a record company/press party sort of a thing, whereby we performed the *Blues For Allah* album live and in its entirety, plus a number of other tunes. Somehow, we had the presence of mind to bring a 16-track, which was the state-of-the-art technology in those days. So, we recorded the shows on 16-track. We also broadcast the show live over, I think, KSAN. But they actually taped it and didn't play it live, but played it the next day, and edited a great deal of it out. So nobody on the outside got to really hear the whole thing. Finally, the tapes went back to the vault and stayed there forever, and finally when this project began to happen I was going through ... well, I have Dennis McNally, and I have Dick Latvalla. There's a number of people in our scene who are taper aficionados, not to mention all the general tape people. So, I started collecting and wound up with maybe a choice of 20 different shows to consider for the first release, and so, after carefully listening to them all and trying to fit it in with all the other requirements and things that needed to be done, I arrived at that show.

*Relix:* The CD is very clean. It's almost crystalline, and that sort of takes away from the live feel of a tape.

*Healy:* You've got to remember that the Great American Music Hall is a very small place, so it doesn't give the impression of large audiences. Two of the 16-tracks were microphones that were in the audience. The main theme of the vault releases in one word is honesty. Most bands, including ourselves, whenever they prepare live tapes for release, there's a lot of cosmetic stuff that goes on, replacing guitar parts, drum parts, and vocal parts and so on and so forth, and there was a large controversy in our scene about whether or not we should doctor the tapes before we release them. There's a whole contingency of us that think we should be doctoring them. My own personal opinion is that part of the definition of the vault tapes is to present them in the original fashion, the way they really were and not do all of that stuff. It took me a year to convince everybody that that would maybe be the best approach. So, when I mixed this show down, I didn't use any processing or equalization or any gimmicks or tricks. It's absolutely straight on tour recording and tour mixing techniques, and I built the mix around the ambient sound in the room. So, believe it or not, it very much carries the characteristics of what it actually sounded like in that room. Again, it's a very small room, so I think if you're imagining that it should have a large, huge ambient sound, that is a misnomer because I would have had to synthetically create it to make it sound like that. It wasn't there.

*Relix:* It's just naturally clean.

*Healy:* Well, yeah, it's very clean. I think what I've done is, I've achieved the essence of honesty in reproduction of this. I didn't manipulate it, I didn't doctor it, and I intentionally set about to do it that way. Also, you have to remember that it was sort of a formal affair, and it wasn't necessarily Deadheads in the audience, it was record company execs and the media, so the audience wasn't screaming and raving and flipping out like they typically do at a show. These are all things that contribute to the reality of it. Actually, that's a misnomer, it isn't very, what you call, clean. What I call clean, by the way, is not distorted, but the reason why what you said, which I gather to mean lack of ambiance is because whatever ambience was there is there.

*Relix:* So, you did all the mixing yourself?

*Healy:* Yes. I'm in charge of the vault release project. Probably because of the number of years I've been here and because I've mixed all the tapes. So, I think that the consensus is that I probably am one of the most likely ones to do it.

*Relix:* Since it is impossible to release the entire back collection of tapes on CD, do you foresee a time when the band might make the archives available to Deadheads directly?

*Healy:* That idea has been kicked around a lot, and I'll tell you where that idea is right now. We've just recently, as I've described to you, put together a room that is solely for listening and digitizing and working with the tapes. I think later on, one of the considerations is to maybe have a mail-order basis or something, whereby if you have a specific show in mind, you can write in and then we'll make you a CD or a tape of it. It'll be along those kinds of lines.

*Relix:* That would be interesting!

*Healy:* We've thought about it, it's definitely in the dialogue. If it happens at all it has to be consistent with the whole unfolding of the larger scale picture of it. But the answer is yes, there's a good chance that that could happen in the future.

*Relix:* It's an interesting perspective, really. So many tapes are available anyway, but such poor quality is in circulation. How's the tapers section been working out? Do you still feel in control of it?

*Healy:* Well, the tapers section has been a mixed blessing since day one. My own philosophy, since I'm an engineer and a recordist, I'm naturally sympathetic with it. The main friction is the tapers colliding with the rest of the audience that could care less about the tapes, but are there to enjoy the show. What happens is, the tapers tend to become abusive to the rest of the audience, and they push people out of the way and set up their equipment and force people to not talk in the vicinity of their microphones. Those are all things that are really anti-Grateful Dead, and so a few years ago, before I formed the tapers section, the mandate was laid on me by the band to do something about the tapers, and it was like there would be no more taping because it was the type of thing that was only *allowed* to happen, but was by no means a *right* that anybody in the audience had. So, at the last minute, somebody came up with an idea. I think it was my wife that said, "Why don't you form a tapers section?" The idea being that if all the tapers will go and be in one section, in return for that we'll sell tapers tickets at the same price for that section, and if you're in that section with your ticket, you actually have rights. And the idea of that is to get everyone together and to get them out of the general dispersion of the audience whereby they were trashing the rest of the audience around them.

It's unfortunate, but life has people who can't seem to enjoy a good thing, and always have to be pushing at it, and there's been a number of people pushing up front, which is something I don't understand because it doesn't sound good up there, anyway. But I think it's a combination of getting away with something and thumbing your nose at authority, which is kind of ridiculous in our scene, because it's not like our scene is an authoritative kind of scene.

Over the last few shows, in Las Vegas and in Sacramento recently, I've been having the guards bust people up there, and if you get caught, you get busted and you get thrown out of the concert. In the future, I think I'm going to confiscate the equipment permanently and throw people out, because it's a situation that I'd really rather not have to deal with. But since I've by vacuum become the defender of the tapers, then it's on me, and if I don't stop that from happening then there's going to be another mandate to end it completely, and I don't really want to do that, and most people are cool. I provide the section for the tapers there, right in the center so they get a good stereo blend and everything, and our spirit is to try to really make it right. But people continue to violate it. Now the trend is moving towards reserved seating, so the typical scenario is that some 16-year-old kid will come to me crying, saying that he and his girlfriend stood in line for five hours to get a ticket, and they got to their seats and some taper came at the start of the show and beat them up and threw them out of their seats, saying they want to be there, and that's actually what the tapers have been doing.

I try to provide everybody an honest trip at it. I'm not trying to hurt anybody. All I want to see is harmony at the show. I want everybody to get away with whatever they want to, but the bottom line is there must be harmony at the shows. And so the very people who tape the shows, that pull those shenanigans, are the self-proclaimed knowledgeables of the spirit of the Grateful Dead, so I don't really understand that myself. It turns out, to add another little twist to it, that the people who are doing most of the bootlegging are the ones who are doing this. There's this one guy who I don't need to name who knows that we already know who he is. What he does is, he buys other people equipment and tickets and instigates getting them up front. This is one of the guys who's at the root of all the [bootleg] CDs that are coming from Italy and Japan. He may not know it, but he's going to fall. But the point is that that's very un-Grateful Dead and it's very un-humanistic.

*Relix:* In true Grateful Dead fashion, many Deadheads will not even buy the stuff, but on the other hand, there are others who will.

*Healy:* It's mind-boggling, you set out to do something nice, and you get trashed for it. It's really amazing, and it's too bad. And again, I'm not directing it at most tapers. Most tapers are really good people and very conscientious about that kind of stuff. It's like the old famous few sour apples. I hate to use all those dumb clichés, but it's kind of like that. It's a sore subject, because the last few weekends I've had to really deal with it heavily.

*Relix:* Back to the *Vault* release, what made it come about now?

*Healy:* This is something that we all, and I particularly, have been considering for years. This is no spur-of-the moment thing. And in those years, we've tried as hard as possible to consider every aspect of it and hopefully the end result being the nicest presentation that can be had. It's something that we sincerely care about. And yet, for instance, the long box packaging is something that is a terrible waste of paper, and I would like to see it abolished personally. Have you seen the new box?

*Relix:* I think the small cardboard packaging is very unique.

*Healy:* Well, people are complaining about it. I got a stack of letters this morning from people disgruntled about it not being in a plastic box.

*Relix:* The cardboard could wear out.

*Healy:* So what? Everything wears out. It's not meant to last forever, is it?

*Relix:* We'd like something to pass on to the grandchildren.

*Healy:* Well, I'd like it also, but a higher priority is our planet, and those are the motivations. People come onto me as though I'm intentionally interfering with their desires, and it had nothing to do with that. It had to do with trying to look out for our planet. I think that if everybody from a musician's point of view, everyone that's doing records, got together and said no more long box, the record companies and record stores could adapt, they could adapt to anything when it comes down to it. It's just a question of enough people being aware of the severe waste.

*Relix:* They have to know that the consumer knows it, and the demand has to be that it change.

*Healy:* Well, it's typical of Grateful Dead fashion. We've always been the leaders of new ideas, and they've always been deemed radical, but many of them have wound up becoming accepted standards. So this is just another one of those examples, I'd say.

*Relix:* Well, go for it, because this is a good one. On another note, have you seen changes in audience taping with the new standards of equipment available now?

*Healy:* Yeah, the audience has very sophisticated equipment. It's largely digital and they use good microphones. And our sound system has really gone through a number of significant changes. The sound in the audience is outrageously good these days, and so that, plus the better quality equipment that the tapers have, and I think the tapers, particularly the older ones, are learning more and more about the ways of doing it. I've heard recent audience tapes that are quite nice sounding. I applaud all those people, basically, I'm on their side; I'm a taper at heart. So I'm glad to see them doing well.

*Relix:* At one point, you had been experimenting with an FM broadcast method during one tour. Was that working out?

*Healy:* Yes, but what happened is that the FCC was about to come down on me, so I had to stop doing it. In order to do it with good quality, I had to use more power than they allow you to have. The amount of legal power the FCC will give you without a license is enough power to go about 20 feet. So it doesn't really work. I was directly in violation. And people like the FCC would love to come down on people like us, so it started getting hot, and I got a few indications that they were about to make an issue out of me, so I backed off for a while. That's not to say I won't ever do it again, but I've decided to let it rest for a while, and I'm gonna do it on more of a hit-and-miss basis. And so I would say that the answer to the tapers is that if you were to bring a tuner, bring a little Walkman radio that you can plug into your tape deck or something, because you never know when I might be doing it again. But officially speaking, I've never done it.

Relix: What are some of your favorite venues from the perspective of sound?

*Healy:* First of all, outdoor playing is a joyful celebration to me. The worst outdoor venue is infinitely more desirable than the best indoor venue. Unfortunately, we are in sports arenas most of the time, mandated by the size of the audience that we're playing to. And sports arenas probably care more about everything else *but* sound. When civic committees raise bonds to build these places, one of the things they always say--it's like the famous campaign speech stuff--is, "We're gonna build a new sports arena/music arena." That's part of how they raise the money and sanction to do it, but then when it comes right down to it, little or no effort goes into it—just like campaign promises, all the good stuff gets shined on.

Because of that, there are only one or two arenas that have fairly decent sound. I think that one of the nicest sounding indoor arenas is Brendan Byrne in New Jersey. That is one of the few places where they actually did put some effort into acoustic properties. It makes it possible to sound fairly good in there. It ranges all the way from that to just awful bellowing, echo holes.

One of the challenges to me over the years was, in view that we're stuck in all these awful sounding places, to try to endeavor to create equipment and procedures and techniques that minimize the echoes and the undesirable aspects of it. I feel that my sound crew guys and I are probably on the cutting edge of the best ability to deal with acoustics and indoor venues and stuff like that. There are many times when we play the Oakland Coliseum, which is not a bad place, but it's not a good place, it's somewhere in the middle, as an example. When we play three or four nights there, by the second night it's remarkably good sounding. It's amazing how 20 years of studying like that has actually taught us techniques and caused the development of procedures and equipment to actually do something about it.

I go to other shows, and I can't believe that people buy tickets to those concerts and don't demand their money back. Some of the shows I see are just awful sounding. You can't tell the difference between guitars and voices and stuff. I know that our shows are much better than that, even though there are things that I'd like to see get better and I'm of course continuously on the case of developing new ideas and better equipment. Our system is going through a real big change right now. We're right on the verge of digital sound. We have pretty much all of the elements together, and we're just heading towards the final stretch to completely close the loop and create a sound system that is fully digitally based. I think the reason why that's significant is because it will give us the ability of computer power to deal with the acoustic properties of a place. So, in essence, it's going to come down to giving us the best-yet handle on how to make an awful sounding hall sound good.

*Relix:* When you schedule a venue, a computer diagram is created that allows you to design the sound system. When you get to a location, the entire set-up is blueprinted out, and then the crew and you set up speaker locations, seating advantages, etc.

*Healy: There* are not too many days off on the road. First of all, it's prohibitively expensive to be on the road with our entire crew. The object is to put a tour together that conforms with the amount of time we want to be on the road and fits realistically into the different cities. We get an architectural layout and then do scale drawings of the venue. We have a special computer that runs a program called Autocad , which architectural designs are based on. We scan into the computer the architectural drawings in a given venue. Also, already in the computer, we have the size and shape and the ability to project any configuration of our loud speakers and of the stage itself. You can take that computer and build any stage inside of a venue, and then you can set the sound system up on it or around it, in any way you want.

The computer can also show projections of what each speaker does and how far the sound travels and how wide and how high and low and areas of dispersion. From all of that, you plot the sound system at any given venue, and the object is to try to devise a set-up that yields smooth, even sound for every seat that you're selling tickets for. It helps keep the sound off of areas that don't have people in them. It keeps it off walls and ceilings, because those are all elements that add to the echo and reverberations in the halls. The reason for it is to be able to devise a set-up that's most desirable visually and aurally for everybody, and has minimized all the undesirable effects.

It also goes for outdoor shows. The difference between that and an indoor place is that it's much larger. There's not only the stage, but there's also the sound reinforcement, speakers, towers and stuff like that. They're all carefully designed and drawn into the different venues to reflect smooth, even coverage sound everywhere. So, yes, a lot goes into planning a show. This all happens months before we actually leave to go on the road. Then, of course, after drawings are completed in the computer, it's printed back out into blueprint fashion and the blueprints are duplicated and distributed to the builders of the stage and the builders of the sound system and the seating people, to let them know where to put the seats and so on and so forth.

*Relix: You've* experimented with many different sound techniques. What are some of the more successful techniques you've picked up?

*Healy:* The Wall of Sound itself was probably the big workshop. In the early '70s, by the time we started to construct the Wall of Sound, that was probably our third or fourth generation sound system. In the early days of sound reinforcement of all audio, it really came from research done in the '20s and '30s by Bell Labs, who at the time was the authority on sound reinforcement, and they did everything from designing loud speakers for theaters to making air raid sirens, which used a similar technology. So, that was all the real research that was done, and the textbooks and all the information you could get really stemmed from that era of research.

By the time we got to our third generation sound system, we had already exhausted all of the technology and research that had been done previous to us. Yet we had questions we needed answered in terms of the pursuit of better sound, and there was nowhere to get information. It became obvious that we were going to have to create a model whereby we could test their hypotheses and new ideas and stuff that we were coming up with. And that was basically the crux of the Wall of Sound.

The Wall of Sound was a culmination of ideas from me and a number of other people that were, like, sound audiophile and designers, and some of them were mathematician-based people. Some of them were loudspeaker design people, some were electronics design people, and some of them were musician sound mixer people, and that was more the area that I was in. But in order to move to the newer technology, it required incorporating all of these people, so it was a group venture. There were some various people, like Alembic, who played a role in it.

They didn't really design and build it, but they did do some consultation towards it. There were a number of other people--a guy named John Curl, a guy named John Meyer. I don't want to name a lot of people because I don't want to burn anybody. What I'm trying to say is there was a cumulative endeavor by a half a dozen really knowledgeable sound people and really knowledgeable mathematicians. By the time I got to where I was asking questions there weren't really answers for, I noticed that the other sound freaks around me were in the same dilemma. So, we got

together and decided to do something about it, and that became the Wall of Sound. It was predicated on raising issues and then finding solutions for them. Without going into tremendous detail, I think that the main thing to say about it is that while it was extremely extravagant, it was very effective. It provided knowledge and answers that still haven't been exhausted.

It gave us the grounds for another 20 years of research and development, and by the mid-'70s, when our nation's economy and government crapped out on us and everything skyrocketed, the Wall of Sound was already nearly prohibitively expensive, in terms of both money and energy. When that happened, it pushed it over the top and made it impossible. We were working eleven months of the year, we were broke all the time and we were fried. That's in fact why we took a year off, because we were just exhausted. When we did that, we also retired the Wall of Sound, the theory being that, okay, it served its purpose, and now it's time to come up with the next generation that takes into consideration as much of the technology that we learned from it, as well as incorporates efficiency in terms of size and the ability to move it around the country and how much time it takes to set it up.

The Wall of Sound is like all other test endeavors, it's not practical on a day-to-day basis, and it's designed to be able to develop information. It wasn't designed to be practical; it was designed to give answers. Now that we had the answers, it was time to regroup, scrap that system, and come up with the next generation, which began to address the practical issues in how long it takes to set it up, how many people it requires to set it up, how many trucks it takes to haul it around. Those became the new important considerations.

The system that we have now has kind of accomplished the best of both worlds. The sound is as good as or better than the Wall of Sound, and is also definitely less complicated and costly and time-consuming to set up and move around. I think the centerpiece of it all was the Wall of Sound, and from that, technology has been sent ahead instead of backwards for the first time in history.

*Relix:* A *Relix* reader sent me some pages from a book on sound reinforcement, and the Wall of Sound was pictured. Alembic is listed as the credit. Nowhere does it mention the Grateful Dead, you, or anyone.

*Healy:* The Grateful Dead put up all the money for it, all the energy for it, and all the inspiration came from a number of people, myself and John Meyer and John Curl and people like that. As a matter of fact, they wound up actually being removed from it because they were in it for business and we were in it for knowledge and technology. I can assure you that it would have happened even without Alembic. I don't mind helping to set the story straight.

The name Alembic was derived from Owsley. He's the guy who came up with it, because he's actually an alchemist. And the original Alembic was Owsley and I, and a guy named Bob Matthews.

*Relix:* What was one of the most unusual venues you had to work the sound system into?

*Healy:* I get asked that a lot, and the best answer I can derive is that over the years now, we've played every place a number of times and in every place we've played I've had horrible times and then I've come back and had wonderful times, or vice versa. So, I used to think that I had favorite and non-favorite places, but now I think it has more to do with who I am and what I'm doing and the band and the day and where the moon is and Lord knows, whatever. The things that make a given show more exciting, or not exciting, really fun and edifying or not rewarding, have to do with things that aren't that tangible. It has to do with moods and atmospheric conditions. Like in cold weather, the sound doesn't sound as good as in warm weather. And the human elements and stuff have more to do with it than the actual venues themselves. Because, as I say, I think all of us would agree that we've had wonderful and horrible times in the same places on different occasions.

*Relix:* I heard about an experiment you tried in Egypt where you piped the band's sound into the King's inner chamber in the Great Pyramid and wanted to mic it back out. That sounds    interesting. Did    it    work?

*Healy.* Um, no. It almost worked. And it worked sporadically. There's no electricity over there, no anything over there. So, everything you have, you have to bring yourself. The distance between the stage at the base of the Sphinx and the King's Chamber of the Great Pyramid was maybe a quarter mile, and we had wireless radio rigs that sent and received the signal to and from the chamber. For some reason--and this is where it can get into the cosmic aspects if you want it to--the equipment would just work intermittently. It would all be working, but the signal wouldn't get from one place to the other. So, who knows. Maybe the King himself didn't dig his bedroom being used as an echo chamber.

But I did spend the night in the King's Chamber. They have tours in there, but between five in afternoon and nine the next morning, they lock the place up. We conned them into locking us in there for the night. Me and David Freiberg and, I think, Jerry and somebody else went in there. We took acoustic guitars and harmonicas and spent the night in the King's Chamber playing music and witnessing the acoustic properties of it, which are very, very unique. For the size and shape of the room, it doesn't sound at all like any other place that has that size and shape. It has its own unique characteristics, and it was a very warm and friendly feeling. The density of the stone from there to the outside means that the place is so incredibly quiet. It's like you're not on the earth. It's like you're in outer space or something, like a whole different place. But it was a very interesting experience.

The experiments were interesting, and from time to time the echo thing worked, but It didn't work totally. I don't think the importance was whether or not it worked, the importance was the fact that we took a shot at it. To get into the King's Chamber you have to climb this long ladder thing, kind of a board walkway, and there was no real safe place to put all the wires that went from the inside of the King's Chamber to the outside where the radio links were, and that got destroyed. Just a lot of stuff happened. And getting the show itself on was monumentally difficult over there. With no electricity, we had these old funky generators, and just kept trying to get them to run. At a show like that you have to be a diesel mechanic and a sound maker and an electrician and a stage constructor. You have to be able to do a little of all that stuff if you want to survive.

*Relix:* Can you give us some insight into the use of MIDI technology?

*Healy:* Basically, MIDI amounts to the ability to control and manipulate musical instruments via computers.

*Relix:* The band seems to be going further into it. Does that affect your working with the sound?

*Healy:* It makes it easier because ultimately, it isn't just the band. I'm into MIDI myself, a lot of what I do and the ability to process sound, I use MIDI, too. I'll tell you what my analogy is. Imagine yourself as an artist, and back in the early days the biggest thing that an artist did that made him or her famous was you made your own canvas, and you stretched it yourself, and you dyed it

yourself, and you made your own paints and stuff. I look at it as, the use of the computers and the use of the digital technology and the use of any kind of technology helps me create a smoother, flatter, nicer stretched canvas with more uniformed tone to it and gives me better, richer colors to paint with. It really makes my job more desirable, because it gives me more flexibility in the creative aspects of it.

*Relix:* Garcia was quoted as saying, "We're starting to deal with the possibility of having a permanent venue of some kind." Can you speculate as to what that would be like?

*Healy:* Some variations go from someplace like Shoreline, for instance, that we would do two or three months a year there, some long run, and the idea would be people would come like they go to Disneyland or something. That's one variation, but now there's some other new possibilities. We're now working on an exhibit of high definition TV, HDTV, and we will do that the next time we play at Shoreline in August. The program will originate there. It will be distributed there. And it will be distributed to theaters around the country.

High definition TV is an infinitely higher resolution than regular TV as we know it. The screens will be 40 feet wide, which is the width of our stage. So, the scale will be one to one, and the picture and color and texture will be absolutely pure, even better than 35mm film. It'll rival 70mm film, extremely good quality. And then each one of these places will have a custom-specified sound system that will go with it, so that each place will have an immensely beautiful picture and an immensely great sound system. This is a test, another one of the Grateful Dead's firsts that we're famous for, and this will be our first

endeavor at high definition TV.

There's only six of these projectors that can project high definition TV in the country, and the idea is that from Shoreline, we'll send a signal to the satellite, and then it will come down into these six cities that we have yet to pick. And then each one of these six systems will go into one of those theaters, and it'll be like a custom exhibit. So that's another possibility. I don't think that it's really known yet whether the place will be a place where people actually come to or will exist in the form of some electronic conveyance.

The thing is that it's difficult and expensive to tour, and I think we might be getting to a place in our lives where being on the road all the time isn't that desirable. So, the object will be to get a place that's more consistent with the time that we have to spend on it and still enable our fans to see and hear the music. Those are just some suggestions and ideas, but I don't think that it's necessarily become a fixed reality yet, it's something that's still an exploratory,

Buckminster Fuller once designed for us, that I have the blueprints for, like a floating venue that looked like a spaceship and held about 10,000 people. The object was that we could go to different cities and have our permanent set-up, like the carnival shows, and that's another possibility. That happened about 15 years ago, before he died. He came up with a design that worked similar to a dirigible. You could take on or remove buoyancy, and you could float to a different city and then you could lower it and tie down and everybody would come and see the show. That's a more space futuristic version of it, but it certainly is a good idea. I would like to see something like that happen, I don't know if it will happen in my lifetime, but it sure would be nice.

## Grateful Dead Word Search

| B | M | n | P | Y | J | d | q | n | v | T | O | I | R | r | l | b | W | K | q |
|---|---|---|---|---|---|---|---|---|---|---|---|---|---|---|---|---|---|---|---|
| N | i | C | h | g | T | i | Q | i | W | s | o | R | w | i | X | C | r | s | M |
| d | o | l | i | t | T | A | t | n | x | D | a | M | Q | b | P | A | H | t | r |
| C | i | D | l | w | Z | I | b | h | a | n | F | o | v | y | c | R | t | E | J |
| r | F | v | n | G | e | k | C | k | q | T | d | r | n | e | p | g | i | P | L |
| u | S | n | n | N | r | H | D | i | m | M | f | n | I | r | y | D | h | W | h |
| U | h | l | z | k | s | a | e | g | p | f | q | i | s | G | c | S | O | T | S |
| W | T | Z | g | i | r | i | h | F | M | G | w | n | e | f | u | v | i | F | i |
| G | p | i | r | T | e | g | n | a | r | t | S | g | n | o | L | h | m | v | x |
| c | U | q | F | D | d | h | e | d | m | J | h | D | o | h | e | u | K | y | b |
| p | f | v | i | w | n | t | r | R | M | W | i | e | J | c | s | y | r | B | T |
| i | M | a | A | x | u | S | N | h | i | x | p | w | y | u | o | q | W | P | k |
| N | A | O | P | b | a | t | u | n | c | s | o | X | e | o | o | e | U | e | v |
| H | f | J | P | q | S | r | t | E | k | R | f | c | s | T | L | r | n | m | E |
| I | K | A | h | q | l | e | b | Y | e | I | F | f | a | f | X | o | M | H | o |
| n | z | I | y | r | r | e | J | u | y | d | o | U | C | W | N | m | e | X | b |
| K | R | w | Q | l | e | t | i | M | a | T | o | m | R | a | g | I | k | B | z |
| R | b | P | a | i | M | b | a | F | p | e | I | f | t | b | e | I | Q | Y | L |
| h | d | n | I | M | B | C | v | v | g | h | s | i | f | g | n | i | K | u | K |
| H | d | e | R | B | S | y | w | G | e | y | F | E | J | b | K | F | V | u | E |

Ship of Fools
Pigpen
Kingfish
Merl Saunders
Long Strange
 Trip
Casey Jones
Winterland
Morning Dew
Loose Lucy
Haight Street
Ace
Phil
Mickey
Fillmore
Jerry
Touch of Grey
Bill Graham

**by A. Klosterman**

Ché Graham

Tom Constanten on the Guiding Light

John Rottet

Antique pick up stick game found in curio shop in Maine. Jack Staws not from Wichita, but from Milton Bradley, Springfield, Mass.

John Rottet

Beth Drumming at the edge of Stealie Mat

Anna Swain

IN HONOR OF THE LIVING, IN GRATEFUL MEMORY OF THE DEAD

Robert Clark

BROKEN ARROW

HAVE A GRATEFUL DAY
KEYSTONE STATE
SYF

Lisa & Michael Hiliadis

Brian Powell

Franklin's Tower

On our way to Deer Creek

Joel in Tucson

# VINCE WELNICK

## BY TONI A. BROWN

Photo by Rob Cohn

*Relix* had the good fortune to interview Vince Welnick back in February, 1991. His enthusiasm was catching, and we had a great conversation about the changes in his life surrounding his induction into the Grateful Dead. Since our interview, spring tour has come and gone. Some of the newness may have worn off by now. But Vince is a welcome addition to the band by all the accounts that have crossed my desk. If you want to get to know him a little better, read on.

**Relix:** A good place to start would be with your history. I have seen the Tubes, so, when you became a member of the band, I was a little intrigued. The Tubes were a theatrical conglomerate, so much was going on on the stage. You performed some rather racey stuff. Just before you joined the Dead, I'd heard that the Tubes were considering going back out on the road or reforming in some way. Is that so?

**Welnick:** There was a little bit of talk about it, but it's kind of on hold because of my situation with the Grateful Dead, which I gave utmost priority over the Tubes and Todd Rundgren. The Tubes at the time weren't touring with Fee [Waybill], sometimes Prairie [Prince] wasn't available because he had other musical gigs, and I wasn't always around because of [my work with] Todd Rundgren, who's a little more steady band, and who at the time was doing an album.

**Relix:** Were you approached by the Dead?

**Welnick:** They didn't approach me, I approached them. I had heard through the grapevine about Brent and my wife Lori called Mimi Mills, who used to work for the Tubes and now works for Bob, and said, "What gives?" She put me in touch with Bobby, and he said, "Bruce Hornsby is in the band now, and we want a synth player who can sing high harmony," which I can do. So they said that they were auditioning. There was one guy that I thought was going to get it, Tim Gorman. He just toured in Japan as the Tim Gorman Band, so he had his own thing going, but perhaps my vocalization helped because I was pretty

strong in the high harmonies.

**Relix:** When did you start playing keyboards?

**Welnick:** I saw my mom playing boogie woogie when I was a baby, and that caught my fancy.

**Relix:** What kind of music do you prefer now?

**Welnick:** Everything, I like it all, except I'm not too keen on opera. But I like Coltrane, Hendrix a lot. I like the Four Tops, Stevie [Wonder], Marvin Gaye, Captain Beefheart. I like lots of various people, including soundtracks. When I started playing, a man in school got me into classical piano for starters. I did a couple of years of that and then went into pop.

**Relix:** Do you think classical prepared you for the Grateful Dead?

**Welnick:** It helped, although it's been a long time since I've played the classics. The thing that helped was the Tubes, because we played a wide variety of music. I kind of identified with the Dead from the beginning, in the '60s. I lost track of them in the '70s when I started going out on the road with the Tubes.

**Relix:** So you hadn't seen the Grateful Dead since the '60s?

**Welnick:** No, I saw them twice. I saw them in Phoenix at the Circle Theater, and I saw them in L.A.,when I lived there, at the Shrine. I listened to them live. In fact, *Anthem Of The Sun* I listened to.

**Relix:** So I guess you basically came in from a non-familiar background of what they were up to now. Did they just pile tapes on you so you could familiarize yourself with their material?

Photo by Rob Cohn

Artwork by Glenn Harding

Artwork by Alfred Klosterman

**Welnick:** I got so much stuff. They were very helpful and generous. They sent me everything on CD and cassette, including a CD player because I didn't own one, and they gave me a list of songs I might want to learn for the audition, which was helpful. There are a few songs that we've never practiced, that we just do.

**Relix:** Do you feel comfortable enough to just go in there and play?

**Welnick:** It's hard to feel uncomfortable because they are so friendly and personable. The first time I saw Bobby and Jerry, I wanted to play with the band. When I heard about the audition and my wife was pushing for it, I thought to myself, well, I'd like to know if they want me in the band, then maybe I'll decide if I want to be in the band. I was used to being free and didn't really know what I wanted to do, but then it sounded intriguing to me because they're such a great band. They represent the '60s and a really great time in my life, which I still feel in my heart even though my hair is falling out. But then I met Bobby and Jerry, and it wasn't a question of bucks or fame, I knew I wanted to play with these guys. Then I went to audition and met Mickey, Bill, and Phil, and they all had the same kind of vibe about them. Then I was sitting there by the phone waiting for a week. Yeah, it was a crazy week, but I practiced hard. I really wanted to play with them, and I tried my damnedest, and I didn't know how the audition went. It was like a blur. Next thing I know, I'm in my car on the freeway wondering what happened.

**Relix:** When you do shows with Bruce Hornsby, is it difficult to stand out? Did his early presence help in your transition because you could lay back and listen more, or did you just dive right in?

**Welnick:** I played with him there about the same way as I play when he's not there. Because of the nature of the synthesizer and the piano, we play different registers and don't really step on each other much. I play about the same way, but more to fit in with the sound because you have two keyboards there and you don't want to have them dropping out. It makes it more subtle and richer at the same time. It depends on who's playing what, and I notice that Bruce sits out a lot and comes in on embellishments. I try to play textures, and I try to be conscious of what's going on lyrically. I try not to step on words or play louder than Jerry. I try to hear what Bob's doing, and I can pick up Phil really easily, but Bobby, sometimes, I have to get him pumped through the monitors.

**Relix:** The Dead's fans have a unique outlook and approach to life. Has this affected you in any way?

**Welnick:** [Laughs] Yeah, probably in every way. Let me count the ways. Yeah, I mean, my whole life is different now. It would really have to be a whole separate interview just to go into that.

Photo by Rob Cohn

**Relix:** When you get up onto the stage and you see this sea of color and you feel this love emanating from the audience, it must be amazing!

**Welnick:** Well, one can't be too cocky here, either, because I'm new at this game. I'd imagine some of the fans are probably looking in another direction when they're relaying their admiration out. But I feel the ripple here and there when I reach for a solo or go for something that may stand out in a small place somewhere in a song and get recognized. But I read magazines and what's said, and I realize that even though everyone's having a whale of a time up there, they are listening to every note. I mean, you can't slip one by on them.

**Relix:** Do you have any ideas about what you'd like to add to the Grateful Dead?

**Welnick:** Well, I just like to collaborate with them on songs. Right now, we're still in rehearsal, getting me warmed up in existing songs. There is some talk going around that we might sit down and pair off with various people and write some songs. And I'd like to be on their next record and have an influence in a good way. How, I can't say, because we've never written together.

**Relix:** But you do write?

**Welnick:** Yeah, and I don't like to write alone. I write mostly music, and I wrote a lot of music for the Tubes. My wife and I co-wrote "Feel It" on Todd's new album. And I like writing with people. I have a lot of song ideas that are different styles, and I don't want to carve too deep into the Dead's feelings. So that's where it becomes a test of how to work it into the context of what we have here. But I figure if I just leave the songs open enough or work with them at this very moment, it will breathe life into it.

**Relix:** So you don't think you'll be introducing "White Punks On Dope," "Mondo Bondage," and other Tubes material into the band?

**Welnick:** Well, if Jerry wants to wear the big shoes, I'll play the songs.

**Relix:** Do you feel that your performance with the Dead has altered your style at all?

**Welnick:** Yeah, I get to solo ten times more than ever before, and it's a real kick. There's lots of open improv jamming, and that's one thing that I really like. The Tubes had some room for improv, but with the Dead there's places in practically every song, which is unlike any band I've ever played in. My style is changing, and Jerry and Bob or Mickey or Bill or Phil lay a CD on me of a keyboard player (like Jerry turned me on to Little Feat), and you know, just give me a taste, and I want to hear and see everything. It's like checking it all out and trying not to be too lazy when I'm home because there are times when I tour for 200 days a year. I try to keep practicing. But I think half of this learning experience is listening. And I do listen a lot.

**Relix:** How did you like the Dead's European tour?

**Welnick:** It was great!

**Relix:** Considering that you were such a new kid at that point?

**Welnick:** Well, I had been to Europe before. The Tubes were probably more popular there than in America, and I was just in Germany, but this was a different thing. For instance, I wasn't sharing a room with somebody in the band.

**Relix:** You've been on the San Francisco music scene for so many years, but you didn't get the recognition of being any sort of a front man with your previous bands. Being with the Grateful Dead, every member is a front man, every member is crucial to the whole. Did you miss the solo status before?

**Welnick:** No, the plan of attack the Tubes took in the beginning, the first concept was that just standing up there playing was boring, and we wanted to fool around more. The second one was how do you remember seven guys' names when they're not nearly as big as the Beatles? You take one guy, you put him up front, you dress him up weird, and you make him a household item. Of course, the idea was to get one guy out there and at least one name, it's better than trying to jam seven people down in front. I was gratified in that I had a lot to do with the music, which is what I did best. And being a piano player, you've gotta sit down sometimes, so you're not exactly Mr. Excitement there on stage. I didn't mind sitting where I was sitting. They were playing my music, and just because a light didn't go on saying, "Vince wrote this," I felt in my own mind that I got to take center stage often enough. With the Grateful Dead, I think it's always gonna gravitate towards the obvious. I don't expect to jump off the keyboards, run up there, and grab a microphone in the center of the stage and entertain people. It's not going to be that way.

**Vince Welnick and Toni Brown
Photo by L.D. Kippel**

**Relix:** The plight of the rainforests came to much public atttenion via the Grateful Dead. They have gotten behind a number of concerns and their endorsements have done mankind a tremedous amount of good. They have that impact on their fans. How does it feel to have such power?

**Welnick:** Scary, it's thrilling. I got a lot more lines on my face from smiling all the time. Everyday is like Christmas. It makes you want to get up early and start the day.

**Relix:** What are some of your favorite Grateful Dead songs?

**Vince Welnick as a "Tube"**
**Photo Courtesy Capitol Records**

**Welnick:** There are too many to mention, but some of my favorites are "Eyes Of The World," "Terrapin," "Box Of Rain," "Scarlet Begonias," "Bird Song," "Victim Or The Crime." I like "Black Peter," I love the bridge in that. I like the fact that Bobby knows all the words to all these Dylan songs. I like to see Phil sing more.

**Relix:** So would everyone in the audience.

**Welnick:** It's funny. We were at a rehearsal learning songs off *Workingman's Dead* and *American Beauty,* which have some pretty lush vocals, and a lot of them are very close together. It's hard to tell where to go on it. So I'd be singing a part, and I'd say, "Does it go like this?", and Phil would say, "No, more like this," and he'd just nail the part. So I'd say, "Phil, why don't you sing it?" He goes, "I can't do that, I can't sing that range." Meanwhile he just did it, right there. He feels his range is more down on baritone, but he sure nails it. "Attics Of My Life," I want to bring that back.

**Relix:** "Unbroken Chain," it would be great to hear some of this material. It seems like you like some of the Weir/John Barlow stuff as well as Hunter who is a very strong force with the Grateful Dead lyric-wise.

**Welnick:** He just showed me in *Box Of Rain,* his lyric book, there's a great deal of lyrics that are unpublished as Grateful Dead songs that he might have done himself, but said that it could be open to new musical interpretations.

I saw him at rehearsal yesterday, and he said to have a crack at some of the words, and I hope to get to do it with him. Jerry and Bobby talk about doing this drum machine party, that is, lay down some drums and party with it. And I've been over to Mickey's a couple of times and tossed him some ideas. I've been to Bill's house, and I'd like to get everyone involved in songwriting without any preconceived, which I'm sure they don't have, notions when they go into it. Just do whatever comes.

**Relix:** Mickey has brought some interesting percussive music to the public's attention. He's got such an intense feel for world music.

**Welnick:** Yeah, I checked his rainforest tapes, which was 22 hours up in a tree getting all of the cycles. From the first cycles of the day and then superimposing native songs over the top.

**Relix:** You have a lot of interesting and creative forces at work here. I think you may have found a very interesting home.

**Welnick:** It's fascinating. He took me over there, and he started playing some things we do on his major speakers down in his studio, and my God! That could be the answer to male birth control. Just stand down there for two seconds, and you'd be good for the whole day.

**Relix:** So any unusual ideas you ever come up with, here's your outlet for them.

**Welnick:** I did one piece where we found a cow out on the road, Lori and I. It was Saturday night, and a farmer was out doing the Saturday night thing. He was gone all night, so he had to keep the cow out in the pasture, and it was making some big-time noise, so I went out and recorded it on cassette. Some time later I'm playing this and I'm going, "Wow! It seems to be pretty consistent in its tone quality." I found out this cow was going in the key of C, big time. So I laid down this track of "boogie woogie" and recorded it while I played the cow going off at random intervals and just let it be the lead singer. It came out real cool. The cow sings. And if I get a loss for songwriting ideas, what I do a lot with 13 cards off a deck, the aces are one, the jacks are 11, queens are 12, and the kings are one again, and the 13th card I deal is the key that the song would be in, and I run out three sections of four chords that go with the 12 cards that have been dealt. And they decide what the intervals are and juxtaposition it to intervals of a melody or a chord change. It makes its own tune, for better or worse. Sometimes you get too many sevens or nines in your hand, and you know you get a weird sound. But for the most part, you can come up with ideas you never dreamed possible.

**Relix:** Now, you're going to be coming up with really weird things. But I'm sure you're finding that the Grateful Dead will give you your voice and your space, and you'll be able to do things, and they'll add to those things, and I think we're going to see a lot of you out there. I know it's a short time, you've only been with them a few months. It's just a beginning for a band that's been around for over 25 years. You have a long strange trip ahead of you.

**Welnick:** Once I get toilet-trained, there'll be no stopping me. ∎

**Artwork by Alfred Klosterman**

**Artwork by Glenn Harding**

*Artwork by Glenn Harding*

Vol. 18
No. 3

$4.50 U.S.
$5.50 Can.
£5.00 U.K.

# Relix
music for the mind

GRATEFUL DEAD'S
VINCE WELNICK

NED LAGIN
— SEASTONES

Summer Issue

COUNTRY SPECIAL

EXCLUSIVE INTERVIEW:
Peter Rowan
Poco
David Grisman
New Riders of
the Purple Sage
Country Joe McDonald
Kentucky HeadHunters
and others...

May/June, 1991

Artwork
by
Gary Kroman

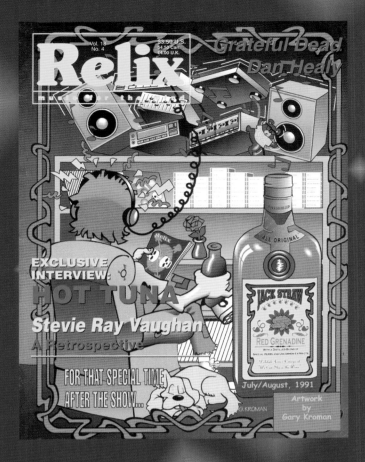

Vol. 18
No. 4

$3.50 U.S.
$4.50 Can.
£4.00 U.K.

# Relix
music for the mind

Grateful Dead
Dan Healy

EXCLUSIVE
INTERVIEW:
HOT TUNA

Stevie Ray Vaughan
A Retrospective

FOR THAT SPECIAL TIME
AFTER THE SHOW...

JACK STRAW
ALL ORIGINAL
RED GRENADINE

July/August, 1991

Artwork
by
Gary Kroman

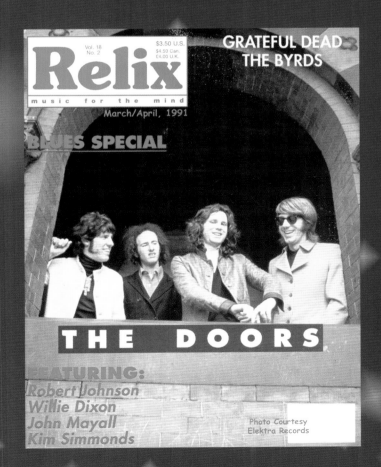

Vol. 18
No. 2

$3.50 U.S.
$4.50 Can.
£4.00 U.K.

# Relix
music for the mind

GRATEFUL DEAD
THE BYRDS

March/April, 1991

BLUES SPECIAL

# THE DOORS

FEATURING:
Robert Johnson
Willie Dixon
John Mayall
Kim Simmonds

Photo Courtesy
Elektra Records

Vol. 18
No. 6

$4.50 U.S.
$5.50 Can.
£5.00 U.K.

November/December

# Relix
music for the mind

Grateful Dead
Stories, Photos, Reviews

SPECIAL
YEAR END ISSUE

Artwork
by
Gary Kroman

# Relix Records

Relix founder Les Kippel's enthusiasm for merchandising dovetailed nicely with his love for the behind-the-scenes action of the music business. He started dealing an array of collectibles aimed at *Relix* readers, and the profits helped keep the magazine afloat. Rockin' Relix / Relix International was born as the merchandising division of the company.

Kippel went on to become one of the top sales reps for Bill Graham's Winterland Productions, the world's largest license holder for music-related merchandise. Through merchandising, he built significant associations with a variety of stores that were critical to the future success of an as-yet undeveloped enterprise.

In 1980, Grateful Dead lyricist Robert Hunter suggested that Les start a record company. Relix Records was born. "I have a split personality," explained Kippel. "It's split between me as Relix Records and me as a fan. The fan in me directs me, and often the businessman in me holds me back. But the fan in me will push to make something happen. And often it costs me money, but I never really felt the bottom line was about making money. To me, the record company bottom line was always about getting musicians out on the road and getting the music out to people."

The first Relix Records release was Hunter's *Jack O' Roses*.

It wasn't easy to run a record label, but Les was an astute businessman. Most of the small independents that emerged were having trouble collecting payments for the albums they shipped. Relix was in a great position---working with the same stores that carried the magazine and merchandise, they had to keep their payments current in order to receive the next issue of the magazine and the latest rock paraphernalia. Without planning, it was strategically brilliant.

As the magazine's publisher, I was naturally ready to help in seeking out talent for the label. I also spent my free time promoting the artists on the label. Before the Internet, this was a daunting task. Shipping hundreds of albums to radio stations and reviewers was time-consuming and expensive. Follow up was tedious. The artists on the label didn't see much of the groundwork that went into putting out their projects, and with a market that was experienced in tape trading, it was tough going as far as selling the product. The label did well on one front---it gave exposure to musicians who would not have done as well elsewhere. With the magazine's promotional and advertising support, Relix Records existed for 20 years.

Relix released more than 120 records and CDs, including material from a "who's who" of the psychedelic / country rock / blues music scene: Jorma Kaukonen, Hot Tuna, the New Riders of the Purple Sage, Tom Constanten, Kingfish, Wavy Gravy, Dinosaurs, Merl Saunders, the Flying Burrito Brothers, Zero, Savoy Brown, Commander Cody, Johnny Winter, Solar Circus, Max Creek and many more.

---Toni Brown, 2009

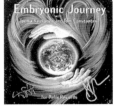

# WE ARE EVERYWHERE

Steve Menard & friends

**Todd Fabbro**

Virginia

ENTRANCE TO GRATEFUL ACRES

**Jay Whitmeyer**

**Mark Kraynak**

Dead Fish

## THE DANCING BEAR PUB

Your Choice ................. $12.⁹⁵

2½ lb. Prime Rib
1¾ lb. Baked Stuffed Lobster
1¼ lb. Boiled Twin Lobster
Surf & Turf · Queen Cut Prime Rib & 1¼ Lb. Boiled Lobster
All dinners include salad, choice of potato & vegetable

Every Friday, Saturday & Sunday, 2 P.M. to Midnight

20 Old Granite St., Manchester, NH          666-0000

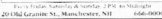

**A'vin Knox**

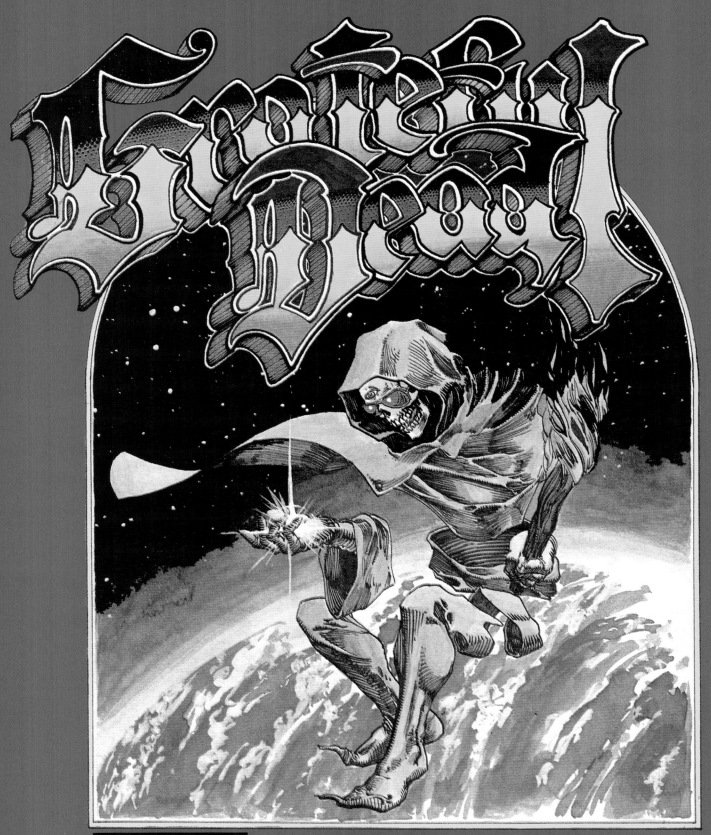

Artwork by Gary Kroman

# GUITARS
## I HAVE OWNED

### By Kim Simmonds

I remember my first guitar well. Like a first love it holds fond memories in the back of my mind. I had bought it from a mail order company whose advertisement I had seen in the rear pages of the *Daily Express*. It didn't cost much, which was just as well, because I was only 13 at the time with only a small paper round to bring me in any income. I had not had any previous musical training apart from beating on a cymbal in elementary school, and so feeling a little foolish and pretentious, I told no one else in the family about my acquisition until it arrived on the doorstep of our South London house. "What on earth is this?" my mother said when the delivery man showed up with a large rectangular box. I had been waiting excitedly for two months for its arrival. The advertisement had promised a delivery date no later than 30 days from receipt of the order, and I had been getting quite worried if I'd ever see the guitar or even my money again. Now it was on my doorstep. "That's my guitar, probably," I replied nonchalantly, and before she exploded I explained the situation, including the important part that it was all paid for, and then I took it to my bedroom. That was when I received my first shock. On opening the box I found that the guitar had arrived unassembled! And furthermore, it was no mistake, for there in front of me were assembly instructions. I hadn't anticipated this, but with the optimism of youth I dived straight into the task at hand and 'lo and behold within an hour I had a beautiful acoustic guitar in front of me. At least to me it was beautiful, but there was one problem - how to tune it! Well, I skipped by that little encumbrance and with the strings at least in place I presented my new instrument to the family in the downstairs living room. I even had the audacity to pretend that I could play and everyone remembers that I did actually play a Chuck Berry riff! From that moment there was no turning back and the guitar went everywhere with me. To school outings, to church socials and to all my friend's parties. It turned out that I could actually strum fairly well but don't ask me what key I was playing in!

My next guitar was an electric, a Hofner, and I had seen it in the local music store. It was costly, and so it should have been, with its glossy red finish that reminded me of the more expensive American Gibson guitars, and its contoured semi-acoustic body complete with two pick-ups. The problem here was how to pay for it. Enter my father. I had tried to arrange a payment plan, but was underage, and my dad came to the rescue with his checkbook. I figured that the best way that I could pay him back would be by learning to play it. I picked up a small amplifier and started a gruelling time-table of eight hours practice each day. As I was going to school at the same time, it didn't leave much time for anything else. Needless to say, my homework never did get done, but I did learn to play the instrument!

On turning professional, at the age of 17, I purchased an American guitar. A Fender Tele-caster. It was "state of the art" at the time and was finished in a beautiful cream color. I made my first records with it and then, flush with success, I exchanged it for a more glamorous Gibson Flying V model. This guitar kept for many years, and I eventually sold it. Nevertheless, the guitar continued to be associated with me and many fans would constantly ask me, "Do you still have the Flying V?" Rather negatively I would have to answer "No." Naturally, as time went by, I began to wonder what had become of it. Then, during a concert in San Francisco, a guitar collecter arrived backstage with none other than the old Gibson itself. It was a prize in his collection, and I happily signed it for him. Its market value had increased enormously in the interim period, and I was very happy to see it appreciated and in good hands.

My favorite guitar would definitely have to be the 1953 Gibson Gold Top Les Paul. What a sound! Clear as a bell. It went through a lot with me, including being stolen on a tour in Germany (it was returned) and narrowly escaping being crushed by the wheels of an equipment truck. I had worn the finish away on the top front from contact with a bracelet, and a belt buckle had guaged the back. Still, as far as I was concerned, the blemishes only served to add further charm to the old instrument. "Get rid of that antique," some people would say. "Use something more hi-tech." But I clung to my piece of history and turned my nose up at their suggestions. I had it with me on a show that I played in New Orleans. Now it is customary on show nights for there to be a sound check earlier in the day, and at these checks my guitars are taken out of their cases and put on stands to facilitate easy access. This particular day a stand was missing and the Gold Top was temporarily set against an amplifier. It was leaning there at a forty five degree angle instead of being snug in its stand, and a jolt from a member of the lighting crew toppled it over and the head stock was broken from the guitar neck. I saw none of this and on arrival an hour later, I was taken into the dressing room and asked to sit down. I knew something bad had occurred. Robert came straight to the point. "Your Gold Top has had an accident. It's broken. I'm afraid you may not be able to use it again." I was heart-broken, but I had suffered broken guitars before, and so I accepted the situation as best I could and then played that night with a spare Les Paul. I actually managed to get the Gold Top repaired. Unfortunately, the Los Angeles shop did a poor job and the guitar never felt the same again. I occasionally take it out of its case nowadays to practice a little, but try as I will, something is always missing and I inevitably end up sadly putting it away with a heavy sigh.

The guitar you always remember is the "one that got away." The instrument that I am talking about that I would liked to have owned, but never did, was a Gibson Switchmaster that was being sold privately by a fellow musician. A large bodied jazz instrument from the late '40s, it came with three pick-ups and was huge. The dark sunburst finish was classic. The cost of the guitar bothered me, and so I thought about it and I thought about it, and eventually procrastinated for so long that someone else purchased it. A week after it's sale I was window-shopping amongst the music stores, and there in the window hanging proud and majestic was the Switchmaster—for sale at double the price!

Eventually, I ended up owning 30 guitars and found that with a growing family I had a

**Savoy Brown – 1980**

problem storing them in the house. The solution was to be found by placing some in the attic, some in my brother's attic and the remainder in my parents' spare room! The situation was such that I couldn't remember what guitar I had where, and inevitably, during the course of a few house changes and an emigration to America, some were lost. To this day, I can't figure out where my 1962 Fender Stratocaster is. Probably collecting dust in an attic somewhere. ∎

*Kim Simmonds is the founder of Savoy Brown. The band still tours with Dave Walker on vocals, and their British blues-based sound is still your best boogie bet around!*

# history of the

# jerry garcia BAND

Steve Clark

### BY CARY KROSINSKY

a look back at the history of the Jerry Garcia Band reveals an interesting evolution and a rich body of work. It wouldn't seem that Garcia, who also fronts the Grateful Dead, the most active touring band in the history of rock 'n' roll, would have much spare time. He has, however, managed to pursue among his other musical interests, a long relationship with his own band.

Existing as a necessary outlet for Garcia, who has stated in previously published interviews a need to be constantly touring live, the Garcia Band provides an opportunity to experience his music on a more personal level. With the Dead, Garcia's playing is part of a larger ensemble. His own band offers the opportunity to examine his individual style and taste more closely.

The Garcia Band's forte is unique interpretations of generally established rock, rhythm and blues, gospel, reggae and country standards. At times, they completely alter contexts of songs. For example, "Knockin' On Heaven's Door" and "Dear Prudence" are reggae in nature when performed by this band. "Tangled Up In Blue" becomes an uptempo show stopper. Others are well-played in their original form, such as the classic gospel song "My Sisters And Brothers," and the bluesy "Think." The Garcia Band has also provided an alternate vehicle for Hunter-Garcia penned tunes. There is no specific, easily definable history of this band, rather, a trail of sound to follow that would finally evolve into the Jerry Garcia Band in 1975.

Jerry Garcia met bassist John Kahn at an informal jam session at The Matrix (a club) in San Francisco. The relationship they struck eventually led to the formation of Jerry Garcia's solo band.

Garcia and Kahn, intrigued by the possibilities of collaborating, were introduced to keyboardist Merl Saunders through a mutual acquaintance, San Francisco musician Nick Gravenites. Garcia, Kahn and Saunders played for the first time at The Matrix. They would go on to form the Saunders-Garcia Band with former Creedence Clearwater Revival guitarist Tom Fogerty, and drummer Bill Vitt, which reached a creative peak in 1973. Always jazzy and unique, with a little funk mixed in, a sample of their work makes it clear why these musicians wanted to get together. The Fantasy Records recordings of *Live At The Keystone,* and *Keystone Encores Volumes One and Two,* all recorded July of 1973 in Berkeley, affords an opportunity to hear this sound. The long, interesting versions of "Like A Road" and "My Funny Valentine" are of particular note. Further examples of the successful jazz-rock-funk of these players can be found in renditions of "Expressway (To Your Heart)," "The Night They Drove Old Dixie Down," and "After Midnight." The September 6, 1973 concert at the Capitol Theatre stands as the best existing evidence of the band's high energy, high quality interpretation, which was done during this period (available through tape trading).

Having previously accompanied Saunders on his recordings of *Heavy Turbulence* and *Fire Up* (also on Fantasy), the Saunders-Garcia Band, while Merl's in name, was becoming Jerry's in spirit. As 1974 unfolded, Jerry went on to release his second solo album (titled simply *Garcia* like his first solo release). This one, unlike the first which was mostly Grateful Dead backed and related, was the first true effort of what would soon be the Jerry Garcia Band. Songs like "That's What Love Will Make You Do," "Russian Lullaby" and "He Ain't Give You None" would gradually be introduced into Garcia's live non-GratefulDead performances. Saunders, meanwhile, was continuing to expand on his own unique sound. The two seemed to mesh less fluidly, as manifested in the subsequently

**Jerry Garcia Band - 1978**
**Keith Godchaux, Maria Muldaur, Donna Jean Godchaux, Ron Tutt,**
**John Kahn and Jerry Garcia**

Photo by L.D. Kippel

Photo Courtesy Sumertone Records

**Merl Saunders**

renamed Legion of Mary.

During the Dead's hiatus, which started in late 1974, Legion of Mary enabled Garcia to play extensively and added Martin Fierro on saxophone and flute to the existing Saunders-Garcia personnel. Fogerty had departed a year earlier. Their playing only succeeded occasionally. Some disappointing material, such as "Wondering Why," left the band members asking just that question.

Saunders and Garcia parted amiably in 1975 (they briefly reunited in 1979, in the mostly funk band, Reconstruction), and the first official Jerry Garcia Band was formed. Garcia, with Kahn on bass guitar, added Nicky Hopkins on piano. With him, Hopkins brought world-class credentials, having sat in with the Rolling Stones on one of their best albums, *Exile On Main Street.* The quartet was completed by Elvis Presley drummer, Ron Tutt. These four musicians established the sound that the Garcia Band is

Brad Peña

**Albany 1980**

known for today. Interpretations of "Catfish John" and "Mission In The Rain" (both from Garcia's 1976 release, *Reflections),* and Saunders-Garcia established tunes such as "How Sweet It Is (To Be Loved By You)," and "That's A!right Mama," led the way.

Jimmy Booker added some soul when he briefly replaced Hopkins in the start of 1976, but he soon departed and was replaced by Keith and Donna Godchaux. The Godchauxs stayed until their combined departure from the scene in early 1979, helping solidify the groove that the Garcia Band settled into during the late seventies. This combination toured frequently and were perhaps best personified musically by the 1978 release, *Cats Under The Stars.* "Reuben And Cerise," "Rhapsody In Red," and "Cat's Under The Stars" were successful examples of the rock-oriented, smoothly-grooved sound of this rendition of the group. "Gomorrah," a slow, sweetly-paced tune, also typifies the play of this time. Their live performances now featured quality backup singing, including for a time Maria Muldaur, famous for the hit song "Midnight At The Oasis." In addition, the Garcia Band of 1977 through 1978 seemed as close in sound to the Dead as it ever would.

Following the departure of the Godchauxs and Garcia's time with Reconstruction, the Garcia Band was reformed and re-worked. In 1981, Melvin Seals joined the band on organ, continuing a trend toward a rhythm and blues and gospel feel. Backup singing fell to Liz Stires and Essra Mohawk (replaced by Dee Dee Dickerson and Jackie LaBranch in 1982), incorporating even more soul into the mixture. When David Kemper took over on drums in 1983 and Gloria Jones replaced Dickerson in 1984, the transformation was complete, and the modern day Jerry Garcia Band was in place.

Unfortunately, Garcia was forced to cut back on his solo playing in 1985 when health became an issue. Following his collapse in 1986, he used his band to facilitate his comeback through some fairly inspired performances at The Stone in San Francisco. The experience seemed to add a renewed sense of commitment to Garcia's solo efforts.

The late summer and fall of 1987 brought about the unquestionable peak of the modern version of the Garcia Band. In August, they warmed up with a fine concert at the Greek Theatre in Berkeley, sweetened by the guest appearance of Bonnie Raitt. September presented the opportunity for the legendary stand at the Lunt-Fontanne Theatre in New York City. Garcia was playing Broadway. The intimacy and aesthetics of the room prompted performances of an intensity that will be difficult to match again. Rollicking renditions of "Dear Prudence" and the aforementioned "Think," and smooth takes of "Lucky Old Sun" were all made possible by the energetic, everywhere-at-once coordinating done by Bill Graham and his crew.

Hard as it would be to live up to this experience, the group perseveres on their self titled live release, *Jerry Garcia*

*Band,* based mostly on April 1990 recordings. The album is poignant and rich, featuring numerous examples of the various styles that this band incorporates. "Don't Let Go" is the quintessential Garcia Band jam song, "The Way You Do The Things You Do" swings, and there are numbers included that are relatively new to the repertoire. Two of these, "Senor (Tales of Yankee Power)" and "Waiting For A Miracle," resonate with the band's evolution and success.

Unlike his playing with the Grateful Dead, where his rotation has remained basically

Photo Courtesy Nora Sage

**John Kahn with Garcia – developing other artistic abilities**

Tim Seufert

constant for a number of years, Garcia continues to add new versions of songs to the Jerry Garcia Band. The likes of "C'est La Vie," "Bright Side Of The Road," and "Money Honey," as well as rediscoveries of previously played Garcia Band numbers, are evidence of Garcia's continuing interest in his band, and indicates more for the musical future of this accomplished act. ■

Steve Clark

Ralph Hulett

Willie Dixon – 1975

# Willie Dixon

## BLUES GIANT

### by Ralph Hulett

To say that Willie Dixon has played a role in popular music would be a definite understatement. Perhaps instead he can be considered as a towering influence for musicians for over 40 years. All one needs to do is look at some who have recorded Dixon's songs—the Grateful Dead, the Doors, the Allman Brothers Band, Paul Butterfield, Humble Pie, Cream, Jeff Beck, Led Zeppelin, and the Rolling Stones. In addition, various blues contemporaries of Dixon's have paid tribute to him many times over, including Howlin' Wolf, Bo Diddley, and Muddy Waters. Dixon taught Waters "Hoochie Coochie Man" in a small club after Waters became interested in using it, and that tune became a Waters trademark. Dixon may have even taught Joe Louis a few fancy moves back in the 1930s when the two were sparring partners in the boxing ring.

But it is his songwriting for which he is best known. In 1948, Chess Records began using Dixon as a session man, and he went on to become a producer as well. Eventually, he played on at least 200 sessions. Also throughout the 1930s and 1940s, Dixon played the blues circuit, which was the North in New York City and Chicago during winter and spring, then in the Delta area of the South during harvest time. People in the agricultural economy had money then, and it was only natural for them to come and hear the blues, since it was one of the musical forms that had grown out of plantation life. Dixon was fascinated by the country, and his love for it gave birth to a song covered by the Dead, the Doors, the Stones, and Howlin' Wolf, "Little Red Rooster."

"I've always loved the country," Dixon says. "But I hardly got to live there at all in Vicksburg [the Mississippi city where he was born in 1915] before I got taken away to the city. I never got to go back, and the people living there live in a way that's really important to me. That's what I tried to show in that song—what it was like, with the hounds baying, chickens running around in the barnyard, folks getting up with the sunrise."

Dixon would end up playing for years with Waters and interacting with a who's who of blues performers on the road—Little Walter, Otis Spann, Jimmy Rogers, Big Walter Horton, Junior Wells, and James Cotton. Dixon's status as both a songwriter and stand-up bass player grew, first with the blues community in America and then in Europe. A great deal of the blues' influence on British rock in the 1960s was due to the tours by American blues musicians that Dixon organized.

"I thought that those people over there should

get to hear blues firsthand instead of just hearing about it," he says. "So I got together the International Folk Blues Festival by signing up everyone I could—Vicky Spivey, Muddy Waters, Howlin' Wolf, Chuck Berry, Bo Diddley, Sonny Boy Williamson, and Big Joe Williams. That was in '61, and the Blues Festival went over and toured Europe every year until 1970. Lots more people got exposed to blues, and we got to play for new audiences, which was good, too."

By 1969, British groups such as Peter Green's Fleetwood Mac were making Chicago-style blues their own. Dixon recorded with them a number of times. "I first worked with Peter Green in London, then later in Chicago," Dixon recalls. "His group was trying lots of different stuff in the studio. They were fun to work with, but they also took the blues seriously whenever they played it. At Chess Ter-Mar [Studios] in Chicago, they did lots of people's things. They worked together with me, J.T. Brown, Shakey Horton, Otis Spann, and some others. We all enjoyed those sessions back in '69."

The fruit of these efforts was *Fleetwood Mac In Chicago* on Blue Horizon Records. Green, whose inspiration was Elmore James, did James covers ("I'm Worried," "Madison Blues"), and there were vocals by Spann on his numbers ("Someday Soon Baby," "Hungry Country Girl"). Other bluesmen were featured as well, and of course Dixon played his stand-up bass. The recordings displayed a real sharing of ideas and material, and this closely coincided with Dixon's altruistic entertainment philosophy. Dixon believes that professionals in music ought to share their knowledge with others who are working their way up. There is potential for newcomers because the industry has grown so much since Dixon began recording in the 1940s.

Although he has been hugely successful as a songwriter, Dixon still feels he has room to improve. "I got a lot of what I wanted on records, but other stuff was what Chess wanted to do," he says. "From my experience, it's that way anywhere. And it's the same with contracts. Then there's always those players trying to work their way to a higher level, without a contract."

Dixon has said he feels artists should be allowed to earn no more than a certain amount, around half a million dollars. Artists who reach this ceiling could then tutor others at different career levels to help them reach greater success. But what about those near or at the top who are afraid of being edged out of their positions?

"Those guys on top shouldn't worry about that because nobody stays on top forever anyway," Dixon says. "The guy who gets to level one's sometime gonna slide back to level two, so why worry about it? He just oughta enjoy being on top while he's there, live off the interest from his $500,000 and be able to help others. That would be time better spent than the top guy just spending energy to make more money for himself."

Much has come out of the sharing concept that Dixon has helped spread. A few examples are the *Super Blues* Chess series that featured Waters, Diddley, and Howlin' Wolf, Blue Horizon's *Fleetwood Mac In Chicago*, and Liberty Records's *Hooker And Heat*, which features Canned Heat and John Lee Hooker.

Keeping up with the times is another thing that Dixon has managed to do. He upgraded and modernized many of his old classics on Columbia Records's *I Am The Blues* at the start of the 1970s. In 1986, he co-wrote the song "Don't Tell Me Nothin'" with former Band frontman Robbie Robertson, and performed it on the soundtrack to the film *The Color Of Money*. But Dixon's career was really kicked back into high gear in 1988, with the release of *The Chess Box* on Chess/MCA Records, a 36-track, two-CD retrospective of his work that included performances by Dixon, Muddy Waters, Howlin' Wolf, Little Walter, Bo Diddley, Lowell Fulson, Koko Taylor, Sonny Boy Williamson, Eddie Boyd, Willie Mabon, Jimmy Witherspoon, Otis Rush, and Little Milton. The set, which sold surprisingly well, was a testament to Dixon's talents as singer, songwriter, producer, and backup musician. Also in 1988, Dixon released his first new album in years, *Hidden Charms,* on Bug/Capitol Records, and in 1989 his autobiography *I Am The Blues,* co-written by Don Snowden, was published by Quartet Books.

Though he is 75 years old, Dixon has returned to the concert circuit recently, performing, for example, at the Benson & Hedges Blues Festival in New York in the fall of 1990. He is a direct and sincere conversationalist in spite of his age, and comes off as a very humble man for all his accomplishments. Influences in music come and go like waves—they lap on current sounds and change them just as water shapes the shore. Then the water recedes, only to return later. Dixon's impact on music has indeed withstood the test of time; in fact, it can be thought of as a continuing tradition. But after all, that is exactly what blues music is. ∎

YUKOTOPIA OPENING PARTY (l-r): Takashi Gion, Kenichi Shibaki, Sandy Rothman, Masuo Sasabe, Akio Okusawa

# Yukotopia

## BY SANDY ROTHMAN

Tucked away in the northeast corner of Tokyo's incomparable metropolis is a newly-opened hippie hangout called Yukotopia. Get off the train at Umejima station, walk a couple of blocks through a perfectly normal and thoroughly fascinating commercial district, and keep an eye out for tie-dyes in the window. It's not that hard to spot. The bright, primary colors of tie-dyes are especially noticeable in the world of the understated colors which are popular in Japan. Once in the door, you try to figure it out: Is Yukotopia a tie-dye clothing shop? A restaurant? Bar? Live music club ("live house")? A meeting place for Deadheads, environmentalists, spiritual seekers? Like New York's Wetlands, it's all those things and more. As a brand-new club, Yukotopia can take some time to find its true identity.

About a year ago I was walking past a laundromat near my downtown Berkeley apartment when I spotted some Japanese Deadheads washing, drying, and folding their handmade tie-dye t-shirts. I admired their tie-dye work—some of the best ever, many with American Indian themes—and we talked, hung out, shared tea in a Chinese restaurant and exchanged addresses. These Deadheads, after returning to Japan, gave my address to Yuko Tsukamoto (Yukotopia's owner). This past October, Yuko asked me to provide some live bluegrass music for the club's opening night.

I called my friend in the Tokyo area, Masuo Sasabe (the area's fine bluegrass singer and guitarist), and we assembled a band of good musicians and friends—Akio Okusawa on bass guitar; Takashi Gion on fiddle; and Kenichi Shibaki on mandolin. Masuo and I had sung trios with Okusawa five years ago when I was in Japan. It was like old times. I flew to Tokyo on October 7 (the 8th in Japan), and we rehearsed on the 9th for the next night's gig. A big honor for us that night was the attendance of Toru Mitsui and his daughter, witnessing the Deadhead phenomenon in Japan for the first time. Mitsui, an eminent historian, folklorist, and expert on American music, actually wrote the world's first book on bluegrass, published in Japan in 1975. Since that time he has published works on Elvis, the Beatles, Jimmie Davis and his famous song "You Are My Sunshine," and recently a history of blue jeans and the Levi-Strauss Company which is selling very well in Japan.

Yukotopia is equipped with a good sound system and (as with serious Deadheads everywhere) there is no shortage of excellent taping equipment—in this case DAT capability. We were asked to play again during my stay in Japan, which we did on November 3rd.

Helping Yuko run the club are her two younger sisters, her brother, and chef Eiji Onada who recently returned to Tokyo after living in San Francisco and working in local Japanese restaurants there. The club has begun to attract a regular clientele of environmentally-conscious young people, some of them "deep Deadheads" and some of them not. Music seems to be the central theme, and Yuko has been featuring several local musicians—bands and solo performers —on a regular basis. A number of Americans and other foreigners have also been going to Yukotopia regularly, some of them singers or musicians who are welcome to play at the club anytime. With Yuko there, it's a good opportunity for English-speaking people to have a cultural exchange with Japanese friends. Having lived in Berkeley for a number of years, Yuko speaks good colloquial English and is thus the perfect Deadhead mamasan in this setting.

Anyone planning a trip to Japan who'd like to tap into the Tokyo Deadhead network would do well to contact Yuko and think about visiting Yukotopia. The club, along with a couple of other little bars and tie-dye shops (many of which Yuko supplies with candles, crystals, t-shirts, and enthusiasm), is definitely on the map.

YUKOTOPIA 3-7-21 Umejima, Adachi-ku Tokyo 121, Japan 33-886-2996 (phone and fax) ∎

www.yukotopia.jp/pc/contents/english/english.html

**Yukotopia crowd**

**Phish**

# SUMMER MIGRATION:
# THE GREAT AMERICAN HORDE

by Matt Goldberg

Comprised of five bands, HORDE was perhaps rock'n'roll's most notable achievement of the summer of 1992. HORDE is an acronym for Horizon Of Rock Developed Everywhere, and took the form of a new music festival which traveled throughout the east coast in July and August.

The northeast migration of the Great American HORDE—Col. Bruce Hampton and the Aquarium Rescue Unit, Blues Traveler, Phish, Spin Doctors and Widespread Panic—made tracks from Portland, Maine, across much of New York, and included a memorable detour in New Jersey. Playing for a total of approximately 25,000 fans, the HORDE—pioneering young bands, each with its own unique perspective—united under a colorful banner with the common premise of exploring the boundaries of rock.

Each HORDE show consisted of over six hours of live music, almost uninterrupted as a result of the logistical wonders performed by an extended and efficient stage crew and production team. The bands received equal billing and equal time, each playing roughly an hour and fifteen minutes. At successive gigs on the tour, each band's performance varied enough to further reveal to the audiences just how much musical prowess was lurking in the summer air.

HORDE subverted regional limitations by bringing the southern twirls of the ARU and Widespread Panic to upstate New York, and the gritty, upbeat groove of the Spin Doctors to Birmingham, AL.

The Aquarium Rescue Unit of Atlanta, GA opened all of the northeast dates, an appropriate situation considering their masterful improvisation and their attitude toward song structure.

Col. Bruce Hampton explained, "Our idea was to take every kind of music that had purity left (bluegrass, jazz and blues) and let it go.

**BLUES TRAVELER: Bobby Sheehan, Chan Kinchla, John Popper and Brendan Hill   Photo Courtesy A&M Records**

We never rehearse, and while we have a format, I'm not sure what it is."

ARU drummer Apt. Q258 added, "In all the six or so years that I've been playing with Col. Bruce we've rehearsed twice. Some tunes have a definite structure which we stick to, but usually it's free and open enough that if anyone in the band wants to do something as strange as vomit in the middle of a jam we could all respond accordingly."

From Athens, GA came Widespread Panic, a psychedelic confederacy with no qualms about stepping into the Aquarium Rescue Unit's southern-tipped, improvising shoes. Literally. One by one, the members of Widespread Panic came out on stage and started jamming as the ARU was finishing its set, eventually replacing the ARU with Widespread Panic. Add John Popper from Blues Traveler on harmonica and the essence of HORDE takes center stage: musicians who have similar enough outlooks to actually pull off live, whole band segues without disturbing the pelvic swinging of thousands of delighted fans.

Widespread Panic spontaneously combusted in nearly every song, taking jams so far out on a limb that if one was to stop and think about how to catagorize their music, the best part of the show would most likely have been missed—musical traditions which are deconstructed and recombined in ways that often defy categorization, a fresh musical state for the '90s.

Bassist David Schools of Widespread Panic said, "Beyond any musical similarities, the HORDE bands have a common spirit." Keep this in mind and imagine the transition from almost two and a half hours of southern-tinged, breathy jams to the unquestionably urban Spin Doctors. Where the Doctors are concerned, lyrical content carries more of the message and the screw of song structure is tightened just a bit. A Spin Doctors jam is like looking through a microscope, as compared to the more telescopic jamming of the Aquarium Rescue Unit and Phish. The Doctors may cover a little less ground in terms of improvisation, but the trade-off is that they can explore it with exacting detail. At Jones Beach, under gleaming emerald lights, the Doctors took the audience on an extended trip in "What Time Is It," inducing a lengthy guitar-soaked jam with a concretely funky beat.

Chris Baron, singer and songwriter for the Spin Doctors, characterized the HORDE: "All the bands are above a certain level of quality...really good bands...with an ethic of jamming. HORDE gave us all a chance to play some big, important venues."

Gigs at notable venues are synonymous with the exponential increase in the success and notoriety of the HORDE bands in the last year. During the year, the Doctors toured hard and well, bringing the beat and the word to thousands across the nation. As the weather warmed, so did the mainstream aesthetic. In the first two months of summer, the Doctors appeared on "Late Night with David Letterman" and "The Dennis Miller Show," as well as performing at New York City's legendary Lone Star, a gig sponsored by radio station WNEW.

"Music and popular movements operate on geometric curves, rather than straight lines," Baron said. "Once word of mouth reaches a certain point, the numbers take astronomical leaps. What people want suddenly comes to be available."

Unfortunately, one thing that wasn't available was a completely democratic environment for two of the HORDE shows—the July 11th gig at the Garden State Performing Arts Center in New Jersey, and the July 12th gig at the Jones Beach Theater. One of the things about the HORDE tour that made it so notable was the animated, informative and diverse concourse of vending and awareness which traveled with the tour. Concertgoers could wade through environmental and political displays, as well as a small carnival of venders. Controversy arose when

governmental regulations prevented three groups—NORML (National Organization for the Reform of Marijuana Laws), NOW (National Organization for Women), and Planned Parenthood—from participating in the concourse.

Tempers flared as First Amendment rights seemed to be violated. Both Chris Baron and John Popper expressed—onstage and off—their concern over this issue.

"The responsibility I hold," said Baron in an interview, "is the burden of liberty. Theoretically, I'm allowed to say what I want and I'm allowed to distribute the information that I want.

**SPIN DOCTORS: Eric Schenkman, Christopher Barron, Aaron Comess and Mark White**   Photo Courtesy Epic Records

**WIDESPREAD PANIC: Michael Houser, David Schools, John Bell, Domingo Ortiz, Todd Nance and JoJo Herman**   Photo Courtesy Capricorn/Warner

**COL. BRUCE HAMPTON & THE AQUARIUM RESCUE UNIT: Jimmy Herring, Col. Bruce Hampton, Apt. Q258, Matt Mundy and Oteil Burbridge**

Maybe what bands should try and do is to raise everyone to that level of responsibility. The same people that empower us [the bands], empower themselves."

"We really encouraged every group with a grievance and table to come down to the shows," said Popper. "We're trying to stimulate people's thinking; it's an election year and we want to encourage people to vote."

Laying down tune after tune, Blues Traveler's melodies snaked all over the jumping and popping rhythms, inevitably diving head first into a huge gonzo jam replete with screaming guitar solos and frantic harmonica runs. The boys jam to a certain intensity and then maintain it steadily, driving the crowd into a frenzy. At the head of the frenzy, encouraging the crowd to beckon the moon out of the clouds, wearing an ominous, black bird-like mask and strumming an acoustic guitar was John Popper.

At their Jones Beach, NY performance, Phish responded to the seaside location and the audience's willingness with expansive versions of "Divided Sky" and "Fluffhead," as well as newer jam tunes like "Maze." As the closing act on the HORDE tour, Phish continuously revitalized the crowd with their distinctive world of organic jamming, a musical arrangement where the sum of the parts and the whole are one in the same.

The band's high order of live performance comes from a rigorous rehearsal schedule (sandwiched in between an even more rigorous tour schedule), and a dedication to communication, on and offstage. Trey Anastasio (guitarist, singer, songwriter) likens playing with Phish to, "a musical conversation, where one person is playing a phrase, and I'm thinking in contrary terms. I try to come up with something spontaneously that answers against that phrase."

Instrumental in HORDE's conception, execution and success was Blues Traveler. Members of the Traveler family were involved in many levels of HORDE's production for months before the actual events, although it is John Popper who is credited with engineering the tour.

"He put months of work into it...really hard work...putting up with a lot of bullshit, all the bands demands and whatever," Baron said. Popper's sense of responsibility to the community, fostered in large part by the activities of his band, is admirable. He was an unusually visible presence, leading several parades and processionals in and around the various venues.

Traveler guitarist Chan Kinchla continued, "We realized that in addition to the music, there's a lot of people out there doing very interesting things that we're hip to. We want to give them as much of a chance to express themselves as we have. One thing music can do is bring a lot of people together." ■

Bob Minkin

# EDITORIAL

The week of August 10th had many people worrying over the health of Jerry Garcia. A pervasive feeling of dread was growing as dates were cancelled for upcoming shows. Rumors were held at bay as the news slowly came out that Garcia was suffering from exhaustion. The Grateful Dead issued a press release on August 14th. I'll share it with you here...

**FOR IMMEDIATE RELEASE**

*As the week has passed, we've learned that Jerry Garcia's recuperation will take longer than we'd initially hoped. We remain certain that he will return to full good health, but the rest and care he needs will require us to cancel the fall East Coast tour. Jerry is in the care of a physician at home and is on the mend, but it will take time.*

*According to Jerry's physician, Dr. Randy Baker, "Jerry Garcia's health problems are primarily chronic rather than acute. He has some lung disease related to years of smoking and this has put some stress on his heart which has become slightly enlarged. He does not have and has not had fluid in the lungs or kidney failure, and he did not suffer from a collapse. He does have borderline diabetes, which should readily resolve with weight loss. His current problems are being managed with mild medication and he is at home and experiencing no discomfort. Jerry has agreed to a program of stopping smoking, losing weight, exercise and dietary changes. As this is accomplished he should regain good health and continue performing for many years."*

*We realize that this comes as very disturbing news for many people, so let us be clear — he is ill, but the right steps are being taken.*

*As Grateful Dead bassist Phil Lesh commented, "I talked to Elvis this morning myself and he said they already have too many guitarists up there, and he also doesn't need any competition in the postage stamp market." More seriously, Lesh added, "We expect to be performing with Jerry before the end of the year, even though right now he's dead tired."*

*Thank you for your love and prayers,*
*Grateful Dead*

We'll continue to keep you as updated as our publication schedule allows. Everyone at *Relix* wishes Jerry a thorough and speedy recovery.

Now that the Dead won't be touring for a little while, some of you will have some free time on your hands. The current financial crunch is affecting clubs nationally. Support your favorite local bands by getting out to see them while they still have someplace left to play.

With love and hope,
Toni A. Brown

David Grisman, Frank Wakefield and Peter Rowan          Photo by Les Kippel

Frank Wakefield and Peter Rowan          Photo by Les Kippel

Bryan Kraus and Dad playing "Terrapin Station" — Owings Mills, MD

Niles Harris

Black Hills, SD

Steve and Scott Van De Wall — Stratton Mt., VT

# WE ARE EVERYWHERE

Marley and Ken Hoff

Kevin Chrane, Zane Jarod, Ponch and Janis

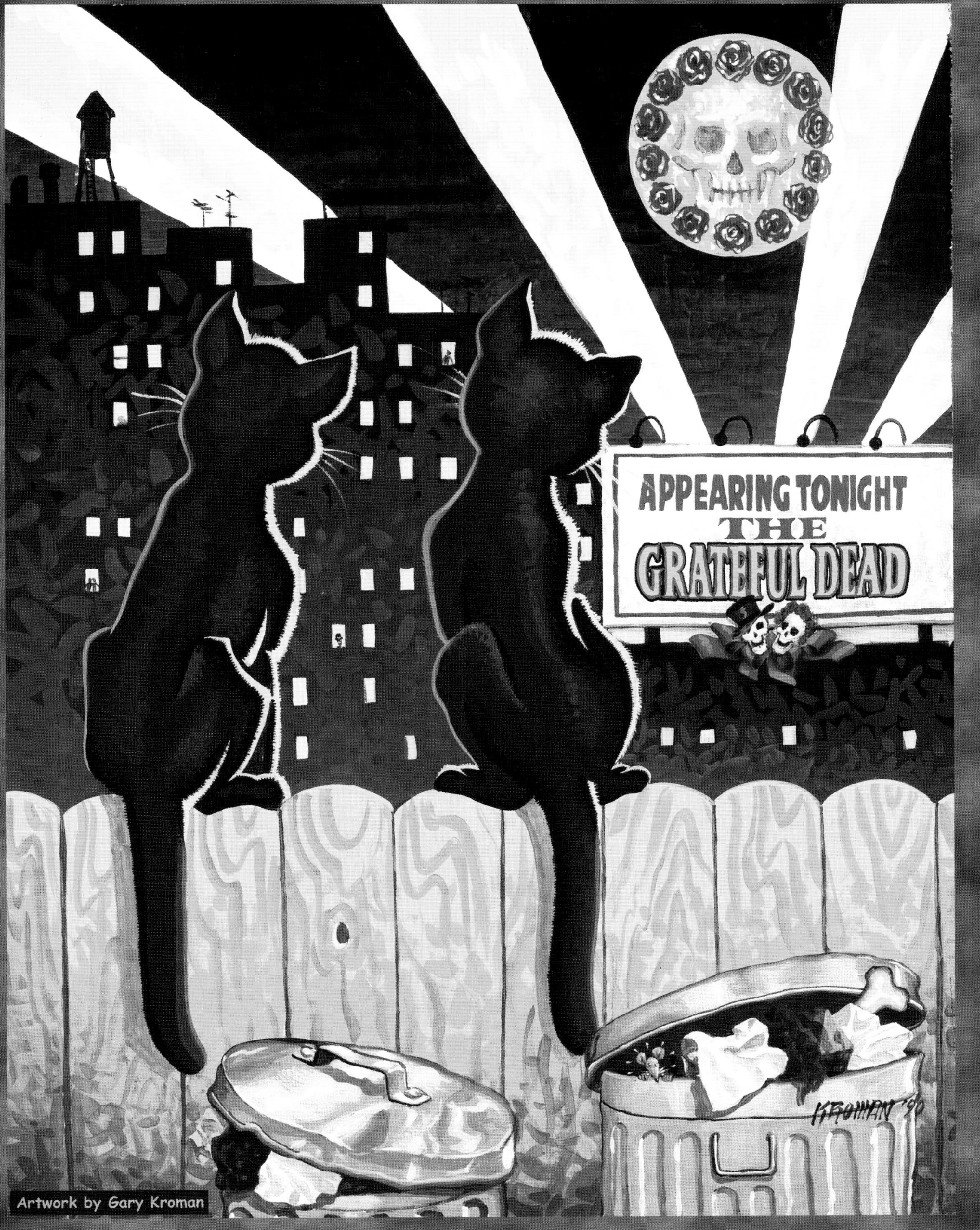

APPEARING TONIGHT
THE
GRATEFUL DEAD

Artwork by Gary Kroman

Mendocino, California

Eddie Orman will be psychedelicizing his '39 Chevy bus

Holly Strickland with Bob Weir on his 49th birth-day, 10/16/96

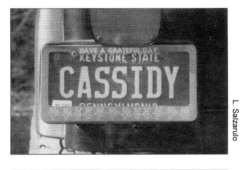

There is a fountain... S.P.A.C. '97

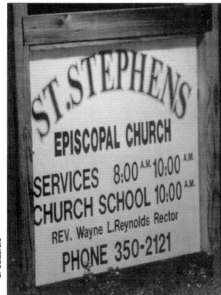

Merl Saunders with Jeremy and Jennifer Weiner

November/December 1992

# RELIX
## music for the mind

Vol. 19
No. 6

*Year-End Special*
## GRATEFUL DEAD
## DEADHEADS

## STEVIE RAY VAUGHAN
## JORMA KAUKONEN
## DICKEY BETTS
## DAVID GRISMAN

$4.5 (CAN. $5.50 £5.00)

Artwork by Gary Kroman

# Bruce Hornsby
## becomes un-dead

### BY JYM FAHEY

After three successful albums with the Range, and a few years as one of the hardest working sidemen in show business, Bruce Hornsby has released *Harbor Lights*. "It's an odd concept to call this a solo album as opposed to the others," says Bruce Hornsby. "This record sounds more like a band playing than the first two records. [The records featuring] Bruce Hornsby and the Range were pretty much comprised of demos, with me playing all the instruments. So those were really more solo records in that sense than this one is. Everyone got tied to the demos so they became the first two records, *Way It Is* and *Scenes From The Southside*. But one reason I didn't want to use the band this time was, well, I was going into a little more complex musical area this time and a couple of guys in the Range weren't that well versed in that more harmonically complex music. They weren't into that."

Bruce handled the musical landscape on *Harbor Lights* quite well, with a little help from friends like Pat Metheny, Bonnie Raitt, and a certain well-known guitarist from Marin County. He says, "Once again, not using the band gave me the freedom to cast the record in the sense that I would have a particular song in a particular style and think to myself who would sound amazing playing on this song? All the guests came out to the house. They all came to work. In Garcia's case, it was easy because we were playing Hampton Roads Coliseum for a couple of days with the Dead on my last Dead tour. So he just came over to the house during the day before the gig."

Some people were surprised when Hornsby started playing with the Grateful Dead. Bruce thinks those folks just weren't paying attention. "The Dead has always had sort of a folk influence, but they've always been really about improvisation, a certain jazzy element. For me, it's been the same way. I've always been influenced by folk music. There's always been sort of a folk influence on my music, but there's always been that jazz aspect too. So I think

Photo by John Rottet

there was always a kindred spirit there. A lot of people wouldn't necessarily get that because in the big picture we come from different worlds. We got on the radio real fast with this sort of wonderful accident, "The Way It Is." Everyone thought it was a B-side, and it became this big hit. So all of a sudden we were catapulted into this hit radio world, sort of typecast into that area. I think a lot of people were surprised when I started playing with [the Dead]. People who don't know much about it probably didn't realize that my band had opened for the Dead two or three times a year for five years before that. We always played with them, and I'd sat in with them a lot. When I was playing with them, they were always talking about working up some of my songs. Some of my songs [on *Harbor Lights*] could be Grateful Dead songs."

Bruce may be more aware of the results of pigeonholing an artist or a band than a lot of musicians. He says that a lot of people think of the Dead as "traditionalists with a back-to-nature approach who are not into technology—when they're completely into that. Probably more so than most any group that I know of."

The problem, as Bruce sees it, is one of getting to know an artist through a public persona, which can sometimes be skewed heavily, on purpose or by accident. "When you have big hits, you have a whole lot of people who know a very little bit about you. And when you have sort of a cult following, you have a small amount of people who know a lot about you. And you know they both have their good and bad points. I think gradually, as the years go by, people are figuring out more of what I'm about. Playing with the Grateful Dead probably blasted people's

one-dimensional notions about me. But I don't do this to get some media profile or some image. It was never about image for me. A lot of my friends couldn't understand why I would just go be a sideman for somebody for a year-and-a-half in the middle of my own career. For me, it was just about a good time and great people to work with and hang with. That's why I did it."

Bruce had to decide between working with the Dead (and nearly everybody else from Don Henley and Leon Russell to the Cowboy Junkies and Liquid Jesus) and refocusing on his own material. He opted for *Harbor Lights*. "When we started making this record in January of '92, I started to extricate myself from the various other musical projects I was doing. Stopped playing with the Grateful Dead, I played with them for a year-and-a-half, about a hundred shows or so. I had a great time doing that. I learned a lot. I got a lot out of it, and I was inspired by that situation and a lot of the other records I was playing on. It was all great input for me and influence. But I felt it was time to get back to me—get back to my own musical projects."

Even though Hornsby is happy with *Harbor Lights* and feels comfortable enough in the recording studio to put one in his Williamsburg, Virginia home, he knows that the magic of making a record is not something an artist can afford to take for granted, commenting, "The recording process for me has always been difficult and elusive. It's so intangible and you can never predict it. It's very maddening in that way. It's so hard to keep your perspective. Imagine if someone straps you into a chair and forces you to listen to the same song 400 times in a row. You think you would be objective about that song? You think you could tell? You think you'd want to hear it again? I think 'No!' is the answer to all those questions. So for me, it's a difficult process. I've always said I've got to find a better way to do it. The piano performances I do tend to be very quick. I tend to just play them. So maybe it's a question of I should just go ahead and play the damn piano first and record everything around that. See if that would work better. Who can say?"

Bruce Hornsby gives the impression of being a regular guy: friendly, polite, intelligent. Why did he decide to concentrate on rock'n'roll piano when guitar was all the rage? He says, "I got into playing the piano because of Elton John and Leon Russell. My brother went to prep school in Connecticut. He was always turned onto this underground music, at least what seemed like underground music to us in Southeastern Virginia. So I remember riding down the Colonial Parkway from Williamsburg to Yorktown and my brother putting in a tape of this song "Amoreena" by Elton John, and it just floored me. It was an amazing, unique sound that I never heard before. I just loved it so much. That, plus the Joe Cocker *Mad Dogs And Englishmen* tape that I loved. My brother had taken a little tape recorder into the Capitol Theatre in Portchester, New York where he had heard this group, Mad Dogs and Englishmen, long before the album came out. It was a great bootleg tape with all this great piano by Leon Russell. So those two tapes I was turned onto by my older brother really got me into playing the piano. That, plus the fact that my parents had a great piano in the house."

Bruce Hornsby made the right choice. He is a successful and respected musician, a family man, and a guy who makes the music he feels in his heart. ∎

Rob Cohn/Dead Images

**Jerry Garcia with Bruce Hornsby**

May/June, 1992

# RELIX

### music for the mind

Vol. 19
No. 4

Neil Young

GRATEFUL DEAD

**EXCLUSIVE INTERVIEWS**

Carlos Santana

Savoy Brown

Blue Cheer

Paul Kantner's Starship

$3.50 [CAN. $4.50 U.K.

Artwork by Gary Kroman

# RELIX

*music for the mind* ™

Vol. 19
No. 5

## GRATEFUL DEAD
## AIRTO

# JANIS!

## ALLMAN BROTHERS
## HORDE
## JACK CASADY

### TAPING TIPS, DAN HEALY,
### BOB BRALOVE & MUCH MORE!

$3.50 (CAN. $4.50 U.K. £4.00)

May/June, 1992

Cover Photo by Jim Cummins/Star File

---

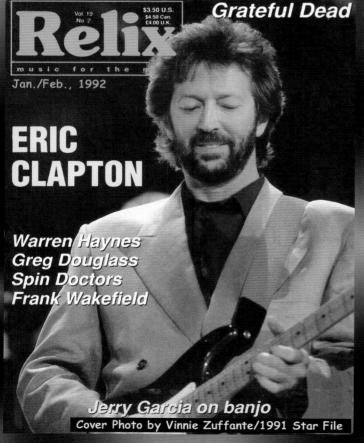

# Relix

*music for the m...*

Vol. 19
No. 2

$3.50 U.S.
$4.50 Can.
£4.00 U.K.

*Grateful Dead*

Jan./Feb., 1992

# ERIC CLAPTON

Warren Haynes
Greg Douglass
Spin Doctors
Frank Wakefield

**Jerry Garcia on banjo**

Cover Photo by Vinnie Zuffante/1991 Star File

---

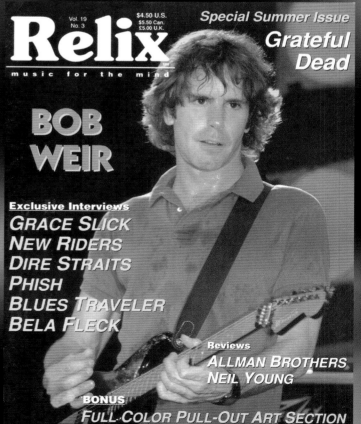

# Relix

*music for the mind* ™

Vol. 19
No. 3

$4.50 U.S.
$5.50 Can.
£5.00 U.K.

*Special Summer Issue*
*Grateful Dead*

# BOB WEIR

**Exclusive Interviews**
## GRACE SLICK
## NEW RIDERS
## DIRE STRAITS
## PHISH
## BLUES TRAVELER
## BELA FLECK

**Reviews**
## ALLMAN BROTHERS
## NEIL YOUNG

**BONUS**
## FULL-COLOR PULL-OUT ART SECTION

Cover Photo by Cathy Miller

May/June, 1992

# Eyes of the World

In an effort to improve life on the planet as we know it, we have devoted this space to environmental issues. We welcome your correspondence.

*"The future's here, we are it, we are on our own."* —Bob Weir

# HEMP

## by David Kopel

This article uses the term "hemp" rather than "marijuana" since hemp is the historical American term for the cannabis sativa plant. "Marijuana" did not come into popular usage until the 1930s, when the Hearst newspapers, spearheading a hysterical campaign to outlaw hemp, successfully associated it with Mexican immigrants by using the Mexican slang "marijuana."

When the plant is cultivated for smoking, all nutrients are directed to the flowers (buds). Care is taken to harvest the plant just prior to full seed. Meticulous clipping can result in smaller plant growth, and higher THC content. But, in cultivation for use as paper and fiber, care is taken to focus on the stalk of the plant, as opposed to the leaf. Hemp plants are known to grow as tall as twelve feet, so the stalk and seeds become the main focus for commercial use. The hemp fiber contains no THC, so don't try to smoke your friend's hemp shirt.

Today, hemp fiber is again available commercially, and being used in clothes. Unfortunately, the federal government's campaign against marijuana makes anything associated with the plant into a counter-cultural item. Accordingly, you can probably buy a hemp shirt at your local tie-dye store, but the folks who shop at J.C. Penney are offered only cotton clothing. As a result, cotton clothing far outsells hemp clothing, and thousands of tons of additional poisons are dumped on the earth every year in order to cultivate cotton.

Because cotton is a natural fiber, many folks think that wearing cotton clothes is environmentally benign. Far from it. Cotton production requires huge amounts of pesticides, as well as massive doses of fertilizer, since cotton wears out the soil so fast.

Hemp, in contrast, is much sturdier, has fewer natural enemies, and hence requires far fewer chemical inputs. Until the 1820s, most American clothing was made from hemp. The Continental Army wore hemp uniforms; the covered wagons that opened up the West were covered with hemp. And when young George Bush bailed out of a fighter airplane during World War II, his parachute was made from hemp.

Hemp can also be used to make paper and indeed was the major paper source until the late 19th century. The first two drafts of the Declaration of Independence were written on hemp paper (the final version was on parchment, which is made from animal skin). Hemp paper is extremely durable, and while hemp is not suitable for replacing all types of wood-derived paper currently in use, increased use of hemp paper could significantly cut the demand for wood paper, especially for uses such as corrugated cardboard boxes, green and white computer paper and paper bags.

In addition, hemp can be substituted for numerous construction contexts, such as production of particle board. An acre of hemp produces as much cellulose fiber pulp as 4.1 acres of wood, according to a United States of Agriculture study.

Using hemp as a wood substitute would significantly reduce the pollution associated with wood processing. For the creation of products from either wood or hemp, it is usually necessary to use sulfur to help separate the valuable cellulose pulp from the lignin which binds the cellulose fibers together; the hemp separation process uses at least 75% less sulfur than the wood process.

When wood is processed into paper, it is bleached with chlorine and results in the production of dioxins, which are then discharged into the rivers near paper mills. In contrast, paper made from hemp can be bleached with hydrogen peroxide, which produces no dioxins.

Hemp makes good carpet backing, too. Unlike currently-used synthetic backing, hemp doesn't emit dangerous gasses that cause some people to become ill in the presence of brand-new carpets. And in case of fire, the hemp carpet backing, unlike its synthetic counterpart, doesn't create poisonous fumes when burned.

Many environmentalists are urging that we reduce our dependence on fossil fuels (such as oil and coal), and begin using greater quantities of biomass fuels, such as corn. For example, under the new Clean Air Act, the federal government requires that the gasoline in most cities include certain percentages of ethanol or methanol. These two fuels are currently made from corn, but hemp can also be used to produce ethanol. Indeed, hemp is considerably higher in potential energy value than is corn. Hemp seed is 30% oil by volume and has successfully been used to make diesel fuel oil, aircraft engine oil and precision machine oil.

Some environmental experts, such as Jonathan Adler of the Competitive Enterprise Institute, argue that the benefits of biomass fuel (such as corn-derived ethanol) are vastly overstated. Even so, since we live in a country where the government is already requiring increased use of ethanol, it makes environmental sense to make the ethanol from the best source available, namely hemp.

Many scientists believe that the increasing rate of burning fossil fuels like coal may, over the long run, increase carbon dioxide levels in the atmosphere which would in turn slow the rate at which heat escapes from the earth, thus causing a "greenhouse effect" and global warming. While there is great scientific debate over the rate at which the greenhouse effect could be occurring, if it is occurring at all, many people believe it would be prudent to reduce the amount of carbon dioxide emissions.

The United States Department of Agriculture has a research team dedicated to reversing global warming. In meetings with hemp activists, the researchers agreed the increased cultivation of hemp could have a dramatic effect on global warming. Most importantly, hemp-based fuels could reduce use of fossil fuels. In addition, greater use of hemp might result in less use of wood and less deforestation. (The deforestation benefits would be relatively small, since most wood which hemp could replace is grown in tree farms where new trees are planted as mature ones are harvested.)

The activists asked the USDA researchers if the researchers would propose to their agency greater use of hemp, which everyone agreed would help reduce global warming. The researchers said no; proposing more use of hemp could ruin their careers, since hemp was marijuana and marijuana is illegal. "You cannot use something illegal," one researcher said. "Not even to save the world. Period."

Much of the information for this article came from Jack Herer's book, *The Emperor Wears No Clothes* (HEMP/Queen of Clubs Publishing).

MEDICINE  PAPER  FUEL  FIBER

**Border Artwork by Michael Raye Smith**

# What a Long Strange Trip It's Been!

## FROM TOURING WITH THE DEAD TO TOURING FOR THE DEA

### by I. M. Foolish

I was busted in 1989 with, what was told to me by the "powers that hold the keys," 500 hits of blotter acid. This was the beginning of one of the weirdest trips I've ever taken in my 36 years. I thought this sort of thing always happened to somebody else, but could never happen to me. Then again, I. M. Foolish.

My first goal in sharing this story is to prevent you from repeating my mistakes, and secondly, I would like to give you some insight into "the powers that hold the keys" and what they know and don't know about our lifestyle.

It was brought to my attention by "the powers that hold the keys" that I was facing 10 to 20 years in prison for this little blunder and would have to do at least 12 years before parole would be considered. I mentioned to you that I am foolish, but I am not stupid, so I tried to figure out a way that I could beat the rap and try not to celebrate my fiftieth birthday in prison.

I had no money, no relatives who were willing to help me out, and no knowledge of the legal system that I found myself thrust into. That's why I had to depend on my own great thinking. I'll remind you, however, that my great thinking is what put me in this predicament to begin with, so you can just imagine the options that I explored.

After several months of driving myself and everybody around me crazy, I reluctantly concluded that I would go on tour as an informant for the DEA. I know what you're thinking, and no, I did not participate in or have anything to do with anybody else getting busted. When push came to shove, I took the money and ran. As it turned out, I did pass go, I did collect over $200 dollars, and then I went directly to jail. Needless to say, this was not the thinking of a rational mind.

The DEA jumped at the opportunity to have someone like me in their corner. The only problem was that my loyalties to my Deadhead brothers and sisters turned out to be greater than my previous belief that anything I would do would be advantageous to my situation. In fact, the DEA made it very clear that they could promise me nothing, except maybe a nice letter saying that I helped them, but there would be no guarantees.

Regardless of our fears of the DEA, I have found that they are nothing more than overpaid modern versions of the Keystone cops when it comes to dealing with Deadheads. They are afraid of us and our way of life, and they made it quite clear to me that there is only so much that they are willing to do to infiltrate our rank and file. Fortunately, they were also not very well informed as to where we were in regard to parking lot openings, etc., and they were consistently in the wrong place at the right time.

Based on my experience, you might find it helpful and rather educational to know how the DEA goes about its business.

1. They never travel alone.
2. They will not freely hug one of us.
3. They will not share our food or drink.
4. They will not do any deals on the "shakedown" as they fear a mob scene.
5. A male agent will never wear a skirt.
6. They will not sample any psychedelic drug before purchasing it.
7. They won't front money, not even for a second.
8. They will not forsake a shower, therefore, they smell like cops.
9. They always want to make a large buy, but not right on the spot.
10. They have been known to trade tickets for substances (even small amounts, making you tempted, an easy target).

Please use these little tidbits of information to your advantage.

Another issue that I feel is very important to understand is entrapment. Remember that just because you ask a cop if he is a cop, and he says that he isn't, does not mean that he has entrapped you. Don't forget that they are known to lie, so don't fool yourself into believing that this will save you later in a court of law.

When I finally went to court for my charges (without any outside help), I was sentenced to five years in the State Prison. This was over three years ago. I was offered an early release program, which, to my dismay, I took about 30 months ago. It was originally supposed to be a 16-month program, but I have been in it for over 30 months. I haven't done anything to violate this strict program, but I've been penalized because I have been unable to come up with $1,600 in fines. Perhaps $1,600 doesn't sound like a lot of money to you, but to me it may as well be $16 million. Let me point out, though, that I did *not* write this for the money, and I will leave it at that.

In any case, I must submit to two urine tests a week and go to countless meetings. I was also forced to relocate to a police state for the duration of this program as I wasn't a resident of the state in which I was busted. Needless to say, this has separated me from my family and my Deadhead friends. Oh, and no Dead shows either; it's against their rules. I also have a strict curfew that I must adhere to, so life hasn't been easy. I guess the grass isn't always greener on the other side of the prison fence, but I have to admit that it still beats sitting in jail.

There are a few more lessons to learn from my experience.

1. If you need to deal drugs, be careful. Try to do business with people you know.
2. "The powers that hold the keys" believe that the flags we fly at the shows are some sort of advertisement for our drug trade, so fly yours high and proud. We could really screw them up on this one.
3. Don't turn in the people that love you. It will gain you nothing!
4. "The powers that hold the keys" have been known to tell you just about anything, except the truth. They don't make guarantees. They use you up then lock you up.
5. Keep a lot of money on hand for legal fees should you get caught.
6. Know the legal ramifications before getting thrust into the system.

And finally, please forgive me for considering working against the lifestyle that is ours and ours alone. Even though I've given up my freedom in the process, I've come to realize that there are more important things in life that are just too precious to give up. ∎

# TAPING TIPS

## by Alan J. Wallace

If you've been trading tapes long enough that storage space and other considerations are becoming a concern, it's time to shift your focus from quantity to quality.

Beginning tape collectors can't afford to be as choosy because they have to have something, anything, to work with. But at some point (it might be 150 hours for one person, 1,500 for another), you'll start to wonder why you're hanging on to those virtually unlistenable 14th-generation '87 audiences.

If you're looking to upgrade your tapes and get access to the really killer stuff, here are six steps to consider:

1. Become a more critical and objective listener. When considering whether to get or keep a tape, base your decision on how it sounds. Set aside generation hype, tales of how somebody's cousin got it directly from the hot dog guy who ran into Phil in the backstage men's room, etc. Ask yourself not only if you like how it sounds, but if it sounds good enough to interest others. Of course, there are exceptions, such as the only tape you've seen of a show you were at and loved, but unless there's sentimental value, let the tape stand or fall on its objective merits.

2. Beware "grade creep." Hopefully, you've built your collection enough that you've had to revise and expand your list several times, and in the process, your tape's quality has already improved somewhat. That means a tape that was A+ on your first list probably is an A or A-now, and your current list should reflect that fact. When somebody orders an A+ tape from your list, they're expecting to hear your best. And always take list grades with a grain of salt, and expect others to do so, too. Until you've heard somebody's A+ tape, their list grades don't mean much.

3. Don't automatically dismiss audience tapes, but again, be choosy. While everybody loves a crisp, low-gen soundboard, a lot of fine (and bad) audience tapes are being made. When you find an audience tape you like, try to find out what sort of mics were used and how. Mic choice and placement comes down to personal preference, but those factors, along with taken-for-granted details like getting the levels right, is the most important factor in how an audience tape sounds. Once you know what you like, you can seek it out, and others who like tapes from the same kind of mics will be interested.

4. Check other copies of tapes you already have, especially older soundboards. Many times, these tapes have annoying flaws such as cuts, flips at bad times, etc. It's often possible to find copies that don't. It's also worthwhile to check just to see if the other copy sounds better.

5. Build an "other" list. Traders who go to the trouble of collecting several thousand hours of Dead usually have a wider range of musical interests. If you have just 150 hours of Dead, you probably have little to offer such a person, but if you also have 50 hours of "other," you just might have something there that'll pry out a killer copy of a Dead show in exchange.

6. Act like you know what you're doing. If your aim is to trade with people holding thousands of hours, be advised that they tend to be busy people with little time for bull. If you're responding to a taper ad that asks people not to send blanks, don't. If the ad is seeking only specific shows and you don't have them, don't waste that person's time. And remember it's not a race. Find a comfortable trading pace, which will vary from trader to trader.

Here's one other idea the taper community might want to embrace, one that would improve quality for everybody. Remember that FM signal sound wizard Dan Healy was sending out from the board in spring '88, only to have the nasty old FCC shut him down? Well, given the newfound regard for the Dead at high levels in Washington, maybe we should all be writing letters to the band, the White House, our elected representatives, and the lords of the airwaves, urging a solution be found that would allow the signal to resume.

Just think of it: no mic stands to lug, no crowded-pit contortionism, no need even for a taper section...and anybody with a decent Walkman and a ticket can walk away with a listenable, virtual soundboard copy of the show.

How about it, people? ∎

Photo by John Rottet

---

# Helpful Hints while on
# THE ROAD

In addition to being an avid Deadhead, I am also a Criminal Defense Attorney, formerly an assistant state attorney (an assistant D.A. or assistant prosecutor depending upon which part of the country you reside), and am consistently amazed at the number of "Deadheads Behind Bars," and the complaints about law enforcement's presence at shows.

First of all, the arrest problem, a fairly recent phenomenon at Dead shows, is due largely to the fact that fellow Deadheads openly advertise their drug use by displaying paraphernalia in open view and having things such as bumper stickers with marijuana leafs, as well as shirts, which condone drug use. Maybe it's what you believe, but it's not the way to keep on Leo's good side.

While I would be the first one to defend one's First Amendment rights to display such bumper stickers and the like, it is just plain stupid, given the social unacceptability of drugs in our current society. Accept it or not, it is no longer 1969, and the laws are vastly different now than they were then. Ask our fellow Deadheads behind bars for the total weight of packaged LSD, facing interminable minimum mandatory sentences. While many of our fellow Heads Behind Bars are not criminals by any means, their careless conduct caused their apprehension.

Other common problems I have personally seen include, but are not limited to, the following;

1. Openly advertising "doses" in the crowds. If you sell to an undercover cop after advertising this way, I suggest you deserve to be in prison, but on a charge of stupidity! Recently, at RFK, I approached a young man who was openly selling "doses," and told him he was an idiot for doing this. He appreciated and followed my advice, but only after telling me he was currently on Bond, facing felony drug possession charges in Virginia. Why didn't he learn the first time, and why was it necessary for me to dissuade him from openly dealing dope?

2. Blatant disrespect for law enforcement and local security. Like it or not, these people must be dealt with from arm's length, and do not look the other way at concerts. Do not mock, torment, or "goof" on them, as they will have the ultimate goof when you are arrested.

Continues...

## Helpful Hints While On THE ROAD (Continued)

3. As aforementioned, never display bumper stickers or wear shirts on the way to the show, which openly advocate drug use.

4. Keep roach clips, other paraphernalia, and contraband securely encased in the trunk of the car, with no personal identification in close proximity to the contraband. Do not smoke marijuana in the car, as the smell of marijuana gives Leo probable cause to search the entire car (and, arguably, the trunk and closed containers secured therein).

5. *NEVER* consent to a search. You do have the right to refuse (although Leos rarely tell you this).

6. If contraband is found, never admit to knowledge. Always refuse to answer questions "based upon the advice of counsel."

7. *IMPORTANT:* If placed in a police car with a potential co-defendant, say nothing in the back seat to each other. Almost all police cars are equipped with tape recording devices, and, at least in Florida, the courts have held that there is no expectation of privacy in the back of a police car and any incriminating statements can, and are, admitted against you in court.

I have noticed recently at the shows that the fans seem to be especially destructive and filthy vis-a-vis their garbage in the parking lots. Same with the use of fireworks in the parking lots, and those dangerous balloon salesman who are destroying your brain cells and the ozone. All this does is increase the presence of security, give all Deadheads a bad name, and further limit the venues which will put up with us. You need to realize that, not only are the rowdies making fools of themselves by being rowdy, they ruin everyone's experience and increase everyone's chances of getting busted for something.

Remember, Deadheads, use your common sense and life experience when on the road and at shows. The more arrests made at a local venue means more money into that county's coffers. In other words, it is clearly in local law enforcement's best interests to make as many arrests as possible. Politically, it looks good for the local sheriff as well.

If further advice is requested, or if you have any questions, I offer advice to Deadheads on criminal matters nationwide, taking tapes in trade for my advice.

Michael B. Rubin, Esquire
Attorney at Law

Artwork by Mike Zmuda

## Editorial

The Grateful Dead has asked me to bring to light a problem that has gotten out of control. The sale of bootleg and counterfeit merchandise has simply got to end. While the band allows its music to be recorded, video taping at Dead shows is absolutely forbidden. They've asked before, but a recent lawsuit against a video bootlegger has forced them to come down more heavily on this matter. This time, they are quite serious.

Following is a copy of a recent press release issued by the Grateful Dead:

*Ripping off the Grateful Dead, percussionist Mickey Hart once remarked, is like stealing from Santa Claus. The band that gives millions to charity, that permits its audience to make audio tapes—who could be grinch enough to loot the most generous rock band ever?*

*Among many others, hundreds of grinches, who had been selling their bootleg merchandise at Grateful Dead concerts, had their merchandise confiscated during the band's recent East Coast and Midwest summer concert tour as part of a series of lawsuits filed by the Grateful Dead in New Jersey, Michigan, Ohio, New York, Kentucky, Illinois, Indiana, and D.C. The Dead estimate that tens of thousands of pieces of illegal merchandise, from t-shirts and other clothing items to stickers, posters, and lyric books, were seized pursuant to Federal court seizure orders and under local anti-counterfeiting and anti-vending laws, enough to overflow the capacity of the storage semi-trailer at several venues.*

*Additionally, a Federal Court unsealed the file and entered a $15,000.00 judgement (which was stayed by agreement) and permanent injunction against a defendant (with much harsher penalties should he violate the injunction) against the sale of unauthorized videotapes of Grateful Dead concerts. The defendant agreed to the issuance of the injunction.*

*The Dead is still Santa Claus in spirit, but the band has the right to control how it can be commercially portrayed. The issue is not particularly about money—no one knows how much the band loses to counterfeiters, and no one is sitting around calculating the figure. It's a matter of what's right: If the Grateful Dead wants to put out a t-shirt, a sticker or a whatever, only the Dead has a right to do so, and to determine and assure the content and quality.*

*Even a grinch should be able to figure that out. Those who don't get it will have judges explain it to them.*

*—Grateful Dead*

Another matter that needs to be addressed is that of the Grateful Dead Ticket Office. In response to a number of letters we printed from readers angry at being shut out of Grateful Dead shows by not receiving tickets via GDTS, I'm happy to announce an overwhelming response in support of GDTS and the work they do. The folks at the Grateful Dead ticket office do an extraordinary job in filling the enor-

mous number of requests they get for each show. Just follow the directions you get from the hotlines, and have the requests postmarked the date stated and you have as good a shot as anyone (and a better chance than if you stand on a ticket outlet line).

On October 14th, we'll be holding a multi-celebratory event at Wetlands Preserve, 161 Hudson Street, New York City. We'll be celebrating the 20th anniversary of *Relix* magazine, and Relix Records will be celebrating new releases by Dead Ringers, Tom Constanten, and Solar Circus. Dead Ringers (featuring Tom Constanten, David Nelson, and Barry Flast) and Solar Circus will be joined by special guests for a great night of music. We hope you'll join us in the festivities.

See you around!

Toni A. Brown, Publisher

Artwork by Alfred Klosterman

Rob and Bobby with Tipper and Al - Tennessee Inaugural Ball - Photo by John McMillin

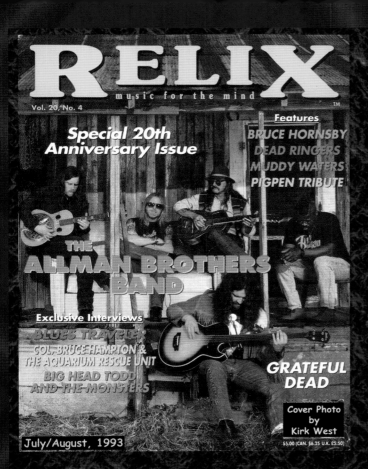

# RELIX
## music for the mind ™

Vol. 20, No. 4

**Special 20th Anniversary Issue**

**Features**
BRUCE HORNSBY
DEAD RINGERS
MUDDY WATERS
PIGPEN TRIBUTE

THE **ALLMAN BROTHERS BAND**

Exclusive Interviews
BLUES TRAVELER
COL. BRUCE HAMPTON &
THE AQUARIUM RESCUE UNIT
BIG HEAD TODD
AND THE MONSTERS

**GRATEFUL DEAD**

Cover Photo by Kirk West

$5.00 (CAN. $6.25 U.K. £3.50)

July/August, 1993

# RELIX
music for the mind

**HOT TUNA**
SPIN DOCTORS
PHISH
**PSYCHEDELIC SPECIAL!**

PIGPEN, MOBY GRAPE, SPIRIT·LOVE

Cover Photo by Chuck Pulin/Star File

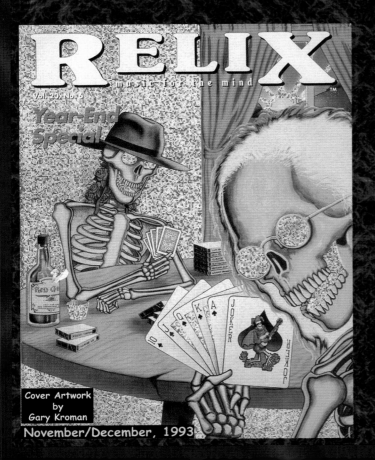

# RELIX
## music for the mind ™

Vol. 20, No. 6

**Year-End Special**

Cover Artwork by Gary Kroman

November/December, 1993

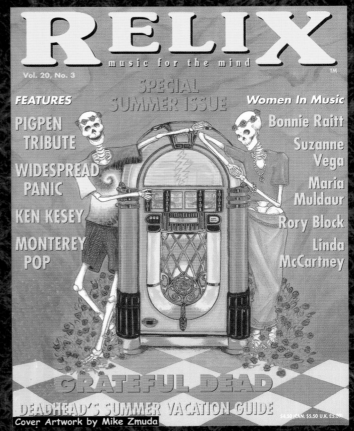

# RELIX
## music for the mind ™

Vol. 20, No. 3

**SPECIAL SUMMER ISSUE**

**Women In Music**

**FEATURES**

PIGPEN TRIBUTE

WIDESPREAD PANIC

KEN KESEY

MONTEREY POP

Bonnie Raitt

Suzanne Vega

Maria Muldaur

Rory Block

Linda McCartney

**GRATEFUL DEAD**

DEADHEAD'S SUMMER VACATION GUIDE

Cover Artwork by Mike Zmuda

$4.50 (CAN. $5.50 U.K. £3.50)

# TOP TEN VERSIONS OF DARK STAR

*by Cary Krosinsky*

"Dark Star" is a song that is appreciated by many people in many different ways. Although compiling a top ten list of "Dark Star" variations is difficult (since everyone's taste is different, and some versions are hard to come by), the attempt has been made in the framework provided.

1) The *Live Dead* version—pieced together from shows performed 2/27/69 through 3/2/69 at the Fillmore West in San Francisco. This studio-composed hybrid of live segments sets the high standard for comparison. This version has probably been the catalyst for more people becoming Deadheads than any rendition of any other Dead song. (But you already knew that.)

2) 2/13/70 Fillmore East, New York City, NY: A delicate, beautiful reading is given here as Garcia gracefully rides the sound waves with his guitar. Grand stuff—the best of the many Fillmore East versions and, arguably, the best of the lot.

3) 6/24/70 Capitol Theater, Port Chester, NY: Broken into three parts, the song is a sort of homing beacon for a brilliant set. The first verse of "Dark Star" sweetly segues into "Attics Of My Life," only to return to a "Dark Star" jam. This leads crazily into a high strung "Sugar Magnolia" (one of the first) and returns home, finishing the song with the second verse. The high energy continues into the immediately following, spectacular version of "St. Stephen."

4) Europe '72—various sites: It would be impossible, and not fully representative, to only select one of the versions played on this tour. The Dead were playing at their best as an ensemble, and each version was distinct. Anyway, 4/8/72 Empire Pool, Wembley, England featured the Dead at the Glastonbury Fayre Festival where they played a building, symphonic rendition. 4/14/72 Tivoli Theatre, Copenhagen, Denmark provided a look at a solid, classic performance in a *Live Dead* vein. 5/4/72 Olympia Theatre, Paris, France featured pristine playing, filled with clarity. At one point, the music prettily conveyed water delicately falling. And 5/11/72 Civic Hall, Rotterdam, The Netherlands had a long, spacey, varied version.

5) 8/27/72 Old Renais-sance Faire Grounds, Veneta, OR: The Dead at their finest. Jams cascade successfully and reach repeated crescendos. Much of the time is spent in the so-called "X Chemistry" zone. Lead, rhythm, bass, and piano are on and in the flow. If *Live Dead* set the standard, this set a new one.

6) 2/15/73 Dane County Coliseum, Madison, WI: A unique, peaceful, summery version. Would be well suited for playing during a summer car trip.

7) 10/18/74 Winterland, San Francisco, CA: The last version for over four years was led into from the most interesting take of Ned Lagin and Phil Lesh's "Seastones" (a piece of music similar to a quiet space jam that would follow a latter day second set drum solo). This long, dynamic piece serves as a fitting send off to the more psychedelic era of the Dead.

8) 12/31/78 Winterland, San Francisco, CA: Revived for the closing of Winterland, this is a surprisingly interesting rendition. Spirited and high strung, both verses were wrapped around an excellent "Other One." Makes up the best parts of a classic Dead set.

9) 7/13/84 Greek Theatre, Berkeley, CA: A full moon, the summer solstice, and the Greek Theatre. So is it surprising that two verses of near perfection transpired? The only version for nearly eight years was inspired, and clear proof that on any given night the Dead are capable of almost anything.

10) 3/29/90 Nassau Coliseum, Uniondale, NY: The Dead meet great jazz. Branford Marsalis, who had never practiced with the group, was invited by Phil to sit in, and he meshed seamlessly with the band, serving, without question, as a full fledged seventh member for a night. This show arguably qualifies as the most successful performance by a guest star. The entire second set was played at an elevated level as evidenced on the version of "Eyes Of The World" featured on *Without A Net*. And mostly due to Marsalis, "Dark Star" reached a plateau that had not previously been heard. This version provides a clear picture of the value of inspired improvisation, as does the whole history of this song. ■

## Editorial

The deeper I delved into the subject of mandatory minimum drug sentencing and carrier weight injustices, the more appalled I became. Not only are the current laws unjust, but there is a marked discrimination against Deadheads in the "War On Drugs." Musical preferences and lifestyles are being used as evidence against drug offenders. More people are serving extensive prison terms for non-violent drug offenses than ever before. That number is growing daily.

Let's join in making our voices heard above the political battle cries. We are not here to advocate drug use, but to have laws changed so that criminal sentences fit the crimes. Read the material presented in this issue and pass the information on. This is a plight that affects everyone on some level.

The war is getting closer to home, so arm yourselves with pens and write your congressmen now.

I've received dozens of in-depth letters from incarcerated Deadheads and have never been more passionately moved to help bring about change. We can and will make a difference.

Let's enter 1994 with the optimistic conviction to make this a better world to live in.

With love,
Toni A. Brown, Publisher

A. R. Klosterman

Artwork by Alfred Klosterman

January/February, 199?

# RELIX
## music for the mind
™

Vol. 20
No. 1

20 YEARS STILL WONDERING

GRATEFUL DEAD
BOB DYLAN · SANTANA
JEFFERSON STARSHIP
AND MUCH MORE

Artwork by Gary Kroman
from a photo by
Ron Delany

# RELIX

### music for the mind

Vol. 21, No. 1

™

STEELY DAN
THE BAND
BLIND MELON

# DRUG WARS
## HEADS BEHIND BARS

EXCLUSIVE INTERVIEWS
# VINCE WELNICK
# BOB WEIR
# DAVID GRISMAN

January/February, 1994

Cover Artwork
by
Gary Kroman

by Jack Dawg

# THE WAR IS ON

## THE CRIMINAL JUSTICE SYSTEM AND THE WAR ON DRUGS

A combination of flawed drug laws, including "mandatory minimum" sentences, strange rules for measuring quantities of LSD and a new Drug Enforcement Agency focus on Grateful Dead concerts, have put 1,500 to 2,000 Deadheads in jail. Many of them are non-violent first offenders who must serve mandatory (no possibility of parole) sentences, some as high as 20 years.

Just five years ago the number of incarcerated Deadheads was fewer than 100. But in recent years, the parking lots at Dead shows have become easy targets for undercover DEA officers, and the war is heating up.

Take the case of Christian Martensen, who was a devoted Grateful Dead follower. In 1991, when his van broke down, a fellow Deadhead offered him $400 to find someone who could sell him LSD, and he did it. The "Deadhead" was actually a DEA agent.

At the trial, Martensen, then 22, learned that the law would prosecute him for the same LSD that the agent bought elsewhere. The other shock was that he would not be prosecuted for the amount of LSD, but for the full weight of the LSD including the blotter paper it was on. The law also carried a mandatory sentence for this offense: five years for the sale of one gram or more, ten years for the sale of more than five grams.

Judge Vaughn Walker didn't like the idea of sentencing this young man who wasn't even in possession of LSD to ten years in federal prison, so he defied the law and sentenced Martensen to only five years. Due to the U.S. Supreme Court's Chapman Decision, which upholds this method of measuring LSD, the appeals court judge was required to issue a new ten-year sentence.

Thousands of young Deadheads are now doing time under similar circumstances. Outraged and angry, the inmates, their friends and families, plus concerned lawmakers and legal professionals are now banding together to fight these injustices.

"It's not that we don't believe in punishment for drug offenses. We're saying, 'let the punishment fit the crime,'" says Julie Stewart, director of Families Against Mandatory Minimums (FAMM), one of the leaders in the fight to get drug laws amended. "It's sad to hear the stories of these young people who make a mistake and have their lives ruined. They deserve a second chance."

Started in 1991, FAMM now has 21,000 members. It also has the support of the American Bar Association, the National Association of Criminal Defense Lawyers and the prestigious Federal Courts' Study Commission, among others.

Some judges, whose hands are tied, also oppose these flawed drug laws. They are forced to "go by the book" and can't take important, relevant factors into consideration. Many judges have called for the repeal of drug laws, recognizing the failure of the war on drugs. These judges feel that the goal of drug enforcement should be to get people off drugs, not to fill up prisons. Meanwhile, the crime rate and drug abuse continue to rise.

Of the 89,743 federal prisoners as of November 1, 1993 (the most in history), 62 percent are drug offenders. Half are first-time offenders, and 80 percent are non-violent. A staggering 3,000 mandatory minimum sentences were handed down in 1992.

Even with the best intentions, changing drug laws and stopping the discrimination of Deadheads is not easy. FAMM has had some success in changing the U.S. Sentencing Commission guidelines, but as long as Congress keeps the mandatory minimum laws firmly in place, there will be no relief.

Why do judges, lawyers, police and anyone else who works in the realities of the legal system oppose mandatory minimums while members of Congress support them? The answer is simple: politics.

"A politician can stand in front of the C-SPAN camera and say, 'I am for stiff mandatory minimum sentences' and people think he is actually doing something to stop crime," says Stewart, who was very disappointed after she testified before the Crime and Criminal Justice Subcommittee of the House Judiciary Committee in July, 1993. "They didn't want to learn anything. It was little more than a forum for the members of Congress to pontificate about how tough they are on drugs and crime."

Two hopeful initiatives have failed to go anyplace. Representative Don Edwards (D-Calif.) sponsored a bill to completely repeal mandatory minimums (with 35 cosponsors), but even he has been quoted as saying the possibility of passing it are "pretty slim." Another bill, the Sentencing Improvement Act, sponsored by Senators Strom Thurmond and Alan Simpson, has become so watered down that FAMM has withdrawn its support for it.

"Mandatory minimums were tried and failed in the 1960s; they were all repealed in 1970," said Stewart. "Then, in 1986 we had the well-publicized cocaine-related death of (Boston Celtic basketball star) Lenny Bias. Drug use was up, and it was an election year," said Stewart. So the politicians got in the act and mandatory minimums came back. It is an attractive way for lawmakers to go on record as being anti-crime without having to pay anything. "But it is costing us millions in overcrowded jails," said Stewart.

Thankfully, though, there is a system in this country for controlling prison sentences: the U.S. Sentencing Commission. Every year, this commission reviews federal sentencing guidelines. It is here that FAMM has actually made progress. Last March, FAMM addressed the LSD weight issue at a hearing of the sentencing commission. As a result, on November 1, 1993, the guidelines were changed.

The carrier is the object that the LSD is transferred on. This may be a piece of blotter paper, a sugar cube or whatever. The entire weight of the carrier is then included as part of the drug. Thus, a person's sentence depends almost completely on the carrier they choose. For example, 100 doses of LSD in pure form weighs five milligrams, which would result in a 10 - 16 month sentence; as a gel, the weight would be 225 mgs., resulting in a 2 1/4 - 2 3/4 year sentence; on blotter paper, the most popular carrier, the weight would be 1.4 grams, resulting in a 5 1/4 - 6 1/2 year sentence; and on a sugar cube, the weight

John A. Young

---

### MANDATORY PRISON TIME
**Minimum federal sentences for people convicted of drug trafficking, based on quantity of the drug:**

#### Ten years minimum, no parole:
1. One kilogram of heroin
2. Five kilograms of cocaine
3. Fifty grams of crack cocaine
4. 100 grams of PCP
5. Ten grams (2,000 doses) LSD
6. 1,000 kilograms marijuana or 1,000 plants
7. 100 grams of methamphetamine

#### Five years minimum, no parole:
1. 100 grams of heroin
2. 500 grams of cocaine
3. Five grams of crack cocaine
4. Ten grams of PCP
5. One gram (200 doses) LSD
6. 100 kilograms marijuana or 100 plants
7. Ten grams methamphetamine

would be 227 grams, resulting in a 15 1/2 - 19 1/2 year sentence.

For instance, Stanley Marshall was arrested and charged with leading a conspiracy to distribute LSD on June 22, 1988 in El Paso, Texas. He had less than one gram of LSD, but since it was carried on about 113 grams of paper, he was charged with conspiracy to distribute 113.3 grams of LSD. If he had been sentenced based on the weight of the actual LSD, he would have spent approximately three years in prison. Instead he was sentenced to 20 years.

At the March 23rd commission hearing, parents made emotional pleas that the law was unfair and should be changed. Also, FAMM presented a study showing that LSD sentences were not even closely related to the amount of LSD involved in many cases. The change was strongly supported by the Public Defender Association and had no opposition.

The resulting modification removes the weight of the carrier from the sentencing formula and substitutes a formula based on doses: one dose of LSD is now set at .4 mg. "We wanted it to be set at .05 mg., the amount the DEA set it at, but they decided to make it eight times higher, at .4 mg." says Stewart.

Thanks to the U.S. Congress, this decision will not affect the mandatory minimum sentences that are still set at five years for a gram of LSD or above, and ten years for five grams or above. What it will do is prevent people from being sentenced to terms *higher* than the mandatory minimums. And people already sentenced by the old guidelines can possibly have them changed.

For example, someone who had a thousand hits on heavy blotter paper that pushed the total weight over five grams would have gotten a ten-year sentence. The new weight guideline, at .4 mg would put his total weight at only four grams so that he would qualify for the mandatory minimum of five years at under five grams.

"At least it's a start," says Stewart.

The other problem facing Deadheads is the DEA's new focus on Grateful Dead concerts as a way to stop the distribution of LSD. Since 1990, the federal government has tripled spending, personnel and arrests for LSD. Gene Haislip, head of LSD enforcement at the DEA says, "We've seen a marked pattern of LSD distribution at Grateful Dead concerts...that has something to do with why so many (Deadheads) are arrested." Of about 500 LSD offenders in federal prisons, more than 80% are Grateful Dead fans. That doesn't include the other 2,000 or so Deadheads that are in state prisons.

The DEA's strategy for attacking LSD is the same they use for all other drugs: try to bust the small fry and get them to turn over evidence to reach the bigger suppliers. "Snitching," therefore, is encouraged in order to get a lighter sentence.

Robert Moody

Endangered Species. © Deadheads Have Become An

---

## COMPARING TIMES FOR CRIMES

How the prescribed prison sentence for a first-time offender with $1,500 worth of LSD compares with sentences for other federal crimes:

| CRIME | Minimum | Maximum |
|---|---|---|
| LSD possession | 10.1 | 13.9 |
| Attempted murder w/harm | 6.5 | 8.1 |
| Rape | 5.8 | 7.2 |
| Armed Robbery (gun) | 4.7 | 5.9 |
| Kidnapping | 4.2 | 5.2 |
| Theft of $80 million or more | 4.2 | 5.2 |
| Extortion | 2.2 | 2.7 |
| Burglary (carrying a gun) | 2.0 | 2.5 |
| Taking a bribe | .5 | 1.0 |
| Blackmail | .3 | .8 |

1- No parole is available on any sentence

Source: US Sentencing Guidelines Manual; Drug Enforcement Aministration

**From: USA TODAY 12/17/92**

---

"The people at the very bottom who can't provide substantial assistance end up getting the worst sentences," said U.S. District Judge Terry J. Hatter, Jr. "That means we end up punishing these people at the bottom of the drug business more severely than those at the top." Hatter is one of the many judges who has spoken out about the great injustices of mandatory minimum sentences. "It's a dehumanizing aspect of the justice system...We're dealing with numbers instead of people."

Regardless, the DEA is not easing up on LSD offenders or Deadheads. According to *USA Today*, Deadheads routinely have their musical tastes, dress and lifestyle used against them in the criminal justice system. It should come as no shock that Deadheads are subject to more police searches than most. To many cops, a Dead bumper sticker is probable cause to pull you over. If he smells the slightest trace of marijuana, he has probable cause to search you and your car. Knowing this, you should not smoke marijuana in your vehicle, especially if you're anywhere near a Dead show or have any bumper stickers that imply that you like the Dead.

Although many Deadheads like to let there freak flag fly, they shouldn't fly it too high. Keep a low profile, and you're much less likely to get busted or harassed. It's not necessary to let the world know you're a Deadhead! When you're on the road, try to blend in. After all, you don't have to look like a Deadhead to be one. Above all else, remember that if you can't do the time, don't do the crime.

How do the Dead feel about this? According to the band's spokesperson Dennis McNally, "We tell them that shows take place In the real world and they will be exposed — sometimes doubly so — to real world penalties. But it's hard to educate 19-year-olds. They can be mind-bogglingly naive. They be-

---

lieve they're doing a non-violent, positive act, and they want to share it with the world." There have been numerous radio ads, and newsletters distributed at venues and with mail order tickets that say the same thing in different words: *don't do it.*

Everybody seems to be aware of the chances they're taking, yet people still openly take and sell drugs on tour. Most people seem to think they're untouchable. The bottom line is that if you get caught with LSD, you're going to jail, most probably for a long time. A first-time offender with $1,500 worth of LSD is looking at 10.1 - 13.9 years, which far exceeds attempted murder with harm (6.5 - 8.1 years), rape (5.8 - 7.2 years), armed robbery (4.2 - 5.2 years), theft of $80 million or more (4.2 - 5.2 years), etc. As crazy as this is, it's the law.

What can you do? Write to your Congressperson and let them know how you feel. I know you've heard it a million times, and you might not think it will help, but every letter they receive is registered and tabulated. Join FAMM (1001 Pennsylvania Ave. N.W., Suite 200 South, Washington, D.C. 20004). This organization is the leader in the fight to change the LSD laws. The Grateful Dead support this group, and you should too. All donations are helpful.

"Our most important accomplishment has been getting politicians to face up to this issue that they used to be able to easily avoid," says Stewart. "When people speak out, it does make a difference."

You also might want to consider dropping a line to one of the more than 2,000 fellow Deadheads behind bars. Many of them are folks just like you who were in the wrong place at the wrong time or who made a mistake. Their lives are filled with darkness and being surrounded by violent criminals can't help. A quick note letting them know that someone cares can make all the difference.

Moreover, if you see someone openly selling drugs, explain the consequences. Above all else, stay clean, be cautious, suspicious and invisible...and remember that the reason we're all in this is for the music. ■

---

## Doing Time for LSD

*The amount of prison time that a person convicted of an LSD offense will serve depends almost entirely on the weight of the material that is used to carry the drug, not on the weight of the drug itself.*

*For example, 100 doses of LSD weigh about 5 milligrams, enough to justify about a year in prison under federal sentencing guidelines. The same amount of LSD, dispersed in sugar cubes, can result in a sentence of nearly 20 years.*

| CARRIER | WEIGHT OF 100 DOSES | GUIDELINE RANGE |
|---|---|---|
| ■ Pure LSD | 5 milligrams | 10-16 months |
| ■ Gelatin capsule | 225 mg. | 2¼-2¾ years |
| ■ Blotter paper | 1.4 grams | 5¼-6½ years |
| ■ Sugar cube | 227 grams | 15½-19½ years |

### LSD VS. COCAINE OR HEROIN

One other result of including the weight of carrier material is that LSD offenses are punished much more severely than cocaine or heroin crimes, even though those drugs are considered much more dangerously addictive.

For instance:

● The sentence for one defendant who sold 12,000 doses of LSD was 20 years in federal prison.

● To receive a sentence of 20 years in prison for selling heroin, a person would have to sell 10 kilograms, enough for 1 million to 2 million doses.

● To receive a sentence of 20 years in prison for selling cocaine, a person would have to sell 50 kilograms, enough for 325,000 to 5 million doses.

Source: Chapman vs. United States, U.S. Supreme Court case No. 90-5744. Majority opinion by Chief Justice William H. Rehnquist, joined by six other justices. Dissent by Justice John Paul Stevens, joined by Justice Thurgood Marshall.

Los Angeles Times, July 27, 1992

Artwork by Gary Kroman

# THE BEAT ROAD NEVER ENDS

## BY JOHN GRADY

*"...the only people for me are the mad ones, the ones who are mad to live, mad to talk, mad to be saved, desirous of everything at the same time..."*

**Jack Kerouac**
**On The Road, 1957**

Neal Cassady, rapping and panting at the wheel of a shiny, new 1949 Hudson, blasted down a Texas highway with his buddy Jack Kerouac at the dawn of a new American era. They were searching together—searching for kindred spirits, "mad ones" in touch with the flames of life.

The adventures of these poet-wanderers separated them from the conformity and accepted standards of behavior of the 1950s. Unlike the A-bomb-dropping prejudice and hate-filled America that they knew all too well, they looked for one of compassionate truthfulness and camaraderie, of honesty and a "laying bare of the soul." And they could find it any-where—in the dismal firelight of a railside hobo camp or under the neon glow of a deadbeat barroom sign.

Their search never ended.

Today, new restless wanderers of the soul, some gathering in rowdy "poetry slams" staged at Paradise Lounge at 11th and Folson in San Francisco or the Nuyorican Poets Cafe in the lower east side of New York, are among a worldwide group of artists, writers, musicians and "grungey" seekers of all description who find the restless spirit of the Beats inspiring.

The Beats, those bongo-beating, free-loving poets of the 1950s, perpetuate in those searching for more out of life—"desirous of everything at the same time." Just as the Grateful Dead. who acknowledge a heavy Beat connection, renews itself decade after decade, the Beats keep on carrying on as well. Here are a few vital signs:

• Rhino Records released best-selling, multi-disk collaborations like *The Beat Generation,* featuring classic Beat readers and improvisers plus jazz music.

• William S. Burroughs released his own CD, *Spare Ass Annie,* on Island, and collaborated on new tunes with Nirvana's Kurt Cobain and with singer Tom Waits on a "pop opera" called "The Black Rider," produced in New York.

• Allen Ginsberg published a new book of poetry this year, *Cosmopolitan Greeting,* and Rhino Records will release a 4-CD collection of his recorded work, including collaborations with Bob Dylan, the Clash and more.

• New poets and writers carry on in Beat tradition with journals like *Bouillabaisse,* published internationally by Alpha Beat Press in New Hope, Pennsylvania and *Rant* published by Literary Renaissance in

Louisville, Kentucky.

Most people have heard about the hitchhiking visionary Jack Kerouac or his sidekick Neal Cassady, the space cowboy who directly linked the Beats with the Dead. "Neal at the Wheel" drove Kerouac cross-country in the '50s as well as the Merry Prankster bus in the '60s. But not that many have read the Beat books or know where they came from. Who were these Beats, anyway?

### Beats, Books and Be-Bop

The unbroken chain of beat inspiration springs from a library full of past and present books. New readers constantly pick them up and experience the verve, the excitement of discovery in life. The messages in this free-form, "spontaneous" style of poetry and prose, which liberate jumbles of previously unspeakable innermost thoughts (with both good and bad results), eluded early, inhibition-laden critics who were simply too shocked to understand. "That's not writing, it's typing," sniffed author Truman Capote about Kerouac in 1958. He was also likened to a "slob running a temperature" and was vilified in the press. But the Beats couldn't be laughed away. Deeply personal and confessional, infused with spiritual insights, Kerouac's books have, one by one, returned to print and continue to sell well today. Previously unpublished works, including his Buddhist *Some Of The Dharma,* are slated to be published in coming years.

Classic Beat titles include Kerouac's *Dharma Bums* with wanderings through snow-capped mountains and frantic North Beach hipster action; Neal Cassady's Skid Row insights in *The First Third;* the sci-fi, cyber-sex-shock of Burroughs' *Naked Lunch;* Allen Ginsberg's renegade *Howl* (which tested and beat the nation's obscenity laws in 1957); Lawrence Ferlinghetti's fantastic *Coney Island Of The Mind;* Gary Snyder's Zen-like love of nature in *Turtle Island;* and the night words, ravishing under Michael McClure's *Jaguar Skies* and Gregory Corso's angry *Gasoline.*

The Beats be-bopped strongly through the late 1940s and 1950s. They experimented with drugs, religion, sexuality, politics and other sensitive subjects—with some disastrous results. Both Cassady and Kerouac flamed out; their premature deaths came before 1970. But they were pioneers, and they were always painfully honest.

"They gave themselves permission to fail and make mistakes, they accepted each other as they were, warts and all," says Dave Christy, a poet and publisher of *Bouillabaisse.*

The Beats, led by Neal Cassady, were always, even in the worst situations, able to laugh. While "beat" meant "beaten down," it also meant "on the beat" and in the groove with a certain "beatitude," a shining beauty despite life's harsh-

ness. They could laugh at the superb "holy goof" it all was. So they started their own circus. They created the Bus. They established a counterculture—without even trying.

Beat inspiration touched millions in the 1960s, including a young Minnesota folk singer named Bob Zimmerman (Dylan), a moody L.A. poet

Photo by Herb Greene

**Neal Cassady**

and art student named Jim Morrison, a scruffy Bay Area banjo player named Jerry Garcia and a sensitive Texas blues singer named Janis Joplin. It even crossed the Atlantic to touch a youthful band called the *"Beatles."*

The Beats continued their search for enlightenment and kicks when a group of people, including Snyder and Ginsberg, met at poet Michael McClure's San Francisco apartment in 1967 to plan a celebration of consciousness—the Human Be-In. The search continued with Cassady dancing wildly to a band called the Warlocks during extended "Be-Ins" at *One Flew Over the Cuckoo's Nest* author Ken Kesey's California canyon home. When Cassady went back "on the road" as "Speed Limit," the driver of the Merry Prankster's bus, the Beats' impact on America exploded.

### Beats Then, Beats Now

The story of the Beats gravitates around Jack Kerouac, born March 12, 1922. He grew up in a tightly knit, French-Canadian family in mill-working Lowell, Massachusetts where he became a high school football star. Always hungry for new ways of seeing, feeling and knowing, Kerouac shrugged off the responsibilities of his Columbia University football scholarship, dropped out and went looking for "kicks" in 1948.

He met his "mad ones" in New York City—the junkies, hustlers and bebop musicians he felt were in touch with real life. There he met

# THE BEAT ROAD NEVER ENDS

**(Continued)**

Burroughs, a refugee from a rigid WASP background (he was an heir to the family calculating machine fortune) who took lessons in life from intense Times Square insiders like Herbert Hunke, and Columbia student Allen Ginsberg, who, not unlike his poet father, was another "mad one" hungry for the passions of life.

And, in a New York City apartment in 1946, Kerouac met the visiting Neal Cassady, his "Western kinsman of the sun," a Denver street urchin whose father was a down-and-out wino. Cassady, a street-wise con artist who grew up stealing cars and cruising with young, feminine conquests, was a volcano of energy, the "fastest man alive," who would inspire not only Kerouac, Burroughs and Ginsberg, but whole generations after them.

The media images of the Beats, however, which were lampooned in caricatures like the "beatnik" Maynard G. Krebs (played by actor Bob Denver on the TV show *Dobie Gillis*) didn't really capture the truth.

"The Beats were seen as hooligans with no morals seeking a wild time," says Christy. "But they were sad about the state of the world, they wanted people to feel their sadness and tragedy. Theirs was an alternative world of beauty and openness that touched people and brought them together."

A newfound capacity for revealing innermost feelings and fears, and a desire to shed restrictions and inhibitions, appears to be coming back into style. At poetry readings around the nation, people are taking to the microphone and revealing their inner thoughts to strangers. That willingness to create a trusting feeling, one almost of family, could be the strongest legacy of the Beats.

"The group we have, it must be about eighty scattered around the world, is like a family," says Christy, who together with his poet wife Ana, publishes their "Post-Beat Independents" journal with submissions from Europe, Asia and India, as well as both North and South America. *Bouillabaisse* publishes the work of original Beats, like Ginsberg's tribute to writer Carl Solomon (who died in 1993), Charles Bukowski: "if only there were magic people to help get us through" or Prankster Ken Babbs's "A Dream Life," along with new writers. Christy says they "don't try to emulate the Beats, but carry on what they were up to."

The willingness to break rules and try new things is evident in the pages of *Bouillabaisse* where a horoscope chart of Carolyn Cassady (Neal's wife who has published her own books, including *Heart Beat* which was made into a Hollywood movie) appears along with original artwork and cartoons. Of course, it's mostly poems, like "Oz" by Alice Olds-Eilingson: "Where honesty is the last syllable of recorded time—and the funniest" or "Tribal Performance" by Frank Moore: "infecting that outer world with the virus of new alternatives and new possibilities."

Across the generations, the spirit of the Beats continues.

Says Christy: "There is a drive to find more in life that we share with the Beats. They showed people that there's more to life than what their fathers told them, more to life than a gray flannel suit. They got America groovin' and rockin'. We, like them, celebrate beauty, nature, sexuality. We may be down and out, but we can still enjoy ourselves. It's a kind of tribal feeling, a feeling of love." ∎

# How I survived Rock 'n' Roll and discovered fame without guilt

## BY TOM CONSTANTEN

It was like a glimpse of Rock 'n' Roll Heaven. A galaxy of stars in one room, a name dropper's paradise, schmoozarama. The 1994 Rock and Roll Hall of Fame induction ceremony was a mammoth event, the kind that brings out the P. T. Barnum in you when you try to describe it.

It was below zero in New York that January evening, but inside the Grand Ballroom of the Waldorf–Astoria Hotel a blaze of music, memories and souls was about to ignite. The Waldorf–Astoria, fabled in song and salad, synonymous with class and prestige, even insists on the double hyphen.

The magnitude of the event got to everyone, invitees and inductees alike. Where else would Paul McCartney read a rambling, touchingly personal love letter to John Lennon before presenting an award to Yoko Ono, or Jeff Beck clarify his love-hate relationship with Rod Stewart whose award he was accepting? Levon Helm even looked good by not showing up.

As in the oft-imagined afterlife, there were the reunions with old friends and the making of new ones. If I could do it, I'd have picked up the needle at the end of the evening and played it over. At least once. It went by so fast, and there was so much to catch up on. I hadn't spent so much time with my friends in the band in years. To see Phil, mellowing like an imperial cognac, or Mickey, in his glory back in his old stomping grounds, was worth the trip already. Vince I'd seen a couple of times backstage at recent shows, but that just made it all the better to see him again. But then to catch up with Bill's underwater explorations and Bob's ventures in Central America was like awakening in the most pleasant sense.

The festivities started, for me at least, in Dennis McNally's (the Dead's publicist) hotel suite. He did his exalted dance by shuttling and juggling interviewers and interviewees between the two rooms and the several radio and television crews that were there. Bob extolled the value of fruit bats as pets to Mickey as the cameras set up, then went on to explain his aversion to tie-dye to the interviewer. Phil was his usual articulate self, renewing his answers every time a new microphone was clipped on him. Mickey raved on about the many reasons for the importance of it happening in New York.

There was even tape left over for a question or two for me. It felt nice to be included.

A brief moment to freshen up, and it was time for cocktails and **The Main Event**. The hotel staff, evidently used to biddable corporate types or docile conventioneers, took more than half

Hornsby, Hart, Lesh, Kreutzmann, Weir, Constanten and Welnick

an hour of "please sit down so we can start the dinner service" announcements before the aisles were clear enough to serve the food. Among the people seated at the table with Beth and me were the Bruce Hornsbys and the former Mrs. Brent Mydland. I'd never had the pleasure of meeting her before, although I'd encountered Brent briefly. We hobb-nobbed with Paul Shaffer, a couple of members of the Spin Doctors, and Willie Dixon's wife and daughter. Somehow it all seemed so easy.

And we weren't the only ones socializing. There's no way to calculate how much wheeling, dealing, cajoling and hand-shaking went on. It was a super-party with industry execs, artists and every manner of middlemen pressing the flesh and their points. It could've gone on for hours, but for one obstacle: the show.

You can read elsewhere who presented the awards to whom and what was said in acceptance. I was too buzzed to keep it all straight, although I was quite alert for the moment when Dennis beckoned me to the side for our walk backstage. The time had come! We were led through the big doors at stage-right, past the kitchen ("It really is like *Spinal Tap*!" quipped Phil) and around to the hall behind the steps to the stage. And there was Bruce Hornsby, brilliantly expostulating on the band's history and significance, trying to keep a straight face while Bob and Phil gesticulated. Then up the steps to the presentation, and around to the press room for the questions and flash bulbs. Meanwhile, on-stage Bono waxed poetic on Bob Marley. The things you miss when you're in the eye of the hurricane. And then, not even stopping for a cigarette, back to our seats for the rest of the show.

The encores were (your superlative here)! As in an all-star game, the players made it an extraordinary event. Bob Weir was joined by Bruce Hornsby and Bill Kreutzmann (as well as

Continues ...

# How I Survived Rock 'n' Roll and dicovered fame without guilt (Continued)

Chuck Berry, Paul Shaffer and the CBS Orchestra, and a few others) in a comfortably moving "Wang Dang Doodle." I listened hard to pick out Bruce's solo. It really didn't make me feel any better to see somebody else's underamplification problems. (Doesn't anyone know how to mix keyboards?) In any case, what I could hear of his playing was stunning.

The stage changes were quick and efficient, scarcely five minutes between tunes. It was like the way they shuttle players in and out of old-timers games, inning by inning. Except, of course, these "old-timers" hadn't lost anything off their fastball. Chuck Berry rolled over Beethoven one more time, Ziggy Marley got us all together and feeling all right, Axl Rose and Bruce Springsteen "Came Together," and Eric Clapton finally got his wish and joined the Band for the grand finale, "The Weight."

Four quick hours were suddenly over.

But not the evening. Up in Bob Weir's suite, Our Band was roasting and toasting. Phil's smile looked permanent. John Popper reached into his bandolero and presented harmonicas to his admirers (Beth and I both got one), and *SNL* comedian Tom Davis contributed his soul-loosening bon-mots. As if I needed another honor, I finally got to meet John Barlow.

After a while, a few of us went up to the 37th floor to Phil Spector's suite, where another party was in progress. As we walked in, Chuck Berry was at the grand piano. Now, take it from me, Chuck Berry is not a pianist. But he is a musician, and he practically has a patent on the I-IV-V chord progression and its permutations. So his playing made sense and had a lot of charm and sophistication for all its rambling and occasional fits and starts. He was about to

leave when Phil Spector stopped him, wanting to play a duet. Now, Phil Spector is neither a pianist nor a musician, judging from the abortive attempts to get his boogie off the ground. "You take the high part," Chuck Berry suggested, and it worked — for about two bars. At that point, Berry made the most delicate, courteous, quickest exit I've ever seen. With Beth's prodding, I filled the void at the piano and got through "Dejavalse" and "Boris The Spider" pretty well, according to people's responses. Then Spector wanted the piano back. It was time for an Elvis tribute.

I'd love to have gone on playing, but hey, the man definitely earned his way there, and it was his party, too. There was plenty of euphoria to go around.

With visions of sugarplums, the evening really ended. It was a dizzying honor, one that was hard to comprehend. The real honor, though, was in my friends inviting me. I wondered why they had. They'd never heard me in playing shape, well prepared, playing an instrument I felt comfortable with. And they've given me much more, in many senses, than I could ever repay.

All I can do is chalk it up to their great good nature. For all their wisecracks and sarcasm, that's what I'll always remember them for. ■

Artwork by Alfred Klosterman

Tom Constanten    Photo by L.D. Kippel

Tom Constanten and Toni Brown - On the Road    Photo by L.D. Kippel

Brian and Michelle Hinton with Toni
Poconos, PA

Courtney Lee and Jordan Lee McClutchy
Palm Harbor, FL

Skip DuVall

Griffith, IN

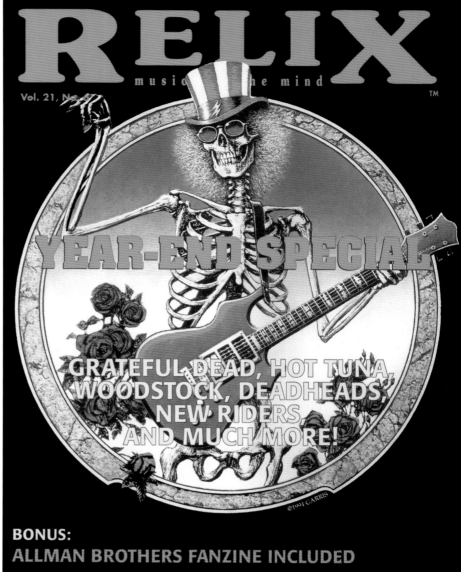

# RELIX

### music for the mind

™

Vol. 21, No.

## YEAR-END SPECIAL

## GRATEFUL DEAD, HOT TUNA, WOODSTOCK, DEADHEADS, NEW RIDERS AND MUCH MORE!

©1994 GARRIS

## BONUS:
## ALLMAN BROTHERS FANZINE INCLUDED

### Cover Artwork by Philip Garris

Anna and Tom met thru the Relix classifieds

we are everywhere

Amy, Dave, Connie and Terry in Medina, OH

# RELIX

music for the mind

Vol. 21, No. 3

SUMMER
1294
SPECIAL

**GRATEFUL DEAD**

BOB DYLAN
THE BAND
SUN RA
HOT TUNA

**DEADHEAD'S
SUMMER VACATION GUIDE**

# BILLY KREUTZMANN
### keeping time

## By Roger Len Smith

Photo by Rob Cohn/Dead Images

Billy Kreutzmann spends half the year underwater. The Grateful Dead's original drummer took up scuba diving several years ago when he made it out to the big island of Hawaii for a vacation with bandmates Jerry Garcia and Bob Weir. Kreutzmann, who immediately took to the sport, gets in his wetsuit as much as possible when the band is not touring.

Having been the drummer for every Grateful Dead gig since its beginning as the Warlocks in 1965, Kreutzmann has probably played more rock gigs than any other drummer in history. With the Dead's total concert tally running somewhere around 3,000 shows in almost 30 years, it's certain that Kreutzmann has seen his share of certain guitarists' rear ends.

Musically, Kreutzmann is more the timekeeper

jam or a "Dark Star" from the early '70s to hear Kreutzmann's *swing*.

Kreutzmann has also had his share of side ventures. Along with virtually every member of the Dead, Kreutzmann performed on Garcia's first solo album, and he co-authored the psychedelic staple "That's It For The Other One" with Weir. He collaborated on the successful *Rhythm Devils* soundtrack to *Apocalypse Now* with Hart in 1980 and put together a "cover band" with the late Brent Mydland and Santana alumni Alex Ligertwood and David Margen in the mid-'80s.

Kreutzmann's latest side interest has consumed quite a bit of his non-Grateful Dead time. In fact, the drummer has just put the finishing touches on a 48-minute documentary on diving, sea life and ecology that very well may end up on the always interesting Discovery Channel. Called "Ocean Spirit," the video was filmed during a trip from San Francisco all the way to a remote island off the tip of Baja, California.

In late November, I reached Kreutzmann the morning after the first night of a three-night run in Denver, which began the final shows of 1994.

### How are the shows going?

We had a great night last night. It was our first night in this little group of eleven shows.

### How did the Ocean Spirit video come about?

It's a very serious underwater deal. We went from San Francisco—before Halloween a year ago—down to San Diego, and we ended up going all the way down to the tip of Baja and off to Scorocco Island, which is about 250 miles southwest of Cabo San Lucas. It's no man's land out there. Nobody goes there, mostly because it's owned by the Mexican government and, on the island, they have a 400-man Mexican navy base. It's not a tourist place, and they guard that island. They know what they have.

### How did you get there?

The captain of our boat (the Argasea Venture), Bill Belmont, his mother was once mar-

ried to the president of Mexico. I wish I could remember the guy's name, there's been many of them. But that kind of helped.

### Did you film the entire journey?

We did most of our principal photography there. We got all of the days of shooting. We had one large underwater Betacam in a big housing, a giant monster thing. It's big to me, because it weighs about 100 pounds out of the water. And we had a bunch of Hi-8's, and a land-based Betacam for interviews and things. It has a heavy environmental message.

### Will it be on the Discovery Channel?

We're in negotiations right now. I would love to be able to tell you that I've got a firm release date, but not yet. It's right up their alley. I'd like to do this as a balance to the Grateful Dead, I mean the Grateful Dead doesn't play everyday. This is really fun.

### Certainly Mickey has plenty of side projects...

I don't think he's ever hurting for stuff to do (laughs). One of my rooms at my place, you walk in there, you'd think you walked into Jack's Dive Locker (in Hawaii). It's all wetsuits, and we also do a lot of ocean kayaking and surfing.

### In the video, there's a scene where you encounter over 20 giant sperm whales.

Yeah, as we were going back, we got the best reward. We knew we were doing something right. One of our guys spotted these big blows off the bow about a couple hundred yards off. Sperm whales are interesting because they breathe off the left side of the head, so you can tell what kind of whale it is right away and the blow goes straight up. Anyway, we saw all these things, a pod of sperm whales. So, we immediately got in our away boat and jumped out on them. We got a lot of film of them.

### Did anyone swim with them?

Oh yeah, I could have touched them. I did a lot of camera work with this, too. That's part of my goal—to learn how to do underwater camera work. We had three passes at them. I thought there was eight, and I went back and looked at the film later on and, of course, there was like twenty animals. They stack up, there's four on the surface, and they're tiered down below. They swim like that to protect themselves. Most of the shots we did we free dove, we didn't use scuba. I think that allowed us, I'm sure of this, to be closer to the animals. We

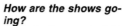

Photo by Rob Cohn

of the group whereas Mickey Hart tends to fill in percussive colors around the beat. The shows from 1971 through 1974 featured Kreutzmann as the only drummer in the band while Hart was on hiatus, and the Dead had a slightly more jazzy feel on certain songs. Kreutzmann did an admirable job holding down the groove in a musical soundscape that previously featured two drummers. Kreutzmann is indeed a very jazz-influenced drummer, citing legends Art Blakey and Elvin Jones as influences. All one has to do is listen to a "Playing In The Band"

Photo by Ralph Hulett

shot about 70 hours, and we used 48 minutes.

**And you rode a manta ray?**

That was one of my goals. It was almost 20 feet. I want to go up to Alaska and get into cages and film polar bears underwater, which nobody's done. There's plenty of on-top stuff. And, always have a message of ecology, and, especially a message of hope. Always have boundless amounts of hope that we can change this thing. We don't always have to be wrecking it. The ocean, people still think it's a dumping ground.

**Synthesizer music appears on the video.**

Bob Bralove and I were the main musicians on the video. Good soundtrack. What happens for me is when the project is done, I'm on to the next project.

**Your son Justin is a young filmmaker.**

Well, I'm not sure what he's doing with film right now, but he did the biggest selling video for the band so far, *The Making Of 'Touch Of Grey,'* that sold more than the actual video did.

**How particular are you with your drum sounds—in the studio or in the concert setting?**

Oh, totally, they have to be perfect.

**Do you like to use certain reverb or effects?**

I do, but it's only what I hear, it doesn't go out to the house. My snare drum—I put a little wetness on it, a little reverb. I can't hear the house, but the drum sound has to be perfect or I'm...freaked! The snare, I want it to be bright, you know, I want it to last a little longer, so I put a little reverb on it. You can hardly notice it.

**How is the new ear monitor system working out?**

They're about the coolest thing that ever came down the pike. They're just ear monitors and we have six different mixes, each guy has his own mix.

**It seemed that the guitar players had a hard time adjusting to it at first.**

It was hard for me, too. You don't get any bass on them, there's no low end, it's just a little tiny speaker in your ear. So you have to get used to it, but you do.

**They never get too loud in your ear?**

You're in control of it. They're pretty sensitive, you can't blow on them. If you get sweat on them, you don't dare blow on them. I've ruined a pair of them by doing that. I didn't know better. You're sound is much more clean, and you can have sounds that are much more enveloped. They're really fun, I'm glad we got into them. It's way fun.

**Who inspired you when you started playing drums?**

When I started playing, I listened to Elvin Jones like crazy. He was with John Coltrane. I liked him a lot. I still like Art Blakey, he can still play, God bless him.

More modern guys: I like the guy who plays for Sting—Vinnie Colaiuta. Amazing, he's just wonderful. He's one of the most amazing drummers. But Sting never puts together anything sloppy. I like Peter Gabriel's music a lot, now. I saw this TV thing, it was kind of hard to watch ("Secret World Live"). It was far out and real risky to show a band that way, you know. They have that long runway and he runs up and down it, and people are dancing. I mean, it takes a risk, which is okay. that's good. Like, we're just the opposite, we just sit up there and play. I've never seen Jerry do any somersaults or jump up like Townshend used to do. Gabriel and those guys play to samples, they don't play anything off the top of their head, if you know what I mean. They play to prerecorded stuff, like a modern metronome. It works fine. You can use a click track to your benefit because it's keeping the beat, and you just think about it like another musician.

**Airto Moreira has sat in with the Dead many times on percussion. He plays completely live, no preconceptions.**

He's the best. He's a primal percussionist. You know what it is? Unlike people that grow up and learn to be musicians, he was *born* a musician. Nothing wrong with growing up and

learning how to do it, but he has God on his side. It was in his body when he was born.

**Jim Keltner is a studio drummer who never liked playing live very much.**

I'm 180 degrees the opposite of Keltner. I'll sit in a studio and go, 'shit, what do I do now?' You put me in front of an audience, I know what to do. I wish there was some kind of magical drug that I could take and go in the studio and do the stuff I do live. I don't come from that place of memorizing chops. I know how to do it and I can do most of the rudiments, but I don't give a shit about that.

**Do you prefer playing percussion as opposed to the drum kit?**

Not too much. I really love playing on the drum set. It's one of the most fun things to do. I love the bass drum. I like the real simple stuff with nice fills every now and then.

**Would you do a project like Go Ahead again?**

That was a real fun band, I gotta tell you. That was a kick in the ass. But after Brent's

Photo by Bob Bromberg

demise, there was just nowhere to go with that. I find that I do better in the Grateful Dead if I have a completely different influence coming in, like diving. I need that. I need to have two different things and then when it balances, it's working great. Mostly because I've done the Grateful Dead for 30 years, you know. You really need to have other influences in your life period. That's just how it is. And I'm not ever gonna play golf!

**Diving and drumming must keep you in pretty decent shape.**

Drumming is pretty physical. I quit smoking five years ago. They say it takes about five years for your lungs to repair, that's probably true. It made me feel a lot better, I don't smoke anything. My lungs are really precious. When you're out wave-riding, kayaking or surfing in Northern California, you wanna have stamina. Those waves are relentless.

**What newer artists do you listen to?**

Melissa Etheridge. I like her a lot. She just sings it from her heart. I gotta be honest with you, when I'm not doing the Grateful Dead, I'm not out listening to a lot of music. I'm usually in a place that I can't listen to music. I let my music just come out from my heart, the way I feel. I feel real clean and I go out and play, that's good enough for me. Like Airto a little bit. I don't know any other way to do it. (Laughs) ∎

Photo by Ed Perlstein

Artwork by Clay B. DuVal

# PHISH

## NO FEAR OF FLYING An Interview with

# Mike Gordon

## by Toni A. Brown

**H**aving a conversation with Mike Gordon, bass player for the band Phish, is somewhat like the first year of algebra. Everything put before you has a greater meaning, and each tidbit, no matter how insignificant at the time, is relevant to a greater whole. Most importantly, you have to pay attention to get it all.

But, unlike algebra, Gordon held my psyche and mesmerized me for two-and-a-half hours. Right before my mind, he wove an intricate tapestry of theorization and metaphysics. His insights are profoundly remarkable. This interview, much like Phish's music, was improvised in spite of a carefully researched list of questions.

The members of Phish are analogous to a fireworks display: four sky-rockets that go off individually, which are accompanied by a lot of sound and upward spiraling that reach its zenith in a blazing cacophony of simultaneous brilliance, with very little warning.

Its music is often compared to the Grateful Dead, but this is not an accurate measure. Yes, like the Grateful Dead, Phish has a propensity towards jamming. But it's the '90s, and Phish takes the concept to an entirely unrelated level. Frank Zappa and Sun Ra are more influential in the band's overall sound than any other artists, although Phish is unique. These four intellectuals combine their talents in differing degrees from one night to the next. The band shares a warped sense of humor with its loyal audience through a convoluted interplay of music, effects and stage antics.

Phish had its biggest year in 1994. The band grossed $10.3 million on tour selling 600,000 tickets to 99 coast to coast concerts, and sold 550,000 records. On December 30, 1994, Phish appeared on *The David Letterman Show* and then went immediately to perform a sold-out show at Madison Square Garden, followed by a sold-out Boston Garden New Year's Eve concert. The band was invited back to *The David Letterman Show* in July, 1995.

Fans keep in touch with Phish through its five-times-a-year newsletter, *Doniac Schvice*, which has 85,000 subscribers, and on the Phish Net, a computer news group. Since it appeared on the Internet four years ago, the site, to which 40,000 Net surfers have access, features instant fan reports on concerts, set lists and lyrics to Phish tunes. Discussions on the state of the Phish scene and its style of improvisation is also common Net fare.

The Phish phenomenon started in Burlington, Vermont in 1983 and has spread across the country without benefit of a hit record, major radio airplay, MTV videos or the cover of *Rolling Stone*.

Anastasio (30), who grew up in Princeton, New Jersey and plays lead guitar, contributes most lead vocals and has a hand in composing most Phish songs. He is the band's only married member.

Drummer Jon "Fish" Fishman (30) is the son of a Syracuse, New York dentist. He is the band's jester, a free spirit who often performs wearing goggles and a house dress—if he wears anything at all.

Bassist Mike Gordon (29) is a native of Sudbury, Massachusetts. His father founded the Store 24 chain. He is a filmmaker and has a great business sense. Before Phish became too big, he kept the books and answered all the fan mail.

Pianist Page McConnell (32) grew up in Basking Ridge, New Jersey. His father, a pediatrician and research scientist, helped develop Tylenol. He drove the van in the band's formative years.

Anastasio started the band in 1983 when he posted flyers around the University of Vermont campus seeking fellow musicians. Fishman, Gordon and another guitarist responded. While that lineup started jamming that year, it wasn't until 1985, when McConnell joined the group, that today's version of Phish really started.

McConnell, at the time, was a student at Goddard College in Plainfield, Vermont. He collected a $50 finder's fee for each when he persuaded Anastasio and Fishman to transfer to his "popular in the 1960s and 1970s" counterculture college with its population waning in the 1980s.

The unnamed fifth member of Phish left the group that year when he became a born again Christian and went off to play in a band with televangelist Jimmy Swaggart.

That year, in November, 1985, Gordon had his own intense, personal religious experience. As he was playing in the band, he felt himself transported into a transcendent state of ecstasy. "It was the peak experience of my life—the time I felt most myself," says Gordon. "I knew I wanted to do this the rest of my life. Now I'm living to try to create and share the kind of experience I had in 1985."

Phish feels that Vermont and its slowed down, non-confrontational style of life has had a huge impact on the band's music. One of the first places Phish ever played was a tavern in downtown Burlington called Nectar's.

"When we used to play at Nectar's, it was so laid-back. We'd play three sets a night, just feeling our way as a band," says Anastasio. "It was such a mellow atmosphere that we were free to stretch out and experiment, to attempt outrageous things and make utter fools of ourselves." Phish dedicated its 1992 album, *A Picture Of Nectar*, to Burlington restaurant/impresario Nectarios "Nectar" Rorris.

Word about this free-form and funny new band spread from campus to campus as the band toured over the mountains into New Hampshire, to small clubs like the Stone Church in Newmarket, NH, up through Maine, including the downtown Portland club scene, and then down into Massachusetts and Boston.

On January 26, 1989 the band, still relatively unknown, rented the Paradise Club in Boston.

When Phish easily packed it with its loyal followers, other clubs wanted to get in on the action.

October 17 and 18 also became Phish milestones when the band sold out two shows at the Great American Music Hall in San Francisco. (Imagine a Vermont band without a record contract selling out a prominent West Coast venue!)

Phish, which never plays the same show twice, permits—and encourages—the taping of its concerts. The band is hoping that its latest two-disc double live album, *A Live One* (Elektra), will capture the excitement, spontaneity and humor of its concerts.

Phish has five other albums out on Elektra Records; *Hoist*, the 1994 release, sold a respectable 250,000 copies. Its four earlier albums—*Junta*, *Lawn Boy*, *Picture Of Nectar* and *Rift*—sold a combined 300,000 last year. *Junta*, Phish's first and most popular recording, still sells 1,500 to 2,000 copies a week.

In addition, Phish does a brisk business in T-shirts, caps, posters and decals through the Phish Dry Goods Department, a mail-order operation that runs out of a small shopping center outside of Lexington, Massachusetts.

Phish's manager, John Paluska, began booking Phish into college bars around Northampton while he was a student at Amherst College. His company, Dionysian Productions, maintains Phish as its only client. Clearly, Paluska has

Page McConnell, Mike Gordon, Trey Anastasio and Jon Fishman

his hands full. Worrying over the band's growth in popularity, he is concerned that the band sold out Madison Square Garden in four hours. "Phish is like hot coals, the last thing we want is a brush fire," he says. He works to keep the price of concert tickets as low as possible so fans can attend multiple shows per year. He also works with ticket agencies to insure that Phish tickets get into the hands of fans, not scalpers. Additionally, he must deal with the problem of bootleg recordings surfacing in the marketplace.

Amy Skelton, a fellow UVM student who was the only person to show up at Phish's first gig in Burlington, is Phish's official "First Fan." She divides her time between her 200-acre horse farm in Maine and serves as Phish's merchandising manager when it is on tour. She is now armed with a federal injunction that permits her to confiscate the numerous bootleg T-shirts and souvenirs that she comes across. Skelton has also been placed in charge of outside security at the shows. One of her chief targets: the nitrous oxide vendors selling $5 balloons full of happy gas at shows.

The biggest fear among "Phishheads" is that their favorite band will become commercialized. This was exemplified by the band's unfulfilling foray into music videos. Bending to pressure from the record company, Phish finally produced a video with an underwater aquarium theme for its song, "Down With Disease." Fans and the band hated it.

"It was a totally farcical, ridiculous thing to do for other people's reasons," says Fishman. The end result of this project was the band reaffirming its belief in musical integrity, not commercial success.

For the members of Phish and its fans, the band is more of a family than anything else. Gordon, for example, invited his grandmother (two weeks before she died) on-stage in Boston on New Year's Eve. His mother, artist Marjorie Minken, paints Phish's stage backdrops. Anastasio's step-grandfather joined him on-stage several years ago in Arizona.

For Phish, this family is a long-term commitment. The band members have repeatedly stated that if any one of them quits, it will be the end of the band.

Every time it plays, the band invites its listeners to be part of this family circle.

This intimate ride into the philosophies and theories behind Phish's music via Mike Gordon is a perfect primer to better understand the intensity of the music this band delivers.

*You'll have to forgive me—much of my reference is going to come from the Grateful Dead. But I see you as being the next progression, except that I can't compare the music — the Grateful Dead jam. But you take it to another level.*
**Gordon:** Yeah, it's different. I think it's exactly what you say. It borrows on some of the same philosophies as well as philosophies from other groups. You know, there's the Frank Zappa influence and groups not found in pop music, but in other styles. But it takes a certain philosophy of jamming, in allowing the music to be, allowing the group mind to develop and the music to take on its own thing where the individuals aren't controlling it, which the Dead definitely believe in. It adds a consciousness where some of the jamming is on more of a conscious level, and we're making decisions, as a band, to suddenly switch the jam in a different direction.

We actually practice jamming exercises, and I think it's the sort of thing that the Dead have never believed in—to practice jamming. But, with us, we've found that it's listening exercises because, if a gig is good, it's always that we're hooked up as a unit and we're listening to each other and are very aware. If it's ever a bad gig, it tends to be when different band members are in their own worlds and aren't aware of each other. So we do exercises in our practice room at home to make sure that we can hook up and that each person can hear each band member and react to each other …

Someone once described it as a herd of buffaloes that were going fast through a field and suddenly took a left turn together. But there are other people who actually described it, this sort of new direction in improvised music that we're taking, as being sort of the coming together of Dionysian and Apollonian val-

**Mike Gordon**

ues where the ecstasy of the Dionysian ritual is combined with the consciousness and thoughtfulness of the Apollonian ethic and combined into a new art form. In terms of modern music, some people have said that's what's happening with us.

**Page McConnell**

*Your music is very elaborate, but many of your lyrics are somewhat repetitive, like going for the sounds and textures of the words as opposed to the actual meanings of the words.*
**Gordon:** The lyrics have gone through changes over the last few years. Most of our lyrics are written by Tom Marshall, a friend of Trey's from before high school. I've written maybe ten of our songs, and Trey himself has written a bunch. But most of them have come from Tom and Trey working with Tom. The words came from word play where the syllables and the way they sound are as important as what they mean—little phrases that might be little intellectual and emotional triggers, but the way they connect together is real up-in-the-air for interpretation. Our albums, especially our first three albums, reflect that. If you can make sense out of the lyrics then it's a real fantasy world with strange characters. At a certain point, we really wanted to sing about something, things that we could sink our hearts into and really believe. I think when you say the musicianship has been more significant in our career than our singing, we've actually worked with singing teachers and we had a barbershop quartet teacher for a while, different people and different concepts. It's been an effort to try to catch up the singing to the musical side of things.

In a 20-minute song which has five words, those five words are much more meaningful than are some with a hundred words. A few albums ago, we wanted to sing music that we could feel more, and there was an effort to write things that were a little bit simpler and easier to grasp onto and about real, serious subjects. If there was a turning point, it might have been *Rift,* which is loosely a concept album about someone sleeping at night and dreaming about his girlfriend, and the rift is a rift in a relationship as much as anything. Ideally, lyrics will have meanings on different levels, but that was roughly the concept. And all the songs fit together in that scheme.

All these ideas that I've been thinking about are sort of popping into my head, and I feel another tangent coming on. I'm good at going off on a tangent and remembering where I came from. Sometimes I talk about my peak experience in November of '85. We were playing for [a few] people in the middle of nowhere at Goddard College, and I've definitely grown since then and I've learned how to achieve those levels of consciousness in music and new musical levels since then. But I still consider that to be my peak experience. How transcendent it was. (Mike Gordon was transported into a transcendental state by the music, and he now compares the experience to flying or swimming.) So when I think about growth, there's change and there's continuity. I think that for me it's important to remember that there is an underlying, universal thing that stays the same, and that there's a goal to return to it.

In terms of growth and change, it's an argument that comes up between me and Trey and it has for the whole 12 years. He and Fish especially say their philosophy is originality and innovation. That's important to me, but the way that I define the musical experience is that it's not actually an artistic experience for me. It's not art that's driving me forward, and [it's not] being creative and innovating and trying to be new and original, which are artistic values. For me, it's more of a religious thing, where surrendering to the moment, meditating, are the supreme ideals for me.

*Where do you think you'll be in ten years?*
**Gordon:** Usually, we talk about our goals, and we never predict the future. We like to think that certain ideals that we had would stay, and one of them is that idea of evolution. Having the music continue to change so that we would be writing new songs and trying new things, and I guess the other is that some things would stay the same. That brings it back to the same thing, the continuity that we'd still be able to get on stage and sort of fly.

David Vann

**Trey Anastasio**

*Do you ever have a night where you just don't feel it?*

**Gordon:** Yeah, yeah. There used to be nights that were horrible. I think that we've gotten to a point where, even if things aren't clicking quite as well, it's still okay. We're more likely to say, "Well, tomorrow will be okay." It's a bad feeling to leave a gig, especially if the last song was bad, because then, as musicians, we'll spend the next 24 hours till the next gig in a bad mood and we've just let people down and let ourselves down. If that happens, it's usually because different people in the band are distracted or they're in their own worlds. There are other reasons. It could be that the acoustics are bad and we couldn't hear each other and we couldn't hook up for that reason.

Often, we get off the stage and analyze what we did, probably more than most bands. Maybe a little bit too much. Actually, I'm thankful for it because we're so good at communicating, so open, that even if we go overboard sometimes, at least it gets our feelings out. Sometimes it's not clear, there's a lot of communication that goes on on-stage. Even just eye contact. But sometimes, we'll get the wrong message. Trey will look at Fish and Fish will think that he's sped up the song too much. Really, Trey is trying to say "You're not hooking up with me." These days, it's usually not bad but maybe not as great, and sometimes it's just unpredictable. It'll just happen and it's definitely the nature of taking risks and improvising.

*Do you go out with set lists?*

**Gordon:** Trey actually writes out a set list, which ends up being a sketch of what we'll do. We'll veer off from it. It's more of a list of ideas in case we can't think of what to do, we'll return to it.

*Do you find that you just pick up on things and go with it?*

**Gordon:** I never see a set list myself, actually. But, yeah the best sets are sets where it just goes up on tangents. I like this idea of playing with structure, and sometimes we'll just start jamming between songs for no reason, and occasionally, we'll break up on a tangent in an unexpected place, like between two verses of a song, or we'll cut a song in half. But going with the flow works out the best. Trey writes the set list in an effort not to repeat songs. He gets a computer printout of what we played last year in the same place, what we played the last couple of nights and anywhere in the region recently so that we can be as different as possible. And then he writes a set list, and then we veer off from it. Lately, almost every night, we've been having at least one unplanned jam which is thirty or forty minutes long. We don't know when it's gonna happen or if it's gonna happen. So the set list really gets forgotten.

*You do a lot of Beatle covers.*

**Gordon:** We have a lot of respect for the Beatles as songwriters. We asked people to vote on what album they wanted us to play. They sent in letters through [our newsletter] *Doniac Schvice.* [Incidentally, the name of the newsletter has no overt meaning.]

The Beatles' *White Album* got the most votes, so we learned that. The songs were simple, but to learn all of them and all the harmonies in two weeks, it wasn't all that easy and that was just the second set of a three set gig. It was a five-and-a-half hour gig. But we still play some of those songs. The Beatles were extremely creative in the studio with songwriting, and I think we all have a lot of respect for that.

The first album I ever listened to was *Abbey Road*, which my parents had. My first few years, that was the only album that I ever listened to.

*Phishheads and Deadheads. There is a huge crossover audience amongst the younger crowd, and it would seem that both audiences embrace similar values.*

**Gordon:** There's a bit of a difference in the mentality. With us, with the band members, we just like any music that's good. There's such a wide variety of music being listened to. Actually, Trey is really into checking out what's going on with current music. His favorite band's Pavement now. We all went to the New Orleans Jazz Festival, and Trey has been playing with Michael Ray, who was the trumpet player in Sun Ra's band. Sun Ra was another big influence on us.

At the New Orleans Jazz Festival, for anyone who hasn't gone, there's like 60 bands a day and that's just at the festival. Then there are all the clubs. One of our favorite things to do is, after we play, to go out to different clubs and to see music and to meet other musicians with different ethnic backgrounds. If music has passion and is being made with the right intent, then we like to check it out and maybe be inspired by it. Hopefully, with our fans, they have that same attitude. I actually went to a club last night where there was a Phish cover band that only played Phish songs. (Laughter) I actually laid low in the back. I wanted to learn some new bass lines for our songs, which I did. (The band that Mike saw was the Phins, which was actually Franklin Turnpike doing a rare show of Phish covers during the summer Phish tour. The Phins were joined by Solar Circus keyboardist, Jason Crosby.)

The point that I'm getting to is this country is rich in music if you want to find it. In the nooks and crannies of this country, there's just incredible culture. I think that anyone would be better off to be interested in discovering some of it.

I'd like to think that by being inspired by an eclectic group and by coming up with music that has different influences, rather than following the trends, that we try to draw on all kinds of influences. People would be encouraged, our fans would be encouraged to try to discover for themselves what's out there rather than limiting themselves to just one band.

*Do you encourage taping or do you simply tolerate it?*

**Gordon:** It's not just tolerate, it's more towards encourage. We sell taper tickets, and that's another thing the Grateful Dead were probably a model for.

When we did our first tour, which was to Colorado for two weeks from Vermont, people had already heard about us because of tapes, and word of mouth has always spread through tapes. So it's been helpful for us. Also, maybe in a little way, it encourages us to be spontaneous. If people are taping every night, we're not going to be playing the same show. If we have a great experience playing, why not let people have a souvenir of it, even if it's not the same experience listening to the tape, it's something. We got a lot of flack—actually Elektra has been a great record company. They understand that we're a phenomenon. We were before we signed with the record label, so they let us do what we want. Taping's a big issue though, with record companies. They're not too big on it. But they let us do it, and it's questionable whether it affects record sales. Of course record sales, though we'd like to sell records, it's not our big goal.

*Your new album,* A Live One, *captures your live ambiance. Your fans are probably going to like it better than they liked the more produced albums. Who's idea was it to do a live album?*

**Gordon:** It was inevitable. It always made sense. But we wanted to wait until we really had the facilities to do it right, the right kind of recording equipment. We wanted to do it a long time ago. The fans have been asking for it for a while. Finally, the way that we decided would be right to do it was by taping every night on 32 tracks. So it took two months of listening to our own music to try to pick tracks,

David Vann

**Jon "Fish" Fishman**

*Who are some of your bass influences?*

**Gordon:** I didn't really spend a lot of time listening to any single bass player. The first time I sat down to learn bass lines, I think it was Big Brother & The Holding Co. (Peter Albin), that Janis Joplin, sort of Motowny sound.

Actually, the first time I decided I wanted to play bass in a band was when I was around 14 and my family was in the Bahamas. There was a band called the Mustangs that played by the poolside at the hotel. They were great. My dad and I were standing inside the pool and listening, and the bass could just vibrate you, whereas the guitar could make pretty melodies, but the bass could actually vibrate your whole body. I really liked that physical thing, and I told my dad at that point that if I ever were in a band when I got older, that I would want to play bass.

I would say that Phil Lesh and Bootsy Collins are probably my two favorite bass players. But with Phil, first of all, it seems like he makes it a meditation. Second of all, he's got this way of making the ups and downs, the peaks and valleys of the bass line, be the only thing that matters. It's like physically, you are being vibrated at your knees and in your chest. What does it feel like to just go up and come down? With other bass lines, with some of the Motown bass players that are so great, certain bass players, you'll hear like a melodic use of the scale. But there won't be so much attention to the ups and downs. Like, they'll jump in a way, so it's almost less important, the physical nature of it, of the high and the low notes. In the case of Phil, I think he's a person that embraces just the pure kinetic physicality of the note. I really like the way that happens.

We went to see Bootsy Collins in New Orleans after we played, and it was just wild. It was the slowest, funkiest groove, and this club was packed with people just getting down. It's also funny the way humor can enter into the equation with notes that sound funny, which I suppose is just another emotion in the sea of emotions. With Bootsy, there's definitely a lot of humor that goes on.

*What are some of your favorite songs to perform?*

**Gordon:** It varies. We just wrote nine new songs, which we're playing since the mixing of the live album, and I like a bunch of them. I like one called "Theme From The Bottom," which has a lot of underwater themes again. There are a couple of songs that we actually wrote as a group, just jamming and taking pieces and writing songs. That was one of them. There's another new one called "Free," which almost sounds like a Southern rocker. I really like playing that one, but the jam in the middle of "Free" is all textural. Trey just plays one note and jams on texture for the whole jam, making it sound different. We do some bluegrass. In the last tours, I'd play banjo, the keyboard player plays upright bass, we would have all acoustic instruments. Now we do this four guitar thing. I actually listen to mostly bluegrass myself.

The song "Ginseng Sullivan" by Norman Blake, we started doing again, which is a bluegrass song that we do with the electric instruments, and I've really been liking that one. It's just a simple song. My favorite songs are probably the songs that end up being the most open-ended, where we can take it to the furthest places, but then it's not the song that's being appreciated. It's the ability to get away from it, in a sense. My favorite songs are probably originals, but we were at Waterloo and we played "Waterloo," an Abba song, and we had John Popper from Blues Traveler come up and play with us, and I kind of liked that. Trey didn't like it. He ended it in the middle.

*What are some of the songs that you get the best audience response to?*

**Gordon:** Well, they like songs that we haven't played in a long time. They really like the obscure ones. There's a song called "Punch You In The Eye." They really like that one. Seems like what they like the least is what we've been playing a lot. They like new stuff. Some people have a hard time adjusting to the change of having new songs in the repertoire, but in general, they really like to hear [songs like] "Theme From The Bottom." People have been saying that they really like it. But since it's a song that starts out with just the high hat and the instruments come in one at a time, it's not a song where there would be necessarily a big roar when we started playing the song.

*You've made the vacuum a viable instrument.*

**Gordon:** Vacuum, trampolines, the big balls. Actually, on New Year's Eve we rode across Boston Garden in a hot dog while playing wireless instruments, and that was wild. We had the hot dog lowered down onto the stage while James Bond music was playing. We got on the hot dog, and it raised up pretty quickly. It went all the way across Boston Garden to the cheap seats, as they call them.

*I know it was a tofu hot dog, too. (Laughter)*

**Gordon:** Not only that, but it was Kosher. We actually had a rabbi come to kosherify it, so my grandmother was happy.

*I know you did an interview with the Jewish Press recently.*

**Gordon:** I tend to do a bunch of those. I actually had a strong Jewish upbringing. In my grade school, everyone spoke Hebrew for half a day, every day, from third grade on. They were fluent. I was a little bit behind. I didn't pick up on it like the rest. And now we play a couple of songs in Hebrew. We sing them. One's a prayer, and one's a folk song.

My dad was actually a leader in the Jewish community at the time of the Soviet Jewry movement, helping Jews who were denied exit visas to get out of Russia. He was a national leader of that. I feel like, in some ways, I'm doing something for Judaism, too.

*Until I went to your shows, I thought, "Hey, we were it. We were the end all." But we weren't, and it's such a great feeling to see that it didn't end with us. And it's still evolving.*

**Gordon:** If you look at people that are very successful, being disciplined and applying themselves is almost a bigger chunk in terms of importance than having creative ideas. It takes commitment. When we first started jamming together in dorm rooms, 12 years ago, I actually thought that we didn't really click together in terms of how we sounded. I think it was beneficial that we didn't because we had to practice five days a week. It took a lot of discipline, real commitment and a sense of vision—all those things over the years. Some people sort of define commitment and love the same way. I think that the audience picks up on this sense of commitment, and they in turn become committed to the situation. But in a way, that's almost like a family value coming out. Whether it sounds good or bad, at any given moment, at least we're gonna be in it for the long haul and try to make it as good as possible.

*Do you think that you'll cross over to an older market at some point, once it discovers who you are and what you're doing?*

**Gordon:** It's happening a bit and I guess I'd like to think so. Bruce Hampton, a friend of ours who I have a lot of respect for, says that it's important to always be child-like, but not to be child-ish. So in that sense, it would be nice to think that we would always have a child-like sense of exploring and innocence and that older people who have that attitude would become interested in our music. And also, that we would continue to explore the more mature and darker innards of the mind with our songs, and that would stretch out towards people that are more mature, sort of from both angles. I could see it happening.

*We live in a very pop-oriented culture. We've been force fed music that is, perhaps, more melodic than some of yours.*

**Gordon:** We're very dissonant, sometimes. Trey's mentor, Ernie, is a composer of neoclassical music with a Big Band influence. They're into atonal fugues, and the way that Ernie writes, you hear a lot of dissonance, but there's a form to it. It's not just clashing notes because they clash. It's for a reason. It's to try to stretch certain limits and to do it in a thoughtful way. So, for the listener, it's a matter of opening your mind to be able to accept that as being something desirable. Trey likes to quote Stravinsky: "Run from beauty and it will follow." I guess it's true that maybe when people

get older, they get a little more set in their ways which, to some degree, makes sense because you're learning, you're testing out your values.

Age doesn't mean that you necessarily have to be locked into the expected. Sun Ra always said to "Expect the unexpected." That's a philosophy we try to embrace, and for anyone to be part of our family, they would have to tap into that. ■

**Phish Rides the Big Weiner**
**Photo by David Vann**
**New Years Eve 1999/2000**

**Phish**

I saw Phish perform before they released any recorded material. Even back then, they transcended Dead cover band status. The major jam entity that they were destined to become was apparent early on.

There were so many bands passing through the *Relix* pages and NYC's Wetlands Preserve. I spent most of my time juggling the magazine and hanging out at the club that became a mecca for live music fans. Blues Traveler, the Spin Doctors, Joan Osborne, Warren Haynes---every night was incredible, and Phish's appearances built them a following in that hallowed hall.

By the time Phish's first self-released project, *Junta*, arrived on my desk, I knew this band was different. There was no longer any comparison with the Dead, or with any other band.

When Garcia died in 1995, the young jamheads who lived on the fringe of the Dead scene followed Phish on their merry journey. The music was very different from what the Grateful Dead had given us, but there was a strong improvisational kinship. It was another generation, and it thrived in its own carnivalesque way until Phish called it quits in August 2004.

Trey Anastasio, Mike Gordon, Page McConnell and Jon Fishman all went their separate ways and played in a variety of musical formats.

As this book hit deadline, Phish had just played a three-concert reunion in Hampton, Virginia in March 2009.

Check out Phish.com for more on what this legendary band is up to!

---Toni Brown, 2009

**RELIX** — music for the mind

Vol. 21, No. 4

WOODSTOCK '94

EXLUSIVE INTERVIEW
**CARLOS SANTANA**

ON TOUR
**PINK FLOYD
TRAFFIC
PHISH**

JANIS JOPLIN
SKIP SPENCE
ALLMAN BROTHERS DRUMMERS

Cover Photo by Jeff Mayer/Star File   July/August, 1994

**RELIX** — music for the mind

Vol. 22, No. 3

SUMMER SPECIAL

Jefferson Starship
Los Lobos
Subdudes
Jayhawks
Xanax 25

The 30th Anniversary of
**The Grateful Dead**
Commemorative Issue

Deadhead
Summer
Vacation Guide

Photo by Gene Anthony-Colorized by Mike Young   May/June, 1995

**RELIX** — music for the mind

Vol. 22, No. 5

**JERRY GARCIA**
1942-1995

FRANK ZAPPA
SOLAR CIRCUS
BOB MARLEY
WIDESPREAD PANIC
BOB DYLAN

**PHISH**

Cover Photo Courtesy Elektra Records

March/April, 1995

**RELIX** — music for the mind

Vol. 22, No. 2

GRATEFUL DEAD

**LED ZEPPELIN**

**EXCLUSIVE INTERVIEWS**
Bonnie Raitt
Tom Petty
Black Crowes
Flora Purim
Jimmy Vaughan
Richie Havens

Rolling
Stones
Revisited

Cover Photo Courtesy Swan Song Records

As we go to press:

## Grateful Dead 30th Anniversary Summer Tour — July 2, 1995 Deer Creek, Noblesville, Indiana

*NOBLESVILLE, Ind. (AP) - Several thousand people rioted Sunday night outside a Grateful Dead concert, throwing rocks and bottles and damaging some police cars before officers used tear gas to disperse the crowd, police said.*

*Four police officers were hurt, said Cpl. Clint Bundy of the Indiana State Police.*

*He said the riot began in the parking lot of the arena, when 3,000 to 4,000 people rushed the security wall behind the stage and tore it down, prompting officers to call for help.*

*Two hundred state, county and local police officers responded to the riot.*

Needless to say, the second show at Deer Creek was canceled.

What the heck is happening out there? It's not as if the band hasn't implored their fans to take heed—no tickets, stay home! Through our pages, with mail-order tickets, via handouts at shows, by recorded announcements—we've all heard the message a hundred times.

Okay, so over 3,000 people broke down the gates at Deer Creek and the Grateful Dead has lost another venue. (Things didn't go too smoothly at Highgate either.) It's amazing how it's nobody's fault yet everyone is so quick to point a finger someplace else. Just because they charge a $10 parking fee at a venue is no reason to think you own a part of the lot (I wonder where all that money goes. The Grateful Dead were unaware of a parking charge, believing that the cost of parking at Deer Creek was included in the ticket price). Yes, *you* had a ticket to the show, but what about the four people that drove in with you that didn't? What about the tour hounds that not only don't have tickets, they have no money to exist, draining energy from the fragile scene? What about the people inside that cheered the gate-crashers, even assisting in helping to tear down the fences?

Problems are not new to the community. Way back around 1970, a bomb threat was called in to the Capitol Theater in Portchester, New York during a Grateful Dead show. They had all of us early show goers exit the theater, and then let everyone back in, including a few hundred folks that were outside waiting for the late show, or had just came down to soak up a little color. It actually seemed cool at the time. But when a similar

occurrence took place at the Fillmore East a short time later, we worried about a trend. Well friends, look where it's gotten us.

Crashing gates is not a new tendency in the world of rock 'n' roll. It's not new in Dead-land. None of this makes it right. You can't look at one another and shift blame around. We are each individually responsible for what we do, and no matter what I ever thought or hoped, we *can't* police ourselves. It only takes one selfish individual to start something irrevocable. One person leads and hundreds (even thousands) follow.

What kind of society have we become that we all think like cattle? It's time to think for yourselves! Think about what your actions will do to people and things around you. Think about what it will do to you. Think about what you'll have to go through to find another band willing to put up with this type of insane scene. Think about who you're hurting when you act selfishly.

So, thousands of people got into a Dead show for free. Whoopee. And with that, we lose one of the best venues the Dead were still welcome at. What a way to show your appreciation to a band that has given its all to the road for thirty years!

Grateful Dead publicist Dennis McNally said, "We object to this sort of behavior. It's characteristic of some youth. Unfortunately, when you have a public event, you can't dictate necessarily who's going to show up." He went on to state that over 15,000 ticketless people showed up at Deer Creek. It isn't just the violent acts of a few thousand, it's the irresponsibility of many more that makes it so difficult for the Dead to play anywhere nice. The band will be relegated to stone fortresses in the future, and the final consequence is that the band will be forced to stop touring altogether.

Please remember that "if you fall, you *do not* fall alone."

Toni A. Brown, Publisher
Relix Magazine

Artwork by Glenn Harding

# RELIX

## music for the mind

™

Vol. 22, No. 6

**30 years of The Grateful Dead** A celebration

# JERRY GARCIA
## 1942 - 1995

# YEAR-END SPECIAL

Artwork by John B. Murphy
November/December, 1995

# JERRY GARCIA
## REMEMBERED

### QUOTES FROM FRIENDS AND ASSOCIATES

There's no way to measure his greatness or magnitude as a person or as a player. I don't think any eulogizing will do him justice. He was that great, much more than a superb musician with an uncanny ear and dexterity. He is the very spirit personified of whatever is muddy river country at its core and screams up into the spheres. He really had no equal. To me, he wasn't only a musician and friend; he was more like a big brother who taught and showed me more than he'll ever know. There's a lot of spaces and advances between the Carter family, Buddy Holly, and say, Ornette Coleman, a lot of universes, but he filled them all without being a member of any school. His playing was moody, awesome, sophisticated, hypnotic and subtle. There's no way to convey the loss. It just digs down really deep.

Bob Dylan

Being guitarists and being a part of the San Francisco music scene together, Jerry and I shared a special bond. He was a profound talent, both as a musician and as an artist, and he cannot be replaced. I take solace in the thought that this spirit has gone to join the likes of Bill Graham, Jimi Hendrix, Marvin Gaye, Miles Davis and other greats who have left us much too soon.

Jerry's in the light. We come from light, and we go back to light—so we're the ones who are feeling bruised, and I'm sure he's fine. Jerry really cared for the higher good of all people. He was a reincarnated American Indian. That's what a hippie is: a rainbow warrior. And in my heart and in his heart, he had the best intentions for all people. I'm sure he's standing in the light that has no shadows, you

**Bob Dylan**

know. I keep saying that to live is to dream and to die is to awaken. He's awake…and we're still dreaming.

The world has lost a special human being, and I join his family, his many friends and his millions of fans around the world in mourning this tragic loss.

My sincere condolences and prayers go out to Jerry's family.

Carlos Santana

Jerry was a traditionalist and a pioneer, embracing America's musical past while forging into the future. He understood how music can be a way to experience the unknown. This quest became a fountain of positive energy. How often does a lead guitarist play so selflessly with the idea of overshadowing the existence of ego? Every speck of me wishes he was still alive.

Mike Gordon
*Phish*

A very gentle and unassuming man who brought so much joy and love into people's lives through music. I can't think of a more profound and beautiful accomplishment at the end of a lifetime.

Trey Anastasio
*Phish*

I can't really be sad because I don't think that's what it's about. I can miss it, and I will miss it. But I think part of living is dying. I think out of everything, that's what the Grateful Dead's music was—to celebrate life. Dying is just an inevitability, so I would imagine Jerry would want everyone not to really become depressed about it. I mean, of course you're going to be sad if the man's music touched you, but at least we got 30 years of it. For me, it's sort of silly because I haven't even been following the band as long as people who've been doing it for 25-30 years.

Opening for the Grateful Dead was the hugest thrill of all. Out of every opening gig we've ever done, that's the one that means the most. For the Dead to let us play on their stage and

**Carlos Santana**

**Mike Gordon of Phish**

**Trey Anastasio of Phish**

Garcia with David Grisman

Photo Courtesy Acoustic Disc Records

on his face for most of the show, and then, when we asked him out to play with us, he looked like a kid on Christmas morning. It meant a lot to us then and now to know that he had such respect and admiration for our music. We will miss him terribly.

Steve Berlin
*Los Lobos*

We have lost a lot of giants recently who revolutionized the music out of the San Francisco Bay Area. I guess right now, Bill Graham is asking Jerry if he has the right stage pass!

I played on a couple of albums with Jerry and he was wonderful to us younger musicians. I'd been called in to do rhythm tracks and played a solo on one that Jerry would overdub later with his own solo. He heard what I'd done and said, "Let the kid have it." So, he let my solo stand instead of his. You can imagine what a boost that was to me, a 17-year-old musician, to have that kind of compliment paid by Jerry Garcia.

Craig Chaquico

Jerry Garcia has been a fixture in my adult life since I was in college. In terms of people who've inspired me and lifted my spirit, he's that person.

Ben Cohen
co-founder of *Ben & Jerry's Ice Cream*

When I hear about the death of any artist or talented person, whether I'm a fan or not, I feel

play to their audience was the best thing we ever got to do.

In the face of time changing and of music becoming more corporate than it has ever been, Jerry always stood and took his same position. He never changed, never bent down to any false idols. The positive side is that at least we got to be plugged into something, whether it was your first Dead show or your thousandth Dead show. If it touched you, then I think you were changed forever.

Chris Robinson
*The Black Crowes*

Jerry told me when we first got back together five or six years ago that his doctors gave him six months to live if he didn't quit smoking. And, you know, after about five years, I got a little less nervous. He seemed—I don't know, he never acted sick; he may have been

in bad shape or looked sick, but he was always right on top of it. And from what I understand, he was that way...it was just that his body gave out. He was always full of life and piss and vinegar, and he was always very funny.

Jerry and I were friends for over 30 years. It's impossible to put into words the profound impact that he had on my life, both musically and spiritually. His love for and commitment to good music of all kinds was 100 percent. I'm honored and privileged to have known him and shared so many wonderful moments. As one of his thousands of admirers, I will miss him deeply from this day forth.

David Grisman

I've known Jerry about 25 years. We did quite a few sessions together in the early '70s. He changed my life quite a bit. We just started smiling and laughing the moment we met, and that's what I remember of Jerry. He let me know where he was coming from, that music was really from his heart, it was not a financial thing. It opened my eyes to just getting purely into music and not thinking of anything else, just the beauty of it. That's the way our records came out.

He was a very warm human being. I will miss him. The music community will miss him. But the one thing he left was the music, and we've got some great things to listen to.

Merl Saunders

On behalf of Los Lobos, I offer my deepest sympathy to all of Jerry's friends and family. To all of us, Jerry was like a favorite uncle whose joy and excitement whenever we played together was like a benediction. I particularly remember when we opened for the Dead at Laguna Seca in 1988. Jerry had ducked behind David Hidalgo's amp with this huge smile

Photo by L.D. Kippel

Merl Saunders

Jorma Kaukonen

Photo by L.D. Kippel

bad. The Grateful Dead were a real roots band; they were there for their die-hard fans, so on that level I feel sort of simpatico with them. And today, there are all these bands that came into being directly because of the Dead. I don't often say this, but I did get into some of their music, like *Workingman's Dead* and *American Beauty*—"Ripple" is a great song. Chelsea and I represent two generations of [Grateful Dead] fans. [Garcia] was just a great talent. He was a genius.

President Bill Clinton

Jerry and I sort of spring from the same well. We're basically folk musicians who have gone a long way because of other things. And one of

Photo by Phyllis Antoniello

**Bruce Hornsby**

almost a singing sound to his guitar playing. It always reached me on a real emotional level. He was a deep old soul to me, a deep old musical soul, and I'll miss him a lot.

Bruce Hornsby

He had a flock. He didn't choose it. He didn't say, "I want to be a big icon and guru," to what is now several generations. But I think it was because, in his own unassuming way, he made himself completely an instrument of that higher good energy, which is the real reason people need music so much. They don't get their money's worth most of the time, but with Jerry Garcia, they sure did.

Maria Muldaur

I was with Delaney & Bonnie & Friends the first time I toured with the Dead, in the 1970 train tour across Canada (Festival Express) when they sang "Drivin' that train, high on cocaine." Garcia threw the press off the train. We were havin' so much fun, and they came on the train and were blowin' our trips. It was the best tour I've been on.

Kenny Gradney
bassist, *Little Feat*

Jerry Garcia was one of the original American icons. He played naturally and beautifully.

Ornette Coleman

This guy was himself, and that's rare, especially in entertainment, where people change according to how the breeze flows…[but] the spirit wasn't just in him; he shared it. It's like he was drinking at a well and a lot of other people came and drank from it too. The well's always

Photo by C.J. Fandel

**David Crosby**

going to be there, but we won't see somebody quite like him for a while, if ever again.

Arlo Guthrie

There is not a sentence in the world that could respectfully do justice to the life and music of Jerry Garcia.

Branford Marsalis

Jerry Garcia's passing is a loss to my generation and my children's. For decades, fans have traveled miles to hear his mellow voice and stirring guitar. Garcia and the Dead have been exemplars of a uniquely American brand of freedom.

William F. Weld
*Governor of Massachusetts*

Musicians and people who love music have lost one of the brightest, most articulate minds of this generation. He was an amazing guy, probably one of the brightest, most articulate musicians alive. If I had to pick one person to be our spokesman, it might very well have been him because he thought for himself. He was not the kind of person who would tell you what he thought you wanted to hear. He would tell you what he genuinely was thinking, and it was usually in an interesting and insightful way. He had an extremely bright mind. He was a great man, a friend and the creator of an incredible amount of wonderful music.

David Crosby

the things I like to remember him best by is his roots music: the bluegrass and the blues and the traditional American music. Of course, he created a whole genre of music himself, but I liked it when he went back to that wellspring. It's ironic—I've been regressing and going back to my roots, old-time and spiritual music, and I'd hoped that at some point, Jerry and I could get together and do something. But that's not to be.

Jorma Kaukonen

I always felt a close connection to Garcia, and I think he felt similarly. The best nights were when we would get into these intense jams where we would go back and forth, trading off musically. We had great duels, always pushing each other. He had a beautiful tone,

I think it's harder for people who don't subscribe to the cultural phenomenon of the Dead to appreciate the quality of some of the songs. If somebody else were to take "Stella Blue," say, and record it like Mel Torme would record it, you would hear what a beautiful song it is. That's not to say that Jerry didn't sing it beauti-

Ralph Hulett

**Arlo Guthrie**

courtesy Warner Bros.

**Elvis Costello**

Dave Patrick

**Joan Baez**

Gregory Ruhe

**Paul Kantner**

fully himself, but he sang it with the awfulest voice. I don't think he had any pretensions of being Caruso. He just had the right voice for his songs.

Elvis Costello

When I formed Arista in 1975—and this was tremendously touching to me—Jerry said to me, "We don't know who is going to be on your label, but we want to be a part of it." That personal testimonial and that show of support just show the kind of qualities Jerry had. The fact that they believed in me and what the new company was going to be about—they endorsed it and stayed with Arista for all these years—has been very, very meaningful to me.

Clive Davis
President, *Arista Records*

Jerry was a kind man as I knew him, who never turned down a request from me for a benefit, from Cambodian refugees to AIDS. My son, Gabe, and I mourn his passing deeply. May he be free now of the demons he tried all those years to suppress and feel the gratitude of hundreds of thousands of fans as he heads toward the light. May he be greeted on the other side by music, dancing and tranquillity of heart.

Joan Baez

Jerry Garcia and Mountain Girl lived down the hill from me; I was still in Quicksilver, barely, and we tried to put together this thing where people would hang out at [engineer] Wally Heider's and record—Crosby, [Paul] Kantner, me, Grace [Slick], Graham Nash, Garcia and Weir. We'd try to play these songs. I'd drive there with Garcia in his old Bentley.

One night, we were coming back over the back roads between Bolinas and Novato—there was nothing out there—and we spotted something in the sky. We looked up, and this weird thing was moving there. There was this white light, and it moved across the sky, and all of a sudden it got huge. It looked like a *Star Wars* explosion, then it disappeared. We stopped the car and got out. Jerry said "If that was a UFO, it sure was unidentified to me!"

David Freiberg
bassist, *Quicksilver Messenger Service*, *Jefferson Airplane/Starship*

I returned today from the big island of Hawaii and while there, went down into the lava off the coast of Kona, which was one of his favorite spots, and dropped a fire in the ocean.
The universe is a cold, indifferent place if you don't believe in Jesus. As Jerry Garcia said, "[Rock 'n' roll] provides what church provided for in other generations." The Grateful Dead went a long way toward providing something appropriate to this current universe that worked. Jerry was the master of that particular paradigm. He was an exquisite man despite all his faults, many of which we all have. Let us all remember exquisite men.

Paul Kantner
*Jefferson Airplane/Starship*

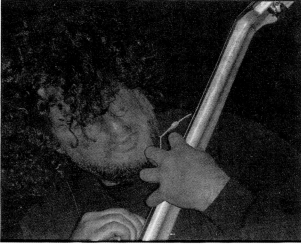

Gregory Ruhe

**Rob Wasserman**

[Bobby and I] were on the road when it happened. Actually, a friend of mine woke me up, and I sort of stumbled around in a daze, and I called back home to find out if it was really true. I went over to Bobby's room, knocked, and he hadn't heard about it. I never thought I'd be the one to tell him that kind of news. I don't know why it had to be me, but actually I was glad. It's much better than hearing it from a television. It was really up to Bobby whether we performed the night Jerry died. I was ready to cancel it if he wanted. But he had no hesitation. He said Jerry would want us to play 'cause that's what he was all about. Bobby's incredibly strong, and I think that night was the best performance I've heard him do in the seven years I've known him—the best, the deepest and the most emotional. I think what's happened is that…his best friend is now part of him more deeply.

Rob Wasserman

Jerry Garcia and the Grateful Dead did as much for mankind as any president.

Grace Slick

Jerry was a great warrior. If he was a good leader, then we don't need him anymore; it should be time for people to become active and follow instructions, and his instructions were fairly simple. He's just a straight-out Christian acid-head, speaking of love and mercy and mischief, all those wonderful things from the '60s.
Jerry knocked a chink out of the wall and let the light shine through, and it's up to us to keep that light shining through, or someday we are going to have to answer to him.

Ken Kesey
*author*

# PART FIVE
## A Lovely View of Heaven, But I'd Rather Be With You
### (Hunter/Garcia)
## The Post-Jerry Garcia Years

When Jerry Garcia died on August 9, 1995, there was nothing that could have prepared me for the loss, or the grief that followed. It was compounded by the immediate onslaught of media that showed up on the *Relix* doorstep. It somehow fell to us to find something responsible to say. I spoke out in defense of our Deadhead family, explaining that we were not "jobless wandering drug abusers" (as they were reporting), but were about music and love and family. I changed many reporters' interview courses, even bringing some of them to tears.

The problems in the scene back in 1995 had reached epidemic proportions, and in hindsight, it was obvious that the end was upon us. It would have been easier for the Dead to call it a day before it got that bad, but as I see it, the band did what it always did: answered our call for more!

When Garcia died, we had a close-up picture of him on our cover (not an unusual occurrence). Newsstands became a media backdrop, reporters holding up our summer issue for the world to see. Santana performed the following morning on a New York-based national television news show, and the cover was taped on the bass drum right above Carlos's head. Wherever I looked, *Relix* was there. I admit that it bolstered sales to heights we'd never seen, but I would have preferred to have Jerry back.

While compiling the material for this book, I approached the Dead's dark days with trepidation, knowing full well that the pain of losing Jerry would hit me just as hard as it had done almost fifteen years ago. It did.

The Grateful Dead called it quits the following year, and Deadheads fanned their musical fires by going to the Furthur Festivals, and by finding other music to dance to. Phish took on some of the displaced family, and, in an amazing twist, live music flourished.

The absence of the touring machine that was the Grateful Dead meant the money that normally went in that direction became available to other live music ventures. The jamband scene that was born in the *Relix* pages flourished, and new bands had a chance at building a fan base. The festival circuit boomed, with tons of musical options available . . . all because the Grateful Dead's fans needed somewhere to go.

*Relix* continued to write about the Dead, their new solo ventures as well as many retrospectives. We also expanded our coverage of the other wonderful music out there, and we moved forward. We had to. . . .

Of Note: In the fall of 2008, the members of the Grateful Dead reunited, performing several benefit concerts in support of presidential candidate Barack Obama. There was still a spark there. As we completed preparations for this book, Grateful Dead Spring Tour 2009 was under way. *Keep on truckin'* . . .

---Toni Brown, 2009

# Editorial

## "It's official."

The news came down hard and fast… the Grateful Dead have called it quits. No more sitting at the edge of my chair, waiting for news of rehearsals. No more pestering the Dead's publicist, Dennis McNally, for the latest word. No more anticipation of that next show, of who would be playing, of what they'd be playing. No more anticipation, period.

I suppose it couldn't be any other way. Jerry Garcia is gone, and things could never be the same. And after thirty years of sharing their magic and devoting their lives to the music, the Grateful Dead deserve to come up for air. But…the day the announcement came, it was as if the knife that had been plunged into my heart on August 9th, 1995 was turned, and finally, removed. Yes, there was more pain, but there was also long needed closure.

Most Deadheads responded that the Grateful Dead's announcement was the right one. Some optimism has surfaced regarding the fragmented members and their potential output. Bob Weir's Ratdog is touring successfully, Mickey Hart is finishing the mixes on his new album and the remaining band members are listening to live and studio versions of the new songs, trying to come up with an album. Promoter John Scher has been working on a "Deadapallooza" tour, expected to feature Ratdog, Mickey Hart and Hot Tuna, which is anticipated for next summer. H.O.R.D.E. officials expect the summer of 1996 to be their biggest yet, and they'll be making a special effort to include Deadheads as part of the trip.

It's true, the Grateful Dead have called it a day, but we Deadheads have more than enough life in us to see us through. Thirty years of music, thirty years of inspiration. The band is packed and gone, but that doesn't mean the party can't go on. Gather with friends. Have picnics, parties, jams and drum circles. Go see your favorite local bands and check out some national acts. We've come so far…don't pack your tie-dyes away if you like wearing them. I've said it before…we've etched our place in society, and the Deadhead culture is thriving. We are a minority, but we must continue to be recognized for our humanity, responsibility to our planet, our individual ideals, our freedom, and most of all, our incredibly good taste in music.

Life is ahead of us—just look back every now and then and remember what we had. Then look ahead and see what will be. Your day is what you make it, so make it count!

*We weren't just an audience, we became part of the event. The energy was passed on as a gift—it is our responsibility to perpetuate the dream. Dream on!*

As always…in love and light,
Toni A. Brown, Publisher
Relix Magazine

Artwork by Serratore

Artwork by Glenn Harding

*There is nothing like a* **Grateful Dead CONCERT** 1977 Tour

Artwork by Gary Kroman

Artwork by A. Klosterman

# GRATEFUL DEAD BOOK REVIEWS

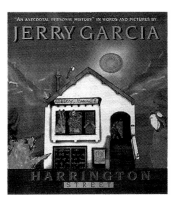
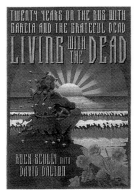
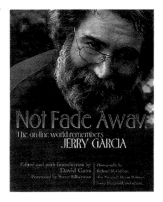

In the aftermath of Jerry Garcia's death, an incredible surge of books have surfaced, chronicling everything from the band's brightest moments to Garcia's autobiographical *Harrington Street*, to excerpts from the Internet following Garcia's death. Many of these books, however, were in the works before Jerry died. We have attempted to review the most noteworthy of these recent publications. Several other books are on the horizon, and we will cover any worthwhile projects in future issues.

## HARRINGTON STREET

"An Anecdotal Personal History" in
Words and Pictures by
Jerry Garcia
Delacorte Press
$22.95 ($29.95 Canada)

This full color, hard cover autobiography chronicles Garcia's life from his earliest remembrances to his tenth year. The handful of topics he delves into in this journal are...well, disturbing. This is an excellent primer into the world of demons that must have plagued Jerry through his life.

One can only hope that Garcia found peace in putting this book together. His wonderful illustrations capture a stark essence of emotion. Colorful and intriguing, *Harrington Street* is one for the collection.

## LIVING WITH THE DEAD

Twenty Years on the Bus with
Garcia and the Grateful Dead
Rock Scully and David Dalton
Little, Brown and Company
$24.95 ($33.95 Canada)

Written by Rock Scully, who managed the Grateful Dead from 1965 through the mid-'80s, *Living With The Dead* is a powerful biography filled with everything you might not necessarily have wanted to know about the band. This is, perhaps, the most interesting tome that has been written about the Grateful Dead to date. But note that no punches are pulled, and this tell-tale volume does its job of de-mystifying the Dead.

This biography was in the works long before Jerry Garcia died. Scully may be jaded as an ousted family member, but the history seems to have been handled realistically. (He claims to have provided an honest portrayal.) Scully does a fair job of bringing the early Bay Area scene into focus (if that's possible).

The book is illustrated by a handful of frequently seen photos by often published photographers.

## NOT FADE AWAY

The On-Line World
Remembers Jerry Garcia
Edited by David Gans
Thunder's Mouth Press
$14.95 ($20.95 Canada)

At first glance, this book will move you, if for no other reason than the fact that it has many never before published photos of the Grateful Dead. Photographer Richard McCaffrey broke out the stash for this one. Other photographers featured include the legendary Jim Marshall, Baron Wolman and others.

When the news of Jerry Garcia's death hit, Deadheads worldwide turned to the Internet to express their sorrow as they sought information, solace and companionship. Many beautiful tributes appeared, and this book captures some of the sentiments that appeared on-line. Especially touching is the fact that this book is by Deadheads for Deadheads. Ken Kesey, Carolyn "Mountain Girl" Garcia, David Grisman, Wavy Gravy and other '60s luminaries are featured.

This is the first book produced primarily from the Internet, and it is a wonderful tribute to Garcia, brought forth by one of the principal personalities of the Deadhead community, David Gans. Gans is also host of the syndicated radio show, *The Grateful Dead Hour.*

## THE WISDOM OF JERRY GARCIA

Wolf Valley Books
$8.95 U.S. ($12.95 Canada)

This tiny volume consists of 90 pages of one-liners, all excerpted (without the author's permission) from David Gans' previously published interviews with Jerry Garcia that appeared in his book, *Conversations With The Dead.* Take the money you would have used to buy *Wisdom*, and buy the complete *Conversations* instead. Now, *that* was a fine book.

## VOICES FROM THE EDGE

Interviews by David Jay Brown
and Rebecca McClean Novick
The Crossing Press
$14.95

*Relix* readers will recognize these writers' names as having done the Garcia interview

that coincided with his death. In this book, these two talented interviewers speak with some of the most important thinkers of our time. In addition to the Garcia interview that graced our pages, you will find conversations with such challenging innovators as Ram Dass, Jean Houston, Annie Sprinkle, Alexander and Ann Shuglin and many other remarkable individuals. What unites these unusually perceptive people is a common ground of creativity, deep compassion, personal courage and childlike curiosity.

## KIND VEGGIE BURRITOS

Recipes For Touring, Tailgating,
Camping and Home
Written by Deadheads Everywhere,
Compiled by Beth Livingston
Photos by John Rottet
$8.00 by mail-order

This grassroots book is filled with wonderful recipes submitted by Deadheads. Grateful Granola Bars, Cosmic Charlie's Cashew Tahini Spread, Bread for Your Head, Kind Fattie Veggie Burritos and many other delightful dishes make up this delectable book. John Rottet's great photos adorn the pages. You can order the book by sending $8.00 to Beth Livingston, 909 Sussex Lane, Cary, NC 27511-3813. All profits will be donated to SEVA and the Rex Foundation.

# Video Review

## DEADHEADS

A Tye-Dye Movie
By Brian O'Donnell

We admit that we missed reviewing this video when it was received several years ago. In light of Jerry Garcia's passing, all things have taken on a different perspective, and this 60-minute documentary, covering 10 years of the Deadhead scene, is a beautiful portrayal of the many things that Deadheads hold dear. Culled from hours of parking lot footage, this video will keep the spirit alive through its many colorful moments. Recommended for the archives.

# FRAGMENTS

## by Toni A. Brown

**A**shes, Ashes: Deborah Garcia and Bob Weir, in a private farewell, waded into the swirling waters of India's holy Ganges River and released Garcia's ashes on pieces of paper bearing farewells from members of the Grateful Dead. The ceremony was held secretly near the holy city of Rishikesh on the upper Ganges as dawn broke April 4, after a lunar eclipse. The ceremony was attended by Weir, Deborah Garcia, three of her friends and a small film crew documenting the event for the widow.

Joel Selvin of the *San Francisco Chronicle* reported that the family of Garcia was furious. Neither Jerry's brother, Cliff Garcia, nor any of his four daughters was notified of plans to take the remains to India. Daughter Annabelle said, "This was done 100 percent without our knowledge. It is gut-churning, to say the least." Ex-wife Carolyn "Mountain Girl" Garcia was also stunned by the news. "There was no reason to take Jerry's ashes to India, a country he'd never been to, and dump them into the most polluted river on the face of the Earth," she said.

Annabelle, who lives in Eugene, Oregon, said she and her sisters planned to travel to the Bay Area to spread her father's ashes in the Pacific Ocean in accordance with his ex-

pressed wishes. "We all feel left out," she said.

Weir said, "It came to me in a flash, in between being awake and asleep." Weir took the plans to a band meeting where it was approved unanimously. He said that only a few handfuls were spread in India. The remainder

The drum circle, an integral part of life on the "Deadlot" during a Grateful Dead concert, as depicted in Andrew Behar's *TIE-DIED: Rock 'n Roll's Most Dedicated Fans*. An ISA Releasing Limited film.
Photo Courtesy *TIE-DIED: Rock 'n Roll's Most Dedicated Fans*

will be scattered during a ceremony outside the Golden Gate.

**Hornsby Deadication:** April 12 at the Fillmore featured an energetic set by Bruce Hornsby and his band. To the delight of the crowd, Bob

Weir stepped onstage during "Sugaree" and joined Hornsby on "Western Skyline." Weir took lead vocals on "When I Paint My Masterpiece" and followed it with a great version of "Jack Straw." Phil Lesh then took over the bass chores on a "Truckin'>Lovelight>Not Fade Away" segue. They all came back onstage for an encore of "The Weight," with everyone singing a verse.

It's heartening to know that the spirit still soars and the occasions still arise.

**AT&T&GD:** When you get put on hold trying to reach a live entity at the phone company, you might not mind the wait. Recently, they have put a music loop on the line which includes the Grateful Dead's "Uncle John's Band."

**Summer Gravy:** Calling all grown-ups who want to go back to summer camp...Let Wavy Gravy refresh your cosmic giggle. Wavy Gravy hosts Winnarainbow for adults again this year, June 17–23. A professional staff offers classes in music, juggling, clowning, stilt-walking, unicycling, art and mask-making, trapeze, improvisation and more. Activities range from the physically demanding to "no sweat."

The emphasis of Winna-rainbow for Adults is on shared creativity among all participants. Each year's camp experience is uniquely defined by that year's staff and campers. You will experience everything from a mini-rock concert to a meditative labyrinth on their wooded ranch in Laytonville, California. There is a three-acre swimming lake and a 350-foot world class waterslide. Zero's Steve Kimock is this year's guitar guru.

The cost is only $450 for a week. Part time

*TIE-DIED:* Grateful Dead fans on the "Deadlot"
Photo Courtesy *TIE-DIED: Rock 'n Roll's Most Dedicated Fans*

stays run $70 a day. Prices include three meals per day, including a vegetarian option. For more info, call 510-525-4304.

**Dog Moon:** *"...where the Dog Moon howls with a cry so full of loss it brings tears to a dead man's eye."* Wordsmith Robert Hunter, the man

**TIE-DIED:** The next generation of Grateful Dead fans
Photo Courtesy *TIE-DIED: Rock 'n Roll's Most Dedicated Fans*

whose lyrics will continue to be quoted as long as there's an ember of Grateful Dead reminiscence, and likely beyond, recently published *Dog Moon* (DC Comics). Exquisitely illustrated by Timothy Truman, this horror-fantasy love story is expressed distinctively, transporting it beyond the standard tale of romance. When the tracker of lost souls falls in love with a mysterious woman, his existence is replaced by a surreal odyssey that exposes him to nightmarish, yet profoundly moving sights and experiences. This **64-page one-shot** is available at your local comic shop, and is priced at $6.95. Also available—*Dog Moon* temporary tattoos.

**Tie-Died:** The Deadhead documentary, *Tie-Died*, that opened in theaters in September, '95 will be available for rental in April through BMG Video. About six months later, it will become a low-priced sell-through title.

The film appeared in about 130 theaters nationwide, but didn't draw the attention it deserved. In light of the upcoming Dead-less summer and, the future without our communal gatherings, this film should be seen, if only to relive the memories. Director Andrew Behar's uninhibited parking lot footage incorporates a variety of colorful personalities; a colorful calliope of sights and sounds. Professionally presented, this film was not slapped together in response to Jerry

Garcia's death as some might suspect due to its original release date.

Included with the video is a special bonus, the eight-minute documentary, *A Conversation With Ken Kesey.*

**Tye Dyed:** Brian O'Donnell may well have inspired the *Tie-Died* movie project with his own more grass-roots *Deadheads* film. Filmed over several years and released a few years ago, the splices of parking lot music are worth the price of admission alone. Well worth owning for the archival aspects of our community. ($23—Flying Eye Prod., Box 243, Sullivan's Island, SC 29482)

**Phish Surrenders:** Trey Anastasio and Jon Fishman of Phish, Marshall Allen, Michael Ray and Damon Choice of Sun Ra Arkestra, Marc Ribot and John Medeski of Medeski, Martin & Wood, Kofi and Oteil Burbridge of Aquarium Rescue Unit, along with Bob Gullotti and James Harvey appeared for two nights at The Academy in New York City for a live concert in support of *Surrender to the Air* (Elektra).

Phish spent the spring in the studio, so there was no spring tour, but they did appear at the New Orleans Jazz Festival. This summer, Phish will be appearing in France, Germany, Italy and the Netherlands along with Carlos Santana.

The Phish hotline number is 802-860-1111 and its taper hotline number is 802-658-8273.

**H.O.R.D.E. All Access:** A CD-ROM from Philips Media provides viewers with front row seats to the festival, as well as backstage exploration of the scene before the crowds arrive—users can sit in on intimate interviews with the artists, climb aboard tour buses and venture around the main stage to learn about guitars, drum kits and sound systems. With a click of the mouse catch performances by Blues Traveler, Dave Matthews Band, Ziggy Marley and Sheryl Crow. Addition-

**TIE-DIED:** A veteran fan bicycles through "the lot" at a Grateful Dead concerts

ally, the Aural Fixation feature offers a jukebox with music from over 40 H.O.R.D.E. bands past and present.

The CD-ROM replicates the festival's strong presence of activist groups, and users can visit the food area, which features a vast cookbook written by the artists themselves. Users can also tap into a detailed look at more than 30 microbreweries from around the U.S. With interactive software like this, you won't have to leave your air conditioned house this summer!

For H.O.R.D.E. info, call the hotline, 212-582-0228, or check out the Web site at http://www.media.philips.com/horde. ∎

Peter Shapiro, director of *A Conversation With Ken Kesey,* and Ken Kesey in front of the Magic Bus, "Further"

# ROCK SCULLY

## Living with the Dead

by Toni A. Brown

Excerpt From Volume 23, No. 1

**R**ock Scully and David Dalton's Living With The Dead: Twenty Years On The Bus With Garcia And The Grateful Dead *appeared on bookshelves shortly after the death of Jerry Garcia. Scully managed the Grateful Dead from 1965 through 1985, and this tell-tale biography serves as a valuable historical perspective of the Dead's early years.*

*I recently met with Scully and Dalton. They both commented that, in the editing of the book, the publishers may have lost certain perspectives. We touch on some of those topics here.*

*When Les Kippel started* Relix *in 1974, the Grateful Dead organization didn't seem very enthralled with the premise of a magazine about the Grateful Dead, even though it was actually more about taping and the experience than the band.*

**Scully:** Well, it wasn't me! (laughter) I don't know. It could have been a number of reasons. One of them might have been our publicist. I recently did an interview with *High Times,* and they have the same history, having difficulty supposedly with the Grateful Dead doing interviews, and here we were one of the premier acid-taking, dope-smoking bands and not talking to *High Times.* We were unaware of a lot of this stuff.

*Was it difficult to interest the Grateful Dead in doing interviews?*

**Scully:** We never could understand or believe that there was such an interest that a magazine could be founded on that kind of a fan base. If I had told them about Dead Base…the Dead Base guys didn't have all that much support either, 'cause most of us were computer illiterate. I mean, this is a long time ago. Now, I don't know what we'd do without them. And *Relix* actually chronicled San Francisco music. I don't know why this is my first interview with you.

*I don't know why.*

**Scully:** Nobody ever called me. (laughter) But I have seen countless quotes from other places, how everybody's talked to *Relix.* Everybody admires the organization.

*In the early years, the Grateful Dead organization seemed very uncooperative about taping.* Relix *started as the First Free Underground Tape Exchange, and taping, at that time, was highly unacceptable.*

**Scully:** Those taping sessions, the only ones that I was ever worried about, as manager, had to do with our live recording. And if we were doing a live recording, we didn't want anybody else to record it live either because we were going to sell it. We had a very delicate balance with our record company, whatever record company we were with at the time, whether it be Arista or Warner Bros. or whatever. We had

a real difficult time convincing them that live recording was an acceptable way of selling Grateful Dead records.

The Grateful Dead, I don't think, really had any difficulty with *Relix* or the live tape exchange. I had to bust balls basically to convince Warner Bros., for instance, that broadcasting live was an acceptable way of marketing the Grateful Dead. Live broadcasting was something that the record companies were very much against.

*It was a very early time for that. Now a lot of bands, like Phish… their record company understands that live taping is a remarkable marketing ploy.*

**Scully:** I love Phish. Starting out, there weren't that many people that taped. *We* taped *everything.* In the early days, for at least the first ten years, you'd find at least two, three, four or maybe the whole band, sitting in my living room in a hotel suite listening to that night's show. It's how

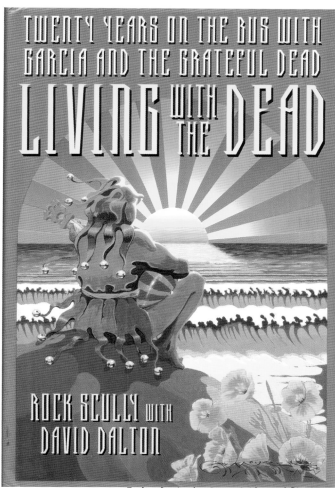

TWENTY YEARS ON THE BUS WITH GARCIA AND THE GRATEFUL DEAD
LIVING WITH THE DEAD
ROCK SCULLY WITH DAVID DALTON

Jacket Design by Steve Snider and Biz Stone
Jacket Illustration by Stanley Mouse

we learned to get better, how the band critiqued themselves, figured stuff out, yelled at each other. But it made it better the next night. Not only that, it reminded them of what they did that very night. They would go on [the next night], and without fail, *not* play the same songs. Even after they had figured out how to do the songs better, they'd go on the next night and do a whole new set of songs. And everybody wondered "How do the Dead do it? They never repeat themselves!" We did fifteen nights at the Fox Warfield and immediately came to New York and did six nights at Radio City Music Hall, and they only repeated themselves five or six times. They have a big book of songs. They don't write a set list, so how do they remember this stuff? Well, one of the ways is by listening to the tapes.

By the very nature of all of this stuff, there

was a time when we were getting worried by our record company to not allow people to tape. Why will the Deadheads buy a live record when they can get the tape? But we didn't care because the Dead really never survived on record sales.

We didn't sell that many records. I was the only one that was out there pushing them. I mean Garcia was out there saying, "We don't make good records," over and over and over again. "We don't make good records."

*You have a long track record with the Grateful Dead. When do you feel that the Grateful Dead's most productive time might have been?*

**Scully:** That's hard to say. I think that by reading the book, maybe you'd understand that the early days, the transition from blues to what Warner's called "psychedelic music" was definitely a turn. And it was a turn for the better.

Continues…

It's when the Dead were at their jazziest. Very experimental. But I don't think that had that much to do with the band's ability to understand what was going on with their music. Then, when they got next to people like the Buffalo Springfield and Crosby, Stills, Nash and so on, they started to understand and be encouraged. Even Kesey and I encouraged them to get back to where they started from. Not just the blues, but bluegrass and country western. So perhaps, the most creative turn of energy was the *Workingman's Dead, American Beauty* period and the incorporation of their, I can only use the term psychedelic, jazzy extended jam stuff. This is when shows were like four hours or all night at the Fillmore East, that kind of thing. The reintegration of their original roots, because Garcia was a banjo picker and they originally had a bluegrass band, and to bring back some of that ability with electric music, with electric instruments, and then to reincorporate their jazz stuff. You'd have things like "Friend Of The Devil" and "Uncle John's Band" and these extended "Lovelight's" and songs like that.

*Having that first set with the New Riders added a whole dimension to the band. That was a really fun time. Was that an era when experimentation was at its peak?*

**Dalton:** Basically there were two factions in the '60s. There were people who wanted to sort of keep doing what they could actually play and the other people who wanted to press on, like Lesh and Garcia. I think there was a tension always between the songs and the experimentation like when you know you've got *Anthem Of The Sun*, which is a lot of long jams, and then you've got *Aoxomoxoa* where they tried to actually do songs that still make it psychedelic. You got to the '70s and they basically went all the way back to their kind of folk origins again, but looked at [them] more profoundly. All those old folk songs they thought they'd bypassed, gone into the stratosphere. Now they went back and they said, "Gee. These are gems." Like "I Feel Like A Motherless Child" suddenly seems like "Wow! Now I know what it means! My God!" (laughter)

*Do you feel that taping helped the Grateful Dead's popularity?*

**Scully:** I'm sure of it. Yeah. That and the live broadcasting. The records, as Jerry said, weren't always that good. And so taping and broadcasting really helped a lot.

**Dalton:** First of all, they were much better live than in the studio. But also, it kind of generated this whole Dead Base thing where you could only *hear* them live, and everybody wanted to be at every concert which generated all those Grateful Dead jokes, you know...

**Scully:** "Who are the Grateful Dead and why are they following me?" (laughter)

**Dalton:** People wanted to hear every tape of every variation and also because it's sort of

like the trajectory of the vibe at these concerts. Who knows what he's gonna do next...We're talking about a religious experience here.

*The Grateful Dead were always at an innovative peak technically. Between Owsley's financial backing and otherworldly views and Healy's productivity...Was there a source of pride among the band, having all this technical stuff that no one had even thought of?*

**Scully:** Yeah, there was.

*Was there envy from other bands? Did they want to use your equipment?*

**Scully:** Absolutely. We ended up loaning out our speaker cabinets to the Rolling Stones, developing sound systems for promoters and nightclubs, how to provide the power if you were using stereo. The whole idea of stereo in live performance was unheard of. Most shows were just like Fender amps and whatever you ended up with. You'd show up and go "Oh, my God." You know, blown speakers and speaker boxes hanging in the wrong places. The weirdest sounds. One of our early gigs in New York was at the Cafe Au Go Go...the one where Frank Zappa was upstairs and we were downstairs blaring into the brick wall, with the sound coming back at us. We ended up actually developing a system so that the band could hear themselves and play better. And if it hadn't been for Owsley, and if it hadn't been for Dan Healy, and Bob Matthews and so on, we would've sounded lousy forever.

**Dalton:** It changed the speaker industry. Altech Lansing—Bear (Owsley) went to see them, and they wouldn't change a thing. And what Healy did was he rented these speakers, more than

Gene Anthony

they needed, and they would blow out in two or three songs. Every night. So the rental people started calling Altech Lansing and saying, "You've gotta make speakers that can carry this amount of amperage." So then they started making bigger amps with more power. I'm still amazed. This hippie band that developed the most hi-tech sound in rock 'n' roll.

*That innovative door of perception was open...*

**Dalton:** Speaking of that, Bear told me the other night that his revelation about the sound system came when he was at one of the Acid Tests and he *saw* the sound coming out, and he realized what he was doing wrong. And the

direction it was going was not in the direction he had anticipated. (laughter) I have to look at my notes, but this is acid at work.

*The Wall of Sound that the band used in 1974 was a monstrous sound system, though cumbersome, to say the least. What happened?*

**Scully:** It was too expensive.

*Immediately afterwards, in 1975, the Grateful Dead took a hiatus. Why?*

**Scully:** It was so much work. Carting that thing around. Going to Europe. Taking this thing wherever we were booked. We played out in Roosevelt Stadium and got rained out. It was the first time we ever got rained out. It took us so long and so many guys. We had a giant system and had to cart all of those speakers up without any hoists or anything and everybody's backs were breaking. After running that system around the United States and taking it to Europe and so on, we were exhausted. It did have a significant role to play in our year long retirement.

*When the Grateful Dead began soliciting for its mailing list, it took years before we heard anything from them. Were you overwhelmed and surprised by the response?*

**Scully:** Totally. Yeah, we were. You know, we started it out with the Golden Road to Unlimited Devotion. Then we put our "fan club" information on that Europe album with the eight-page color photograph book of the tour inside. We were overwhelmed with that.

But this is when we started realizing that we could actually communicate with people that were coming to hear us and actually set up a hotline and sell Bill Graham our own tickets.

*For decades, Deadheads have held this purist, mythical overview of the spiritual aspects of the Grateful Dead. Is there a basis for that mystique?*

**Scully:** I really think so. There is a true, wonderful heart in what the Grateful Dead do. It has to do with their belief in their audience and what they're doing. There's a belief and a faith and a love of life and a love of peaceful exchange and a smile and a dance that goes on in human relationships that the Dead really encourage and really encourage the Dead. And if it hadn't been for that, there would be no Grateful Dead today.

*Did you feel that it was time for people to know what was happening behind the scene?*

**Scully:** My intention wasn't to de-mystify or knock them off of their pedestal or bring anybody down about how human the Dead are. And they are basically human beings that have their doubts, their fears, their insecurities and their flaws, warts and all, just like all the rest of us. They're not God on a pedestal smiling down beneficently on their loving public. We had our warts just like everyone else has their warts, and we think good of ourselves sometimes and think bad of ourselves sometimes. But mostly, the spirit has always been really forward, progressive, righteous, on with the world, let's survive and let our kids grow up to be cowboys. (laughter)

**Grateful Dead at the Panhandle, Golden Gate Park, 1967**

**From the archival history of the Grateful Dead scene**

# CRAZY FINGERS

### by Paddy Ladd

**Lori signing "It's Alright"**

**I**n the midst of the unique creative space with its two different dimensions, the Grateful Dead and the Deadheads, many tributes to the eternal inventiveness of the human spirit have emerged over the past 30 years. One of the strangest of these is the Deafheads, for how can such a uniquely *musical* experience be accessible where there are no ears to hear?

Not unlike Heads, many deaf have sought a whole new life experience and lifestyle since the '60s. They often sought access, but felt unwelcome. As the torch of that era passed to the Dead, some deaf, searching for the larger experience of life, plucked up the courage to peek a little closer to what was happening at Dead shows. Over the last ten years, a number were able to press their noses to the glass of the GD experience, and a few, with Eileen Law's help, even occasionally squeezed through to good seats.

The door, however, was finally unlocked by Dan Healy, whose own father was deafened. Some of us finally caught up with him on December 30, 1989, and found that rare thing—a hearing person who knew what crap hearing

**If you get confused, watch the signing play—Deafheads, Giants Stadium 1995**

aids really were! He had even made a hearing aid for his father himself (sure would have liked to have heard an Alembic model). He understood that even partial deafness results in horrible distorted sound quality. Even a soundboard tape can sound like an audience tape recorded from out in the lobby! So Healy got the band to heed our suggestion of a DeafZone—a place close enough to use our eyes to translate noise into music and to use balloons through which to feel Phil, and joy of joy, the Rhythm Devils.

The Zone began at Cap Center in March 1990, and for the next three years, aided by Carob, Annette Flowers, Steve Marcus and

Ruby, hundreds of deaf fans gained the chance to experience something they never dreamed of. Right off, one signed, "The way the crowd moved, I could almost *see* the music." They were no less fascinated by the scene itself. "Here they don't stare when I sign," exclaimed one happily. Indeed, that was the whole point. In a scene made up of perceived misfits, deaf folk were becoming accepted as another exotic rose in the bouquet. Thus I will never forget the reaction of man mountain Steve at the last show, when he turned to me at the end of that song we all love so well and signed, "Terrapin—that's my *home*."

But for those with no hearing at all, an important dimension was missing—a way of demonstrating the music and words visually. The search was on for Deadheads who could sign—for no outsider could ever successfully transmit this special experience. After three years, Lori Abrams manifested herself, and the next piece of the jigsaw puzzle was in place.

Venues, promoters and GDP alike had a hard time adjusting to this new dimension and its requirements, but slowly over the next two-and-a-half years, things improved with help from people like Vince, David Gans and Steve Silberman. Unlike other bands, where learning 20 songs was enough, we had to deal with 150 played at random, most written by two poets, with depths of meaning that required 30 hours of study and practice on each to even begin to do a good job! Each show required two signers to do it all justice. Lori got help at times from Bren, JR and myself, but mostly Lori had to grow whilst "on stage" alone.

Slowly, a beautiful thing began to happen. We began to feel we were a genuine part of it. More and more hearing Heads would come up and watch entranced, even swapping their seats to do so. Understandably, for in this special arena where all knew the words, they could see them take form in the flesh and watch all those characters dance their stories out. They could see Shannon and Jack Straw argue, Cassidy die and Cassidy born. They could observe the shaman and his initiate in "Broken Arrow," the chase across the badlands of El Paso, could stand alone on a distant moon, or climb Terrapin with the other Seekers. In so doing, they could get glimpses of lyric meanings which, like us, they had never thought about until hands brought them to life.

It was a powerful testimony to the unique qualities of this language that deaf people had

created in the face of scorn and banishment for much of the preceding century. At last it seemed possible, amidst a special group of people famous for saying "Yes" to life, that deaf and hearing people could finally come together as one. The crazy dream of people signing to each other across the four corners of the coliseums seemed within reach. Afterwards, Heads would come up and vow to bring their deaf acquaintances, friends, relatives and even their own deaf children to future shows. And so the Zone grew, so much so that by July, 1995, thousands had passed through it.

For those with no hearing at all, a new world

**Photos Courtesy of Paddy Ladd**

**Paddy Ladd signing during "Stagger Lee"**

opened up. One of them was so mesmerized by his first Chicago show that he promptly traveled to New York, where after two similar experiences, he sat back in his seat, tears running down his face, and signed, "I'm home. *I'm finally home!*"

All of this was created by word of mouth and hand. After the last Summer Tour, we felt the time was right to go fully public, explain ourselves in the deaf and Dead media, recruit and expand. Your scribe finally agreed to join Lori as the necessary second signer, and bought his plane ticket for Boston. And then suddenly, the world grew dark and mean, and all that we were building, this unique human experience, came crashing down.

Deafheads are unable to hear tapes, shows being the only place to appreciate the Dead, and have thus had all our doors slammed shut on our "home." As I write, we hold our breath to see if something may yet emerge from the ashes. And if not, we may ask you all to help persuade the Grateful Dead to add signing to the Dead videos that get released, as that is all we will be left with!

Nevertheless, thank you to our boys for letting the words come to life in our hands and bodies, even for such a little while. Thanks to Jeff and Grover, to Amy, Cameron and Dennis, and everyone else who helped us shed a little light from our crazy fingers. ∎

# WE ARE
# EVERYWHERE

Dave Yasui with Harie Siluwal Prasad in Kathmandu

Shah Safari's Dead embroidery in Kathmandu, Nepal

David Yasui

David Yasui

Steve Clark

Nicholas

Toronto Deadheads

David Yasui

David Yasui

Toronto

Andrew S.

N. Raleigh, North Carolina

Lori Young

Ft. Lauderdale, Florida

Cary Paul

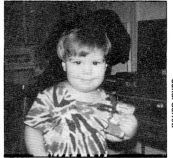

Sandi Garrett

Blake

Rick Passaro

St. Maarten

## What's Become of the Baby?

**by Christopher Sheridan**

One cold night in November 1985, during the Dead's visit to Brendan Byrne Arena, a friend of mine opened the trunk of his car and produced two stacks of basic black-on-white bumper stickers: "We Are Everywhere" and "Reagan Knew." Since Reagan's public speaking days are over, "Reagan Knew" remains undisputed. "We Are Everywhere" seems to have abruptly become "We Are Nowhere."

Since the "Living Dead/Deadapalooza" tour was announced, there has been speculation as to what to expect from a "Return of the Living Dead" concert. We know that stadium shows, as we've come to know them, are gone for the foreseeable future. Those of us who filled those stadiums can only reflect on running through the Soldier Field parking lot in a rainstorm or being busted in 100 degree Louisville.

But as warmer weather approaches and we experience the changes that the sun brings, our souls will ache to hit the road. Those who have taken these excursions will agree there's nothing like a tour of the northeast country in early June before the crowds get on the highways.

Although the Dead is gone, it's up to us to meet our own needs. A desire to reconnect washes over us. Some Deadheads are pessimistic about the future; others feel that the community spirit will remain alive in the alternative "Living Dead" scene. And there are those who foresee much more definite splintering in alliances. Many are quick to point to what they see as a division among the Heads: those who had rejected a way of life and stood naked looking for another, as opposed to those who took a week off in the summer and escaped the corporate or academic drudgery to spend some time with those for whom they held existential allegiances.

In any case, the interactions in the parking lot strengthened our relations. The "Shakedown Street" lot scene also celebrated the American entrepreneur and the spirit of capitalism. The complexity and richness of its makeup, coupled with its overall carnival atmosphere, served as our church for many years. Not everyone who learned the hustle on Shakedown will just slip quietly into the mainstream. The Summer Tour served a key purpose for us spiritually in many ways.

GD Productions will probably continue to look for "copyright infringers," but original craft work, food, juice and water have proven over time that they reliably convert to gas money. The idea is that we all buy-sell-swap-give everything we need to each other, so that all of us can get by, get to the next show, the next high time.

But if we let Shakedown Street die, we'll let an important means of communication within and between us break down. Where will our communal activities take place? Where will the hackey-sack kicking and live tape blaring occur? Although we all had the occasional affinity to sell nine cases of imported oatmeal stout out of the back of our vans, we went back to our day jobs soon enough. Between tours we disappeared.

Many of us have turned to the Internet to make necessary connections and stay in touch, but it can only do so much. On the Internet we're still safely fractured by our individual ID numbers and technical and social limitations to amassing online.

"Return of the Living Dead" will serve as a conduit for remaining Deadheads to create and reinvent social bonds with one another. The majority of us will branch out into the plethora of "modern Hippie" bands, from Dave Matthews to Rusted Root. Others—older members of the Dead crowd—may stop going to shows altogether, maybe catch "Living Dead," CSN and Chicago, the Allmans.

One thing is for sure—those who lived the experience are thinking about it. The rush of happiness at making two hundred bucks selling beer and getting a free ticket doesn't fade easy. It wants to repeat itself into another experience and another. "We Are Everywhere" is now applied to the police. If you have bumper stickers of any kind, make sure that not so much as a seed can be found should your van be taken to the brushless car wash.

A few might hold the view that "If you build it, they will come" and that will certainly be true this summer, as Deadheads everywhere will have to face the dog and reconcile themselves to choosing an escape. A good many of us might stay home, give up the ghost. A good part will turn to camping. Others will look for any of the remaining Dead members' appearances. The last group are those destined to search for the outdoor improvisational guitar sounds to fuel their interstate romps.

A quickly growing alternative may be the personal tour. We may design our own tours. We may take our vacations as usual, planning with friends and obtaining tickets not only for "Living Dead," but perhaps Phish, Hot Tuna, Allmans, H.O.R.D.E., Traffic or any of the lesser known bands of incredible talent.

The advantage we have now is what we've learned from faithful touring. The freedom now is in choosing a variety of shows in different venues and setting our own pace for our immediate groups. This way, we'll all run into each other crisscrossing the highways.

We will be more diffuse, but we will still represent large pockets of the ticket-buying public. Hopefully, those of us who have internalized the mottoes (such as "Keep The Scene Clean") will practice them in whatever parking lot we end up in. ■

KLOSTERMAN 95

A. R. Klosterman

Oakland

Greensboro

# Children Of The Dead

**By W. Marc Ricketts • Photos by W. Marc Ricketts**

There aren't enough pages in this magazine to describe all of the differences between a Grateful Dead concert and one by any other artist. One that is usually apparent is the number of children present.

As we feel the sadness of losing Jerry, let us not forget to celebrate those that will follow. Birth and death. You can't have one without the other. This was made clear to me when 20 days after Jerry's death, I wel-

Colin Jerome Ricketts

comed Colin Jerome Ricketts into the world. His only show was in utero, but like the many children that have experienced the magic, it probably touched him on some level.

Theirs is perhaps the purest joy. No time spent wondering if this is the night that "St. Stephen" gets resurrected. No bitching over hearing "Corinna" for the sixth time this tour. We should learn from them. The wheel is still turning. ∎

Oakland

Laguna Seca

Shoreline

Laguna Seca

Frost

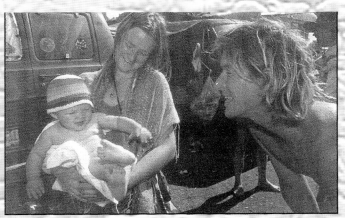

Atlanta

# MIA'S FAIRY TALES

## "ENCHANTED ROSES"
BY MIA L. BEANE

(A/K/A David Sporrong)

Once upon a time there was a band of musicians who played enchanted music...

Whenever the musicians played together the music would compel anyone with a pure heart, free spirit and open mind to dance...and dance... and dance...

The musicians traversed the land for many, many years, attracting many, many new dancers along the way...

One day one of the musicians, a stout, compassionate guitar wizard with long white hair and a big white beard went to weave his magical web of melody with the angels...

The other musicians and dancers felt lost, how could they possibly play and hear the enchanted music without the guitar wizard?!

The music stopped, the dancing stopped...gloom and sadness covered the musicians and dancers as they gathered around a memorial for the guitar wizard...

When out of nowhere a little barefoot girl in a tattered white dress appeared...she dug a small hole, planted a single seed, turned and silently walked away...

Presently an enchanted rosebush grew from the seed...a rosebud appeared... as it bloomed the sweet melodic sounds of the guitar wizard's magic wand pealed from the flower...

Other roses joined in, each rosebud blooming, each flower playing in consort, magically, miraculously, the same enchanted music the band had played lo those many years...

Enraptured the dancers leapt to their feet and danced and hooted and hollered and laughed and hugged...the magic was back!

In the midst of the gaiety and uproar the little girl in the tattered white dress reappeared, unnoticed she gently plucked the guitar wizard's rose, turned and silently walked away...

SNAP.

Meanwhile the other musicians music continued to blare from the roses and the dancers continued to dance...and dance... and dance...

Although now the enchanted music would take different shapes and forms, it revealed something to the dancers, they realized they could carry on the magic... they could plant seeds!

And that's just what they did...soon enchanted roses bloomed and flourished throughout the land, spreading peace, love, fellowship, and much, much dancing...

For the magic, music and message of the guitar wizard could never die...and they all lived hippily ...... ever after!

Artwork by Miki Saito

# Editorial

Almost a year has gone by since the Deadhead community was knocked off its axis. Summer tour 1995—plagued by disaster, almost a premonition of worse events to come. Looking at our future with doubt and concern, worrying whether or not the Grateful Dead would be able to continue touring. The heat of August—Jerry's birthday on August 1. Then that day we thought would never come though it was smack in our face inevitable—August 9, Jerry Garcia died. Devastation and regret invaded our once happy landscape as reality swept over us like an angry tide. After some months of speculation, anticipation and expectation, the remaining members of the Grateful Dead called it a day.

How many of us still well up in tears at the oddest memory triggered at the weirdest moment? Why do our hearts leap when the car passing on the right exhibits a Dead sticker? Who wonders if the parents of the 12-year-olds at the mall bought those Dead tie-dyes, or if the kids bought them themselves? Life has become an endless volley of questions. The biggest question is, "Where do we go from here?"

The Furthur Festival looms ahead as a final vestige of hope. A final place to shake our bones together, perhaps for one last time. One last chance to gather those phone numbers of folks you only caught up with at shows. A last ditch attempt to salvage all that was warm and wonderful about gathering together under the hippie banner. It doesn't matter anymore that it's not the Grateful Dead. What matters is that the spirit remains alive, and it's our place in the cosmic scope to guarantee that one final thing.

With the living spirit, we soar on to new horizons as we continue to grow. Our memories remain bigger than life. Feed them and let them flourish like a beautiful flower.

As we were preparing this issue, a barrage of sad news reached us. John Kahn, bass player with the Jerry Garcia Band, died. That was followed by the news of Timothy Leary's dramatic departure. Then came the news of the death of Steve Cripe, the woodworker that built Jerry's latest guitars (Lightning Bolt). Regrets to all of the families and friends of these people who have each given so much to our community.

*What a long, long time to be gone, and a short time to be there.*

With love,
Toni A. Brown, Publisher

# The Furthur Festival

*Saratoga, New York*
**by David Lubell**

T he Furthur Festival's stop at the Saratoga Performing Arts Center in Saratoga, New York, proved much more mellow a gathering than the Grateful Dead shows there in the 1980s. Even the Dead's publicist Dennis McNally, spinning around the parking lots before the show in a golf cart, looked relaxed. McNally, happy with ticket sales, estimated the crowd at 20,000, though the final count was closer to 30,000. When asked about the tour in general, he confirmed the tour's looseness: "Everybody's having a helluva time. It's nice and laid-back."

Though a laid-back affair, the show was run with military efficiency; each set was timed to the minute, and there was no downtime between them. **Hot Tuna** was the first major act to hit the stage, launching into "Death Don't Have No Mercy" precisely at 4 p.m. Its tight set was, unfortunately, played to an almost empty shed, save for the few hard-core Tuna fans that knew the band was opening the festivities. It's unfortunate that arguably the best band on the bill played so early in the day. Regardless, the boys satisfied with such classics as "99 Year Blues," "Keep Your Lamps Trimmed And Burning" and "Embryonic Journey." Jorma Kaukonen and Jack Casady were flying from the start. The highlight of the set, though, was Michael Falzarano's turn on vocals, leading the band through the scorching, self-penned "Just My Way."

Unfortunately, this reviewer missed much of John Wesley Harding and Alvin Youngblood Hart, as breaks were needed to recharge the old batteries for the seven-hour plus show.

Barry Nathanson

**Vendors on tour**

Jon Weiner

**Bob Weir with RatDog**

Most attendees had the same idea, as Harding and Young also played to a virtually empty amphitheater. The breaks afforded us time to check out the expansive vending area set up inside the concert grounds.

About 20 vendors pitched everything from tie-dyes to candles to photos of the Grateful Dead. Key-Z Productions had a booth, selling copies of Ken Kesey's works and Tom Wolfe's Electric Kool-Aid Acid Test. The most interesting and possibly, most successful aspect of the vendor's village was the CyberTent, an area set up with six Macintosh computers that offered concert-goers a chance to send e-mail to friends and take part in live chat sessions. A video diary of the tour was even being kept, where fans had their pictures taken along with their comments on the tour.

We got back to our seats in time to see **Los Lobos** play an outstanding set. Guitarists David Hidalgo and Cesar Rosas led the band through a wonderful version of "Evangeline" and cuts from its latest album, Colossal Head. The group's powerful rhythm section was reminiscent of Santana's legendary percussion. A cover of Neil Young's "Cinnamon Girl" garnered the first real ovation of the day, and the band kept the crowd on its side by dropping the chorus of "Turn On

**Setting up before the show**

Your Lovelight" into a rocking version of "I Got Loaded." A killer "Bertha" ended the set (making one almost expect "Good Lovin'" to follow), and gave the crowd a taste of things to come. Pete Sears, Hot Tuna's keyboardist, joined Los Lobos for much of its set.

**The Flying Karamazov Brothers** provided between-set entertainment. Their juggling and other assorted acts were amusing,

but the general feeling in the crowd was that the Karamazovs went on too long. The most interesting aspect of their act was when one Brother told of how they opened for the Grateful Dead in Oakland years ago and, under the influence of some "Owsley '69," backed their tour bus into Jerry Garcia's new BMW. In an act of repentance, the crowd was encouraged to chant "You asshole" to the ensemble, the same reaction Garcia had when initially told of the accident.

**Bruce Hornsby** pulled out some surprises in his hour-long set, rearranging some of his own songs while dropping in some crowd favorites. The "Spider Fingers" opener was more jazzy than usual and journeyed through Thelonius Monk's "Well, You Needn't" and Wayne Shorter's "Footprints." A Latinized version of "Scarlet Begonias" drew an understandably loud ovation and featured a chorus of George Benson's "On Broadway" for good measure.

The biggest surprise, though, was his stellar rendition of Bob Dylan's "Tangled Up In Blue," which was seamless despite the fact that Hornsby needed to refer to lyric sheets. "Pastures Of Plenty" featured a surprise appearance from opening act Samba Nova (who played before Hot Tuna) for an impromptu percussion jam. Blues classic

**Samba Nova**

Jack and Jorma

**Mickey Hart's Mystery Box**

**Bob Weir with Bruce Hornsby's Band**

Hot Tuna: Pete Sears, Jack Casady, Harvey Sorgen, Jorma Kaukonen, Michael Falzarano and Dave Ellis

"Mystery Train" rounded out the set and left us anticipating even bigger things from Hornsby later in the show.

The hour that had been allotted the unknown quantity of the tour, **Mickey Hart's Mystery Box,** was ample time to show the crowd that, while the Grateful Dead are no longer, Hart still likes to push the musical envelope. It's easy to classify what Mystery Box does as percussive dance music. But even those not prone to frequent a nightclub or disco couldn't help but dance to the infectious grooves laid down by Hart's crew. The Mint Juleps, the British vocal sextet doing most of the crooning for Mystery Box, were fabulous and added wondrous textures of harmony to Hart's percussion machine.

Mystery Box's set featured mostly cuts from the recent CD and proved Hart to be an engaging and entertaining frontman. It's clear he relishes the spotlight, but has no problem deferring to his talented group. While Hart as vocalist on cuts like "Only The Strange Remain" and "The Sandman" was a bizarre sight for many Deadheads, he clearly proved he can lead a band as well as back one.

The major deviation from the CD-based set was a rap-style version of the Dead classic "Fire On The Mountain," which featured an under-miked Bob Weir on rhythm guitar. Jack Casady also joined in on bass and was clearly having a ball trading licks with Hart's bassist Habib Faye.

When **Ratdog** took the stage at 9:30 p.m., the lower portion of the amphitheater was filled, as was most of the balcony, which provided us with the perfect vantage point to check out the jamming to follow. Weir chose mostly familiar material (covers and Dead songs) for his set. This clearly was the right tactic, as the crowd responded favorably. After opening with a tight working of Leiber and Stoller's "Youngblood," Weir pumped up the crowd with "I Need A Miracle."

Matt Kelly, on harp, nobly took a shot at Jerry Garcia's leads in the song. Al Green's "Take Me To The River" followed and led into a beautiful "Blackbird," with Weir on acoustic guitar. An interesting combination of "This Time Forever>Shades Of Grey" quieted the crowd a bit, but Bobby performed each impeccably, switching from electric to acoustic during the segue. The crowd perked back up during an extended "Cassidy," which felt a bit disjointed as keyboardist Johnnie

Johnson had not returned after being absent for the preceding two songs. Bruce Hornsby jumped in to fill in the obvious gaps, and soon the song was spiraling into space.

After one of bassist Rob Wasserman's famous solos and a tight "Josephine," Weir chose to end his set the only way he knew how on this particular day…with "One More Saturday Night." Hornsby, Hart and Hornsby's horn section joined in as the crowd sang along and shook their bones.

The all-star jam that immediately followed Ratdog featured many different musicians coming and going at all different points in the songs, making it difficult to chronicle just who played on what. Regardless, the jam session was a great opportunity for all involved to stretch out on some good old-fashioned rock 'n' roll.

"The Weight," the first number and a real crowd-pleaser, had Hornsby and Weir trading verses. It was followed by an absolutely smoking "Good Lovin'." The Mint Juleps then came out and lent their superb vocals to Jackie Wilson's classic "(You're Love Keeps Lifting Me) Higher And Higher," a tune that caught many by surprise, but left everyone dancing up a storm. By then the crowd was transfixed, and Weir led the ensemble through a wild version of "Gloria." Casady, jumping up and down and stalking the stage, seemed to have more fun than all his counterparts. A rocking "Satisfaction" followed and abruptly ended the show; not even the standard Bob Weir "Thank you all, good night" followed.

As the house lights came up and the musicians left the stage, we were left to ponder what we had seen. It was tough to immediately analyze the proceedings, although no analysis was needed. Quite simply, it was a great time that helped fill a gaping void in our collective souls and that's all that mattered. And while it wasn't a Grateful Dead show, in some ways it was better. None of the problems that accompanied the Dead in recent years (except for the traffic jams) were visible, and that put everyone at ease. Hopefully the success of this and other Furthur shows will lead to a continuation of the tour next year.

Artwork by Glenn Harding

Keep it on, keep it on. Just keep on keeping on, folks.....

Artwork by Miki Saito

SPACE > THE WHEEL
MIKI SAITO.

BOUND TO COVER JUST A LITTLE MORE GROUND!!

# My Evening With The

# ALLMAN Brothers Band

## A Reluctant Deadhead Rekindles His Love For Live Music With A Rather Obvious Choice

### by Anthony Head

I've had a revelation that has helped me through concert withdrawal and could possibly help many fellow Deadheads find their way back to live music, if they haven't already.

After countless Grateful Dead shows that left me totally spoiled, I had all but given up on concerts. But, then I finally attended my first Allman Brothers Band show. I may just be preaching to the choir, but allow me to revel in this zest. And though I wouldn't call myself a Peachhead just yet, I may have taken the first steps of another long, strange trip.

I should point out that from the first time I heard "Jessica" playing from behind my older sister's perpetually closed bedroom door, I have always loved the Allmans' music. But, I've been on the halcyon bus with the Dead for the past 15 years and, during that time, if I ever had the good fortune to find a couple of bucks in the bottom of my pockets, my first reaction was to send them to a certain post office box in San Rafael, California to score some floor seats.

Still, I didn't ignore other great acts like the Allman Brothers Band. I've got Eat A Peach on vinyl, Live At Fillmore East on cassette and Greatest Hits 69-79 on CD. I've listened closely to my friends rave about their shows. Hell, even my 50-year-old aunt Jeannie has seen them. (She liked them, but thought that the solos were too long and too loud. Isn't that the point?)

So, when the opportunity recently came along, I scraped together the cash and purchased a ticket. "But," I said to the lady in the box office perhaps a little too sternly, "they better play 'Jessica'." As I turned away, I punctuated my request with "and 'Melissa,' too." "No, dear, my name's Ruth," she replied kindly.

The ambiance of the evening was immediately inviting. Nestled among the trees of Los Angeles' Griffith Park, the Greek Theater is a fabulous spot for any show. It seats a mere 5,000, but as I leaned back and marveled at the stars shining overhead, the Greek became as vast as it was intimate. Dayglow tapestries of magic mushrooms filled the stage and brought a psychedelic curl to my lips as I studied the crowd and inhaled drifting smoke from Marlboros, clove cigarettes and some very kind weed. Well, it certainly smelled like a Dead show.

Tie-dyes were outnumbered by black T-shirts and leather—lots of leather. Lots of cowboy hats, too. Curiously, there weren't too many wallets not leashed to belt loops with intricate silver chains. It wasn't the same rainbow-infused gathering that followed the Dead from show to show, but it was a style I could live with.

Finally the lights dimmed, and a familiar feeling of anticipation rose within me and everyone else. I knew by the ovation that this assembly was eager to celebrate—to be as much a part of the show as the band itself.

With nearly 30 years of touring to back them up, the Allman Brothers Band once again took the stage, and without hesitation launched into "Statesboro Blues." A tight "Midnight Rider" followed and, for the very first time, that song truly spoke to me. I looked over the crowd of Harley Davidson-loving road warriors (both real and wanna-bes) and the lyrics made sense; this was an anthem. Personal liberty was cherished, and the open road was a symbol of their freedom. (Of course, the video screen behind the band that showed a long desert highway helped me with that realization, as well.)

Just like my first Dead show, I didn't know the words to every song. I didn't even know every song for that matter. But, I know great Southern blues when I hear it, and Warren Haynes belted out some of the best. I was a bit disappointed that Gregg Allman took more of a supportive role for most of the evening, letting his organ do the singing which allowed for some stellar guitar work from Dickey Betts and Warren Haynes. At times, their rollicking licks were like two tornadoes whirling within each other. At other times, they were so amazingly synchronized, you'd swear it was a single guitar.

At one point, as those guitars were dueling, I turned to Dave, the guy dancing next to me, to point out the incredible pale moon that was rising slowly above the stage. He acknowledged it, and then asked, "Hey, did I hear some 'Franklin's Tower' in that last solo?" I was home.

Dave provided some very surreal moments during the evening. He had seen hundreds of ABB shows as well as a significant number of Dead shows. Like many other men in the crowd, he was big and husky, yet he moved as nimbly as a prima ballerina when inspired to do so. Watching him reminded me of that dancing hippopotamus scene from Fantasia. At one point, he passed me his binoculars for a better view of the stage. After I returned them, he plucked out one of the eye pieces and guzzled a long draft of Jack Daniels from a hidden compartment inside. Like I said, Dave blew my mind.

During the show, I remember thinking to myself that while the Grateful Dead gently lifted you up with ethereal playing and swirling epiphanies, the Allman Brothers Band strapped you to the back of its Hogs and thundered down the dusty highway with forceful, gutsy jams that continued without end. Once it got going, you'd better hold on.

The band launched into one of those marathon jams as the moon reached its apex in the night sky. What began as total chaos with each member charting his own musical course turned positively Pink—as in Floyd—with some cosmic solo guitar work from Betts that was reminiscent of "Shine On You Crazy Diamond." And that led the others, one by one, to follow along and then gradually return to a Southern rock groove. The percussionists took over for a spirited session as Butch Trucks, Marc Quinones and Jaimoe beat the skins alone for several minutes before Allen Woody took center stage for an engaging bass solo. Now, call me crazy or call it wishful thinking, but I swear I heard the faint melodies for "Love Light" and "The Other One" filtering through.

Eventually, the rest of the band returned to continue the super jam and, yes, that was clearly the familiar notes of "St. Stephen" ringing out from Betts' guitar. And I wasn't the only one who heard it that time because the large contingency of "Steal Your Face" T-shirts that were scattered around rose up and saluted the stage with cheers and butane lighters as Betts tirelessly played on. (I don't want to imply anything unnatural, but he certainly must sleep with that guitar for it to sing like that.) How massive and seamless was this jam? Check out Dick's Pick II for a reference.

Throughout the night, calls for "Whipping Post" rose from the assembly. The evening ended with an exhaustingly long "Jessica" that even left this veteran Dead dancer a bit sore in the calves. For the encore, the Brothers were joined on-stage by Black Crowes' frontman, Chris Robinson, for a blistering "One Way Out," which must have had five or six crescendos before Betts would finally abandon it to echo off the hills. Sadly, the Allmans never played "Melissa."

Happily, though, the audience did a lot of singing as it marched out into the warm L.A. night. I felt a camaraderie among us—the same camaraderie that kept me with the Dead for so long. The Allman Brothers' music brought people together in celebration, and that's what it's supposed to be about. And while I'm not totally ready to exchange my tie-dye for a leather vest just yet, you'll have to excuse me as I drive my VW minibus to the Harley Davidson dealership to work out a little trade. ∎

# MOONBEAM *IN THE 21st CENTURY*

### "A VISIT FROM JERRY AND THE GOOD OLD GRATEFUL DEAD"

'TWAS THE NIGHT BEFORE CHRISTMAS BUT TIMES WERE NOT MERRY ANOTHER CHRISTMAS WAS COMING AND WOULD COME WITHOUT JERRY.

MAYBE SOME EGG NOG WOULD HELP?!

NAHHH... I'M A VEGAN

DEADHEADS WERE NESTLED ALL SNUG IN THEIR BEDS, WHILE VISIONS OF SUGAR MAGNOLIAS MADE THEM DANCE IN THEIR HEADS.

MY FRIEND HAD SOME INDIGA, AND I HAD SOME HASH WHICH ALTERED OUR BRAINS AND SOON MADE US CRASH.

ZzzzzzZ

WHEN WHAT TO MY WONDERING EARS SHOULD I GLEAM BUT A MELODIC GUITAR LICK WEAVING AN ENCHANTED DREAM.

I RAN DOWN THE STAIRS LIKE A GALLOPING COLT AS IF MY BRAIN HAD BEEN STRUCK BY A HUGE LIGHTNING BOLT.

THERE STOOD A GUITARIST SO STOUT AND SO MERRY I KNEW IN A MOMENT IT HAD TO BE JERRY.

MORE FASTER THAN EAGLES HIS FINGERS THEY CAME THEN HE WHISTLED FOR THE BAND AND CALLED THEM BY NAME...

"ON BOBBY, ON VINCE, ON MICKEY AND BILL, LISTEN TO THAT BASS LINE IT'S GOTTA BE PHIL?"

KA BOOM

"FROM THE FRONT OF THE STAGE TO THE TOP OF THE HALL, NOW JAM AWAY! JAM AWAY! JAM AWAY ALL!"

THEN HE SAID NOT A WORD BUT WENT STRAIGHT TO HIS WORK HE PULLED BACK THE GUITAR NECK AND GAVE IT A JERK.

HIS EYES HOW THEY TWINKLED AS HE SANG EACH REFRAIN HIS SOARING JAMS ECHOING THE VOICE OF COLTRANE.

DAVID SPORRONG

THE BAND ALTOGETHER HAD A SOUND ALL THEIR OWN THEY MADE ME FEEL LIKE A CHILD NOT YET FULLY GROWN.

SOON THERE WITH VINCE STOOD THE BELOVED PIGPEN BRENT, DONNA AND KEITH WITH BRUCE BACK AGAIN.

ST. STEPHEN, LOVELIGHT, DARK STAR, AND DEAL, ESTIMATED, UNCLE JOHN'S, TERRAPIN, THE WHEEL.

THEY PLAYED THEM ALL TILL I FELL OUT OF BED MY DREAM IT HAD ENDED BUT STILL IN MY HEAD

THUD

I HEARD THEM EXCLAIM ERE THEY VANISHED FROM SIGHT "HIPPIE HOLIDAYS TO ALL AND WE BID YOU GOOD NIGHT!"

By David Sporrong

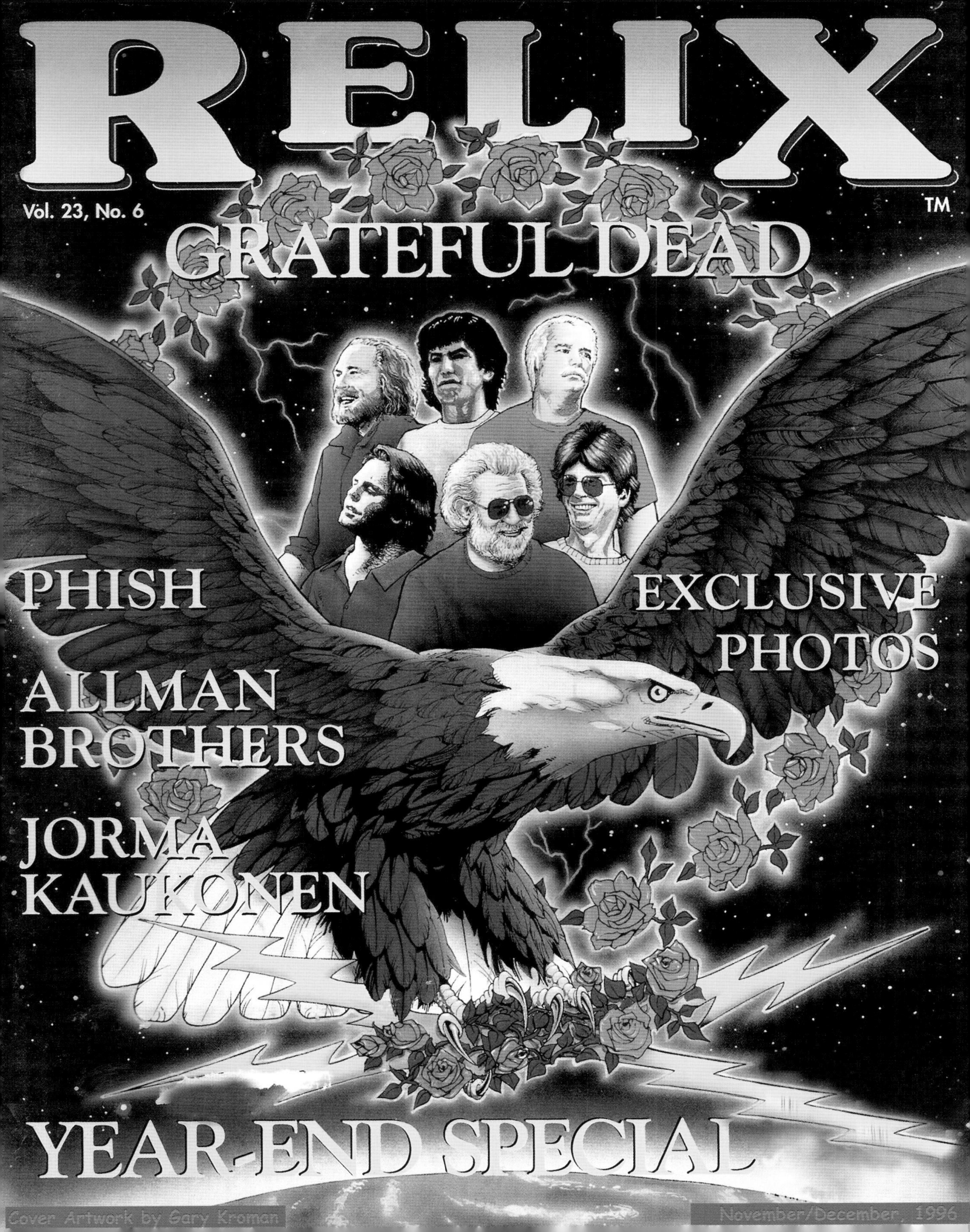

RELIX
Vol. 23, No. 6
TM
GRATEFUL DEAD
PHISH
EXCLUSIVE PHOTOS
ALLMAN BROTHERS
JORMA KAUKONEN
YEAR-END SPECIAL

Cover Artwork by Gary Kroman

November/December, 1996

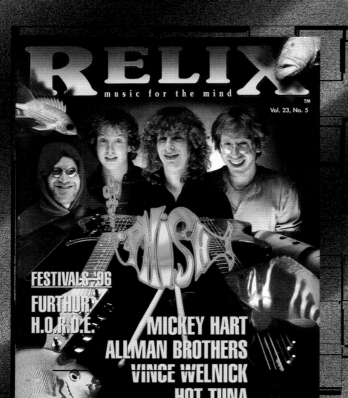

# RELIX
## music for the mind ™

Vol. 23, No. 5

**PHISH**

FESTIVALS '96
FURTHUR
H.O.R.D.E.

**MICKEY HART
ALLMAN BROTHERS
VINCE WELNICK
HOT TUNA**

Cover Photo Courtesy Dionysian Productions
September/October, 1996

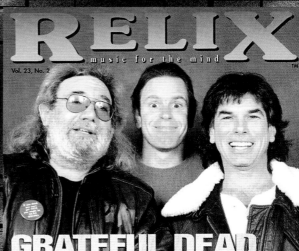

# RELIX
## music for the mind ™

Vol. 23, No. 2

## GRATEFUL DEAD

**Exclusive Interviews**

Bob Weir
Rock Scully
Bob Bralove

**PHISH
RUSTED ROOT
JORMA KAUKONEN
CHRIS ISAAK**

Joe Gallant:
The Blues for Allah Project

Cover Photo by Tom Sheehan/LFI
March/April, 1996

Artwork by Gary Kroman
May/June, 1996

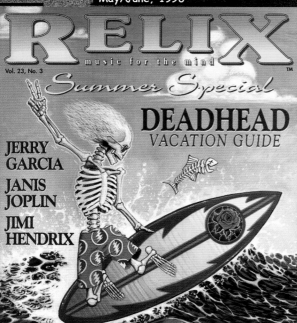

# RELIX
## music for the mind ™

Vol. 23, No. 3

*Summer Special*

## DEADHEAD
### VACATION GUIDE

JERRY
GARCIA

JANIS
JOPLIN

JIMI
HENDRIX

**DEADHEAD**
TRIVIA

Cover Photo by L.D. Kippel
January/February, 1996

# RELIX
## music for the mind ™

**JEFFERSON
AIRPLANE**

**EXCLUSIVE
INTERVIEWS**

Joan Osborne
From Good Homes
God Street Wine
The Nevilles
The Meters
Michael Falzarano

**JORMA KAUKONEN**
Land of Heroes

**GRATEFUL DEAD**
*Carlos Santana
Bruce Hornsby
Hot Tuna*

# Donna Jean Godchaux MacKay
# Playin' In The Band

### by Toni A. Brown

In 1971, the Grateful Dead was at the height of its psychedelic improvisational musical prowess. The group's extended jams and interwoven musical texturing seemed an unlikely place to find prominent vocals of any kind.

When Donna Jean Godchaux found herself singing back-up in the band that year, a new vista for her vocal approach was thrust upon her. Relocated from her home in Muscle Shoals, Alabama, Donna Jean's singing experience had been confined, mostly, to studio session work. She and her husband, keyboardist Keith Godchaux, approached Jerry Garcia at a Garcia Band show at the Keystone in San Francisco. Before they had time to think about it, they were in rehearsals with the Grateful Dead. The Dead's original keyboardist, Ron "Pigpen" McKernan, had left the band due to health reasons on August 26, 1971. Keith's first appearance came soon after, on October 19.

Pigpen returned to his spot with the Dead two months later. Keith stayed on, and Donna Jean soon joined in. By the time Pigpen left the band permanently on June 17, 1972, Keith and Donna had become full-time participants in "the greatest show on earth!"

Unfortunately, Keith was killed in an auto accident shortly after they left the Grateful Dead. Donna Jean has led a relatively quiet musical existence for the past 25 years. She went on to marry David MacKay, a guitarist, with whom she has worked for the past two decades. They have recently released an album, *Donna Jean*, whose material makes stark statements about life and the time we live in. Her clear, clean vocals shine throughout. Gone are the pressures that existed when singing back-up to the most improvisational and untrained vocalists of our time.

Here, the affable Donna Jean shares her history, some road recollections, fond memories and the reasons for her departure from the Grateful Dead.

*When did you start singing?*
**Donna Jean:** I was about four or five, and we lived in Fort Knox, Kentucky. My dad was in the army, and I would sit out on my back porch and sing all the time. There was a little boy next door and I sang so much that it made him mad, and he actually hit me in the head with a hammer. (Laughter) So that was my first initiation into music.

Actually, the guy's sister was an opera singer on the *Firestone Hour*. She had heard me sing and talked to my mom and dad and said, "You need to get her into lessons immediately. She has the potential to be a really good singer." Of course, that never happened. (Laughter) You just never know how things will happen in your life. I just always knew that I wanted to be a singer.

*You started out as a session singer…*
**Donna Jean:** When I was 12, studios started springing up in the Muscle Shoals area. That's when I visited my first recording studio, and I got studio fever. I just couldn't wait until I was old enough to get involved in music. I can't remember if I was 15, maybe 16, the first time I actually recorded. I went to Nashville and did a couple of little demos at Billy Sherrill's studio. I just got the bug, what can I say? And the other thing is, I would always sing harmony. I would learn the lead part and then [my friends and I] would go around singing "Soldier Boy" and all those kinds of songs, and I would always be singing harmony and it bugged everybody—they said it messed them up, but that's the way I learned to sing harmony. I would sing all the harmony parts to every song that came on the radio.

*What did you do before you joined the Grateful Dead?*
**Donna Jean:** I was in a vocal background group that recorded on all the sessions as the music industry began to boom in Muscle Shoals, and I did sessions with Percy Sledge, the *When A Man Loves A Woman* album, and Joe Tex, Joe Simon, Benny King, Neil Diamond, Elvis Presley, Cher, Dionne Warwick, the Boxtops, just a lot of Memphis/Nashville/Muscle Shoals things that were coming out in the mid to late '60s. And then in the '70s, I went to California.

*What brought you to California?*
**Donna Jean:** I just always wanted to go. And I was ready for the next step.

*You weren't out there very long before you joined the Grateful Dead.*
**Donna Jean:** No. In fact, even when I was here, I remember hearing things about the Grateful Dead, and I would go, "Ooh! What a name for a band!" But I never really heard them. When I got out to California, I had a couple of friends who had moved there. Everyone was into the Grateful Dead. Everybody was the way the Grateful Dead fans are. They were just absolutely, thoroughly dedicated and didn't want to do anything except listen to the Grateful Dead, and I thought, "Where in the world is this at?" I just couldn't really relate to it and they would have me listen to the records, and I would go, "Well, I don't get it." And then I thought, "Well, they must be really good looking or something." And so they showed me an album cover, and I went, "No, that's not it." (Laughter) "Okay, what's the deal?" They said, "Well, you have to see them live."

So everyone was going to this concert at Winterland—it was the New Riders, Quicksilver, the Airplane and the Grateful Dead, in

Donna Jean and Toni Brown at the Maritime Hall

that order, I think. So they made me go. I didn't want to because I had to get up for work early the next morning. I'd come to California, kind of giving up music to do something else, just experiment in life a little bit. I ended up going, but I said, "I'm not gonna take any drugs. I'm just not gonna take anything." So we were in the back of the balcony at Winterland and the New Riders came on, and I said, "Hey, they're pretty good." And then Quicksilver came on, and I thought, "Wow, this is really different stuff." Then the Airplane came on, and I thought, "Wow, this is really good." And the Grateful Dead came on, and it was more than music. And I just went, "Whoa! How do they do that!" And I listened to the rest of the concert, and I just could not even believe it. I had not taken anything, and I was just blown away. And so we got home and I couldn't go to sleep, and I just thought, "Man, I cannot believe this! This is the next step, musically, that I want to go." I could detect the spirituality in the music, and I had always had those kinds of leanings anyway, so it was a combination of things that I was really looking for as the next step in my life.

It was around that time that I was introduced to Keith. We had never talked to one another. He didn't know that I sang, and I didn't know he played piano. I was not really telling people that I was a singer. I went to visit with a friend of mine who lived in the East Bay, and she said, "I'm gonna invite Keith over," and I thought, "Good!" So Keith came over, and it was the oddest thing. We had never really talked, but when my friends went to bed, Keith, instead of leaving, we just kind of met in the middle of the room and put our arms around each other, and he said, "I love you," and I said, "I love you, too." We sat down on the couch and talked about getting married. It was just amazing. He and I kind of fell in love, and we had never really talked to one another. He had never heard me sing. I had never heard him play the piano.

When I heard him, I couldn't believe it. I just freaked. That was in the summer of 1970. And we were married in November of that year. It was the end of the next year, '71, when we joined the Grateful Dead. Keith was going to college, of a fashion, and I was working and I got home from work one day, and I said, "Let's listen to the Grateful Dead." Keith said, "I don't want to listen to it. I want to play it." And I went, "Whoa. Well, okay." The Garcia Band with Merl [Saunders] was playing the Keystone in San Francisco. Keith and I went down there and when Jerry was leaving the stage for a break, I just tugged on his arm and said, "My husband and I have something we want to talk to you about." And that was it.

The next week, we were at Grateful Dead rehearsal. Keith and I didn't know that Pigpen was sick or anything.

*Did you have a difficult time fitting in vocally with the Grateful Dead?*
**Donna Jean:** Well, yes and no, because there were two different aspects of it. One was when we were in the studio or rehearsing or getting vocals together, it worked out really well. The studio setting is very different. It's more of a controlled atmosphere and it's much more particular, and you can go over things and do overdubs. You have more of an opportunity to really focus just on the vocals. In the studio, it was wonderful. As you can tell on a lot of the studio recordings, our voices blended really, really well. Then you get on stage, and it's a whole different atmosphere.
*In those days, the sophistication of the monitor systems was lacking...and to sing harmony with anybody, or even just to sing over the instrumentation, you couldn't hear yourself. Did you have a lot of trouble in that environment?*
**Donna Jean:** It was a nightmare most of the time because you could never really hear properly. The answer, if you couldn't hear yourself, was to turn up and then of course, the other person couldn't hear themselves and they

**Closing of Winterland with John Cipollina**

would turn up, and so it was just always so loud on the stage that it was not conducive to having the best atmosphere in order to hit a real true note.
*With the Grateful Dead, no matter how many times you could have sung a song, or rehearsed a song, it was never going to be the same.*
**Donna Jean:** Of course, the vocal harmonies were pretty much the same because you're singing words and you're singing together. Phrasing was always a little bit different. Intonation was always questionable.
*In those days, was it strange being a woman coming into a male dominated industry?*
**Donna Jean:** Maybe I was very naïve, or not paying a lot of attention. I never felt really oppressed. I didn't feel like I was being squashed or anything like that, and maybe that was because of an inner confidence that I had that I was not looking to be something. I was where I wanted to be. I was having fun. I was getting new experiences in life. I had never sung on stage before. All of the work that I had done vocally was in a recording studio. I was a novice on a certain level as far as performing, and so I was not looking to try to outdo anybody or be the big deal. That's not what I was

looking for at that time. And everyone treated me wonderfully.
*When the Grateful Dead brought in the Wall of Sound in 1974, did that monstrous sound system affect your role? Was it more difficult to sing with that set-up behind you?*
**Donna Jean:** Because it was a "Wall of Sound," we were constantly trying to find microphones that would work that would hold back the feedback because we would have to have monitors loud enough to hear over the Wall. We experimented with phase canceling microphones, which were the two mics, one on top of the other, that we had for a while. Your mouth had to be touching the microphone, it was so set to ward off feedback. If you got back even an inch, you would lose the quality and ability for the microphone to pick up. So we were constantly trying to find the right microphone in order to deal with how much sound was coming off that stage. I don't know that we ever arrived. (Laughter)
*When you recorded in the studio, there was such a vast difference from your live performance—your dynamics were able to shine through.* Terrapin Station *and* Shakedown Street *both featured you in fine solo performances.*
**Donna Jean:** That's where I was at home, vocally, in the studio. We would listen to some of the concerts after we got back to the hotel, and I would go, "My Gosh! The vocals sound awful! What in the world is this? Why is it so off key?" I was just trying to make that stretch to discern where the intonation was and what to pay attention to that was on key and who to listen to and try to make the sound come out that you know needs to come out, but you don't know quite how much pressure you're gonna have to put behind that sound to make it come over. Obviously, if you listen to any of the tapes, you realize what a struggle it was.
*At least your confidence was adequate to handle that. But we're talking about a band whose every show is out there on tape...*
**Donna Jean:** Under scrutiny. And it's not like you're in the situation where someone is listening to your performance as it is doctored up later on something. What you hear is what you get. I think that's part of the beauty of it. I think it's refreshing when you compare it to everything that's so processed these days. You get into studios now and if the vocalist is off key, they go note by note and electronically bring it up. It takes hours to do this. Most of the vocals that are out these days are done this way.
*You also sang with the Jerry Garcia Band. Was it easier to sing in that environment than with the Grateful Dead?*
**Donna Jean:** It was a bit easier, of course, because it wasn't as loud as the Grateful Dead, but then again, the variables. Jerry, as a singer, he was off or on, too. You just kind of had to go with whatever was there at the time, and I think

Dave Patrick

Gathering on the Mountain Festival-1998
Marty Bostoff, David MacKay, Donna Jean, Matthew Kelly and Toni Brown

Photo by L.D. Kippel

that's another thing to consider. You had to look at the whole concert, and that's how you measured it. In any song, there were gonna be mistakes. You were gonna have that dynamic going on, and you had to look at the whole concert. "Well, this was a good gig" or "This wasn't a good gig." If you studied it bar by bar, well, that's something you just couldn't do with the Grateful Dead's music.

*Did the band ever walk away from shows unhappy with a performance?*

**Donna Jean:** Oh, my goodness, yes. After almost every concert. Most of the time it was the blame game, depending on who was in the room. I won't elaborate any further than that.

The adrenaline is still there [after a show], and the atmosphere is so charged that you need to have some kind of closure. It's so charged that when you get off the stage, at least in your mind, you're looking for some kind of closure and unfortunately, with the Grateful Dead, it was hardly ever there. When I say unfortunately, I mean for the band members. Everybody's judging the evening based on something different, so that made for some complicated scrutinies.

*You got to do a couple of European tours with the band.*

**Donna Jean:** It was wonderful. For me, it was such a whirlwind. Europe '72 was, basically, when I joined the band. Here I am with this band with this energy that is unlike any other. I'm on stage. We're in Europe. Everything is new. I wish that I could do it again where I could pay attention. For instance, I could see the Eiffel Tower from our hotel room, and I never got out of the hotel room. That's bizarre. Everything was so inward that I never got outside long enough to really take a look around.

*Did you enjoy going to Egypt in 1978?*

**Donna Jean:** I loved Egypt so much, it's one of the fondest memories of my life. We were the first rock 'n' roll band to play in front of the Sphinx. The Sphinx Theater. And of course, it being a first, there was a lot of anticipation and energy and excitement around us. And it was great, all the fans coming. It was pretty amazing that this entourage of [American] Grateful Dead fans followed us to Egypt.

It was a real unique experience getting to play music in front of the pyramids. I have a very special memory. An Egyptian man named Ati had this boat for hire that would go up and

down the Nile, so we hired the boat after the concerts were over. Keith and me, Jerry, Billy and I think Bobby, went on this boat. We took this three-day and night trip down the Nile, and it was incredible. We slept on this little boat. We'd wake up with the sun shining down on us. The Nile is a very narrow river so both shores were visible. When they would hear the boat coming, kids and whole families would rush down to the shore and wave and bring their drums, and they would sing and play the

Red Rocks – 1978

Bruce Polonsky

best music you ever heard for the boats going down the Nile. It was an incredible experience and, of course, we stopped at Luxor and Aswan and toured the tombs and all of the special sites. I loved it so much.

*Well, that's one trip you got outside. You had your son, Zion, with you during all of this. Is he into music?*

**Donna Jean:** He still lives in San Francisco. He has a band called 1978. They're actually starting to play around the Bay Area a little bit. He's doing great. He's 23 now.

*When the Grateful Dead took a hiatus in 1975, you pulled out the Keith and Donna Band.*

**Donna Jean:** I think it was just something we wanted to do. I don't remember having any feelings about it other than just wanting to have our band and play some other songs. Like Garcia had the Garcia Band. It's just another

avenue of expression, and I really enjoyed it.

*When did the Heart of Gold Band come about?*

**Donna Jean:** That was in 1980, after Keith and I were out of the Grateful Dead. Greg Anton and Steve Kimock (Zero) were in it, and we had various bass players.

*What kind of music do you listen to now?*

**Donna Jean:** I listen to everything. I should qualify that—I really enjoy good quality music of any kind. I love good classical music. I love good Irish music, good Scottish music. Actually, Brian Godchaux, Keith's brother, is playing in an Irish band sometimes, and I love that, that classical, true-to-your-country music. I really love ethnic folk music. I love good rock 'n' roll. I mean, hey. That's what we were brought up on. I love good R&B. I just love good music.

*Were there any specific reasons why you left the Grateful Dead?*

**Donna Jean:** Well, this is probably the best time to clarify that. People ask me, "Did you guys quit or were you fired?" The answer is, really and honestly, both.

There was a tour where things had gotten so bad, it was not fun anymore. That's when drugs were really getting to be more of an issue, and there was just a lot of discord in and around the band because of that. And this one tour, I just left. I told the road manager, "I don't have to take this anymore, and I'm going home." And so I left right in the middle of the tour. Keith and I did one more tour after that, but he and I had been saying that we needed to get out of the band. We weren't blaming anybody else.

It's just what everything as a whole was doing to us as a couple, individually, with Zion, and we realized that if we did not make a real serious change soon that it was not going to turn out well. And we were physically, spiritually and emotionally wasted. Literally. Of course, in situations like that, you have to look at your own responsibility, and I'm not blaming anybody. It's just the situation that we found ourselves in, we were in over our heads as far as how it had turned out. We knew we had to make a change. Neither one of us are quitters—we talked for weeks about how to make a change.

Meanwhile, the Grateful Dead...the other band members were going through the same things. They knew that it needed to happen, and so they called a meeting at Keith's and my house, and it was a mutual decision.

When we were out of the band, I felt like a whole load was lifted off me. Not because of anybody or the band, it was the scene and it had wrought things in us that was detrimental to us going on as human beings in a marriage and in a life. What can I say? It just had to happen. It was time. They knew it, and we knew it.

*After Keith died, you had to pull things together for yourself, and I'm sure that was not easy.*

**Donna Jean:** No, it wasn't easy. We had already started the Heart Of Gold Band, and we had played one concert. It was just a few

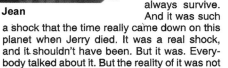

Maria Muldaur and Donna Jean

Photo by Leslie Kippel

days after that that Keith was killed. Greg Anton (the drummer in the Heart Of Gold Band) was so special during that time. I think he's the one who told me that Keith had been in an accident and, of course, I went right over to his house. Greg was right there, and I will always have real special feelings for him. He's a good man. That was really a rough time.

I continued on with the Heart Of Gold Band. That's when I met my husband, David MacKay. He came to play with us one night, and that was that. Like he said, he got the gig and the chick. (Laughter)

*You did some gospel music with him...*

**Donna Jean:** Yeah, we had a gospel band in San Francisco. David and I were involved in a church there, so we did some singing and put out a little record that really wasn't meant to be a big deal. But it was just a nice record with some songs that we had written. And then we didn't really do anything musically for quite awhile and then when we were in California about three or four years ago, we started getting songs together and realized that we needed to get back into music. There were things that were coming up in our throats again. We have something musically to express, and we were real astute that we needed to get back into music. And I just missed it. I missed reaching out and being able to touch people like that. There's something about playing live and being with people that helps bring who you are forward, and there's something relationally that I so missed that it was time.

*The album has more of a rock slant to it, and you've written the material.*

**Donna Jean:** Yeah. It's what you would call a rock 'n' roll album. It's got a little bit of New Orleans flavor on it. There's a little bit of reggae flavor. There's definite rock 'n' roll. There's a couple of strong ballads. So it's a real

well-rounded record, musically.

I do most of the lead singing with Will McFarland. He was Bonnie Raitt's guitar player in the '70s. Will and I do a couple of songs together, and he sings some solos on the record. We wrote some of the material together, and my husband David and I wrote some of the material together and I wrote a couple of songs by myself. But it's a real collaboration. They're strong songs—strong music and strong lyrics. They incorporate things that we're facing today, on the streets. One song is called "Children Of The Night." It's about the struggle with the children as they're trying to find their identity, and they're in the streets; things that we face as a nation.

*When Jerry Garcia died, what were your thoughts?*

**Donna Jean:** I think my thoughts were pretty much like everybody else's. It's something people said was going to happen, but nobody believed it. He would always survive. And it was such a shock that the time really came down on this planet when Jerry died. It was a real shock, and it shouldn't have been. But it was. Everybody talked about it. But the reality of it was not something that I think people really believed would happen.

*We're very lucky in that the spirit that remains is as strong as it is. But people are picking up the pieces now. It's almost two years. But it's an incredible thing that one man through music did so much for so many people. It's a shame that we couldn't do as much for him, although in some ways I guess he got his rewards doing what he loved doing.*

**Donna Jean:** Jerry was like a father to the fatherless in some ways to some people. There was a sense of home or something, finding a place and there was a place for you. People were attracted to that, and people need that. They need a sense of belonging, and Jerry opened that door for people.

One of the last tours the Dead did, I went to one of the shows in Birmingham. I hadn't been to a Grateful Dead concert in so long, and I was just amazed at all the young kids. It was almost like a time warp, and I thought, "My word! This is really and truly the next generation." And what

amazes me is they know who I am. It's shocking—they weren't even born when I was in the Grateful Dead. (Laughter)

Being in the Grateful Dead was an adventure. It was an experience. That's the way people looked at it, which is a different thing about the Grateful Dead. People were not there to critique the music. They were there to have an experience. I think that's another reason why they were so giving when it came to whether the music was great or not. They weren't in it just for the music. They were in it for the experience and for the belonging and the comradeship and everything else that the Grateful Dead was, in addition to being musical. That was part of the attraction.

Getting back to what I was saying, we went to the concert and I got to spend some time with Bobby, which was really great and, of course, all the other guys, and Jerry called the next morning...we were staying at the same hotel, and he called and asked if we wanted to come up and have coffee with him. So we had coffee with Jerry and Deborah, and Jerry and I talked for about two hours about stuff that only he and I knew about, inside experiences that we had had on tour together, and we just laughed and laughed and had the best time together. It was so wonderful for me. I will just always be grateful that I had that time with him. So I got closure.

*What's in store for the future?*

**Donna Jean:** I'm really looking forward to touching base with people again, and I really think they're gonna like the music.

*A lot of people have missed you, so welcome back.*

**Donna Jean:** It's good to be back. You grow in ways that you don't know you're gonna grow, and things happen and progress that take you to the next step or cause you to become more whole in ways, and I have grown in the past few years. Part of that growing is a greater capacity to love, and my heart right now is still full of love for people. Before, even being in the Grateful Dead, I was so guarded. I was not used to being whisked away here and there and I was not in a place in my life to really appreciate and linger with people, and I'm looking forward to that now. I really am looking forward to just talking with people.

*Donna Jean is planning to hit the road in the near future. Be sure to stop in, say hello and listen to the music play.* ∎

Donna Jean and Toni Brown - Magnolia Festival 2008

Photo by Ed Munson

# Jefferson Airplane Word Search

```
R f I F i G z Y B V D U p G b p h F a U
e V P g Q C y o T z B e p b o N P s C U
R I k c a J P C n B a c w s g I V p v K
N q M t d H I h R r r a C i z t s i p y
p H J y Z M o n f Z k r T d i G n h J d
k c b Q B J a c u m g G d b g j e S X W
D M G P a e K r H I x e b Y a g Y n r G
F g t p S s s y t u V a j t j x P e w X
F s a y p J r t x y R o P x m D c d B P
r P B F a g o H F e Q a l y k n i o D d
X v B U m d N r t r u I C u e C r o U r
j I c q W B o i m I i T g p n o Q W h e
A a P U a g h T y a f e S v y t J d a h
X V F w. F W c O g Z g v n I P X e y s t
v j b q O Z r u Z K R J C d u b o e N a
n y e n r u o J c i n o y r b m E I r L
Y H P T X i G v L g s V m C o t I I R s
n M r J y Q A F E I m c i e D w e g I B
T e v o L o T y d o b e m o S o a f G M
B Y V b e v U L P j I H Q O j E R p C N
```

Jack
Volunteers
Grace
Bark
Lather
Jorma
Wooden Ships
My Best Friend
Spencer
Today
Somebody To
   Love
Joey
White Rabbit
Marty
Papa John
Paul
Embryonic
   Journey

by Alfred R. Klosterman

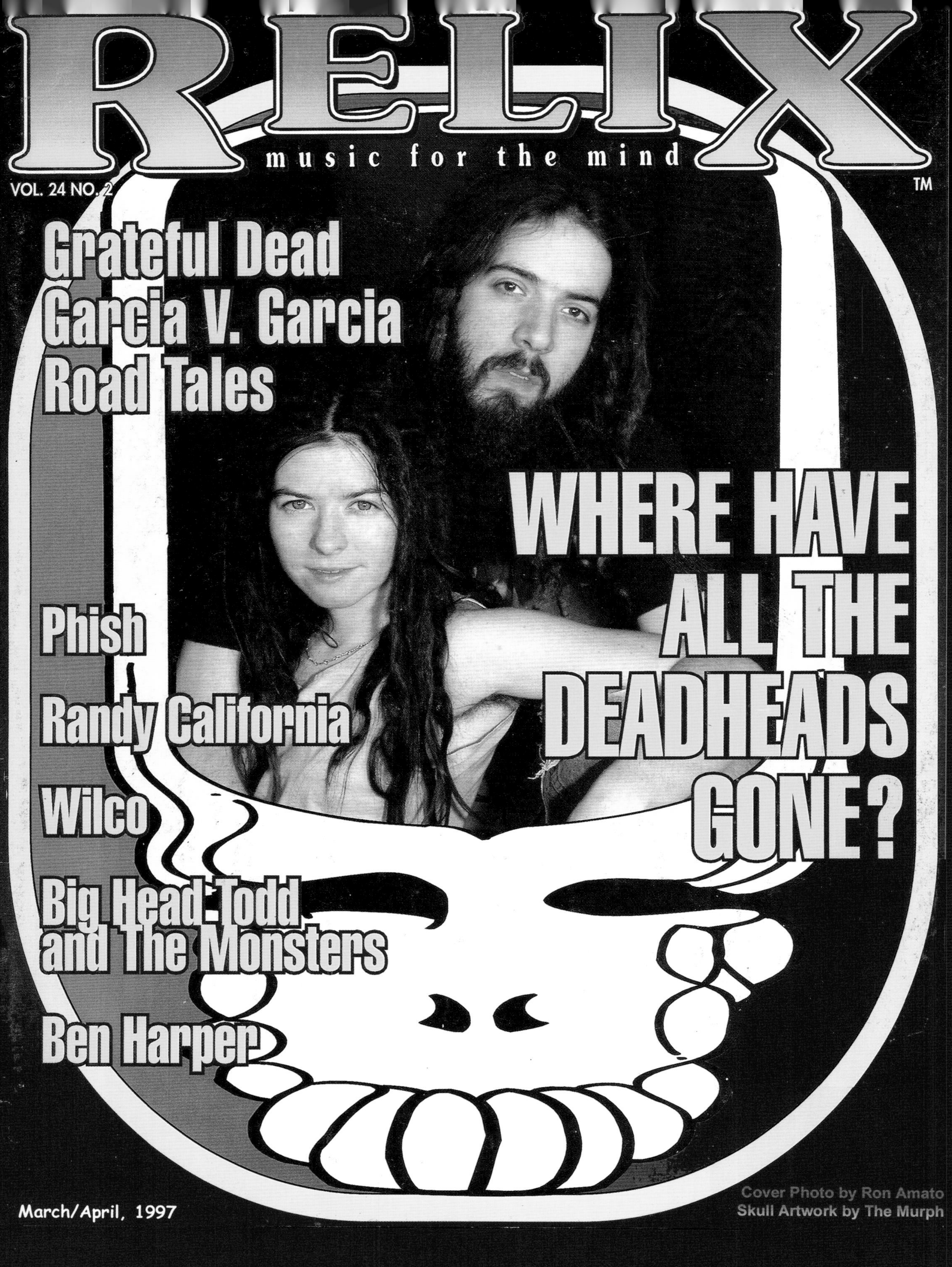

RELIX
music for the mind
VOL. 24 NO. 2
TM
Grateful Dead
Garcia V. Garcia
Road Tales
WHERE HAVE ALL THE DEADHEADS GONE?
Phish
Randy California
Wilco
Big Head Todd and The Monsters
Ben Harper
March/April, 1997
Cover Photo by Ron Amato
Skull Artwork by The Murph

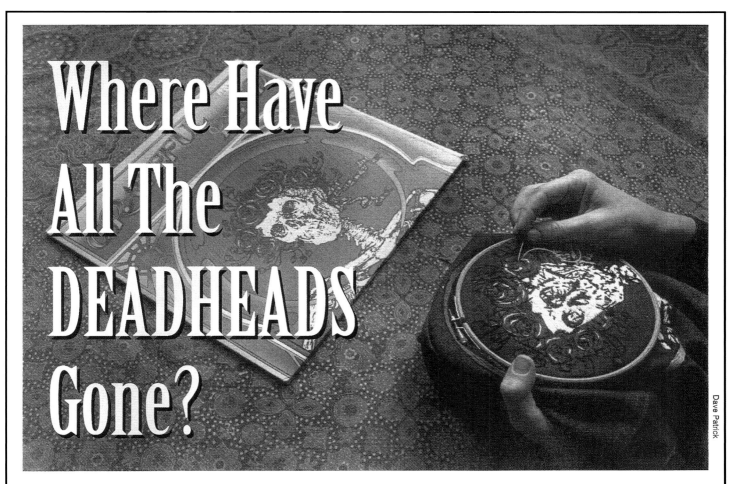

Dave Patrick

# Where Have All The DEADHEADS Gone?

### by Toni A. Brown

Archaeologists have long searched Greece for the true story surrounding the statue of the Colossus at Rhodes, which allegedly greeted ships at the entrance to the city's harbor. But it has been virtually impossible to figure out how such a large structure was erected. Historians have spent eons trying to uncover such mysteries.

We are fortunate to have lived through a time that will be looked upon from the distant future as the awakening of twentieth century culture. Likewise, historians will one day ponder the Grateful Dead phenomenon and its long reaching effects on civilization. Fortunately, the Grateful Dead and its subculture of Deadheads will leave much behind as evidence of what a long strange trip it was.

When Jerry Garcia died on August 9, 1995, life as many knew it ceased to exist. It was a rude awakening—a time to face reality with all of its harsh consequences. With the band's retirement from touring came the end of a way of life, but it also brought about a time of rebirth and continuation. From the ashes, embers still flickered. And from those embers rose the spirit that will allow Deadheads to continue the journey.

Upon the dissolution of the Grateful Dead, the media was quick to cite this as the "end of an era." Hardly. Deadheads have just forged the beginning of something that will thrive long after the memory of the touring entity fades.

The question remains—where have all the Deadheads gone? The scene has shifted, and people have scattered among the many bands that continue to provide valid musical

options. Some went to laugh their cares away at Phish shows, others tried to make it just one more day at Widespread Panic concerts. Independent bands and the club scene have all been provided a jolt of life. Millions of Deadheads have dispersed, and we are now, truly, everywhere.

## One step done and another begun and I wonder how many miles...

By the late '60s, the Grateful Dead had earned a reputation as house band for some of the most experimental events ever held— The Acid Tests and Trips Festival. It was not necessarily the most productive way to hone a musical craft, amid swirling lights and tripping souls. But the music evolved, and the improvisations that grew from those historic moments set the Dead apart from its contemporaries. Though the band's keyboardist, Pigpen, kept his blues spirit intact, the rest of the band found itself inspired by the enlightenment that the then legal L.S.D. provided. The doors of perception were open wide, and the Grateful Dead helped guide us through those doors with its music.

The sound systems of the era did little to get the message across, but the freaks in the Dead camp, specifically Augustus Owlsey Stanley III ("Bear"), changed the way the music industry delivered concert sound with their pioneering concepts. Owsley's innovative approach to sound delivery in the concert setting paved the way for all future concert systems.

The Jefferson Airplane was the first band from San Francisco to get a record deal, Moby Grape came up with a significant album that went largely ignored and Janis Joplin and Big Brother went on to commercial success. But the Grateful Dead made the largest commitment to touring of any band in history.

In 1966, the Dead ventured into Canada, but it wasn't until June 1967 that the band traveled to the East Coast. Most of those shows were at a tiny Greenwich Village club called the Café au Go-Go. The Dead also did a free concert in Tompkins Square Park and one in Central Park. That summer brought the boys to Canada again, and they got additional exposure by playing a few dates in Michigan, followed by Seattle and Denver that September. In December, the band was back on the East Coast, turning in shows in New York and Boston. By April of '68, the Dead became a full touring entity, with Florida, Pennsylvania and a date in Virginia on its itinerary.

Courtesy of promoter Bill Graham, the Dead was invited to play the Fillmore East in New York on June 14 and 15, 1968. The Jeff Beck Group (with Rod Stewart) also appeared on the bill.

It wasn't until early '69, though, that the Grateful Dead put its energies into full-fledged national touring. The band that invoked the spirit with its ever changing array of sound finally stepped out of the confines of California and brought its musical message to a very hungry country.

It was a time of intense change in our society. Revolution and experimentation were paramount in the minds of most youth. The Vietnam War was a uniting front on which we

**Free concert in Golden Gate Park, September 1975**

could all agree—peace and love was the battle cry.

Though San Francisco embraced difference as the norm, the rest of the country was still extremely conservative. Hippies were not unique to California, but most existed in isolated environments. It wasn't easy to find like-minded people to hook up with—until Woodstock, the single most important event in the hippie movement.

We woke up at Woodstock and realized that we were half a million strong! This was the ultimate qualifying experience that encouraged us to stand apart. And from that day on, we didn't feel weird or alone again. Our freak flags flew high, and we embraced the Grateful Dead as our band. We called ourselves Dead Freaks, and a subculture was born.

In our fights for individuality, many of us alienated our birth families. But at a Dead concert, we became part of another family, one that welcomed everyone. That unique camaraderie brought more people to shows in those

early years than the music, which was largely loose and disjointed. But as the Grateful Dead's magic began to congeal, the music improved and provided an important soundscape to our mind altering experimentation. No two Dead shows were alike. Its repertoire grew and its improvisation became more precise. And the word got out. There was nothing like a Grateful Dead concert.

It may be that the single most important facet of the Grateful Dead's growth came through the unauthorized taping of concerts by fans, who later began trading those tapes. The First Free Underground Grateful Dead Tape Exchange was formed in 1971, and with it, the first formal link between Dead enthusiasts was solidified. The more tapes that surfaced, the more people heard them. The best kept musical secret was fast becoming well-known outside of the intimate concert circuit.

The Dead's sound didn't translate well in the studio, but these concert tapes captured some of its live energy. Of course, record com-

pany executives were distraught over the perceived "bootleg" competition, but the notoriety that the tapes created brought an increased audience to the live shows, which ultimately resulted in additional record sales. With time, taping became so culturally intrinsic to the Dead experience that a taping section with special taper tickets was provided at all Grateful Dead concerts.

More and more people wanted to experience the Grateful Dead's music. As the scene itself was very enticing, the family steadily grew. By 1972, the band was on a roll: Bob Weir released his first solo effort, *Ace*, Mickey Hart released *Rolling Thunder* and the band toured Europe and released *Europe '72*, a live collection of its material from that tour.

Monumental change for the band and the Deadhead scene came in 1973 when Pigpen died on March 8 at the age of 27. To the dismay of fans, the band hit the arena circuit. New York's Nassau Coliseum dates March 15, 16 and 19, resulted in the most drug

**Oxford Plains**

**Compton Terrace**

busts at a concert recorded at that time. This was the start of the targeting of Deadheads by drug enforcement in this country. The public outcry was heard by the band who promised never to play the arena again. But the popularity of the Grateful Dead forced the band to remain at the stadium level for the remainder of its career, and Nassau County police continued to bust Deadheads at Nassau Coliseum.

The Wall of Sound that accompanied the Dead in 1974 was the ultimate experiment in sound conveyance. The equipment, which was so expensive and time-consuming to haul around, put such demand on the band that it decided to take a hiatus from touring in 1975.

Deadheads feared for the future of the Grateful Dead, but it was actually an extremely productive year. Solo albums were released including Garcia's bluegrass project, *Old And In The Way*; Robert Hunter's *Tiger Rose* featured guest band members; Phil Lesh and Howard Wales released *Seastones*; *Blues For Allah* was released in September; Bob Weir joined Kingfish and the group released its self-titled album; and the band spent time in the studio rehearsing. In early 1976, Garcia's *Reflections* was released followed by Mickey Hart's percussive *Diga Rhythm Band* album.

By June, 1976, the Grateful Dead was back on the road, to the delight of its anxious extended family, the Deadheads. And despite a couple of close calls with Garcia's health, there it remained until the summer of 1995.

In July, 1987, something occurred that changed the scene dramatically. The band released *In The Dark*, its very first album to achieve commercial success. Suddenly, it had hit singles and a chart-topping album.

It also became more difficult than ever to get tickets to shows. The Grateful Dead's in-house ticket sales office was inundated with requests for every tour. Controversy arose

among Deadheads—a resentment against new fans coming into the scene. The family began to fragment, and problems became more common with too many people showing up at shows without tickets.

The parking lot scene expanded dramatically as well. The real world began to intrude—bootleggers of unlicensed Dead products became part of the scene, and the band was determined to put an end to the negative effect this had on its royalties. The Dead called for an end to vending in the lot, partly to stop the bootlegging of its merchandise, but also because it attracted too many people, making it tough for those with tickets to find parking and facilities.

But, with time, came acceptance. We eventually felt like a family again, only on a grander scale. The young Heads that infiltrated the ranks actually added vitality to the carnival. Shakedown Street grew into a part of the scene that the Dead couldn't control. Veggie burritos, tie-dyes, beaded jewelry, Guatemalan clothing, crafts, incense, original artwork, candles…it was a hippie shopper's paradise. The scents, the colors, the sounds became ingrained in our psyche. We were a traveling circus that moved from town to town.

And many ran off to join that circus. Tourheads became so multitudinous that it was as if a small city followed the band from show to show. Although some venues had trouble accommodating the large entourage and many disliked the problems with drugs and litter, the profits they earned inspired them to invite the band back year after year. Yes, the Dead was shut out of some wonderful venues over the years, such as Red Rocks in Colorado, but the extent of what the band had become was not wholly in its control.

The road seemed endless for the Grateful Dead. We all lived by the credo of "Be Here Now," an apt phrase left over from the early years. No one questioned the future, and we

lived happily, waiting for the next tour. We existed in anticipation of the next time we could gather and feel the vastness of who we were.

In retrospect, there was premonition in the air that last summer. It was the very first time the media so closely chronicled a Grateful Dead tour. After all, it was the group's 30th anniversary. It wasn't as if the Dead hadn't experienced problems before, but this summer was extreme in its casualties. And while we were being scrutinized by the rest of the world, the synchronicity that had previously seemed to hold it all together began to come undone.

The War On Drugs, which had been targeting the scene for years, was on us in full fury. We were easy targets, and the DEA literally set up camp on Dead tour. Garcia looked bad and sounded worse. Lightning struck Deadheads in Washington, D.C., problems arose in Boston, fans were killed in an accident in Missouri and riots broke out in Deer Creek, resulting in a show canceled due to fans' actions for the first time in the Dead's long journey.

While we pondered the events that had threatened to halt the Grateful Dead's ability to tour, we worried for the first time whether there was a future for the band and Deadheads. A month after the Dead's last concert in Chicago, which was thankfully uneventful, we were hit by that fatal blow—Jerry Garcia had died.

The world was unprepared for the outpouring of grief over the loss of someone who had become such an important icon of an era. The media scrambled, and suddenly the Grateful Dead was once again in the spotlight. But Deadheads couldn't have wanted anything less. We needed to mourn quietly. The loss was so indescribably deep, so abstruse that we couldn't share it with those that weren't part of it. It wasn't just that a guitarist had died. This was the head of our family, and suddenly, unmistakably, our lives were changed forever.

Photo by John Rottet

**1997 Covers**

Cover Photo Courtesy Mercury Records

Cover Illustration by Miki Saito
Cover Photo by W. Marc Ricketts

Cover Photo by Henry Grossman

FESTIVALS '97

Cover Photo Courtesy A&M Records

Cover Artwork by Miki Saito

# BOB WEIR AND THE RATDOG EVOLUTION

## Enjoyin' The Ride!

### By Toni A. Brown

When Bob Weir met Jerry Garcia at Dana Morgan's music store one New Year's Eve in the early '60s, fireworks did not light the backdrop. Nevertheless, that moment was the beginning of a musical evolution and Bob Weir, for one, has never been the same.

Weir was born in the San Francisco area and started piano lessons in the third grade. After having trouble with the left-handed bass lines, he switched briefly to trumpet. He then got a guitar and began playing folk, country and rock music with friends.

His fateful meeting with Garcia resulted in the formation of a jug band, which soon included Ron "Pigpen" McKernan. The line-up of Mother McCree's Uptown Jug Champions went through a number of changes, eventually plugging in and becoming the Warlocks, which metamorphosed into the Grateful Dead. This is all well-documented historical fact. What is probably not as well documented is the fact that Jerry Garcia became the unofficial, unwilling icon for that group, dimming the lights on the other band members as far as societal association was concerned. So how does a very young rhythm guitarist build self-esteem when, despite his good looks and blossoming musical ability, the attention is often on someone else?

Weir's first recorded solo project, *Ace* (Round Records, 1972), showed a confidence and versatility few knew he possessed. Accompanied by his Grateful Dead band-mates, he was exceptional both in performance and in the material he showcased.

He went on to join Kingfish in the mid-'70s, but was too busy to give the commitment the band required. The brief foray did give Weir the opportunity to work with current Ratdog crony, Matthew Kelly. Kingfish released a self-titled project in 1976 which featured Weir.

With *Heaven Help The Fool* (1978), Weir emerged with a new maturity. He took an ironic and solid approach to the songs, and though the Dead never embraced the material that appeared on that album, it was obvious that Weir could hold his own in the category of band leadership.

Bobby and the Midnites was first assembled by Ibanez guitars for a trade show appearance. Bobby Cochran (guitar), Alphonso Johnson (bass) and Billy Cobham (drums) were joined by Brent Mydland (keyboards), and the band recorded its self-titled release in 1981. The group toured relatively often between 1980 and 1984 and although the name became well known, the band achieved little success among Deadheads and even less from the commercial market.

When Bob Weir hooked up with Rob Wasserman, he found a unique camaraderie. With quiet intellect, the two merged into a respectable musical duo. Weir was able to pick up his acoustic guitar and step into the spotlight. They toured extensively for a number of years and their relationship grew into Ratdog. Matt Kelly on harmonica and rhythm guitar and Jay Lane on drums added a more rock-driven approach to the predominantly acoustic forays Weir and Wasserman had been delivering.

The Grateful Dead remains an institution in spite of its dissolution. The other band members have kept quietly busy—Mickey Hart played a key role in the 1996 and 1997 Furthur Festival tours, and occasionally plays with a vast selection of world class percussionists, producing a diverse array of world music; Billy Kreutzmann is living in Hawaii and recently completed an album with his band, Backbone, and has performed two low-key shows in San Francisco; Vince Welnick has periodic forays with his Missing Man Formation outfit; and Phil Lesh has undertaken some eclectic projects, including jamming with local musicians, orchestral endeavors and a number of benefits.

The torchbearer role has been placed on Bob Weir, the most likely frontman. With Ratdog already seasoned by several years on the road, the latest configuration has taken hold and is tackling the material that Deadheads have grown to love—a wide selection of Grateful Dead songs. When Garcia died, it took Weir some time to embrace the music that he and the Grateful Dead had made so familiar. Instead, he took sojourns into many diverging arenas—aside from performing some of his trademark songs from his years with the Dead ("Victim Or The Crime," "Looks Like Rain," "Throwing Stones," "Eternity"), he was stretching for more classic material ("Misty," "Fever," "Blackbird").

Weir took his time in reintroducing Garcia-related Dead classics to his audience. Perhaps the need to distance himself for the sake of his personal healing process was the reason. Or it may have been his own need to attempt a different attack on his audience. Whatever his reasons for holding back the Dead material, it was instantly obvious that it was what the fans wanted to hear. Ratdog continues the tradition, much to the delight of Deadheads and new fans alike. Rock on Bobby!

# Ratdog
## The Ballroom, Washington, D.C.

Although many in the Deadhead community have chosen to turn the other cheek to Bob Weir's current musical venture, Ratdog, plenty more packed The Ballroom, an old warehouse in Washington, D.C. The venue's location was not conducive to vending, yet there were still people outside looking for "miracles" and chat-

L. D. Kippel

**Bobby & the Midnites**

ting about past adventures. Before the show, many wondered if Ratdog's set would consist of Weir's old Dead tunes (as most of this year's Furthur Festival sets did) or the blues-based selections from the Ratdog catalogue. The nearly two-hour show last October 19 combined both to form a well-rounded set.

After arousing the tie-dyed masses with a hot "Hell In A Bucket" opener, Weir offered a blues-infected "Wang Dang Doodle." As he did throughout the night, Matt Kelly contributed admirably to this song. Whether he was playing lead guitar, singing a sweet "Big Boss Man," adding nice harmonica fills or pounding on the congas, Kelly's presence was an essential component of the band.

Surprisingly, "Queen Jane Approximately" was strong. Never a favorite at Dead shows, Ratdog did a solid job on this tune. Bob donned an acoustic guitar for "KC Moan," but gave it a flat reading. Normally a solid Ratdog tune, this version faltered from the start and never gained momentum. It was a few more songs before Weir strapped the electric guitar back on; this section of the set proved to be the strongest of the evening.

"Easy To Slip" was bouncy and, before Weir finished the tune, Rob Wasserman and his excellent bass playing took over. Wasserman is the most under-appreciated member of Ratdog. Never a flashy performer, Wasserman let his steady bass playing speak for itself. A hot "Supplication" jam soon followed with Dave Ellis adding some jazzy saxophone lines and the crowd danced wildly. As the jam wound down, the first strains of "All Along The Watchtower" elicited cheers. This fired-up version did not disappoint. As if the band realized the beauty of the previous selections, Ratdog went back into a "Supplication" jam and finished the sequence

with the ending of "Easy To Slip." This arrangement showed the great juxtaposition of Ratdog and Dead tunes, and also provided some of the tightest playing of the evening.

As has become tradition, Wasserman's bass solo hinted at Grateful Dead songs. This evening, Wasserman gave "St. Stephen" a workout and then explored "The Other One." His playing (another tradition in the making) was superb.

Photo by Brian Gold

Unfortunately, the low-point of the evening followed. Jay Lane, who had played his drums competently if not exceptionally throughout the evening, came to the front of the stage. After whispering something in Wasserman's ear, Lane stepped up to Weir's mic and said, "Let's all get stoned." He then took some hits from a joint while a stunned Wasserman looked on. With Deadheads continually fighting a stereotypical image of drug abuse, Lane's antics were both childish and unnecessary. In fact, his actions were downright offensive.

Nonetheless, Bobby soon returned to the stage, and any thoughts of fatigue were quelled by a powerful "Samson & Delilah." The song, a custom at Sunday Dead shows, allowed Weir an opportunity to preach to the crowd. Those assembled enthusiastically sang "*If I had my way/I would tear this old building down,*" which brought worried looks to the faces of the security guards. A laid-back "Throwing Stones" ended the set. "Rock-star" Bob paraded to the front of the stage after the *"We are on our own"* section. As always, the crowd responded enthusiastically and the hard stare Weir gave them in return was his sign of gratitude.

The "Touch Of Grey" encore was an anomaly.

It was eerie as the refrain "*I will survive*" was changed to "*We will survive.*" Hearing Weir sing this number is certainly bittersweet. Everybody realized something was missing, but that didn't stop anyone from singing along and dancing. The song adds another dimension to Ratdog and, although some clearly resented Weir singing a Jerry Garcia song, most appreciated it.

While Bob Weir sang his heart out, something clicked. The lyrics seemed to take on a life of their own. We ARE surviving. Deadheads are continuing their musical voyages and are checking out many diverse musical forms and groups, and dancing when the vibe requires. Still, as Ratdog ably demonstrated, it's always nice to go back to an original source every once in awhile.

—Brad Shafran

## Underestimated Prophet—Ratdog
## Hammerstein Ballroom, New York, NY

Bob Weir and Ratdog blew the roof off the sold-out Hammerstein Ballroom last October 25, in what was easily the most dynamic, large scale, New York area event of this genre since the demise of the Grateful Dead.

Not every New York fan needs to mellow out and hang with friends for eight hours at a wistful "Furthur" Festival. What many need is to go to a funky old place on a Saturday night and go nuts with a great band. Ratdog's sets at the Furthur Festivals seemed to have been overshadowed by the oddly contrived atmosphere of the event. On the one hand, there was Weir, the patriarch, presiding over what amounted to a funeral wake. On the other hand, his act was supported by a half-dozen other bands as if it couldn't carry a show on its own. Weir, Ratdog and the audience seemed genuinely liberated by the lack of pretense at the Hammerstein Ballroom show. It was about Ratdog's music and having fun. Period.

One of the many ironies of the Grateful Dead has always been that the good-looking and athletically graceful Weir was, considering his role in the band, relatively under appreciated. He's written many of the Dead's best and most loved songs (with lyricists Robert Hunter and John Barlow) and, in the band's later years, wrote with the most ambition. He is easily the most underrated guitarist in rock; along with Keith Richards and Pete Townshend, he wrote the book on rhythm guitar (*Europe '72* anyone?).

Vocally, Weir is deceptive. Just as you're about to write off his technique as beside the point (as one could have during the evocative "Black Throated Wind" duet with bassist Rob Wasserman), he'll suddenly surprise you with his phrasing and narrative skills, then astound the listener at the end with masterful pacing and raw power.

As a band, Ratdog is good enough. Rob Wasserman, who is both cerebral and solid, excels on the upright electric bass and has good personal chemistry with Weir. Jeff Chimenti on keyboards, Jay Lane on drums, Dave Ellis on sax and Matthew Kelly on guitar, vocals and harp all contribute with skill and taste. As with any improvisational music, here, the whole is greater than the sum of its parts.

Ratdog's sound, presented with stunning clarity, is lean, nuanced and utterly contemporary.

After the show, someone remarked that "this band is one bearded guitar player short of a great band." When asked to name an existing band that could have topped this show, he got the point. There are obvious reasons why Ratdog is better off, at least for now, without a lead guitarist. Probably the best reason is that Bob Weir is a major artist in his own right who needs the room this band gives him to realize his ultimate direction.

Show highlights? A kick-ass "Hell In A Bucket" opener, a "This Time Forever/Shade Of Gray" segue that reminded us of what a unique ballad writer Weir is, one of the better "Eternity" renditions, an "Estimated Prophet" that showed promise and a spectacular "Throwing Stones," with Weir building to a crescendo during a chord solo on the bridge. The first encore, "One More Saturday Night," did nothing to discourage the crowd, and the finale, "Touch Of Grey," was absolutely gut-wrenching.

Like Bob Dylan and Neil Young, Weir has a major catalog of material to draw from and obviously has the artistry to continuously reinterpret. Perhaps as Ratdog evolves, he'll be inspired to write new songs. Either way, it's great to see him motivated and looking to the future. While Ratdog has the strongest link to the Grateful Dead of any existing band, it sounded more vital, fresher and more sophisticated than any you-name-it-wise-guy jam band half its age. But then again, that's only surprising if you underestimate Bob Weir.

—Rob Wolfson

## Ratdog Stirs Up Old Memories in Boston

If the latest Ratdog tour proves anything, it's that persistence pays. For Dead fans, this was a chance to hear Grateful Dead classics many had long thought, well, dead. For Bob Weir and company, it was a chance to play some of those songs again, building on an audience that had become noticeably nonchalant. The lack of Dead material from Ratdog's early '90s sets had alienated a larger portion of its potential audience.

Winging through the Northeast this past Fall, Ratdog touched down and sold out Boston's Orpheum Theater on Sunday, October 26.

Anticipation was high, especially coming off another successful Furthur Festival this past summer, a show which saw Ratdog and other tour participants include more Dead material in their repertoire. At this point in the band's development, Ratdog's setlist is almost entirely songs played by the Grateful Dead, both originals and covers…and that is clearly suiting ticket buyers just fine.

While the band's arsenal has expanded, so has the lineup. Saxophonist Dave Ellis and keyboardist Jeff Chimenti add a great deal to the overall mix, and with guitarist/harpist Matt Kelly in tow, it rounds out the sound nicely. Not that compadre and bass guru Rob Wasserman didn't create a full sound when it was simply Weir/Wasserman (a.k.a. "The Rockin Ws"), but

this expanded lineup seems to appeal to a wider audience.

Opening the Orpheum show with the blues nugget, "Walkin' Blues," the audience response was much more appreciative than when the tune was played by the Dead. After a brief space jam, it evolved into "Saint Of Circumstance." If the crowd was at all blasé, this quickly got their attention. Everyone was now on board.

Photo by Philip Gerstheimer

Photo by Rob Cohn

One of the more pleasant developments of Ratdog's live sets has been the inclusion of Jerry Garcia material and, on this night, Weir treated the crowd to the rare "Loose Lucy." The crowd was clearly in full swing and although Weir flubbed the *"I got home with two black eyes"* verse, awkwardly adding it at the end in a sort of "Lucy reprise," the crowd took it in stride. Mistakes are, after all, easily forgiven in these circles.

Just when Weir's guitar was starting to come though clearly in the mix, he threw his soundman a curve ball by "going wood." A mini-acoustic set featured only Weir and Kelly (on harp) for "KC Moan," with Wasserman joining in during the segue into a powerful "Victim Or The Crime." Weir practically screamed certain lines on the latter, which Wasserman accentuated with several bombs of his own.

The entire ensemble then returned, and while it looked like Bob might reach for his electric, the band instead opted for one more acoustic tune. A tight "When I Paint My Masterpiece" followed featuring the oft-deleted "dirty gondola" verse.

Flexing its chops a bit, the group launched into what can best be described as a "swing jam," a short, upbeat instrumental that seemed

way off the beaten path for Ratdog. It was quite interesting, although much of the crowd seemed a bit bewildered.

The highlight of the night had to be the solo material combination of "The Winners>Easy To Slip." Weir's vocals were particularly strong, but the house nearly blew a collective gasket as Ratdog stretched out the middle section of "Easy To Slip," wandering into Dead territory with a full out "Lazy Lightning" jam that lasted for several minutes. A stunned crowd hoped Weir would treat them to the lyrics, but Bobby opted to wind back into "Easy To Slip."

A lengthy, jam-filled "Corrina" showed off Weir's excellence as a guitarist and, though not a popular choice in Grateful Dead setlists, this selection received a rousing ovation. Wasserman's famous bass solo unfolded, and his chops shone as he switched from bow to finger-picking to slapping techniques. Few bassists can pull off as consistently an interesting and creative bass solo night after night. The recent Rolling Stones swing through New England may have been on his mind as he led the audience in a massive "Satisfaction" sing-a-long.

Drummer Jay Lane took his cue after Wasserman finished, lighting into a drum solo that gave way to an expected Sunday night "Samson & Delilah." "Sugar Magnolia" nearly lifted the roof off the place and, although slightly retooled with a few additional mid-jam pauses, it sounded as good as ever.

Weir still knows how to work a crowd, taking his famous front-of-stage strolls during the pre-"Sunshine Daydream" jam, and then leaving the stage with the crowd screaming for more.

*"I wanna do a little livin' in your livin' room,"* Weir ad-libbed during a raucous "Gloria" encore. A frenzied, yet appreciative, crowd was clearly happy to get another taste of live Grateful Dead music and, judging by the grin on Weir's face, he was happy to oblige.

Weir and crew seem to have found a happy middle ground with the added material and "new" audience. Let's hope they continue to tour regularly.

—David Lubell

# Editorial

We naturally count off milestones to mark achievements in life. When it came to our attention that we were going to reach our 150th issue, it didn't seem like much. After all, 150 hours of live Grateful Dead music would barely make a dent in anyone's collection. But upon more careful thought, 150 pints of Cherry Garcia is a lot of ice cream, and multiply that by the number of calories in each pint—well, you get the point. So sitting down and looking through the *Relix* archives, there is no doubt that we have achieved something monumental. We have chronicled a musical sub-culture, helped it to thrive and provided enough information to inspire an entirely new generation of musicians. In addition to all of the musical aspects that *Relix* has shared with its readers during its 27 years, there's been so much more. The nurturing of a lifestyle is a responsible task.

When *Relix* came into my hands, I was nervous. I'd never run a magazine, and it was a challenge. But what is life without reaching beyond the dreams and goals we set for ourselves? In calm reflection, the most important thing I realized about my role as editor and then publisher of *Relix* was that I must use it responsibly. No greater tool exists than the media, and I take this position very seriously.

In an effort to take full advantage of as powerful a resource as a magazine, it was an easy decision to provide more than just musical news to our readers—we alerted people to a vast variety of environmental issues, describing how even one person can make a change. We carefully observed the scene we thrive within and cautioned the masses that not everyone out there is a friend. We spoke out against the injustices of the War On Drugs, and the implications of the unjust Mandatory Minimum Sentencing Acts that continue to plague our society. We have given musicians' perspectives on touring, fans' grievances with parking lot problems, and stood strong when East Coast Deadheads took a bashing from their West Coast Deadhead brothers and sisters. We rifled through the gossip to give readers actual news, waded through lawsuits to preserve our right to share that news, and labored with massive egos in the wonderful world of rock stardom. At times we were disheartened, but there was always a stronger hand at play in this entity. It was never about what "*I*" wanted, it "*is*" about destiny and the part we each play in that which "*will*" be.

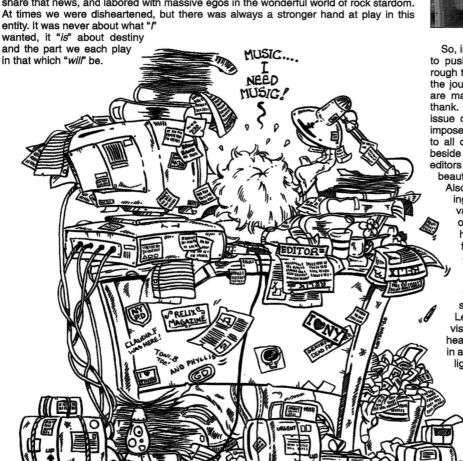

An amazingly accurate depiction of my desk by Nicholas Watson—Toni

So, in the remarkable scheme of things, we continue to push the boundaries, paving a road through the rough terrain of the mainstream and mundane. And as the journey continues, so does the hard work. There are many people behind the scenes that I need to thank. They are the good folks that help bring each issue of *Relix* to you—and in spite of my own self-imposed distractions, they are always there. First, thanks to all of the loyal *Relix* contributors that have stood beside us through the years. Thanks to my friends and editors Claudia Falzarano and Phyllis Antoniello, two beautiful, brilliant women that I adore working with. Also thanks to Rick Spanier who has been designing *Relix* for 12 years, and Jacquie Block, Rick's valued protégé. Ian Brand has taken on many of our most industrious covers in recent years, and his artistry is appreciated. Thanks to Tom Canova for his trusty advice, and Enis Moran who diligently pushes us into the expansive void of cyberspace. Thanks to John Lucchese who helps in the office. And thanks to Les Kippel who wasn't satisfied to just go home after a Dead show—he had to take the show home with him! Les has led the way for tapers, and with the initial vision with which he created *Relix*—as a Deadhead and as a music enthusiast, I thank him. Once in a while you get shown the light…and Les saw the light big time!

The *Relix* Years…they have been the *best* years of my life. A big thanks to you readers, the reason we're here in the first place! It's not just a job, it's an adventure!

Remember to leave only footprints, watch each card you play and let there be songs to fill the air. See you somewhere out there…

In peace, love & light,
Toni Brown

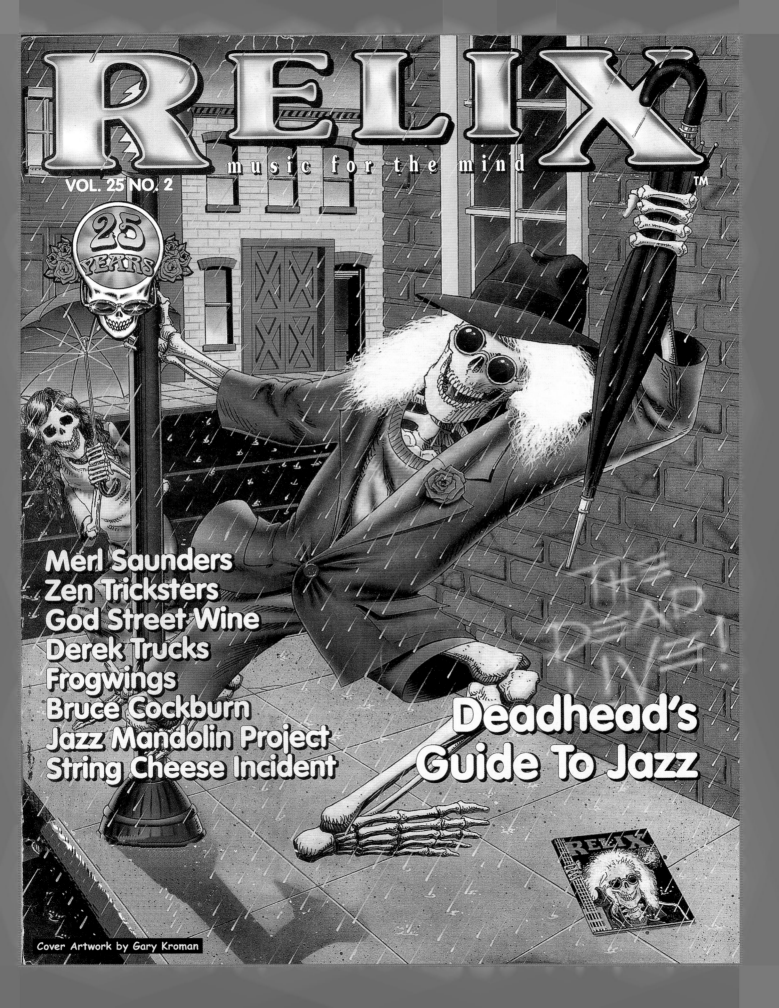

# RELIX

*music for the mind*

™

VOL. 25 NO. 2

**25 YEARS**

Merl Saunders
Zen Tricksters
God Street Wine
Derek Trucks
Frogwings
Bruce Cockburn
Jazz Mandolin Project
String Cheese Incident

THE DEAD LIVES!

## Deadhead's Guide To Jazz

Cover Artwork by Gary Kroman

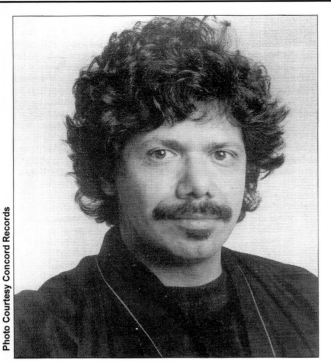

Photo Courtesy Concord Records

**Chick Corea**

**B**ill Graham made history when he booked Miles Davis to open for the Grateful Dead many years ago in San Francisco. More recently, Branford Marsalis and David Murray have brought their jazz stylings onto the scene. A look beyond these familiar jazz players reveals an entire world of new musical frontiers to explore.

Common elements in the music of both the Grateful Dead and the genre of jazz include extended, free-form jams and improvised musical conversations that extend each song's melodic theme. Tape trading is also a part of the jazz scene, although to a much lesser degree than with Deadheads. An interesting aspect of jazz CDs, though, is the occasional inclusion of "alternate takes" of the same song on a disc. Due to improvised solos and spontaneous jamming going in different directions, many jazz discs include two or sometimes three versions of the same song.

Knowing the players is key so here is a brief history of jazz and the musicians who made it what it is today.

In the early and mid-1940s, Charlie "Bird" Parker (1925-1955), granddaddy of the tenor sax, and Dizzy Gillespie (1917-1993), master of the trumpet, created a new form of jazz known as "be bop." The be bop sound featured "small" bands of five to eight players with much more freedom to improvise and jam than did structured "big band" jazz, which was the dominant force in music at the time. Be bop brought fast and furious tempos to the music with solos that were sometimes wild and always much more spontaneous than its big band counterparts.

In the mid to late '40s, Miles Davis (1926-1991) joined Charlie Parker's band and played a slower, more deliberate tempo as compared to the rapid-fire licks of Parker and Gillespie. Davis also brought an unmatched melodic genius and highly personal, sensitive tones to the voice of his trumpet, which provided a beautiful contrast to the "hard bop" sounds of Charlie Parker.

Miles Davis took the jazz world by storm with his 1954 release, *Birth Of The Cool*, an album that had actually been recorded four years earlier and still stands as the prototype for the "cool school" of jazz. Miles Davis became the dominant force in the development of jazz music during the '50s and '60s, giving many of the great jazz players their first shot at the big time as a member of his band.

In 1969, Davis again put his stamp on the direction of jazz (and, ultimately, music in general) with the release of *Bitches Brew*, another groundbreaking album. The new direction infused electronics into the sound while the music itself explored increasingly abstract rhythms and melodies, masterfully articulating the jazz form known as "fusion."

Parker, Gillespie and Davis are just a few jazz heavyweights; listed below are some other key players in alphabetical order.

Art Blakey (1919-1990) is regarded by many as one of the best, if not the premier, jazz drummers. As leader of the very influential Jazz Messengers, Blakey's recordings emphasize his drumming. His music is also rich in melodies due to the talents of his band members who were always among the very best of the day. Blakey also "sat in" with virtually all of the jazz legends over his lengthy career and has performed on many of the great jazz albums that have come to be regarded as classics.

*Caravan* was recorded in 1962 and is a prime example of Blakey's polyrhythmic stylings. It also features Freddy Hubbard on trumpet and Wayne Shorter on tenor sax. This album includes alternate takes on two of the tunes, giving insight into the various expressive possibilities available to musicians of this caliber. Anyone that appreciates innovative work on the drum kit will enjoy the music of Art Blakey. Other titles to look for include *Free For All*, *Freedom Rider*, *Mission Eternal* and *A Night At Bird Land Volumes 1&2*.

John Coltrane (1926-1967) recorded *A Love Supreme* in 1964, almost ten years after he was thrust into the jazz spotlight as the tenor sax player in Miles Davis' "first great quintet" during the mid-'50s. Coltrane's music is noted for its brilliant creativity as well as his unique combination of melodic sensibility and machine gun speed on the horn. His solos create powerful moods, displaying a myriad of textures that range from the smooth, rich, relaxed voice of a seductive sax to frenzied, shrieking intonations that have made more than one listener's hair stand on end.

*A Love Supreme* is actually a four-part epic that achieves some of the same transcendental qualities as "Dark Star." Touted by many of the world's most influential musicians as a source of inspiration and spiritual enlightenment, this is a masterpiece that is a window to mystical worlds and a wonderful soundtrack for adventures in mind expansion. John Coltrane recorded many other great albums including *My Favorite Things*, *Blue Trane*, *Lush Life*, *Soul Trane* and *Giant Steps*.

Chick Corea (born 1941) is another graduate of the same Miles Davis university of jazz, primarily known for his innovative work with the Fender Rhodes electric piano on Miles Davis' *Bitches Brew* album. In 1971, Corea founded Return To Forever, a jazz "super group," which set the new standard for jazz fusion, and featured Joe Farrell on flute and sax, Flora Purim on vocals and percussion, Stanley Clark on bass and Airto Moriera on drums and percussion.

*Return To Forever*, a self-titled 1972 release, paints exquisite musical landscapes

# A DEADHEAD'S GUIDE to JAZZ

## by Lee Abraham

and explores fantasy worlds from another dimension. Corea's music possesses some of the same essence as "Terrapin Station," as well as some of the spaces explored in "Unbroken Chain" and "Birdsong." In addition to ten other Return To Forever releases, the best of which include *Light As A Feather*, *Where Have I Known You Before* and *Hymn Of The Seventh Galaxy*, Chick Corea has several other recordings with both his "Akoustic" and "Elektric" bands that are outstanding. Most notable are *Chick Corea Akoustic Band*, *Alive*, *Beneath The Mask* and *Paint The World*, as well as the 1995 release, *Time Warp*.

Thelonious Monk (1917-1982) is widely regarded as one of the premier jazz composers, as well as being a gifted pianist and influential bandleader. Monk's music is technically complex and occasionally eccentric with quirky twists and turns. His compositions are distinctive, influencing the directions, phrasing and tones of the musical conversations his band engaged in.

A contemporary of Parker and Gillespie from the '40s, Monk was involved in the creation of be bop, yet did not achieve popular acclaim until the '50s when he collaborated with sax greats Sonny Rollins and John Coltrane. *Brilliant Corners* is a 1956 recording that features Sonny Rollins and ranks as one of the all-time great jazz albums. Other standout CDs include *Monk's Music, Live At The Five Spot* (with John Coltrane), *Mulligan Meets Monk* and *Thelonious Monk/Sonny Rollins.*

Sonny Rollins (born 1930) epitomizes the complete jazz musician with his unmatched array of skills that include an incomparably wide range of rich tones from his tenor sax and his effortless phrasing that articulates his melodic genius. Rollins' early career was put on the fast track as a side man for Miles Davis in the early '50s. His subsequent recordings with Thelonious Monk and as the leader of his own bands makes him one of the very best jazz has to offer. Rollins has the ability to touch the soul with a gentle spirituality, occasionally bringing to mind the moods created in "Standing On The Moon," "Must Have Been The Roses" and "Stella Blue."

*Tenor Madness*, recorded in 1956 with Rollins backed by the Miles Davis band, features one of the most eloquent musical discussions ever recorded with John Coltrane and Rollins exchanging points of view on the 12-minute title track. There are too many great Sonny Rollins records to list, but some of the best are *Saxophone Colossus, The Quartets, Way Out West, The Bridge* and Rollins' current 1996 release, *Sonny Rollins +3*, which is a testament to his enduring brilliance.

Joshua Redman (born 1969) is the best tenor sax player to come along in many years, and he has already earned a place in jazz history as one of the all time greats. Son of Dewey Redman, an innovative, avante-garde sax player who has played with many of the jazz giants from the '60s and is still playing today, Joshua Redman hit the jazz scene in 1991 after graduating with honors from Harvard.

Redman's *Spirit Of The Moment* is a two-disc, live recording from 1995 that is chock full of wonderful musicianship and displays the diversity of talents that evoke inevitable comparisons to Sonny Rollins. Other excellent releases include the self-titled *Joshua Redman, Wish, Mood Swing* and *Freedom In The Groove.*

John Scofield (born 1951) has been recording since the early '70s and has been regarded as a virtuoso guitar player since he became a member of Jerry Mulligan's band in 1974. Scofield's reputation grew steadily as he performed in a variety of ensembles, including a brief stint with Charles Mingus in 1977. His tenure with the Miles Davis band from 1982 to 1985, though, elevated his stature in the jazz world to the superstar level.

*What We Do* is a stunning album from 1992 that mixes Scofield's blues influences with his traditional jazz roots and an occasional New Orleans flavor to create a very distinctive sound. *Grace Under Pressure, Groove Elation, Hand Jive* and the 1996 release, *Quiet*, are among the many other gems in Scofield's catalog.

Sun Ra (1914-1993) is easily the most flamboyant and outlandish of the jazz greats. Born as Herman "Sonny" Blount, he changed his legal name to Le Sony'r Ra in 1952 and was known from that time as Sun Ra. He claimed to be from the planet Saturn on a mission here as the "Cosmic Communicator." His free jazz stylings were very innovative and often as eccentric as his outer space imagery and unusual stage costumes, but his contributions to music as both a pianist and bandleader are unquestioned.

*The Futuristic Sounds Of Sun Ra* was recorded in 1961 and is a prime example of Sun Ra's unique sound. Chimes, congas, shakers and all sorts of percussion bring to mind the sounds of Mickey Hart's Rhythm Devils, particularly the *Apocalypse Now Sessions*, but also includes variations on be bop with influences from swing and cool school mixed in. Sun Ra created some of the best "space" ever recorded, with extended percussion explorations that incorporate flutes and other instruments dancing together, enticing the listener to pass through the doors of other dimensions. Other highly recommended Sun Ra works include *Cosmic Equation, Nubians Of Plutonia, We Are In The Future, Magic City, Atlantis* and *Of Mythic Worlds.*

The best place to find out about new and different jazz artists has historically been music and book stores, but the Internet is also a great place to expand your musical horizons. In particular, an excellent source of jazz information is the Northwestern University jazz Web page located at nwu.edu/WNUR/jazz.

Jump in and enjoy the music!　■

Sunshine Daydream　　　　　　　　　　　　　　Artwork by Gary Kroman

**RELIX** — music for the mind ™

Vol. 25, No. 6

Year-End Special

**25 YEARS**

The Other Ones
Hot Tuna
Max Creek
Strangefolk
Deadhead Photo Spread
We Are Everywhere

Rusted Root
Jazz Fest
Reviews
Comix

**RELIX** — music for the mind

Vol. 25, No. 5

**WOMEN IN MUSIC**
BONNIE RAITT
LILITH TOUR '98

**THE OTHER ONES**
SUMMER CONCERTS IN REVIEW

**RELIX** — music for the mind ™

Vol. 25, No. 3

Summer Special

Phil Lesh
Mickey Hart
Bob Weir
Jorma Kaukonen
Jack Casady

**RELIX** — music for the mind ™

Vol. 25, No. 4

**JERRY GARCIA**
ANNUAL TRIBUTE ISSUE
2 Exclusive Interviews
Plus
Garcia: The Banjo Years

Mickey Hart
Widespread Panic
Missing Man Formation
Marshall Tucker Band
Robbie Robertson

Maui

Caleb and Bonnie Hiliadis, Charlotte, NC 3/23/95

Charles Cariello

Rebecca Feld

Becca and Matt in upstate PA

We Are still Everywhere

Joe Ryan

David Saddler

Incarcerated Deadheads Stanley Marshall,
Matt Rosen and Evan Rottman

Joe Ryan

Trisha's "Deadbago" — Sioux Falls, SD

Martin's Grateful collection

Gus and Brook

Chase Monster III

233

RELIX
VOL. 26 NO.5
GRATEFUL DEAD
WIDESPREAD PANIC
CALOBO
SUSAN TEDESCHI
JOHN POPPER
DAVID GANS
SUMMER CONCERT REVIEWS

Cover Photo
by
Jon Weiner

Cover Artwork
by
Una Toibin
Dancing Bears
Reg. TM
Grateful Dead
Productions

RELIX
music for the mind
MILLENNIUM SPECIAL

RELIX
music for the mind
VOL. 26 NO.2
HOT TUNA
BLUES SPECIAL
B.B. KING
RORY BLOCK
JOHN LEE HOOKER
JONNY LANG
GRATEFUL DEAD
PHISH
MOON BOOT LOVER
WISE MONKEY
ORCHESTRA

Cover Photo
by
L.D. Kippel

RELIX
VOL. 26 NO.4
music for the mind
PHIL LESH
EXCLUSIVE INTERVIEW
MOBY GRAPE
NEIL YOUNG
JOHN BELAND AND THE
FLYING BURRITO BROTHERS
PERCY HILL
SPECIAL ANNUAL
GRATEFUL DEAD
TRIBUTE ISSUE
CONCERT REVIEWS,
NEWS AND MUCH MORE!!

Cover by Rob Cohn-
Purple Moon Design

RELIX
music for the mind
VOL. 26, NO3
SUMMER SPECIAL
DEADHEAD VACATION GUIDE
TAHITI
LONDON
DISNEY WORLD
THE RECIPE
MOE.
FOXTROT ZULU
BIG WU
LEGION OF MARY
BILL WALTON

Cover Photo by L.D. Kippel
Dancing Bears Reg. TM Grateful Dead Productions

RELIX
music for the mind
VOL. 26 NO.1 TM
PHISH
STILL SPAWNING
WE'RE JAMMIN'
WIDESPREAD PANIC
JIGGLE THE HANDLE
STEVE KIMOCK
MERL SAUNDERS
RATDOG
MICKEY HART'S
PLANET DRUM
BOB DYLAN

Cover Photo by Loren Haynes
Courtesy Elektra Records

# An Interview With Bob Weir

## The Music Never Stopped

### By Toni A. Brown

Photo by David Vann

It was a hot, early summer afternoon. RatDog was playing at Asbury Park, New Jersey, the former stomping grounds of Bruce Springsteen. It was a shock to drive up and see the boarded up area that was once a major seaside resort. I suppose that when the music moves on, all that gets left behind are the skeletons…

A warm, friendly greeting from Bob Weir wiped away my surprise at the nearby desolate surroundings. His eyes were filled with light and vigor, and his sincere smile washed away the years. His willingness to talk was reassuring as the summer heat brutally beat down on us as we chatted by the pool.

Where can someone begin when there is a vast history and a million unanswered questions? The music is always the best place to start. Bob Weir has kept true to his musical vision in the years since the Grateful Dead has stopped touring. He was hesitant at first to incorporate material from the Grateful Dead's repertoire into his solo touring entities—Weir and Wasserman and RatDog—because this was, after all, his solo career. And once Jerry Garcia died, the sorrow he felt at having lost his longtime contemporary also kept him from delving into the Dead's musical well. Bobby was simply uncomfortable and chose to distance himself from that music for a while. This may have alienated many fans, but Weir feels that he has done things the way he needed to and has not compromised his music for the sake of drawing a crowd.

Selections from the Dead's archives have gradually found their way into RatDog's playlist. But there's the lingering question of whether or not Weir should have pulled this material out just to please his audience. "I have to do what floats my boat," Weir adamantly remarked. "I have to please myself first. Either that or I'm just an act. I'll retire before I'm just an act. I've got to write. There's music that I haven't written. There's stuff that I haven't said, and I'm just getting to it. I think that's probably always going

to be the case. That said, there are also a lot of things that I'm *not* prepared to walk away from, so you're gonna be getting some of the new stuff and some of the old stuff with me. I don't even have a choice in the matter. I have to do it this way."

The first, long anticipated RatDog album, *Evening Moods*, has just been released on Grateful Dead Records. It's Bob Weir's first non-Grateful Dead studio project since the early 1980s. He and the band spent several weeks in Weir's home studio, Ace's, and the songs evolved organically. RatDog then went to Coast studio in San Francisco, and in a live, jazz-like manner, recorded the tracks. Musicians on this album are Bob Weir on vocals and guitars, Rob Wasserman on bass, Jay Lane on vocals and drums, Jeff Chimenti on vocals and keyboards, Mark Karan on vocals and guitars, Eric Crystal on saxophone and Matthew Kelly on vocals and harmonica.

The Dead had been performing "Corrina," the Weir/Hunter composition, for years, but had never released a studio version. (It did appear on last year's live *Furthurmore*.) Weir's approach to the song is distinctively RatDog's, giving it a different feel than the Dead's standard performance. Weir discussed the departure. "It wasn't like, 'Okay, we're gonna do this song different,'" he explained. "Sometimes we decide to do that, but that wasn't the case with 'Corrina' though it has come out substantially different just because the song has been morphing all along. There was never really an arrangement or a feel that was etched in stone or even in glass for that tune. I guess there is now that it's recorded. Once it gets out on a record and hits the airwaves, then that's the definitive arrangement."

Weir had a hand in writing every song, having worked with several contributors. "2 Djinn," "Bury Me Standing" and "Even So" were co-written with Gerrit Graham. Weir's longtime collaborator, John Barlow, contibuted to "Lucky Enough" and "Welcome To The World" with

Andre Pessis. Pessis also co-wrote "Ashes & Glass" and "October Queen." "Odessa," co-written by Weir, Graham and Russ Ellis, seems to have been a crowd pleaser during the last RatDog tour with its rowdy, up-tempo delivery.

At the time of our meeting, news of Furthur Tour 2000 had just been released. With so many other summer tours under way and local festivals popping up everywhere, there was a bit of concern over whether or not the tour would work coming late in the summer and spilling over into fall. Weir was conservatively optimistic about the Other Ones going out on the road again. "Here's hoping that people have had summer jobs," he mused. "I hope we don't run into the empty pocket syndrome. But there will be people there. It's gonna be a little tough, I think, because we're doing it at the end of the summer and into the school year, so we're not gonna get the vacation crowd. The hard core—they'll be there. And the music will be good. We just got together with Alfonso [Johnson] for the first time a couple of days ago and that's gonna go well. I've played with Alfonso before. But the rest of the guys didn't know what they were in store for."

Bassist Alphonso Johnson had been part of Bob Weir's Bobby and the Midnites project. Johnson has also been playing in Jazz Is Dead in recent years, so he is particularly well-versed in the Dead musical spectrum.

There is still the underlying need for Deadheads to gather, and the opportunity to see so many former members of the Dead at once is bound to be enticing. Bob Weir, Mickey Hart, Vince Welnick and Bill Kreutzmann will be joined by Johnson, Bruce Hornsby, Steve Kimock and Mark Karan.

Ziggy Marley and the Melody Makers was announced as this year's opening band for Furthur Fest. This was not an obvious first choice by most Deadheads, but Weir was generous in his explanation of how it came about. "That selection came our way through John Scher and the folks at Metropolitan," he said. "I've got to say that I like the idea. The more I think about it, the better I like it, too, because it's not a huge stretch for anybody. Most of the kids like reggae, and that guy's the real thing. But he's young, too. He's young blood in reggae, and he's good. People are really going to enjoy that."

There are so many good bands out there that have gotten a fair amount of inspiration from the Grateful Dead. Bob Weir is familiar with many of them, even recognizing that Phish was, at one time, a Dead cover band. It was as if the Grateful Dead pushed the musical envelope in mixing musical styles and expanding on the improvisational level at a time when music was already becoming formulaic. His thoughts on the Dead's influence on current improvisational, psychedelic, groove rock are very modest. When asked how he likes hearing other bands interpret the Dead's music, his answer was not surprising. "I'm tickled," he revealed. "I tend to write the kind of music that I want to hear, so it's my kind of music. If I can be evangelical about it here for a moment, it's gratifying to see people doing that. That's our legacy, and I'm thrilled. Not that they need our go-ahead…As far as I can see, it's all good. I mean, we didn't develop this approach to music for no reason at all, or as a conscious ploy or marketing tool; we did it because it's fun and interesting and leaves the music wide open for development from night to night and also from moment to moment. It's gratifying to see other people doing that. The more people who play like that, I think, the better. It's not like this is new. The jazz people have been doing it

for years, and it's an American tradition. We're just bringing it into popular music a little more than it has been seen for a while.

"There used to be more room for improvisation in popular music back in the '30s, for instance, when the dance bands were hot," Weir continued. "That was the ultimate improvisation happening then. Those were jam bands—the Ellington Ensemble, Count Basie, Fletcher Henderson, all those people. They were jam-bands. So what we're doing is not without precedent. Still, it's great to see it come around again 'cause that means I can listen to a lot of bands and really enjoy it. When somebody's playing something fresh, you can hear it. You can feel it. And there's nothing else that supplies that punch. No magnifi-

Photo by Peter Simon          Courtesy PeterSimon.com

Photo by Rob Cohn          Courtesy DeadImages.com

cently rendered road performance is gonna amount to something that's happening right there for the first time. I like to live my life like that, and I like to see other people live their lives like that. I think that's the way it should be."

After spending well over 30 years constantly touring, it's amazing that most of the members of the Dead have kept at the thing they love best—playing live music. Vince Welnick was involved in several projects, including the excellent Missing Man Formation; Mickey Hart has kept busy with a number of percussion-inspired projects coming to fruition in his most accessible project to date—a full band that includes Welnick. Bill Kreutzmann recorded an album with the band, Backbone, in Hawaii where he currently resides, and Phil Lesh has come through a successful liver transplant

and taken up touring with a variety of friends.

With the touring history that has made Bob Weir one of the world's most traveled road warriors, it's a wonder he hasn't decided to kick back and take a breather. With his wife and new baby, he spends more time at home than he may have in the past, but he's not considering it as a way of life. "Maybe I'd take a little time off from touring, but I'm always gonna have a guitar with me," Weir explained. "I'm always gonna be writing or doing stuff like that. I thought of not hitting the road for a few months to do a little wood shedding. Work up a bunch of new stuff. New scales, new approaches, that kind of thing. And sooner or later, I'm going to want to do a little traveling. I'm gonna go to India for a while, Tibet, some other places. Like I said, I'll probably always have a guitar strapped to my shoulder. I've spent some time on some beaches. I like to travel. I like Asia a lot. It's just great over there, and part of my heart lives in Asia. Part of it lives here in America.

"This is a story that I've told a few times, but it bears telling again," Weir continued. "A number of years back, I went to see Count Basie. He was playing the Venetian Room, an elegant nightspot in San Francisco. He came on and the band, they swung like angels, particularly the quartet. Three of the four people in the quartet had been together for 50 years or so. And it was just the most wonderful evening I could have imagined. As it turned out, that was his last gig. After that gig, he went home to his place in Florida, put his feet up and checked out. He was old, real old, and I can't think of a more fitting way to live one's life than doing what one loves and bringing it to people. I'm not in this business to make a killing and go retire in Maui or play golf for the rest of my days. I do this 'cause I have to. I'll probably stop having to do it when my heart stops beating."

This brings us to the matter of the Grateful Dead's treasured Vault, the place where all of the band's live tapes are archived. Dick Latvala was the keeper of the flame for many years until his premature death in August of 1999. Mickey Hart has been quoted as saying, "It would take 20 lifetimes to get the Grateful Dead's music out there." Admittedly, no one could ever replace Latvala, but Weir is enthusiastic about the person that has taken over at the helm. "There's a kid who's working for us named David Lemieux who knows our material," Weir enthused. "It's scary is all I can tell you. And he's not a 'get-a-lifer' either. I don't know where this guy came from...he must have rolled off a cloud. I think they kicked him out of heaven, and he bounced and landed in our Vault. You're gonna be hearing more about him in the days to come. Nobody's gonna replace Dick, but this kid, David, is gonna take a little bit of the sting out of his passing."

With so many years of road time under his belt, it's easy to speculate that Bob Weir has many memorable road tales. When the question came up, he instantly recalled something that happened during the Dead's trip to Egypt in 1978. "One moment stands out, and I don't know why it's coming to me now, but we were in Egypt," Weir laughed. "The first night of three we were playing at an amphitheater at the foot of the Sphinx at the foot of the Great Pyramid. They light it up really nice. There was a light show and all that kind of stuff. It was pretty spectacular. We were not that far from the Nile River. The sun was going down and we start playing, the lights come on, and I hear a mosquito buzz my ear. One lands on my arm and as we're playing, I realize it's dusk and I look around and there's mosquitoes everywhere. I'm figuring okay, this is gonna be a 'Welcome to hell.' I'm not gonna be able to play a note. I'm staring to swat at mosquitoes.

And I'm like, 'How the hell am I gonna do this?,' and just as I'm thinking that, a shape goes by my head real fast. And the full moon's starting to rise now; it's gonna be an eclipse pretty soon.

"Back lit, you can see on the bluffs on either side of the theater, there's these sand dunes, and these bluffs are now ringed with Bedouins on their horses and camels with their rifles over their shoulders, hundreds of them on either side. They had heard that this was going on and came to check it out. Meanwhile, back on the stage, we've got a cloud of mosquitoes and as it turns out, that shape that flew by my head, another one flies by and then another. I look around again, and there are these bats about a foot-and-a-half across. Big fellas, lots of them going after the mosquitoes. So if you back off from this, what you see is the Great Pyramid lit up, golden, magenta, whatever color it was at that moment and the Sphinx also lit up, and the theater surrounded by these Bedouins. And on the stage is the band all lit up surrounded by a cloud of bats! It had to have been one of the most sublime moments that's ever occurred. I left my body. (Laughter) If I had to freeze a moment in time, this is it. Take me now, Lord. This is how I want to remember it."

The subject of Jerry Garcia is never far from Weir's thoughts. In discussing how the scene has changed in the past five years, Weir had some first-hand insight and a little perspective that has been flavored by time. "Jerry's not really gone from me," he said matter-of-factly. "He's breathing over my shoulder about 24-7. That's really simply the case with me. He was always there when he was alive, too. Very little is different for me. In conversation, I just don't have to open my mouth anymore. That's the only real difference."

Weir's sister, Wendy, has maintained a continuing dialogue with Jerry for some time, which she began at the urging of Bob. Her book, *In The Spirit,* contains quite a few of the after-life overviews she has shared with Garcia's spectral self. Bob Weir believes firmly that "We're all with him. Everybody's with everybody always. That's something I learned a long time ago, so I don't freak out when people die. That's a formality."

"As for the scene," he continued, "I think it's very much the same; Jerry was a figurehead of the scene reluctantly, and people ascribed to him all kinds of qualities and notions that weren't him. A lot of what Jerry amounted to for people was conjecture, group conjecture oftentimes, and that's still going on; so what's the change? He's not here anymore, but he wasn't there for them anyway. Had people been able to meet him, their notion of him would have been considerably different. Jerry's something a little different for everybody. But he was that when he was alive, too. So that hasn't changed much either. The thing that has happened was that he died, and people were able to focus on that event and make of it what they would. Aside from that, people's relationships with Jerry are very much the same as they've always been. Just like mine, as far as I can see it."

The Dead has left behind a rare legacy—the Deadhead subculture, which continues to evolve culturally. One aspect that has changed in the past five years is the advent of the Internet and how its sophistication has connected us beyond a word-of-mouth forum, linking the music, linking the gossip, linking the news.

In wrapping up our interview, it occurred to Weir that he was reaching directly to his audience by speaking with *Relix*. Asked if he had anything to add, his simple, honest response was, "I have more to say, but I do it best with my fingers and a microphone."

**Toni's Final Note:** This was the final interview I did for *Relix*. I'd sold the magazine, and within ten months of the sale, I was history. My 20+ years with *Relix* were sublime. Some bittersweet memories came back to me as I compiled this book. I was vividly reminded of the problems in putting a magazine together, and there were moments when I wanted to call it quits. But as we rounded third, the reality hit home—this is not about me or the people who would criticize my intent. It's about a time and a place in history that *Relix* helped create. It's not about one person, it's not about egos, and it's never been about money. It's about music and continuity. *I Live for Music*---the new folks at *Relix* recently put it on a T-shirt. I couldn't have said it better! Dance on. . . .

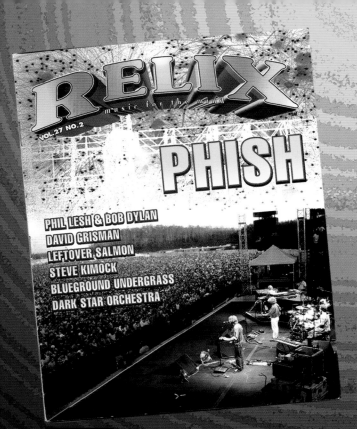

Cover Photo
by
David Vann

Phish Courtesy of
Image Entertainment

Widespread Panic Photo
Courtesy
Capricorn/Warner

String Cheese Incident
Courtesy SCI Fidelity

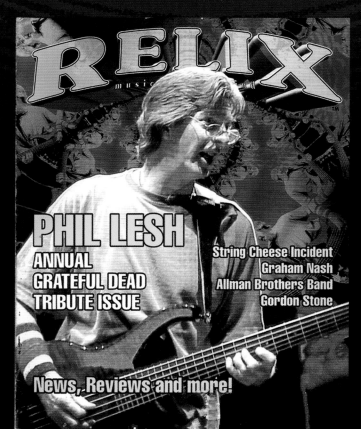

Cover Photo
by
L.D. Kippel

Cover Photos from 2000

Cover Design by Toni A. Brown and Ian Brand

239

# AFTERWORD

IN JUNE 1984, I'D BEEN THE GRATEFUL DEAD'S biographer for more than three years, talking with lots of people and, since I was an academic by training, digging through a mountain of written material, which of course included reading the complete stack of *Relix* that I'd collected over the years. The many interviews were a good source for the band's opinions, of course, but the magazine as a whole was a record of the evolving Deadhead sensibility—and writing a history of the Dead required that viewpoint. After all, Deadheads were part of the band. One day the Dead's office receptionist asked the band during a company meeting about dealing with the press, and Garcia replied, "Get McNally to do it. He knows that shit." And so I became the publicist.

Jerry also said at the meeting that he'd train me, so I went up to his house for my education. He said, "Remember one thing: we don't suck up to the press. Be nice, but don't suck up." Then he fired up a fat one and the talk went in other directions.

This instruction did not apply to *Relix*, which had come into existence in direct response to the band; I certainly didn't have to suck up to the editor, Toni Brown, to get her to cover my guys. The fact was, in the pre-Web era, it was—along with the telephone hotline, which announced show dates—one of our fundamental ways of communicating with our audience. And that was critical, because the relationship between the Dead and Deadheads was like no other.

Jerry didn't do interviews because of ego or to sell anything; that seemed to take care of itself. He felt an obligation, a sort of *noblesse oblige*, to relate to the caravan of pilgrims that had, much to his amazement, formed to follow the band.

And *Relix* led the way. The only (minor) hassle ever was when so many people claimed to be *Relix* photographers that I had to dump it all back in Toni's lap. In any case, we had a mutually beneficial relationship for 16 years from my hiring through Garcia's death in 1995 and beyond. It was startling when, in 2000, my former housemate in graduate school called to tell me that she was working with someone who was purchasing *Relix*; it was the end of an era.

Thanks, Toni. You helped the Grateful Dead more than you'll ever know.

—Dennis McNally, 2009

# ED SAYS...

PHOTO BY TONI BROWN

**TONI HAS OPENED UP SO MANY VISTAS IN MY** life that it would be impossible to express in words all that it, and she herself, mean to me. Although I am an avid music lover and guitar player, I lived outside the Grateful Dead world until I met Toni. I had shut the band out of my musical interest as a result of a complete misunderstanding going back to the earliest days of the Dead. I rebelled against the idea that someone would be designated "Captain Trips." Nobody was captain of my rebellious youth! Little did I know that Jerry hated having that moniker hanging on him. He was nobody's captain, or at least, he never sought that position.

When I first met Toni, I had never heard of her or *Relix*, and had everything to learn about the Grateful Dead. Now I am completely immersed in a beautiful world of music and community. I think that I have a young man's enthusiastic heart with so many years of life experience, and this is what I tried to bring to the mix while working with Toni Brown and Lee Abraham. All the effort on this book has enriched my joyous life with Toni even more. For this I will be forever "Grateful."

—Ed Munson,
Layout Guru, *RELIX, The Book*

## ACKNOWLEDGMENTS

**THERE ARE SO MANY PEOPLE WHO CONTRIBUTED TO THIS PROJECT.** First, I'd like to thank Steve Bernstein for his cooperation in making this book possible. My sincerest gratitude goes to him for keeping *Relix* alive. I would also like to thank Peter Shapiro who has recently stepped in to carry the *Relix* torch forward.

Special thanks to Ed Munson, my sweet new husband and this book's amazing layout guy. Thanks to Lee Abraham for lighting the fire that got this labor of love out of my head and into your hands.

Much gratitude to Les Kippel, Tom Canova, Mike Edison, Mike Lawson, Jeff Tamarkin, Jorma Kaukonen, Dennis McNally, Donna Jean, Crazy Fingers, Jon and Marsha Zazula, Aeve Baldwin, Josh Baron, Dean Budnick, Jonathan Schwartz, the staff at *Relix*, Barbara Brown, Philip Kippel, Susannah Munson, Shelly and Andy Schwartz, Carol and Rick Matzker, Edward Munson, Donna and Bernie Thornton, Al Peller, Jay Flemma and Rena and Bill Burkhart, and in loving memory of Florence and Philip Kippel, Pete Brown, Dick Wilson and Skip Webb.

In appreciation for their timeless contributions, I'd like to thank Jerry Moore, Steve Kraye, Gary Kroman, Monte Dym, Bob Alson, Clark Peterson, Dave Patrick, Mick Skidmore, Phyllis Antoniello, Claudia Falzarano, Bob Bromberg, John Lucchese, Rick Spanier, Enis Moran, Scott Boldt, Pat Breslin, Robert Bryson, Clay DuVal, Glenn Harding, Patrick Moran, Alfred Klosterman, Stephen Martin, Michael Raye Smith, Miki Saito, Mike Shapiro, David Sporrong, Mike Swartzbeck, Mark Tuchman, Nicholas Watson, W. Dire Wolff, Mike Zmuda, Greg Anton, Steve Barancek. Karen Funk Blocher, Bruce Brass, Kevyn Clark, Steve Clark, Jym Fahey, Michael Fasman, Matt Goldberg, John Grady, Anthony Head, Ken Hunt, Karen Kohberger, David Kopel, Cary Krosinsky, Paddy Ladd, Charles Lamey, David Lubell, David Mlodinoff, Steve Peters, Michael Rubin, Esq., Rosina Rubin, Evan Rudowski, Brad Shafran, Christopher Sheridan, Roger Len Smith, Rob Wolfson, Alan J. Wallace, Richard Aaron, Gene Anthony, Amy Bursten, Dennis Callahan, Robbi Cohn, Brian Gold, Herb Greene, Ralph Hulett, Kurt Mahoney, Susana Millman, J. P. Niehuser, Ed Perlstein, Bruce Polonsky, W. Marc Ricketts, John Rottet, Peter Simon, David Vann, Jon Weiner, Buddy Cage, George "Commander Cody" Frayne, Tom Constanten, Jorma Kaukonen, Barry Melton, Sandy Rothman, Kim Simmonds and the many others whose work appears in this book. I'd also like to thank all of the other past contributors to *Relix*—it was an honor to work with you. And most, thanks to the readers who made it worthwhile. Your input directed us, and your loyalty nourished us.

On a final note, I want to acknowledge the many musicians that moved, lifted, inspired and encouraged me, and let me into their lives as they created a place to live in mine. Thank you for a real good time!

—Toni Brown, 2009

# RESOURCES

## CONTACTS
Toni Brown: email at
   TBCommunications@aol.com
Jam 'Til Dawn Promotions:
   www.JamTilDawn.com
Toni Brown's Music:
   www.ToniBrownBand.com
Relix Magazine: www.Relix.com

## PHOTOGRAPHERS and ARTISTS
Richard Aaron: www.RockPix.com
Gene Anthony: geneanthony1@charter.net
Adrian Boot: www.adrianboot.com
Robbi Cohn: www.DeadImages.com
Herbie Greene: www.HerbGreenefoto.com
Ralph Hulett: www.RockRetrospect.com
Gary Kroman: www.GaryKroman.com
Patrick Moran: www.moran784.com
Ed Perlstein: www.musicimages.com
Bruce Polonsky: www.bpphotography.com
Roberto Rabanne: www.RabanneDesign.com
John Rottet: www.well.com/~unkljohn or
   www.flickr.com/photos/unkljohn
Mike Shapiro: www.mikeshapirocartoons.com
Peter Simon: www.PeterSimon.com
David Sporrong: www.alunareclipse.com
Mike Swartzbeck: www.sinkers.org
David Vann: www.DaveVann.com
W. Dire Wolff: www.wdirewolff.com

## WRITERS
Cary Krosinsky:
   http://styluspub.com/Books/BookDetail.asp
   x?productID=179039
David Kopel: www.davekopel.org
Roger Len Smith: www.RogerLenSmith.com
   or myspace.com/rogerlensmith

## MUSICIANS
Grateful Dead: www.Dead.net
Allman Brothers Band:
   www.AllmanBrothersBand.com
Blues Traveler: www.BluesTraveler.com
Boris Garcia: www.BorisGarcia.com

Commander Cody:
   www.CommanderCody.com
Tom Constanten: www.TomConstanten.com
Michael Falzarano:
   www.MichaelFalzarano.com
Crazy Fingers: www.CrazyFingers.net
Donna Jean Band:
   www.DonnaJeanGodchauxBand.com
Dark Star Orchestra:
   www.DarkStarOrchestra.com
David Gans: www.trufun.com
David Grisman: www.Dawgnet.com
Warren Haynes: www.WarrenHaynes.net
Dan Healy:
   www.dozin.com/danhealy/house.htm
Dan Hicks: www.DanHicks.net
Bruce Hornsby: www.BruceHornsby.com
Hot Tuna: www.HotTuna.com
Jefferson Airplane: wwwJeffersonAirplane.com
Juggling Suns: www.JugglingSuns.com
Steve Kimock: www.SteveKimock.com
Barry Melton: www.counterculture.net/thefish
David Nelson Band: www.NelsonBand.com
New Riders of the Purple Sage:
   www.TheNewRiders.com
Phish: www.Phish.com
Peter Rowan: www.Peter-Rowan.com
Melvin Seals: www.jgbband.com
Pete Sears: www.PeteSears.com
Kim Simmonds/Savoy Brown:
   www.savoybrown.com
Spirit: www.RandyCaliforniaandSpirit.com
Wavy Gravy: www.WavyGravy.net
Widespread Panic:
   www.WidespreadPanic.com
Zero: www.Zerolive.com

## MISCELLANIOUS
Wildman Steve Radio: www.WildmanSteve.com
WMNF: www.WMNF.org (Tampa, Florida's
   real radio!) Ed Greene and Doctor J!
Sirius Grateful Dead channel 12
WXPN: www.WXPN.org (Philly's Best)